GLOBALIZATION AND SOCIAL MOVEMENTS

THE POPULIST CHALLENGE AND DEMOCRATIC ALTERNATIVES

THIRD EDITION

VALENTINE M. MOGHADAM

NORTHEASTERN UNIVERSITY

ROWMAN & LITTLEFIELD
Lanham • Boulder • New York • London

Executive Editor: Susan McEachern
Assistant Editor: Katelyn Turner
Channel Manager: Jonathan Raeder

Credits and acknowledgments for material borrowed from other sources, and reproduced with permission, appear on the appropriate pages within the text.

Published by Rowman & Littlefield
An imprint of The Rowman & Littlefield Publishing Group, Inc.
4501 Forbes Boulevard, Suite 200, Lanham, Maryland 20706
www.rowman.com

6 Tinworth Street, London SE11 5AL, United Kingdom

British Library Cataloguing in Publication Information Available

Library of Congress Cataloging-in-Publication Data
Names: Moghadam, Valentine M., 1952- author.
Title: Globalization and social movements : the populist challenge and democratic
   alternatives / Valentine M. Moghadam, Northeastern University.
Description: Third edition. | Lanham : Rowman & Littlefield, [2020] | Series:
   Globalization | Includes bibliographical references and index.
Identifiers: LCCN 2019047111 (print) | LCCN 2019047112 (ebook) |
   ISBN 9781538108734 (cloth) | ISBN 9781538108741 (paperback) | ISBN
   9781538108758 (epub)
Subjects: LCSH: Social movements. | Transnationalism. | Globalization. | Anti-
   globalization movement.
Classification: LCC HM881 .M64 2020 (print) | LCC HM881 (ebook) | DDC
   303.48/4—dc23
LC record available at https://lccn.loc.gov/2019047111
LC ebook record available at https://lccn.loc.gov/2019047112

CONTENTS

FIGURES AND TABLES

FIGURES

TABLES

PREFACE TO THE THIRD EDITION

In 2019, it appeared that populism was gaining ground across the globe. Elections in late May for the European Parliament saw a wave of right-wing populist parties winning seats, although Green parties in several countries won as well, showing the extent of citizen disdain for the established parties. In Turkey, Recep Tayyip Erdoğan was still president and his Justice and Development Party (AKP) still the ruling party, with local elections having largely gone his way. In Israel, Prime Minister Benjamin Netanyahu won yet another election and again sought to form a coalition government with right-wing, religious, and anti-Arab parties. In India, Narendra Modi's Bharatiya Janata Party (BJP) won a landslide victory after already being in power for five years. In the United States, Donald Trump was still president, and on a state visit to Britain in June, he declared his preference for Boris Johnson—a fervent Brexiteer, or advocate of Britain's withdrawal from the European Union—as the next British prime minister. The right-wing populist wave had begun earlier in the new century, but it came to prominence after the Great Recession and became the subject of much scholarship, policy dialogues, and political debates. This third edition, therefore, includes an extended discussion of the contemporary wave of right-wing populism—its origins, features, varieties, and possible challengers. The challengers include left-wing populist movements, youth action against climate change, and a reinvigorated feminism aligned with peace and justice movements.

This book originates from an invitation extended by Manfred Steger when we were both at Illinois State University and he had just taken on the coeditorship (with Terrell Carver) of the Globalization book series. It took me several years to complete the project (2009), and by this time, I was at Purdue University. I decided to focus on what I regarded as three transnational social movements with varied links to globalization: Islamism, feminism, and the global justice movement. In the second edition (2013), which followed the Arab Spring, I included a chapter on social movements and democratization, examining the democratic demands of contemporary social movements and highlighting the democratizing potential of social movements. I interrogate conventional definitions and practices of democracy, pointing out that demands for a robust democracy must include economic rights as well as civil and political rights. Such demands were evident in the social protests and opposition movements of Tunisia and Egypt, and they figured prominently in the critiques and stated solutions offered by transnational feminist networks, the World Social Forum, Occupy Wall Street, and the anti-austerity protests in Europe, Chile, and elsewhere.

As it happens, only Tunisia and, to a lesser degree, Morocco, embarked on a democratic transition. Elsewhere, the hopes and aspirations of the Arab Spring were dashed either through external intervention or internal fissures, or both. Despite the widespread criticisms of neoliberal capitalism and demands for economic justice that had followed the 2008 financial meltdown, parties and governments made no significant changes to economic policy. Many citizens lost houses and jobs; however, no restraints were placed on the corporate and banking sectors, and thus income inequalities continued to grow. Meanwhile, armed conflicts, the ravages of environmental degradation, and continued poverty pushed people out of their countries and into neighboring countries, Europe, and the United States. On top of preexisting local concerns about crime, terrorism, and unassimilated immigrants, and in a context of austerity and income inequality, the migration wave of 2015 set off the right-wing populist time bomb. In this third edition, therefore, I analyze the emergence and spread of right-wing populist parties, movements, and governments and connect them to the ills of globalization that were dissected in the previous two editions. As will become evident and as was suggested in the opening paragraph of this preface, populism is hardly confined to the Global North.

We are living in times of insecurity, instability, and risk, but equally in times of opportunity and possibility. Climate change, war, and economic crisis loom large, while increased militarization by states and violent contention by nonstate actors contribute to a seemingly dangerous world. The challenge of right-wing populism may be the inevitable result of neoliberal globalization and the mismanagement and arrogance of the ruling elites, but it requires sustained opposition and mobilization for change. If the global justice movement—those many disparate advocacy groups, progressive networks, peace organizations, human rights groups, *altermondialisation*, civil society organizations, and social movement representatives that typically meet at the World Social Forum or its regional forums—have thus far preferred to remain fluid, decentralized, and leaderless, the rise of right-wing populism and its capacity for governance suggests that a new vision and model of organizing are needed. Urgently needed is the transformation of the status quo and the building of "another world" that is peaceful, environmentally sound, egalitarian, and just. Can a New Global Left form to sideline the Global Right, including right-wing populisms, and thus realize that goal? It remains to be seen if networks and communities of activists—young people and veterans, within and across borders—can work together and with progressive political parties to craft a new strategy for social transformation. This book is dedicated to those who share that vision. It is also dedicated to the memory of Samir Amin and of Immanuel Wallerstein, both of whom inspired many of the movements and activists described in this book.

ACKNOWLEDGMENTS

Many colleagues and friends have contributed to a deeper understanding on my part of the issues analyzed in this book or have kindly read chapters and provided cogent comments. In particular, my thanks go to Christopher Chase-Dunn, Lauren Langman, Massoud Karshenas, Jackie Smith, and Sylvia Walby, as well as to my Northeastern University colleagues Max Abrahms, Michael Handel, Ioannis Livanis, and Silvia Dominguez. Gizem Kaftan-Yilmaz took two of my courses, and we eventually coauthored an article on varieties and gender dynamics of right-wing populism. Other students provided valuable research assistance: Elizabeth Mohr, Katherine Doering, Chynna Lewis, and Lily Moseley. Finally, I owe a great intellectual debt to two outstanding thinkers and scholars, the late Samir Amin and the late Immanuel Wallerstein.

Acronyms

AKP	Justice and Development Party (Turkey)
ARP	Assemblée des Représentants du Peuple (Tunisia, parliament)
ASEAN	Association of Southeast Asian Nations
ATTAC	Association for the Taxation of Financial Transactions and for Citizens' Action
AWID	Association for Women's Rights in Development
BJP	Bharayiya Janata Party, or People's Party (India)
BRIC	Brazil, Russia, India, China
CEDAW	Convention on the Elimination of All Forms of Discrimination against Women; also Committee on the Elimination of Discrimination against Women (UN)
CFTC	Commodity Futures Trading Commission (US)
COSATU	Congress of South African Trade Unions
DAWN	Development Alternatives with Women for a New Era
ECOSOC	Economic and Social Committee (UN)
ENDA	Environnement et Développement du Tiers Monde
EU	European Union
FIS	Front Islamique du Salut (Islamic Salvation Front, Algeria)
FTAA	Free Trade Area of the Americas
GCC	Gulf Cooperation Council
GIA	Groupe Islamique Armée
GJM	global justice movement
IAW	International Alliance of Women

ICFTU	International Confederation of Free Trade Unions
ICPD	UN International Conference on Population and Development (Cairo, 1994)
ICTs	information and computer technologies
IGO	intergovernmental organization
IGTN	International Gender and Trade Network
ILO	International Labour Organization (UN)
IMF	International Monetary Fund
INGO	international nongovernmental organization
IROWS	Institute for Research on World-Systems
IS/ISIS/ ISIL	Islamic State (short-lived caliphate based in Iraq and Syria)
MAI	Multilateral Agreement on Investment
MDGs	Millennium Development Goals
MDS	Movement of Socialist Democrats (Tunisia)
MENA	Middle East and North Africa
NAFTA	North American Free Trade Agreement
NATO	North Atlantic Treaty Organization
NGL	New Global Left
NGO	nongovernmental organization
NIEO	New International Economic Order
NWICO	New World Information and Communication Order
OECD	Organisation for Economic Co-operation and Development
OWS	Occupy Wall Street
PAS	Pan-Malaysian Islamic Party / Parti Islam Se-Malaysia
PJD	Parti du Justice et du Dévéloppement (Morocco)
PT	Partido dos Trabalhadores (Workers' Party, Brazil)
RWP	right-wing populism
SAP	structural adjustment policy
SEN	Solidarity Economy Network (US)
SDGs	Sustainable Development Goals (UN)
SIGI	Sisterhood Is Global Institute
SMO	social movement organization
TARP	Troubled Asset Relief Program
TCC	transnational capitalist class
TFN	transnational feminist network
UNCED	United Nations Conference on Environment and Development

UNCTAD	United Nations Conference on Trade and Development
UNDP	United Nations Development Programme
UNU	United Nations University
WEDO	Women's Environment and Development Organization
WICEJ	Women's International Coalition for Economic Justice
WIDE	Network Women in Development in Europe
WIDF	Women's International Democratic Federation
WILPF	Women's International League for Peace and Freedom
WLP	Women's Learning Partnership
WLUML	Women Living under Muslim Laws
WSF	World Social Forum
WTO	World Trade Organization

CHAPTER 1

INTRODUCTION AND OVERVIEW

GLOBALIZATION, SOCIAL MOVEMENTS, AND CONTEMPORARY POLITICS

> Men and women make history, but not under conditions of their own choosing.
>
> —adapted from Karl Marx,
> *The Eighteenth Brumaire of Louis Bonaparte*[1]

What is the connection between globalization and social movements? How have people collectively responded to globalization? Have social movements changed to better confront globalization's economic, political, and cultural manifestations and challenges? And how are contemporary social movements and networks affecting the progression of globalization? These are the principal questions posed and addressed in this book. The conceptual framework used to answer the questions draws on Marxist and feminist concepts of capitalism, class, and gender; world-system analysis of accumulation, crisis, and transi-

1

tion; world society (or world polity) research on institutions and norm diffusion; and social movement theories of political opportunities, resource mobilization, collective action frames, and emotions. In so doing, I have drawn on an array of studies, including my own research, and chosen the case-study method to elucidate key features of social movements in an era of globalization—and possible deglobalization. This book analyzes the interrelationship of globalization and social movements; explores the ways that scholarship has sought to address changing sociopolitical realities, such as the rise of neoliberal capitalist globalization, democracy deficits, and new forms of collective action; and provides four case studies: global feminism, global Islam, the global justice movement (GJM), and right-wing populisms. It ends with a discussion of prospects for more coordinated and strategic collective action toward a different world order.

This first chapter introduces the book's subject matter, offers a summary description of the book's chapters, and ends with a series of theoretically informed propositions. First, it may be useful to clarify and define the concepts that inform the book and the social movements examined.

Globalization has been approached in diverse disciplinary ways, but here it refers to the latest stage of capitalism in the evolution of the modern world-system, with economic, political, and cultural/ideological dimensions and features. The consolidation of *neoliberal* capitalist globalization—characterized by an unprecedented degree of integrated and liberalized markets, "flexible" labor markets, powerful financial sectors, and wide income inequality—occurred following the collapse of world communism in 1989–91. That consolidation triggered a wave of antiglobalization protests, which scholars and activists came to call the **global justice movement** —comprising disparate antiglobalization, peace, environmental, human rights, and *altermondialisation* advocacy groups, progressive networks, social movements, and civil society organizations—that appeared in the 1990s and typically met at the World Social Forum (WSF) or its regional forums.[2] I continue to use that term, although some now refer to the broader category of New Global Left, which includes progressive political parties and newer campaigns and networks such as Black Lives Matter.[3] **Social movements** have been defined as sustained contentious politics directed at the state, usually nonviolent and thus distinguished from revolutions. Globalization and its concomitants—open borders and ease of travel, especially within the European Union (EU), and the spread of new information and computer technologies (ICTs)—facilitated the formation of **transnational social movements** and advocacy networks, bringing together activists from various countries around a common agenda. One such movement is **global feminism**, perhaps the longest and most sustained modern social movement, given its origins in the late eighteenth century. Across the world, local or national women's rights groups may set priorities and craft frames differently, but they have tended to coalesce around certain international conventions and norms; and they have formed or joined several *transnational feminist networks*. **Islamism** appeared in the 1980s as a religio-political project and became globalized in the 1990s. As a transnational movement, it ranges from religious fundamentalism to parliamentary politics to militancy and violent extremism. Finally, **populism** is a movement and a discourse, an appeal to "the people" against the "corrupt elites" and the dominant ideas, values, and policies that they have imposed. Because it does not have a defined ideology, populism may take left-wing or right-wing forms. *Right-wing populism* is often reactively nationalist, concerned with "own people first," opposed to open borders, and keen on immigration controls. In this century, right-wing populist parties have won elections or formed governments in an array of countries across the globe, and some are disrupting the post–Cold War world order of neoliberal and globalized capitalist democratization, possibly in the direction of deglobalization—which, ironically, has been an objective of many leftists.

GLOBALIZATION AND THE SOCIAL SCIENCES

In addition to exploring the interrelationship of globalization and social movements, this book examines the ways that the social sciences have sought to address changing sociopolitical realities. The social sciences have long focused on processes and institutions within single states, societies, and economies. Until the 1990s, the terms "global" and "transnational" represented concepts that were either alien or marginal to mainstream social science theories. "International" and "world" were of course understood, but supranational developments could hardly be fathomed. The post–World War II world order consisted of what came to be called the First World, Second World, and Third World—also known as the rich capitalist countries of the West, the countries of the communist bloc, and the developing countries of Africa, Asia, and Latin America. When scholars studied those political and economic regions, analytical frameworks—such as modernization theory, theories of international relations, studies of international development, or the study of women-in-development (WID)—tended to focus on single societies and economies. The emerging field of "new social movements," too, focused on national-level dynamics, and mainly in the West or in "postindustrial society."[4] But no sooner had such theories gained prominence in the 1980s than new developments began to challenge some of their basic assumptions: transnational forms of social movement organizing, and shifts in political economy and global governance that could influence the emergence, course, and consequences of social movements.

Dependency theory and its more sophisticated variant, world-system theory, challenged mainstream social science theorizing, drawing attention to the transnational nature of capital and labor flows and implications for economic and political processes at the societal level, as well as for the reproduction of global inequalities. (There also was a critique of Marxism's emphasis on class conflicts within single societies. However, in *The Communist Manifesto*, Karl Marx and Friedrich Engels correctly predicted the ever-growing concentration of capital and its expansion across the globe. Toward the end of volume 1 of *Capital*, Marx's sardonic comments about the "bankocracy" presage the 2008 global financial meltdown.[5] These points are relevant to the discussion of neoliberalism in chapter 2.) World-system theory was unique in its conceptual and methodological approach. Though it posited the existence of hierarchical "economic zones" of core, periphery, and semiperiphery, it emphasized the structures of the world-system in its entirety as the analytical point of departure. It was also unique in recognizing *waves of globalization* across modern world history, notably in the pre–World War I era of colonialism and imperialism.

The capitalist world-economy has experienced cyclical processes and secular trends for hundreds of years, with various globalization waves (as measured by volume and direction of trade), along with the rise and fall of hegemonic powers (e.g., Great Britain), upward trends in economic and technological development as well as population growth, and cyclical crises.[6] Parallel to these largely economic processes, and closely related to them, has been the evolution of a world polity, characterized by states, empires, modern nation-states, hegemonic powers, international organizations, revolutions, social movements, and transnational social movements. From the 1815 Congress of Europe, which convened in Vienna to establish a balance of power among European states following the Napoleonic wars, to the League of Nations and on to the United Nations (UN) and the EU, states have tried to maintain stability and prevent wars in the world-system. That effort met with failures or with countermovements and revolutionary uprisings: the 1848 revolutions, World War I, the revolutions of 1917 and 1918, World War II, the Cold War rivalries, and the ethnic conflicts of the postcommunist era. Although the 1648 Treaty of Westphalia, in the wake of the ruinous European religious wars, established the principle of state *sovereignty*, powerful states have consistently challenged or undermined the sovereignty of less-powerful states, whether through "tied aid" and conditionalities for loans, economic sanctions, outright military aggression, or more subtle forms of state destabilization. All this occurred even before globalization became a buzzword in the mid-1990s and mainstream scholars began to debate a "post-Westphalian world" where markets or transnational social movements came to dominate and bypass the state.[7]

Scholars also noted the ever-growing power and influence of multinational corporations, the World Bank, the International Monetary Fund (IMF), and (later) the World Trade Organization (WTO), along with the emergence of a seemingly powerful and integrated regional bloc such as the EU and trade groupings such as the North American Free Trade Agreement (NAFTA), the Association of Southeast Asian Nations (ASEAN), South America's Mercosur, the Gulf Cooperation Council (GCC), and the Southern African Development Community (SADC). These institutions of global and regional governance initiated or adopted shifts in the international political economy, which entailed the move from Keynesian or state-directed economic models to neoliberal or free market economic strategies. Numerous studies emerged to analyze "global restructuring."[8] The "structural adjustment and stabilization" policies that were advocated for and implemented in debt-ridden Third World countries in the 1980s and 1990s, the transition from socialism to capitalism in the Second World, and the free-market imprint of Reaganism and Thatcherism in the First World were part of a global process of economic restructuring. Along with these changes arose a powerful ideology of free-market capitalism, consumerism, and "globalism."[9] In chapter 2, I discuss how and why this shift occurred, and what brought about this latest wave of globalization. Here I note that a large literature emerged to analyze globalization in its economic, political, and cultural dimensions.

One group of scholars came to analyze what they viewed as a global tendency toward common values. Echoing arguments made earlier by modernization theorists, proponents of "world society" (or world polity) maintained that structures, institutions, and processes—such as rationalized state tax and management systems, formal organizations, bureaucratized legal systems, and formal schooling—are explicit or implicit carriers of modern values such as rationality and individuality. In the 1990s, emphasis began to be placed on the role of international organizations in the construction of world values. World society theory places primacy on cultural and political institutions and norms, emphasizing norm diffusion and convergences in political and cultural developments, which is interpreted as a kind of global westernization. It posits a tendency toward "isomorphism" in institutions, values, practices, and norms across the globe, indicated by states' membership in intergovernmental organizations and their adoption of international instruments, along with the exponential growth and increased prominence of national and international nongovernmental organizations (NGOs and INGOs). Theorists argue that these are measures of a world culture and a kind of world polity. In this perspective, world culture encourages countries to adopt similar strategies for addressing common problems. World organizations are viewed as "primary instruments of shared modernity," disseminating standards and practices, and international conventions and treaties often provide declarations of common causes and blueprints for change. Social movements and civil society organizations—including human rights and women's rights associations, environmental protection groups, and various other advocacy groups—are regarded as active agents in the deepening of the cultural and normative features of world society. The global diffusion of social media and of cyberactivism are further indicators of world culture.[10]

Scholars discussing cultural aspects of globalization pointed to the spread of "cosmopolitan" values, especially with the rise of "global cities," multicultural policies, and immigration.[11] One consequence of such aspects of globalization has been the capacity for interactions, connections, and mobilizations conducive to transnational collective action. Another, however, has been disquiet and unease with the cultural and normative changes that globalization has wrought.

FUNDAMENTALISM AND THE NEW RELIGIOUS RIGHT

Parallel to the economic shifts that were unfolding in the 1980s, a new phenomenon emerged: the revival of religious movements across the globe that appeared also to take on a political character. In the United States, this movement came to be analyzed as the New Religious Right, and it gave rise to questions about the validity of the "secularization" thesis associated with Max Weber and some tenets of modernization theory. Robert Wuthnow discussed the increasing tendency of American evangelicals to enter the political arena after 1976, and Rebecca Klatch examined the American New Right, including the role of women within it, as a kind of countermovement to the progressive social changes of the 1960s and beyond. Kathleen Blee and Kimberly Creasap located the American New Right in "the alliance of free market advocates and social conservatives . . . [and] the entry of large numbers of conservative Protestant evangelicals into secular political life." In explaining the emergence of Islamic fundamentalism and political Islam, Said Amir Arjomand examined five broad processes of social change generally associated with secularization—integration into the international system; development of transport, communication, and the mass media; urbanization; the spread of literacy and education; and the incorporation of citizens into political society—and showed how these in fact had "fostered a variety of movements of revitalization in the Islamic world."[12]

In the Middle East, North Africa, and South Asia, Islamic movements sought to reinforce religious values, recuperate traditional social and gender norms, and curb Western political and cultural influences. The theorization of these movements fell largely to scholars within Middle East studies and Middle East women's studies, although Benjamin Barber later included them under the rubric of "jihad" movements against "McWorld." Those who studied Muslim-majority countries, as well as scholars of Islam, sought to understand the new movements in terms such as "political Islam," "fundamentalism," "Islamist movements," or "resurgent Islam." The focus tended to be on the dynamics within particular countries that had led to the growth of such opposition movements, but some studies also noted region-wide factors, such as a shared religio-cultural civilization, the presence of authoritarian governments, reaction to changing gender relations, and a shared antipathy toward Israel and its handling of the Palestinian question.

Following the al-Qaeda attacks on the United States on September 11, 2001, "terrorism studies" became widespread, but social scientists such as Quintan Wiktorowicz and Mohammed Hafez studied Islamist movements in terms of social movement dynamics or as conservative political movements. Islamist movements were rarely studied in terms of their relationship to the changing global political economy, although an early work of mine did situate the growth of Islamist movements in global restructuring.[13]

ACTIVISM ACROSS BORDERS

Social movement theorists previously had focused on domestic processes and movement characteristics, but it became increasingly clear in the 1990s that the analytical point of departure would have to take account of the *transnational* and that local-global linkages would have to be theorized. Early theorists of transnational advocacy networks focused on ideational and ethical motivations for the emergence of the human rights, environmental, and solidarity movements. Margaret Keck and Kathryn Sikkink defined a transnational advocacy network (TAN) as a set of "relevant actors working internationally on an issue who are bound together by shared values, a common discourse and dense exchanges of information and services. . . . Activists in networks try not only to influence policy outcomes but to transform the terms and nature of the debate." They emphasized the research, lobbying, and advocacy activities of the TANs that they studied.[14] Still, the 1997–98 mobilization against the Multilateral Agreement on Investment (MAI) in the United States and the Battle of Seattle in late 1999 confirmed that movement interest in economic, inequality, and class issues had returned, and that movements were now prepared to add *direct action* (e.g., mass protests that were sometimes disruptive) to their collective action repertoire.

A new body of literature emerged, therefore, taking these novel departures into consideration, and pointing out that the response to global economic, political, and cultural developments—neoliberalism, war, the decline of the welfare state, and growing inequalities—was taking the form of transnational collective action, including the emergence of transnational social movements and advocacy networks focusing on human rights, the environment, and economic justice. As discussed later in this chapter, such movements and networks were not historically unprecedented, but they did become prominent in the early part of the new century, leading to the formation in 2001 of the WSF.

The financial crises that engulfed Russia, South Korea, and especially Argentina at the turn of the new century bolstered the new transnational movements and, in Latin America, generated a "pink tide" of electoral victories for left-wing political parties in Argentina, Brazil, Chile, Bolivia, Ecuador, Uruguay, and Venezuela.[15] Neoliberalism's next phase was the Great Recession, which originated in the financial sector of the core countries, beginning in the United States with the 2007–8 subprime mortgage crisis. The financial crisis had immediate reverberations (and long-term ones as well) in those developing countries that were closely linked to the global financial markets. Loss of assets and rising unemployment, coupled with knowledge of the stratospheric incomes of economic elites, brought into sharp relief the complicity of states with a model that had wreaked havoc on economies and households. In Europe and North America, growing income inequality and the power of established elites now intersected with frustration over the consequences for ordinary citizens of the economic crisis: whereas banks and corporations were bailed out, ordinary citizens lost jobs, homes, and assets, and had to face austerity policies. In the Middle East and North Africa (MENA), the economic crisis intensified frustration with the slow erosion of the long-standing "authoritarian bargain," whereby states provided citizens with a level of social welfare provisioning and jobs in return for acquiescence to authoritarian rule. The result was the spread of global protests. The year 2008 saw the eruption of labor protests in Egypt and Tunisia, and in 2009, Iranians protested what they saw as a rigged presidential election. In December 2010, a young man in Tunisia set himself alight in frustration over bureaucratic intransigence impeding his ability to earn a livelihood; his act triggered nationwide protests that cascaded across the Arab region, reaching Turkey in 2013.[16]

The year 2011 is notable for the multitude of protests and social movements. We saw the Arab Spring, the European Summer, and the American Autumn. Transnational networks, civil society organizations, NGOs, and radical intellectuals, who usually met at the WSF in Brazil or other parts of the world, expanded when Europeans protested austerity measures following the Eurozone crisis, students in the United Kingdom and Chile protested the rising costs of education, and the *indignados* mounted massive demonstrations in Madrid and Barcelona against unemployment and welfare cuts. In fall 2011, the call for democracy and social justice seemed to engulf the world. The Occupy Wall Street campaign, which began with activists in New York City protesting economic injustices and the financial malfeasance of Wall Street practices, spread across the United States, and in a show of global solidarity, cities across the world held Occupy protests on October 15, 2011, one month after the movement's emergence in New York. With confidence and trust in government declining in the West as well as in developing countries, global social movements redoubled their efforts to draw attention to democracy deficits and economic injustices. The global spread of social protests also saw the global transmission and diffusion of social/economic justice frames. New left-wing political parties emerged ("movement parties"), such as Syriza in Greece, Podemos in Spain, the Left Bloc in Portugal, and the People's Democratic Party (HDP) in Turkey. The United States saw the growing national prominence of democratic socialist senator Bernie Sanders. As recognition of the democratic transition occurring in Tunisia, and in solidarity with ongoing struggles in the MENA region, the WSF met in Tunis in 2013 and again in 2015.

That was the good news. Neither the Arab Spring nor the GJM, however, was able to disrupt the capitalist world-system, much less weaken the hegemon. It is true that the emergence of pro-democracy movements in Iran, Tunisia, Egypt, Morocco, Turkey, and elsewhere—all of which had significant female participation—seemed to shatter popular and social science stereotypes of the region as inescapably authoritarian, fundamentalist, and patriarchal. But the Arab Spring was not permitted to flourish, and there was much confusion about the appropriate international response to events in Libya and Syria. The North Atlantic

Treaty Organization (NATO) intervention in Libya in 2011—in which air power was used to support armed rebels and force the collapse of the regime of Muammar Ghaddafi—spawned debates about the legitimacy of such action, responses from the Left, and the role of violence in this particular "pro-democracy" movement.[17] Code Pink founder Medea Benjamin, along with Charles Davis, pointed out that "democracy doesn't come on the back of a Tomahawk missile," adding:

[I]n 2009 alone, European governments—including Britain and France—sold Libya more than $470 million worth of weapons, including fighter jets, guns and bombs. And before it started calling for regime change, the Obama administration was working to provide the Libyan dictator another $77 million in weapons, on top of the $17 million it provided in 2009 and the $46 million the Bush administration provided in 2008. . . . The U.S. government need not drop a single bomb in the Middle East to help liberate oppressed people. All it need do is stop selling bombs to their oppressors.[18]

It is worth noting that the governments of Argentina and Brazil, led by presidents Cristina Fernandez de Kirchner and Dilma Rousseff, respectively, opposed the NATO intervention in Libya. Nearly a decade after Libya's "liberation" through an ostensible "humanitarian intervention," it remains chaotic and violent, a conduit for people smuggling. Throughout this period, Syria also descended into a violent uprising with violent state response, morphing into an internationalized civil conflict that mirrored what had occurred in Afghanistan in the 1980s.[19] A massive wave of Syrian refugees ensued, pouring into the neighboring countries of Turkey, Jordan, and Lebanon as well as into Europe. Turkey opened its borders not only to Syrian refugees but also to jihadists from across the world who sought to join the armed uprising against the Syrian state.

The unfortunate outcomes of the Arab Spring coincided with the waning of the Latin American pink tide (1998–2014) and with the coming of another development, itself a consequence of economic crisis and frustration with political decision making: right-wing populist movements and new political parties in Europe. A flurry of scholarship now focused on what political theorist Chantal Mouffe calls "the populist moment."[20] If the earliest critiques of globalization and institutions of global governance had come from the Left, now critiques were coming from the Right, calling for a return to renewed national control over borders, economic and financial matters, and political decisions. The United Kingdom Independence Party (UKIP) called for Britain's withdrawal from the EU, launching a movement known as "Brexit" and a referendum won by the "Brexiteers" in late June 2016. Throughout Europe, but also in the United States, Turkey, India, and Brazil, right-wing populist parties and leaders came to power, challenging the globalized order. In one study, world-system scholars Chase-Dunn and Inoue showed a marked slowdown in global trade, and wondered if it presaged another historical period of deglobalization, such as the period that followed World War I.[21] In late 2018, a series of mass protests by citizens—dressed in yellow emergency vests and thus called the Gilets Jaunes—erupted across France, demanding a halt to certain reforms and policy measures by the neoliberal globalist government of President Emmanuel Macron. The next year saw renewed social protests against privatization and income inequality in Chile, strikes by teachers and workers in Morocco and the United States, and mass protests against government corruption and ineptitude in Algeria, Iraq, and Lebanon.

STUDYING SOCIAL MOVEMENTS

Scholars have long shown that the roots of social protest, organizing, and movement building are located in broad social change processes that destabilize existing power relations and increase the leverage of challenging groups. Sidney Tarrow notes that social movements emerged in the eighteenth century from "structural changes that were associated with capitalism," such as "new forms of association, regular communication linking center and periphery, and the spread of print and literacy."[22] Social movements—like revolutions—are thus associated with modernity and capitalism; they are rooted in and triggered by the contradictions of the capitalist world-system. In a Marxian dialectical sense, the contradictions entail both oppressive conditions and opportunities for action, resistance, and change.

Social movement analysis has taken a clear theoretical shape within sociology. There is now an appreciation for the interconnection of political, organizational, and cultural processes in social movements, with scholars arguing that the three factors play roles of varying analytic importance over the course of the movement. Opportunities are critical to emergence, as they are tied to the relative openness or closure of the political system and the state, the stability of the elite, and the presence or absence of elite allies—all of which may be determined by location within the world-system's economic zones, or world-systemic crises or transitions. Pertinent empirical questions are, how does the national political system influence movements? How does movement strategy and structure change in response to political opportunities? How do movements respond to, but also help create, political opportunities? Mobilizing structures—networks, associations, and patterns of recruitment, leadership, and resource mobilization—become more central as the movement develops. Much research has documented the formation and evolution of social movement organizations (SMOs), but research also shows that they originate in small groups or informal networks. Framing processes—the meanings given to action, the formation of collective identities, the ways in which issues are presented through collective action frames—are always important, but they become more self-conscious and tactical over the course of the movement, sometimes with the emergence of a "master frame." Scholars have identified an ongoing process of "frame alignment" or "frame resonance," whereby social movement actors link their claims to interested audiences, often to strategically construct more resonant and persuasive frames that will mobilize people or recruit them to the cause.[23]

The three aspects of social movements are interrelated, inasmuch as the structure of political opportunities can affect resource mobilization; meanings, frames, and identities can be formed in connection with available opportunities, resources, and audiences; and the political context can be influenced or even changed by concerted collective action. In addition, scholars examine cycles and waves of protest, as well as "collective action repertoires" such as boycotts, mass petitioning, marches, rallies, barricading, sit-ins, and acts of civil disobedience. To this list we should add the meetings and conferences typical of feminist action, the suicide bombings deployed by radical Islamists, and the new forms of cyberactivism.

All movements have some structure, but not all movements have major formal organizations that dominate and direct movement activity. According to Luther Gerlach, social movements are "segmentary, polycentric, and reticulate [SPR]." Illustrating his SPR thesis by way of the environmental movement, he shows that social movements have many, sometimes competing, organizations and groups (segmentary); they have multiple and sometimes competing leaders (polycentric); and they are loose networks that link to each other (reticulate). Despite the segmentation, there is a shared opposition and ideology. In the environmental movement, for example, SMOs have ranged from the very radical Earth First! to Greenpeace and Germany's Greens (who later evolved into the Green Party), and on the more moderate side, the World Wildlife Fund. Gerlach argues that the SPR nature of SMOs is very effective, allowing them to be flexible and adaptive and to resonate with larger constituencies through different tactics (for example, direct action versus lobbying and legal strategies). It also "promotes striving, innovation, and entrepreneurial experimentation in generating and implementing sociocultural change."[24] This argument is consistent with more recent scholarship in political science and sociology—such as Keck and Sikkink's work on transnational advocacy networks, my examination of transnational feminist networks (TFNs), Jeff Juris's study of antiglobalization protest networking, and others' works on the WSF—which underscores the openness, fluidity, and flexibility of contemporary network-based movements. And yet, as we shall see, there are weaknesses with the "horizontal" model of collective action.

The role of emotions is important, too, as a growing body of literature points out.[25] Commitment, zeal, moral outrage, solidarity, ethics—these are aspects of social-movement building and participation that scholars oriented toward rational choice theorizing have neglected. No one who examines Islamist movements can deny that there are strong emotional undercurrents and motivations among participants. When Muslim-owned media such as Al Jazeera and Al Arabiyya dwell on bombings in Afghanistan, Iraq, Lebanon, and Palestine, this can be regarded as a movement event that is also an emotion-producing ritual. Similarly, emotions play a role in the feminist and global justice movements. Violence against women is certainly addressed analytically by feminists but is often confronted in emotive terms. The MeToo movement against sexual harassment may have started in the United States in 2017, but it went viral and global, triggered by worldwide outrage over continued harassment and abuse of women at workplaces and public spaces. Activists within the GJM frequently articulate their opposition to neoliberal capitalism and the international financial institutions in moral economy terms. Social movement actors do not simply engage in coolheaded cost-benefit calculations but also express strong feelings about injustices and entitlements. In the United Kingdom, rallies of pro- and anti-Brexit advocates in 2018–19 were highly charged events, as were the French yellow vest protests. European citizens have reacted to both economic insecurity and anger over jihadist attacks by voting for right-wing populist parties.

The presence of emotions such as humiliation, anger, and frustration has been widely noted in connection with Muslim militants, by observers as well as by Islamists themselves. Osama bin Laden, for example, once declared that for more than eighty years Islam had been "tasting . . . humiliation and contempt . . . its sons . . . killed, its blood . . . shed, its holy places . . . attacked."[26] In Tunisia, when the street vendor Mohammed Bouazizi ignited himself in December 2010 out of frustration at his inability to make a living, this seemed to express the frustration of a large segment of the Tunisian population, which had seen its once-vaunted welfare state deteriorate in the wake of neoliberal reforms as well as the global economic crisis. Anger and frustration also could be seen in Greece, Spain, Italy, Chile, Britain, and other countries where street protests and strikes targeted governments, corporations, and banks as the architects of the hated neoliberalism that had done away with the once strong social economy model. In the United States, Occupy Wall Street protesters expressed frustration with the inability of the world's largest economy to provide decent jobs and decent wages, as well as anger at bank bailouts and gross income inequalities.

Emotions are not limited to anger, alienation, and moral outrage. Kum-Kum Bhavnani, John Foran, and Molly Talcott write of the Zapatista movement, "Love of life, love of people, love of justice—all play a role in the core values of Zapatismo."[27] At the antiglobalization protests and demonstrations of the early part of the century, during the anti-austerity protests in Europe in 2010 and 2011, and at the Occupy Wall Street protests of fall 2011, laughter, music, satire, parody, and puppetry—indeed, a festival-like atmosphere—abounded. Strong feelings of social solidarity, unity of purpose, and hope were evident in the Tunisian and Egyptian antigovernment protests of early 2011, which also saw poetry, song, and candlelight vigils. Emotions such as joy, anger, commitment, and solidarity are as important in the social movement experience as are the "entrepreneurial" dimensions that resource mobilization theories of social movements tend to emphasize. For these reasons, elements of the older explanatory frameworks that focused on sociopsychological factors in protest mobilizations cannot be entirely ruled out as anachronistic or unhelpful. Indeed, the concept of cultural framing is rooted in social psychology.

TRANSNATIONAL/GLOBAL SOCIAL MOVEMENTS

Until relatively recently, social movements were not studied systematically in relation to capitalism. The emergence of transnational social movements in the 1990s, and especially the GJM's explicit critique of economic globalization, compelled sociologists to pay closer attention to the political-economy underpinnings of social movement activism. Transnational or global social movements constitute a subset of social movements; they are mass mobilizations uniting people in three or more countries, engaged in sustained contentious interactions with political elites, international organizations, or multinational corporations.[28] A transnational social movement is analytically distinct from, though related to, an international solidarity network or a transnational advocacy network; the latter may identify itself with social movements, such as the feminist, environmentalist, human rights, or peace and justice movements, and thus may be oriented toward social change. In the perspective taken in this book, transnational social movements and transnational advocacy networks alike are structurally linked to globalization, and they constitute important sectors in what scholars call "global civil society." These points are elaborated further in chapter 2.

Whereas theorists of new social movements had projected feminist movements as localized and identity focused, the 1990s saw women organizing and mobilizing across borders in transnational feminist networks, particularly around the effects of economic restructuring, patriarchal fundamentalisms, and violence against women. In the MENA region, movements for women's rights spread, and one transnational feminist network, the Collectif Maghreb Egalité 95, based in North Africa and linking feminist groups in Algeria, Morocco, and Tunisia, mobilized for the reform of patriarchal family laws, criminalization of domestic violence and sexual harassment, equal nationality rights, and greater political and economic participation.[29]

ORIGINS AND ANTECEDENTS

Transnational social movements date back to the late eighteenth century, although in recent decades the scope of transnationalization and the scale of international ties among activists have risen dramatically. As noted, social movements are rooted in, and react to, the contradictions of modernity and capitalism—as also is the case with revolutions. In her study of historical resistance to economic globalization, Zahara Heckscher identifies five episodes between the 1780s and the early 1900s: the Tupac Amaru II uprising in what is now Peru against the Spanish colonialists; the international movement against the Atlantic slave trade; European workers and the First International Workingman's Association; the campaign against the colonization of the Congo; and United States–Philippines solidarity in the anti-imperialist movement of the late nineteenth century.[30] These cases of what world-system analysts call "antisystemic resistance" confirm Marx's many apposite observations about human action and societal constraints, including the famous line from the opening paragraphs of *The Eighteenth Brumaire of Louis Bonaparte*: "Men make their own history," he noted, [but] "they do not make it under circumstances chosen by themselves."[31]

World-system theorists point out that history proceeds in a series of waves. Capitalist expansions ebb and flow in waves of globalization and deglobalization, and egalitarian and humanistic countermovements emerge in a cyclical dialectical struggle. Karl Polanyi calls this the "double-movement," and Terry Boswell and Christopher Chase-Dunn term this "the spiral of capitalism and socialism."[32] Table 1.1, which I prepared for classroom use in 2007 and have updated since, summarizes some of the key events associated with the global spread of capitalism and its challengers during the "long twentieth century"—that is, from the early 1900s to the present century. It draws attention to the salience of, and relations among, political economy, states, and resistance. It also includes some of the key institutions of global governance and international organizations that belong to what sociologist Jackie Smith has identified as two contending global networks: the global neoliberal network and the global pro-democracy network.[33]

The movements studied in this book have historical antecedents in the eighteenth, nineteenth, and early twentieth centuries. The global justice movement (GJM) had echoes of the transnational movements

Table 1.1. Timeline: The World-System, Globalization, and Social Movements, 1870–2019

1870–1914	Economic liberalism, free trade, British Empire, colonialism, competition (France, Germany, and British, Austro-Hungarian, and Ottoman empires)
1914–18	World War I; suffrage movement, socialism/communism
1920s–30s	Breakup of empires; modernity and its discontents; Great Depression; socialism/communism, labor, League of Nations; fascism
1939–45	World War II (United States, United Kingdom, and Soviet Union vs. Germany, Italy, and Japan)
1945	Beginning of decolonization; decline of British Empire, rise of the United States as hegemon (especially after 1953 coup in Iran)
1950s	Cold War (including coups and CIA dirty tricks); emergence of the "three worlds," including the nonaligned movement (Bandung Conference)
1950s–70s	Theories and policies of development (balanced growth, basic needs, dependency, ISI, etc.); era of state-led development (industrialization, etc.); Fordist/Keynesian economics; deficit financing; influence of CEPAL/ECLAC, NAM, NIEO, UNIDO, UNCTAD, ILO, and UNESCO[a]
1960s–80s	Third World revolutions and Western social movements: anti–Vietnam War, 1968 student movement; feminist, environmental, antinuclear, and animal rights movements; Huntington's "third wave of democratization" begins in Southern Europe; anti-IMF protests in Third World
1980s	End of Keynesianism and rise of monetarism: indebtedness due to interest rate increases; structural adjustment policies; Contra Wars in Central America; Afghan war; Islamic fundamentalism; slow decline of Soviet Union; emergence of transnational feminist networks
1989–91	Collapse of communist bloc; end of Three Worlds; publication of first UNDP Human Development Report
1990s	Iraq sanctions, Yugoslav wars, Rwanda genocide; consolidation of European Union; end of apartheid in South Africa; neoliberal capitalist globalization: transnational capitalist class and global governance, flexible labor markets, NAFTA, shift from GATT to the WTO; rise of NGOs, INGOs, transnational advocacy networks; the UN's Fourth World Conference on Women; mobilizations against neoliberal globalization: anti-MAI, "Battle of Seattle"
2000	Beginning of cycle of antiglobalization protests; enactment by global elites of Millennium Declaration and MDGs; Security Council Resolution 1325
2001	September 11, al-Qaeda, invasion of Afghanistan; spread of global Arab media
2003	"War on terror" and US/UK invasion of Iraq
2007–	Defeat of the Doha round, rise of Brazil, Russia, India, China (BRIC); mortgage crisis in United States; start of global financial crisis and economic recession; declining US hegemony and world-system transition?
2011–12	Arab Spring; European protests against austerity; Chilean protests; Occupy Wall Street
2012–2019	Right-wing populist parties win parliamentary seats or form coalition governments; ISIS/ISIL/IS/Daesh emerges in Iraq and Syria ("caliphate" defeated in 2018–19)

[a]CEPAL/ECLAC refers to the UN's Economic Commission for Latin America; NAM is the Nonaligned Movement; UNIDO is the UN Industrial Development Organization; UNESCO is the UN Educational, Scientific and Cultural Organization.

of workers, socialists, communists, progressives, and anarchists during an economic period that Polanyi calls the "great transformation." Many of the older activists in the GJM, including those active within the WSF, were once affiliated with left-wing organizations or solidarity movements, many of the younger activists were involved in labor and economic justice causes, and the writings of Karl Marx are well known to many activists. A key difference, however, lies in the GJM's preference for noncentralized, nonhierarchical, and "horizontal" forms of organizing and of deliberative democratic decision making; it is far more decentralized, diffuse, fluid, and internetworked than was the case with the nineteenth- and twentieth-century Left. Human rights groups abound in the GJM and are a strong presence at the WSF. Some scholars have found similarities between their moral discourse, tactics, and strategies and those of the much earlier antislavery movement in the United States and the United Kingdom. Keck and Sikkink note that the backbone of the antislavery movement was made up of Quakers and the "dissenting denominations"—Methodists, Presbyterians, and Unitarians—who used reportage, conferences, and novels to push for abolition.[34] Reportage and conferences are still used by human rights organizations, as they are by feminist organizations, with the internet revolution helping to broaden the scope of their mobilizing mechanisms and tactics and adding to their collective action repertoire.

Islamist movements are rooted in eighteenth-, nineteenth-, and early twentieth-century revival movements, which in turn claimed to be following the path taken by the Prophet Muhammad in the seventh century AD. Sociologist Mansoor Moaddel has traced the evolution of Islamic modernism, liberal nationalism, and Islamic fundamentalism, arguing that the movements arose in the context of different global developments, resources, cultural capital, and institutional ties. He adds:

> Yet Muslims reached no lasting agreement on the form government should take, the appropriate economic model, the relationship of Muslim nations with the outside world, the status of women, their national identities, and the relation of Islam to rational analysis and rule making. Instead, Islamic societies experienced a sequence of diverse cultural episodes characterized by serious ideological disputes and acrimonious debates followed by sociopolitical crises, ending in revolutions or military coups.[35]

Self-described Islamic governments have come to power in Iran, Saudi Arabia, Sudan, Pakistan, and Turkey, and only in Turkey was the ruling party—the Justice and Development Party, or AKP as per the Turkish acronym—discussed in terms of an example of the compatibility of Islam and democracy, although that changed after 2011 with the party's increasing authoritarian turn. Following the Arab Spring, Islamist political parties won elections in Egypt, Morocco, and Tunisia. The government of Egypt's Muslim Brotherhood–affiliated president, Mohamed Morsi, became very unpopular, triggering new protests, and in July 2013, it was overthrown by a military coup. Tunisia's an-Nahda and Morocco's Justice and Development Party (Parti du Justice et Développement, PJD) have been in government since 2011, though they are not popular with secular and liberal or left-wing citizens. Questions that may be posed include, Are Islamic movements anti-systemic? Can they be democratic and pro-feminist? Are they agents of democratization or of a new form of authoritarian right-wing populism?

The contemporary global women's movement has roots in first-wave feminism, with its focus on suffrage and justice for women, and in second-wave feminism, with its demands for equality and cultural change. Early first-wave feminism emerged with the bourgeois democratic revolutions, and it subsequently brought about international women's organizations around abolition, women's suffrage, opposition to trafficking in women, antimilitarism, and labor legislation for working women and mothers. In the United States, the 1848 Seneca Falls Convention comprised elite women familiar with the details of the French and American revolutions and supportive of the antislavery movement. First-wave feminism later grew to include women disappointed that the franchise was not extended to them when slaves were emancipated and the men given the right to vote. Scholars have identified moderate, socialist, and militant strands of the early feminist movement. Among the SMOs of first-wave feminism was the International Woman Suffrage Alliance (IWSA), formed in 1904. Its methods included speaking tours and rallies, but militants were ready to be arrested, jailed, and force-fed for the cause. Militant suffragists in the United States and the United Kingdom deployed public agitation, civil disobedience, and sometimes violent tactics to draw attention to their cause; the Women's Social and Political Union in the United Kingdom and Alice Paul and her associates in the United States used such methods.

The early twentieth century also saw the emergence of an international socialist women's movement. In 1900, the Socialist International passed its first resolution in favor of women's suffrage, and suffrage became a demand of socialist parties in 1907. Within the Second International, the women's organizations of France, Germany, and Russia mobilized thousands of working-class as well as middle-class women for socialism and women's emancipation. In Asian countries, as Kumari Jayawardena showed, many of the women's movements and organizations that emerged were associated with socialist or nationalist movements. Although feminists and leftists have not always agreed on priorities or strategies, there has been a long-standing affinity that helps explain the involvement of feminists in the GJM and the WSF. Examples of early international women's organizations are the Women's International League for Peace and Freedom (WILPF), the International Council of Women (ICW), the International Alliance of Women (IAW), the Women's International Democratic Federation (WIDF), and the Young Women's Christian Association (YWCA). In promoting women's rights, maternity legislation, and an end to child labor, they engaged with intergovernmental bodies such as the League of Nations and the International Labour Organization (ILO).[36]

Populism is not new, given its long history in Russia and the United States and the deployment of populist rhetoric and policies of various ideological hues in Latin America and Europe. An even earlier manifestation was brilliantly analyzed as "Bonapartism" by Karl Marx, whereby the coup of Louis-Napoleon Bonaparte (the nephew of Napoleon, founder of the First Empire following the French Revolution), led a revolt with the support of small farmers and urban lumpenproletariat against the French bourgeoisie (i.e., the Orleanists and the Bourbons), to establish the Second Empire.[37] Marx argued that the political stalemate and instability in the balance of class forces enabled the Bonapartists to actually preserve and mask the bourgeoisie's power. The term "Bonapartist" came to be used more generally for a political movement that advocates an authoritarian centralized state with a strongman charismatic leader based on anti-elitist rhetoric and conservatism. Vladimir Lenin used the term to describe the counterrevolutionary nature of the Russian bourgeoisie after the July 1917 crisis. In spring 1979, following the Iranian revolution, some Iranian leftists used the terms "populist" and "Bonapartist" to describe the new Islamic revolutionary state.

If earlier episodes of populism, often tinged with nativism, emerged from the contradictions of the transition from traditional to modern society during the early industrial era (e.g., displacements and exploitation), many studies describe the current wave as a backlash against the contradictions of neoliberal globalization, including economic difficulties, cultural changes, and democracy deficits (see chapter 7).

ACTIVISM AND THE INTERNET

Scholars have long examined the extent to which social networks—whether formal or informal—affect movement recruitment and organizational growth. The internet and especially social-networking media are now viewed as significant new mobilizing technologies that help create "virtual communities" or connect various movements, networks, and individuals for collective action framed by a collective identity. In the United States, MoveOn.org—a nonprofit organization and political action committee founded in 1998 to focus on education about and advocacy for national issues—has utilized the internet extensively and effectively to mobilize public action on specific bills, policies, or candidates in favor of progressive politics. In addition to the virtual communities that it creates, MoveOn.org encourages the formation of local discussion and activist groups. Avaaz.org, launched in 2007, is a global campaigning organization with a strong antiwar stance.[38]

The new information and communication technologies (ICTs) inspired research on their role in protest participation. One study showed how mobile phones were used for political mobilization processes, such as the deposing of Philippine president Joseph Estrada in 2002, the election campaign in South Korea in 2002, the 2004 elections in Spain following the terrorist bombing attack in Madrid, and the protest events at the 2004 Republican National Convention in the United States. Social-networking media such as Facebook, Twitter, and Instagram, very popular among young people, are especially useful for purposes of rapid communication during protest periods. In Iran's Green Protests of June 2009, mobile phones and tweets were used to mobilize people for the street protests, record and document the massive nature of the demonstrations, warn activists of police presence, photograph police brutality, and disseminate visual and aural images globally.[39] Throughout the Arab Spring of early 2011, young people used social media to receive information and mobilize others; they captured police brutality on their smartphones, posted images, and celebrated their victory on the web as well as on the streets of Tunis, Cairo, and elsewhere. On October 15, 2011, one month after Occupy Wall Street emerged in New York City, a global day of solidarity took place, with nine hundred protests across eighty-two countries—all coordinated via ICTs.

WikiLeaks—part of a longer tradition and principle of free publication, "open source" information, and news distribution—challenged authorities and governments the world over by releasing classified US documents revealing malfeasance in wars, foreign policy, and global business. According to one report, WikiLeaks had changed whistle blowing, dissident journalism, and the new phenomenon of "citizen journalism" through its regular exposés of state or corporate crimes. Its founder, Julian Assange, an Australian national, unveiled WikiLeaks .org in January 2007, and in publications that were picked up by the *New York Times*, the *Guardian*, *El País*, *Der Spiegel*, and *Le Monde*, it exposed evidence of corruption in the family of former Kenyan president Daniel arap Moi, published the standard operating principles for the Guantánamo Bay detention center, and, most significantly, released in April 2010 a video of a US helicopter attack in Baghdad in July 2007, which killed a number of Iraqi civilians and two Iraqi-born Reuters personnel. An eighteen-minute film called *Collateral Murder* gave a chilling insight into what could be perceived as US war crimes. Assange maintained that an explicit part of WikiLeaks' purpose in exposing US State Department cables and other government documents was to highlight human rights abuses. Subsequently, both the website and its founder became the subject of investigation, personal attacks, and a financial blockade that impeded supporter donations. In response, the chimerical Anonymous collective retaliated by hacking into government, police, and corporate files.[40]

Lauren Langman and Douglas Morris have argued that ICTs permit "internetworking," or connections to diverse networks and movements for social change. Stefaan Walgrave and colleagues examined the ways ICTs may "lower networking costs, extend the reach and diversity of networks, and increase levels and scale of participation," as well as the extent to which digital media "allow activists to combine multiple engagements with diverse causes."[41] Such observations illustrate how ICTs play a role in facilitating rapid horizontal communication and coordination.[42] As one of the "gifts" of globalization, the internet has been an indispensable tool for activists, for both mobilization and the exposure of elite malfeasance. It has allowed for rapid communication and coordination; internet-savvy transnational networks have set up extensive, interactive, and increasingly sophisticated multimedia websites, which make available statements, research reports, and manifestoes, as well as discussion forums, chat rooms, blogs, tutorials, webinars, and digital libraries. Such websites, many of which are linked to each other, create or support communities of activists while also providing them with resources. Peace and antiwar activists can access the US-based Peace Action website or that of ANSWER (Act Now to Stop War & End Racism Coalition), or the websites of the women-led groups Code Pink: Women for Peace and WILPF.[43]

Cyberactivism can cross generational lines, but it is the vehicle par excellence of the younger generation, with their affinity for, and expertise in, social-networking media. As such, the "biographical availability" of youth for protest activity is enhanced by their immersion in the world of ICTs, creating a demographic pool with a potential for rapid mobilization and protest activity.[44] It is important to note, however, that the internet also has been used by right-wing and violent networks, most notoriously by the terrorist group Islamic State (also known as ISIS or ISIL or Daesh in Arabic), which formed in the chaos following the US-UK invasion of Iraq and especially after the weakening of the Syrian state in the wake of its post-2011 internationalized civil conflict. Internet sites and social media also are under constant surveillance by state agencies to monitor citizens as well as real or perceived external enemies. Platforms such as Facebook and Google share individuals' information to advertisers. Reliance on social media sites may encourage what critic Evgeny Morozov calls "slacktivism."[45]

All these developments—the rise of transnational social movements and networks for democracy, justice, and human rights; the growth of militant networks that draw on Islamic symbols; the spread of women's rights movements; the invasion and occupation of Afghanistan and Iraq; the Arab Spring and the NATO intervention to support the armed uprising in Libya; the extensive use of ICTs; and the rise of populisms—are pertinent to the study of globalization and social movements. They present questions about opportunities and resources for movement building, the use of violence in social/political movements and transnational networks, the relationship of war to the global capitalist order, the changing dynamics of the world-system and the role of the hegemon, the salience of masculinities in global processes, and prospects for women-friendly democratic transitions that institutionalize the economic as well as civil and political rights of citizens. These questions are addressed in the book's subsequent chapters.

ORGANIZATION AND METHODOLOGY OF THE BOOK

This book integrates a discussion of theories and empirical documentation of social movements in an era of globalization while also offering an explanatory framework. It analyzes the relationship between globalization—in its economic, political, and cultural manifestations—and social movements, including transnational collective action (both left-wing and right-wing). Chapter 2 takes a deeper dive into the processes and mechanisms that have led to both left-wing and right-wing responses to neoliberal capitalist globalization. Chapter 3 takes up such sociological issues as the agents of the democracy movements, democracy "frames," mobilization processes and organizational features, the populist challenge to democracy, and prospects for a global democracy. The case-study chapters—chapters 4, 5, 6, and 7—focus on global social movements that emerged under the conditions of late capitalism/ neoliberal globalization: political Islam, the women's movement, the global justice movement (GJM), and right-wing populisms (RWPs).

To anticipate the argument, this book shows that each movement connects people across borders around a common agenda and collective identity; mobilizes large numbers of supporters and activists, whether as individuals or as members of networks, groups, and organizations; and engages in sustained oppositional politics with states or other power holders. There are, however, differences. Although Islamist movements are internally differentiated, their grievances, methods, and goals differ in profound ways from those of the radical democratic or socialistic visions of global feminism and the GJM. One key difference is that many Islamist movements seek state power and, like revolutionary movements before them, are willing to use violence to achieve this aim. In contrast, both the feminist and global justice movements eschew violence and have shown a lack of interest in state power, although they do seek wide-ranging institutional and normative changes. Right-wing populists evince a desire for strong political parties, electoral victories, and state power. They have a rather thin view and practice of democracy, and they focus on the defense of cultural values and norms against external influences or threats. This book, therefore, examines the opportunities, mobilizing structures, and frames pertinent to global social movements (see table 1.2 for an elaboration).

Methodologically, the book takes a multi-scalar approach, in that it covers global, national, and local social-movement activism across the Global North and Global South. It is a variant of what Michael Burawoy and his coauthors term "grounded globalization."[46] My analysis of TFNs, for example, grew from both my involvement in feminist groups and my observation of TFN lobbying activities at UN conferences when I was a UN staff member in the 1990s. I have followed developments in transnational feminism since then, including at the WSF. I attended conferences and meetings, conducted interviews, and became a member of two of the ones I have studied. In addition to having consulted the relevant secondary sources on globalization, social movements, the Arab Spring, and the global Islamist, feminist, global justice, and right-wing populist movements, I have examined movement websites and publications. The present book, therefore, synthesizes previous research, including my own fieldwork and published results over the years, while also offering a framework for analysis of complex processes and proposals for genuinely democratic alternatives to the present state of affairs.

I end this chapter with several theoretically informed propositions regarding globalization and social movements, which also presage the book's premises, arguments, and concepts:

1. Globalization is a multifaceted process of social change with economic, political, and cultural dimensions that reflect isomorphism and divergence, new forms of inequality and competition, and transnational forms of organizing and mobilizing. What has been called globalization-from-above is the latest stage of capitalism on a world scale, involving the spread of neoliberal capitalism through investment, trade, and war. Given the capitalist bases of globalization, the inequalities of class, gender, and race are maintained through processes of accumulation and patterns of distribution in the productive, reproductive, and virtual economies

Table 1.2. Social Movement Features of Feminist, Islamist, Global Justice, and Populist Movements

	Opportunities and Resources	Mobilizing Structures: Networks and SMOs	Frames
Feminist	Sociodemographics: women's educational attainment and labor force participation UN Decade for Women (1976–85) and 1990s UN conferences. Resources: women's organizations, donor agencies, European foundations	DAWN, WIDE, WLUML, WEDO, WILPF, World March of Women, MADRE, WLP, Code Pink	Women's rights are human rights; end feminization of poverty; end violence against women; empowerment; gender justice
Islamist			
Parliamentarian	Local support; resources from Muslim states; publicity and support via Arab media such as Al Jazeera	Hamas, Hezbollah, Muslim Brotherhood; an-Nahda	Islam is the solution; establish sharia law; end repression; justice for Palestine
Extremist	US-sponsored Afghan war, 1980–1992; 2003 US invasion of Iraq; Saudi financing; publicity via Al Jazeera	Al-Qaeda and affiliates; various salafist or jihadist groupings; ISIS/ISIL/Daesh	Get "Crusaders" out of Muslim lands; liberate Palestine, Afghanistan, Iraq, Syria; jihad against "near enemy" and "far enemy"; global caliphate
Global Justice	UN conferences of 1990s; occasional support from EU and social democratic governments; *Le Monde Diplomatique;* Workers' Party government of Brazil; rise of left-wing governments in Latin America; information and communication technologies	Third World Network; ENDA; Focus on the Global South; Oxfam; Jubilee 2000; ATTAC; World Social Forum; World March of Women; Occupy Wall Street	Against neoliberal globalization; for biodiversity and cultural diversity (*altermondialisation*); economic justice, ending Third World debt, making poverty history, environmental protection, human rights, antiwar, ending corporate greed and power, "another world is possible," "we are the 99%!"
Right-Wing Populism	Right-wing (and sometimes conservative) political parties; media, think tanks, foundations	Political parties (see chapter 7 for listing); local networks	The people vs. the elites; against globalism, for national sovereignty; "Make America Great Again"; Welfare for "own people first"; controls on immigration and borders

Note: For full names, see the list of acronyms.

within and across the core, periphery, and semiperiphery of the world-system.[47] Periodic crises trigger political responses by ruling classes, ordinary citizens, and organized movements.

2. Social movements—sustained contentious politics by mobilized groups that target states—have been affected by globalization in at least two ways: (a) they are increasingly influenced by forces and factors beyond national borders, and (b) they have expanded their scope above and across borders. Movements that begin within national borders may have supra-national determinants and then diffuse transnationally; examples are the neighborhood effects of the Arab Spring, the global spread of Occupy encampments, the global movement to end violence against women, and the spread of right-wing populist movements.

3. Transnational social movements are related to globalization in three ways: (a) they are responses to the downside of globalization, specifically, neoliberal capitalism; (b) they reflect the global expansion of civil society, the transnational public sphere, and world culture; and (c) they benefit from opportunities and resources associated with the new information and communication technologies. Transnationalization is a deliberate strategy to increase the global reach of social movements and expand movement diversity, representation, and influence. In some cases, as with transnational feminist networks and the WSF, it is a way of transmitting democratization.

4. Social movement theory has emphasized the importance of organizations, but the network form—with its flexibility, fluidity, and horizontal nature—became the predominant form in the post–Cold War era. Although the noncentralized network form, characteristic of the GJM, transnational feminist networks, and the WSF appeared to be most conducive to an era of globalization, it may be unable to sustain itself or challenge the status quo. Research may need to focus more on the weaknesses as well as strengths of "horizontal" versus "vertical" forms of social movement organizing.

5. If neoliberal capitalist globalization was a strategy of the transnational capitalist class to improve the accumulation process and increase profits, the increasing domination of finance capital precipitated the 2008 crisis and the subsequent mass protests, social

movements, political revolutions, and populist wave. Following from world-system theorizing, all these processes coincide with the global B-phase downturn of the Kondratieff wave and the gradual decline of the hegemon. A key question is the extent to which they may be regarded as antisystemic and could presage what world-system scholars call another "world revolution."

6. Globalization and its discontents, including possible deglobalization, present the social sciences with analytical challenges: how to theorize the links between local and global, national and transnational; the capacity of states, social movements, and networks in a world of global capital; the relationship of (fractions of) capital and the capitalist class to various right-wing movements; and the future of the world-system.

7. The study of social movements in a global era calls for an integrated framework drawing on world-system theory and world polity theory for a macrosociological and global perspective; employing feminism for an understanding of the gendered nature of institutions and movements; referring to Marxism for an elucidation of the class-based nature of the neoliberal project and of the propensity of capitalism toward both expansion and crisis; and invoking social movement concepts such as grievances, political opportunities, resources, mobilizing structures, and cultural frames. Such a holistic framework would help accomplish the goal of "globalizing social movement theory."[48]

Combining world-system, Marxist, and social movement conceptual frameworks helps us better grasp the factors behind the emergence and global diffusion of Islamism, feminism, the GJM, and populism. Integrating feminist insights allows us to discern the role of gender, and especially of hypermasculinities, in social movement dynamics, the state, and institutions of global governance.

CHAPTER 2

GLOBALIZATION, ITS DISCONTENTS, AND COLLECTIVE ACTION

Urgent: pouvoir d'achat et dignité pour tous!

—Gilets Jaunes slogan, Paris

Another world is possible!

—World Social Forum

Globalization became a buzzword in the mid-1990s, but before then scholars and activists had been focused on the social and economic development prospects of Third World countries and the damage that had been done by structural adjustment policies (SAPs) in the 1980s. Critiques of the "lost development decade"—which is what the 1980s era of structural adjustments, Reaganomics, and Thatcherism came to be called—intersected with earlier criticisms of the growing power of multinational corporations.[1] Veterans of Third World socialist or solidarity movements, left-wing groups, student movements, anti-Vietnam protests, and peace and antimilitarist causes—some of whom were also active in international development circles—then networked at various conferences to exchange ideas and plan strategies.

This chapter has three objectives. First, it describes how the transition took place from the era of state-led development and Keynesian economic policy to the consolidation of neoliberal globalization. In so doing, it elucidates neoliberal globalization's dimensions, mechanisms, agents, and social implications. Second, it examines the relationship between globalization and contemporary forms of collective action, including the challenge of right-wing populism. Finally, it analyzes the status of the state in an era of globalization and in relation to social movements, including transnational social movements.

FROM DEVELOPMENT TO GLOBALIZATION

Development has its roots in post–World War II reconstruction of Europe and postcolonial nation building. Leading theorists included Sir Arthur Lewis, Albert Hirschmann, Gunnar Myrdal, Raul Prebisch, and Walt Rostow. The 1950s through the 1970s were dominated by policy debates on achieving prosperity in the "Third World" and the formation of new institutions, theories, and forms of international cooperation. (Refer back to table 1.1.)

The 1970s was a time of both horror and hope. The US-supported 1973 military coup d'état against the democratically elected socialist president of Chile, Dr. Salvador Allende, ushered in both a reign of terror and the Global South's first experiment with a neoliberal economic policy framework. In her book *Shock Doctrine: The Rise of Disaster Capitalism*, Naomi Klein highlights this event as the harbinger of the more expansive scope of neoliberalism at century's end and into the new millennium. David Harvey states that "neoliberalization" was accomplished in 1970s Chile and Argentina in a manner that was "as simple as it was swift, brutal, and sure: a military coup backed by the traditional upper classes (as well as by the U.S. government), followed by the fierce repression of all solidarities created within the labour and the urban social movements which had so threatened their power."[2] At the same time, the early 1970s saw the end of dictatorships in Greece,

Portugal, and Spain. In particular, the 1975 defeat of the United States in Indochina and the unification of the Socialist Republic of Vietnam suggested a more hopeful era. The Cold War between the United States and the Soviet Union was in full swing, but the presence of a powerful communist bloc checked further aggression by the United States while also providing moral and financial support to various Third World institutions, movements, and revolutions.[3]

At the start of the 1970s, the "golden age of capitalism," with its Keynesian and "Fordist" production and labor policies, was still in place, as was state-led Third World development.[4] Revolutions and democratic transitions occurred in developing countries and in southern Europe. The decade also saw the emergence of new international organizations supportive of Third World development, including the United Nations Conference on Trade and Development (UNCTAD), the South Center, and the Center on Transnational Corporations. The Society for International Development had been formed earlier, but in the 1970s, it became an important forum for the discussion of development theories and strategies. The United Nations Educational, Scientific and Cultural Organization (UNESCO) promoted literacy and schooling, higher education, scientific networks, intellectual and cultural production, and research on and in developing countries. The International Labour Office, the Geneva-based secretariat of the International Labour Organization (ILO), produced many studies on labor and employment, often from a social-democratic or leftist perspective, as well as conventions and declarations.

The UN General Assembly issued a Declaration on the Establishment of a New International Economic Order (NIEO), which targeted "the remaining vestiges of alien domination, colonialism, foreign occupation, racial discrimination, apartheid, and neo-colonialism." The declaration called for the "establishment of a just and equitable relationship" in terms of trade between developed and developing countries, the "establishment of a new international monetary system" for the promotion of development in the Third World, and "securing favorable conditions for the transfer of financial resources to developing countries." It emphasized the need to "promote the transfer of technology and the creation of indigenous technology for the benefit of the developing countries in forms and in accordance with procedures which are suited to their economies" and the "necessity for all States to

put an end to the waste of natural resources, including food products."
The NIEO would continue to inspire scholar-activists in Third World
solidarity movements and development studies for at least ten years
and was a discussion topic at many meetings of the global Left. For
example, in the 1980s, the Communist Party of Yugoslavia was organizing the Cavtat Roundtable, which brought together Marxist theorists,
socialists, and communists from across the globe in an annual dialogue
that was also an arena for networking and strategizing. Although discussions covered a range of issues, prospects for a new international
economic order were debated at several of the meetings.[5]

By the latter part of the 1980s, however, the NIEO had become a
dead letter. Third World countries had borrowed heavily during the
hopeful years of 1960s and 1970s developmentalism. International
banks were only too eager to lend, and the developing countries needed
the loans to offset the effects of the oil price hikes of 1973 and 1979 as
they continued to implement their development strategies.[6] When interest rates on loans suddenly soared in 1980–82, the Third World was
plunged into what Cheryl Payer presciently had called "the debt trap."[7]
The situation was exacerbated by the collapse of world market prices
for Third World commodities such as copper, coffee, and oil. When
developing countries turned to the World Bank and the International
Monetary Fund (IMF) for new loans to service their debts, to carry
out their development plans, or to guarantee their creditworthiness,
the international financial institutions insisted on policy changes as a
condition for additional loans. In the name of efficiency and balanc-
ing budgets, SAPs called for austerity measures such as cuts in social
spending, public-sector restructuring, denationalization, and the promotion of private capital. These were, indeed, "conditionalities" placed
on indebted developing countries in return for new loans that would
enable them to repay the outstanding debts. The immediate results of
SAPs and the various conditions on new loans were financial transfers
from the Global South to the Global North as a result of debt servicing; deterioration of health, education, and welfare in many developing
countries; falling real wages and incomes; a heavy household burden
on women to compensate for income loss and social service cutbacks;
and the collapse of governments and emergence of conflicts. Within the
women-in-development (WID) community, feminist scholars described
the gender bias of these policies and the social hardships they created.[8]

The international political economy was changing, and new "rules of the game" were crafted. Markets were becoming more integrated and less regulated, and labor practices were growing more "flexible" (that is, easier on employers, with fewer rights for workers); production sites in the United States were moving to nonunion or cheap-labor locations, first in the American South and then in the Global South; financial products were becoming more complex and widespread, taking over pension and retirement plans. In a prescient US-focused 1993 study of what was to come, Mary Zey described the junk bond scandal of the 1980s as "structural embeddedness," eschewing labels like "greedy" or "bad apples" and showing how such reckless banking activities normalized manipulations of the financial markets.[9]

In the course of this global restructuring, more women and migrants were integrated as flexible low-paid labor into increasingly segmented labor markets connected to global commodity chains. Public services, basic provisions, and public goods were privatized and subjected to market principles. Dramatic reductions in transportation and communication costs, combined with the breakdown of Fordist/Keynesian regimes in the core countries, made it possible for firms to coordinate production on a truly global scale. In the United States, neoliberal capitalism entailed deindustrialization and loss of job security; in the United Kingdom, it meant attacking the trade unions first, then slowly chipping away at welfare provisioning.[10] Moreover, in 1984–85 the US and UK governments withdrew from a UN agency that they felt had become improperly radical: UNESCO. The stated reasons for the withdrawal were the alleged bad management of the organization, the left-wing orientation of the programs, and the politicization of debates. The United States was especially opposed to the proposal for a New World Information and Communication Order (NWICO). In 1985, the British government led by Margaret Thatcher followed suit, citing similar reasons.[11]

In concert with the World Bank and the IMF, the governments led by Ronald Reagan in the United States and Margaret Thatcher in Great Britain became the proponents of the doctrine of neoliberal capitalism, which earlier had been implemented in Chile under the auspices of the "Chicago boys"—economist Milton Friedman and his associates from the University of Chicago. Along with the US government, the World Bank and the IMF became the prime agents of not only SAPs in the Third World and neoliberalism in the rich capitalist countries but also the transformation of formerly socialist economies into capitalist economies in the 1990s. As the communist world weakened and then collapsed in the latter part of the 1980s, Prime Minister Thatcher's declaration that "there is no alternative" to global free market capitalism seemed to ring true.

By the 1990s, the shift from the post–World War II era of full employment and welfare creation through government spending and industrial policy to the preeminence of big business, banks, and the operations of "the market" was now complete. The institutionalization of economic liberalism—free trade, free markets, and capitalist globalization—came to herald the end of both the "global age of capitalism" and the "golden age of Third World development." The so-called Washington Consensus (the term was coined by economist John Williamson) became the global framework for economic growth and debt reduction and entailed the following elements:

- a guarantee of fiscal discipline and a curb to budget deficit;
- a reduction of public expenditure, particularly in the military and public administration;
- tax reform, aiming at the creation of a system with a broad base and effective enforcement;
- financial liberalization, with interest rates determined by the market;
- competitive exchange rates to assist export-led growth;
- trade liberalization, coupled with the abolition of import licensing and a reduction of tariffs;
- promotion of foreign direct investment;
- privatization of state enterprises, leading to efficient management and improved performance;
- deregulation of the economy; and
- protection of property rights.[12]

How would the Washington Consensus affect the world's regions and social groups? Economist Paul Streeten's globalization balance sheet suggests who the winners and losers would be (see table 2.1). It is prescient in its insights, but for three caveats. First, globalization has not been good for Global Peace. Second, globalization has benefited a

Table 2.1. Balance Sheet of Globalization

Good for	Bad for
Japan, Europe, North America	Many developing countries
East and Southeast Asia	Africa and Latin America
Output	Employment
People with assets	People without assets
Profits	Wages
People with high skills	People with few skills
The educated	The uneducated
Professional, managerial, and technical people	Workers
Flexible adjusters	Rigid adjusters
Creditors	Debtors
Those independent of public services	Those dependent on public services
Large firms	Small firms
Men	Women, children
The strong and risk takers	The weak and vulnerable
Global markets	Local communities
Sellers of technically sophisticated products	Sellers of primary and standard manufactured products
Global culture	Local cultures
Global peace	Local troubles (Russia, Mexico, Turkey, former Yugoslavia)

Source: Streeten 1997.

certain segment of the female population, notably, Sheryl Sandberg's "lean in" population of high-income women professionals. Third, we now know that neoliberal globalization would eventually adversely affect even the richest economies, while China's economy would become a major beneficiary and a challenge to US hegemony.

DEBATING GLOBALIZATION

In the 1990s, economists including Jagdish Bhagwati, Jeffrey Sachs, and Dani Rodrik, or those who produced the United Nations Development Programme's *Human Development Report 1999*, saw globalization as "Janus-faced," with some capacity to reduce poverty and increase growth but also with a dark side. Dani Rodrik pointed out, "The fact that 'workers' can be more easily substituted for each other across national boundaries undermines what many conceive to be a postwar social bargain between workers and employers, under which the former would receive a steady increase in wages and benefits in return for labor peace." Joseph Stiglitz, formerly chief economist of the World Bank, criticized the "unfair trade agenda" and the absence of democratic accountability in global governance. Guy Standing of the ILO wrote extensively about the challenges for developing countries of global labor market flexibility. In a 2002 report, Oxfam maintained that trade liberalization could benefit developing countries, but not invariably so. The multilateral trade system, the report noted, is weighted against the interests of developing countries because core countries practice double standards by urging developing countries to liberalize while keeping their own markets closed to imports such as agricultural products and textiles. Policy recommendations, therefore, were that investment and trade between advanced and less developed countries should proceed equitably, and development assistance from North to South should increase. The ILO called for a "fair globalization" that would include decent jobs and decent wages.[13] China was not exactly a model of decent jobs and wages, but numerous core-country corporations invested there for its educated, obedient, and low-wage workforce.

For progressives like Walden Bello, Martin Khor, David Korten, Jerry Mander, Samir Amin, and others associated with the World Social Forum (WSF), globalization reproduced great and growing inequalities of wealth and incomes within and across countries. As such, globalization should be vigorously opposed by organized movements starting at the grassroots, local, and community levels.[14] Many in the labor movement across the globe espoused a similar view. Trade union leaders decried the social costs of globalization, such as unemployment, job insecurity, and continued poverty—the so-called race to the bottom—and they called for the establishment of core labor standards, fair trade, democratization of global economic management, a shift of focus from markets to people, and a tax on speculative financial flows. As the global justice movement (GJM) and several transnational feminist networks (TFNs) adopted the idea, a word on the Tobin tax, sometimes known as the "Robin Hood tax," is in order.

As early as 1972, Professor James Tobin, winner of the 1981 Nobel Prize for economics, proposed a tax on international currency transactions—for example, foreign exchange speculation—to reduce the volatility and instability of financial markets.[15] In 1994, he reiterated his proposal, suggesting that the proceeds of that tax be placed at the disposition of international organizations for development purposes.

The idea for such a tax was endorsed by many progressive nongovern-mental organizations (NGOs), including TFNs, and became a principal demand of the French-based group Association for the Taxation of Fi-nancial Transactions and for Citizens' Action (ATTAC), which went on to become a key group within the GJM. The Tobin tax was discussed by NGOs at the 1995 UN Social Summit in Copenhagen but was turned down by most governments. (James Tobin died in March 2002.) In 2011, in the wake of the Great Recession and as part of the rescue of the Eurozone, a financial transaction tax for development purposes was dis-cussed but rejected at a G20 meeting. Back on the Left, scholar-activists such as Walden Bello echoed Samir Amin's earlier call for "delinking" from the capitalist world-economy and in the late 1990s called for *deglo-balization*—rather a far-sighted clarion call, given that it has been more widely adopted by both left-wing and right-wing populist critics.[16]

Was globalization an inevitable product of technological change? Or was it "made" by globalizers? Here, both structure and agency are equally salient. Globalization certainly was shaped by forces such as technology, management innovations, and the market, but it did not just "happen." It was, rather, engineered and promoted by identifiable groups of people within identifiable organizations and states. Behzad Yaghmaian pointed out that the emergence of the neoliberal model of capitalism was part of a systematic effort to lower the social value of labor power and provide the flexibility demanded for global accumula-tion by removing all national restrictions on the full mobility of capital and by imposing a restructuring of the labor market centered on the creation of flexible labor regimes. David Harvey argued that neoliberal-ism, headed by the United States, had aimed for the restoration of class power to a small elite of financiers and corporate leaders, accomplished through forced privatization, or "accumulation by dispossession," as well as by the "virtual economy" of finance capital. Sociologist Leslie Sklair added to Marxian class theory by arguing that the transnational capitalist class (TCC) comprises not only those who own or control major corporations but also other groups whose resources and actions are deemed vital to the process of globalization: neoliberal bureaucrats and politicians, assorted professionals and technocrats, advertisers, and the mass media. Such "globalizers" carefully promoted and dissemi-nated the culture of consumer capitalism, as Sklair demonstrated, or free market ideology, as discussed by Manfred Steger.[17]

William I. Robinson, who like Sklair theorized the TCC, argued that the reorganization of world production through new technologies and organizational innovations was giving rise to an emerging transnational state apparatus (TSA). For Harvey, globalization was the "new imperialism," while for Robinson it was a historic stage in the maturation of capitalism as a driving economic force. In another structuralist position, world-system theorists Immanuel Wallerstein and Christopher Chase-Dunn argued that "globalization" is another word for the processes they have always referred to as world-systemic: integration into the economic zones of core, periphery, and semiperiphery, with their attendant hierarchies of states and forms of resistance, known as antisystemic movements.[18]

Synthesizing these debates in light of the evolution of globalization, we may conclude that globalization was not merely an inevitable stage in the development of capitalism but the result of conscious neoliberal policy making by globalizers (the agents of globalization), including multinational corporations and international financial institutions. Table 2.2 elaborates on globalization's features, agents, and challengers.

GROWING INCOME AND WEALTH INEQUALITY

In the 1990s, global justice activists began to refer to growing worldwide inequalities as a reason for their antiglobalization stance, citing research by economists such as Angus Maddison, Anthony Atkinson, Lance Taylor, and Branko Milanovic. World-system scholars Roberto Korzeniewicz and Timothy Moran similarly studied patterns of inequality between countries from a world-historical perspective. Maddison's study of inequalities between nations since the nineteenth century showed rising cross-national inequalities since the 1970s, while Atkinson documented rising inequalities in the industrialized countries (except in France). Taylor found that globalization and liberalization had not been uniformly favorable in terms of effects on growth and income distribution. Among the eighteen countries studied, only Chile after 1990 managed to combine high growth with decreasing inequality—in contrast to that country's increasing inequality over the preceding fifteen years. In a 2005 book on measures of global inequality, Milanovic found a complex situation including greater inequality within nations, greater differences between countries' mean incomes, and the

Table 2.2. Capitalist Globalization versus Alter-Globalization: Features, Agents, and Challengers

	Features	Agents	Challengers
Economic	Neoliberal/free market capitalism; accumulation via investment, trade, aid	Multinational corporations and banks, the World Bank, IMF, WTO, OECD; the transnational capitalist class	Global justice movement, transnational feminist networks
	Tobin/Robin Hood tax; workplace democracy; robust social policies	Unions, progressive political parties, UN agencies	TCC, pro-business states, World Bank, IMF, corporate sector
Political	Multilateralism, international solidarity, humanitarian operations, diplomacy	Intergovernmental organizations, transnational advocacy networks, international NGOs	US preference for bilateralism or unilateralism; right-wing populist-nationalists
	"Humanitarian intervention" and "preventive war"	NATO, United States, United Kingdom, France, Israel	Global justice movement, transnational feminist networks, peace groups
Cultural	Consumer capitalism, free market ideology, electoral democracy	Multinational corporations, US government, transnational capitalist class, corporate media	Global justice movement; Islamist movements; right-wing populists
	Human rights, women's rights, environmental protection, human security, social justice, peace	Transnational feminist networks, global justice movement, civil society groups, some INGOs and UN agencies	States and corporations prioritizing profits and growth; occasionally local groups

"catching up" of large, poor countries such as India and China. Still, he concluded that, with adjustments for price levels (purchasing power parity, or PPP, income), the bottom 90 percent of the world's population had half of world income, and the top 10 percent had the other half. In simple dollar terms (not adjusted for price levels), the top 10 percent earned two-thirds of the world's income.[19]

As the decade progressed, inequalities worsened in countries such as China, Chile, Iran, Egypt, India, Russia, the United Kingdom, and the United States. A report by the United Nations Development Programme (UNDP), *Human Development Report 2005*, showcased India as an example of a "globalization success," but one with a "mixed record on human development" because of the persistence of pervasive gender inequalities, inadequate public health, and growing income-based inequalities. Among the richest countries, income inequality became especially severe in the United States, but the report highlighted American health inequalities, too. In an extensively documented book, Richard Wilkinson and Kate Pickett show how US income inequality had grown, absolutely and in comparison with Europe, and demonstrated convincingly that many modern social problems—such as the breakdown of community relations, drug use, obesity, lower life expectancy, poor education outcomes, teen birth, violence, imprisonment, and low social mobility—are tied to inequality. Extravagant pay packages for the heads of banks, corporations, and, increasingly, university presidents were marked by lack of government oversight of financial practices. The business model of pharmaceutical companies such as the Sackler family–owned Purdue Pharma involved false claims about its opioid medication, eventually leading to the notorious opioid addiction problem in the United States, disproportionately affecting low-income Americans.[20] Rana Foroohar provides comparative data to show how the United States had become "the land of less opportunity," with less upward social mobility, compared with other rich Organisation for Economic Co-operation and Development (OECD) countries. This problem had been captured by sociologist Katherine Newman as early as the 1990s, when she wrote of the US phenomenon of "downward mobility in the age of affluence." George Monbiot summarized the root of the problem:

> What has happened over the past 30 years is the capture of the world's common treasury by a handful of people, assisted by neoliberal poli-

cies that were first imposed on rich nations by Margaret Thatcher and Ronald Reagan. Between 1947 and 1979, productivity in the U.S. rose by 119%, while the income of the bottom fifth of the population rose by 122 percent. But from 1979 to 2009, productivity rose by 80 percent, while the income of the bottom fifth fell by 4 percent. In roughly the same period, the income of the top 1 percent rose by 270 percent.[21]

Why does inequality matter? After all, apart from their promotion of economic growth, mainstream economists—in academia, policy institutes, and international organizations such as the World Bank—have been more concerned with poverty than with inequality. Inequality matters for the range of reasons that Wilkinson and Pickett noted and more: health and education outcomes, employment prospects, questions of fairness and equity, and the public's trust and confidence in government, institutions, and leaders. In 2015, Princeton economists Ann Case and Angus Deaton wrote of increasing mortality rates among white, middle-aged, less-educated American men, at a time when mortality rates of other men, including blacks and Hispanics, were declining; their 2017 follow-up study referred to "deaths by despair" among white non-Hispanic women and men alike.[22] Inequality also matters because people's perceptions of growing inequality, downward social mobility, and lack of equal opportunity could lead to out-migration, involvement in lucrative criminal activities, resentment of elites and foreigners, or electoral gains for right-wing populists.

In 2000, concerns about the persistence of poverty and poor development outcomes led governments and multilateral organizations to adopt the Millennium Development Goals (MDGs), a set of eight objectives to be reached by 2015 that pertained to ending poverty and hunger; universal education; gender equality; child health; maternal health; combating HIV/AIDS; environmental sustainability; and global partnerships.[23] But neither the logic of neoliberal capitalism nor growing income inequality was questioned, and by the second decade of the new century, it was clear that many countries would not be able to meet the goals, while others would be able to achieve some but not all the MDGs. It was further acknowledged that climate change needed to be addressed, and that development needed to be environmentally sound. Thus, the MDGs were followed by the Sustainable Development Goals (2015–30).

The economic crisis that engulfed the world in 2008 laid bare the excesses of neoliberal globalization, especially its feature of financialization, which had brought about not only gaping income and wealth inequalities but also higher prices for many commodities (including food and fuel), increased market volatility, and governments saddled with growing debt, the result of the over-zealous lending spree that banks had engaged in.[24] But even before the 2008 financial crisis, several other economic crises took place, revealing what Marxists call the intrinsic "contradictions" of capitalism.

There is no doubt that capitalism innovates, but it is also beset by crises, which occur periodically but invariably. Since the onset of globalization, the world has experienced recessions in 1979 to 1982, 1991, 1997 to 1998, and 2001. Because each recession was followed by a growth period, policy makers seemed to learn no lessons, even though the crises in Asia, Argentina, and Russia had been caused by volatility and speculation in financial markets. Financialization proceeded, especially in the form of Anglo-Saxon "casino capitalism" (Susan Strange's apt term), with its increasingly complex and opaque, and ultimately corrupt, financial instruments. In their separate analyses located in feminist political economy, Spike Peterson, Jill Rubery, and Sylvia Walby drew attention to the gendered nature of financialization and the differential effects of the economic crisis on women's well-being.[25] This variety of capitalism produced hedge funds, derivatives, bundled mortgages, mortgage-backed securities, and leveraged buyouts; these were prioritized over the production of goods and investments in infrastructure, giving rise to cheap and easy credit and loans tied up in exotic, and toxic, financial instruments. Because short-term gains were rewarded with huge bonuses on top of huge salaries, traders and investors were encouraged to engage in risky and reckless speculation that eventually led to the bursting of the housing market bubble. In turn, businesses stopped growing or stopped hiring, unemployment rose, prices increased, and household budgets shrank. This is the context in which the Arab Spring, the European mass protests, and Occupy Wall Street (OWS) took place, and it is evidence of capitalism's contradictions and its crisis-prone nature. The power, privilege, and arrogance of the top economic elites constituted the context in which the OWS slogan "We are the 99%" took shape.

GLOBALIZATION, THE WORLD-SYSTEM, AND THE STATE

In such a context, what recourse do states have? One debate about globalization that is relevant to both the global economic crisis and social movements concerns the extent to which the sovereignty of nation-states and the autonomy of national economies have been weakened. In the early days of globalization, some argued that inasmuch as globalization entails "deterritorialization" through supranational economic, political, and cultural processes and institutions, the nation-state as a power apparatus would be superseded. Capital flows and the growing power of institutions of global governance, such as international financial institutions, leave states with greatly diminished options. In one version of this argument, Jessica Mathews held that "the absolutes of the Westphalian system," including "territorially fixed states," were all dissolving. According to Susan Strange, "Where states were once the masters of markets, now it is the markets which, on many crucial issues, are the masters over the governments of states." In another version, fixed and strong state systems had been replaced by networks and flows. For Ulrich Beck, rather than the state as such, "we are living in an age of flows—flows of capital, cultural flows, flows of information and risks."[26] For Manuel Castells:

> Power . . . is no longer concentrated in institutions (the state), organizations (capitalist firms), or symbolic controllers (corporate media, churches). It is diffused in global networks of wealth, power, information, and images which circulate and transmute in a system of variable geometry and dematerialized geography. . . . The new power lies in the codes of information and in the images of representation around which societies organize their institutions, and people live their lives, and decide their behavior.[27]

Others did not go as far as Castells but argued that the activities of transnational corporations, global cities, and the transnational capitalist class rendered state-centered analysis outdated. As noted, Sklair, Robinson, and others theorize the emergence of a deterritorialized transnational capitalist class, with its attendant institutions. Sklair argues that "the transnational capitalist class has transformed capitalism into a globalizing project," while Robinson and Harris write that "the transnationalization of the capital circuit implies as well the transnationalization of the agents of capital."[28] In contrast, Paul Hirst and Grahame Thompson assert that the nation-state remained the dominant form of governance by comparison with more global or subnational levels. Similarly, the study by Suzanne Berger, Ronald Dore, and their collaborators shows that national governments were still able to pursue different policies and maintain distinctive institutions, and they urged caution in generalizing about the extent of economic globalization.[29]

Empirically, states do seem to have lost power and control to markets; the financial crisis of 2008, which began in the United States, quickly engulfed many European countries and others that were integrated into the circuits of global finance capital. Even the US economy, which had led globalization and financialization, found itself facing a collapsed housing market, rising unemployment, growing poverty, and widening income and social inequalities unseen since the early twentieth century. In 2011, Europe's eurozone was in crisis, as Portugal, Spain, Ireland, and especially Greece struggled with huge debts and budget deficits. While some pundits argued that individual governments or political cultures were responsible for reckless spending and unbalanced budgets, others insisted that the affected countries were the victims of a mismanaged and misguided global economic system and unregulated financial markets.

As discussed in chapter 1, social movement theory posits a central role for the state in movement formation and evolution, captured in the wide-ranging concept of the "political opportunity structure." Sidney Tarrow defines social movements as mobilized groups engaged in sustained contentious interaction with power holders in which at least one state is either a target or a participant. Hank Johnston sees social movements as constituting contentious politics, or a broad range of claims against the state that sets the stage for popular pressures through noninstitutional channels (protests and social movements) and possibly institutional ones (party politics and legislation).[30] What, then, do we make of a transnational social movement that targets institutions of global governance such as the World Bank, the IMF, and the World Trade Organization (WTO)? What of the anti-EU movement in the United Kingdom? A brief digression into the main postulates of world-system theory could help with answers.

World-system theory posits the existence of a hierarchical interstate system of unequal states and markets, with a hegemon (the dominant power, economically, politically, and militarily) and economic zones of core, periphery, and semiperiphery. Following World War II, the United States supplanted the United Kingdom as the world-system's hegemon. Scholars argue that toward the end of the 1970s, American economic power began to decline relative to the growing power of Europe, the newly industrializing countries, and, more recently, China. Beginning with the Reagan administration, so the argument goes, successive American administrations sought to maintain American hegemony through diplomacy and free trade, including the Washington Consensus. As with debates on globalization, discussions ensued among scholars over whether we were observing a new phase of US imperialism, the consolidation of an integrated system of global capitalism, or a combination of imperial and neoliberal projects.[31] Immanuel Wallerstein argued that the current world-system was in crisis and in a stage of transition, the end product of which is unknown and cannot be predicted.[32]

As the world-system is the primary unit of analysis, the position of a national state within one or another of the world-system's economic zones, and the relationship between the state in question and the hegemonic power, can shape the emergence, course, and consequences of social movements. Social movements in the democratic countries of the core may have more freedom to operate, mobilize resources, and express dissent (the "social movement society"), while those in peripheral or semiperipheral countries may lack adequate resources or face considerably more repression. Similarly, participation in the global justice movement (GJM) may be shaped by world-systemic constraints: networks and organizations from richer countries are likely to be involved in a more sustained manner and in greater numbers than are those from poorer countries. On the other hand, they are also subject to state surveillance and may find it difficult to mobilize larger support for economic justice or peace, mainly because of the "cultural hegemony" of the ruling elites and the ideological state apparatus (as per theorizing by the Italian Marxist Antonio Gramsci and the French Marxist Louis Althusser).

The world-system also affects social movements in the way that it generates grievances. The WSF, for example, emerged precisely to challenge the dominance of a neoliberal world order, to call for "another world," to protest the excesses of corporate capitalism and its political allies, and to demonstrate an alternative form of deliberative democracy. The capitalist world-system generates various forms of inequalities, including gender inequality; the behavior of corporations, banks, and many governments evinces the kind of hypermasculinity that feminists have long critiqued. Austerity policies that either accompanied the Great Recession or are required for the delivery of IMF loans typically result in social welfare cutbacks that harm lower-income women and their families. Increased military spending by states does the same.[33] The 2003 invasion and occupation of Iraq outraged people across the globe, including millions of Muslims. Capital's search for cheap labor—along with wars, environmental devastation, poverty and unemployment, land grabs, privatizations, and other forms of "expulsions"—created waves of refugees and migrants, or what Marxists would call a reserve army of surplus labor.[34] Open borders and migrant labor may be preferred by capitalists and political elites, but they are resented by many workers and middle-class citizens who fear lowered wages or threats to their culture, values, or security. The response to these aspects of the world-system has come in the form of Islamist, feminist, left-wing justice, and right-wing populist movements. Such movements are multi-scalar; they exist at local, national, regional, and global levels.

That social movements exist within and are shaped by world-systemic processes does not invalidate the salience of the state, which remains an important institution and the target of many social movement actions, as we saw with Iran's 2009 Green Protests, the Arab mass protests of 2011, the anti-austerity protests in Spain and Greece, and more recently, the 2018–19 Gilets Jaunes protests in France and the 2019 antigovernment protests in Algeria, Iraq, and Lebanon. Transnational social movements often target specific states in their critiques and protests. The state continues to matter for at least four reasons. First, neoliberal capitalism requires state regulation in order to function. As Tarak Barkawi observes, "States are not victims of economic globalization so much as they are agents of it."[35] The world-system consists in part of an *interstate* system, albeit one subject to the vagaries of capital accumulation and commodity chain processes across economic zones. And while neoliberalism posits a less interventionist role of the state in general, it does require that states provide the legal and regulatory framework necessary for the functioning of markets and the private sector.

Second, the state matters because international law confers obligations on states for the implementation of treaties, conventions, resolutions, and norms. The state remains the body primarily responsible for guaranteeing the rights of citizens and human rights more broadly. For feminists, the state is the most relevant institution on matters of reproductive health and rights, social policies for women in the workforce, women's physical security, and family law for women's rights and safety within the family. In Europe, among the most ardent supporters of the European Union (EU) project are feminists who support EU directives on gender equality, which their governments must adopt. Pro-democracy social movement activists may protest authoritarian or laissez-faire states, but they expect the state to provide citizens with civil and political rights, as well as the material conditions and means to realize those rights (that is, social/economic rights).

Third, the world-system functions as an unequal hierarchy of states situated across the economic zones. Capital accumulation on a world scale relies on disparities in resource endowments, levels of industrialization, wealth, and power. It is precisely such structural inequalities and the ways in which powerful states may bully weaker states that motivate much transnational protest. Recent examples of pernicious state power are hardly limited to the 2003 US and UK invasion and occupation of Iraq; Israel launched an attack on Lebanon in 2006 and appropriated much of Palestinian territory, and in 2015 Saudi Arabia and the United Arab Emirates launched a brutal bombing campaign against Yemen that persisted at the time of this writing. US allies spend inordinate proportions of their gross domestic product (GDP) on the military, including massive arms purchases from the United States and United Kingdom.

A digression on state capacity may be useful, before turning to the fourth reason. The capacity of states to implement human rights may be compromised by poor resource endowments, by the power of foreign investors, or by foreign intervention, occupation, or conflict. Some states possess the means and the capacity to provide civil, political, and social rights of citizenship but lack the will to do so; instead, they repress any attempts at independent organizing or protest, or they allocate resources to militarism. Across the world-system's economic zones, we can see that state capacity is variable. This has implications not only for economic development but also for relations with civil society and social movements and for movement prospects. Keck and Sikkink suggested that globalization provides social movements with the opportunity of the "boomerang effect," in which advocacy networks are able to bypass their target states and rely on international pressure from other states or from transnational advocacy networks to accomplish their goals at home. And yet the boomerang effect is not always realized. First, international appeals can backfire. In her analysis of the Danish imam delegation's decision to internationalize the contention over the published cartoons deemed insulting to Muslims by traveling to various Muslim-majority countries, Lindekilde shows that the reaction within Denmark was more severe than the imams and their supporters had expected: they were accused of being disloyal and ungrateful.[36] Second, strong semiperipheral states can ignore or withstand pressure from core states or the pleas and demands of transnational social movements and networks. Examples include the Chinese government's repression of the pro-democracy movement in Tiananmen Square in 1989, its continued refusal to consider the demands of the people of Tibet, and its treatment of its Muslim Uighur population, which came to light in 2018–19; the Iranian government's repression of the Green Protests in summer 2009 and continued harassment and jailing of dissidents, including feminist activists; and the Israeli government's constant dismissal of international criticism of its policies toward the Palestinians, and its illegal bombing of Syrian strategic sites in 2017–19. The boomerang effect has been similarly moot for strong states in the world-system's core, especially for the hegemon. Although massive street demonstrations took place across the globe in early 2003 to protest US plans to invade Iraq, the governments led by George W. Bush in the United States and Tony Blair of the United Kingdom ignored them and ordered military action. As of 2019, the US and UK governments continued to sell arms to Saudi Arabia and the United Arab Emirates, despite the horror of their destructive military campaigns against the region's poorest country, Yemen. Celebration of the "justice cascade"—as evidenced by trials for perpetrators of human rights violations within newly democratic states such as Argentina, legal cases brought by governments or NGOs against foreign perpetrators, and the number of special tribunals and cases brought to the International Criminal Court—ignores the fact that malfeasance by the largest or most powerful states, especially the hegemon, will almost always escape prosecution. Thus, although states do have obligations under international law, and it could be argued that they have moral obligations as well, it is usually the strongest states in the world-system that are able to ignore or withstand international pressures.[37]

As we saw in chapter 1, the internet can play an important mobilizing role as well as bypass state secrecy or even reveal state crimes. But it has not been able to supplant state security and intelligence services, which continue to monitor and sometimes disrupt dissident websites. The Chinese government regularly monitors and shuts down dissident sites and has set up an internet firewall. In the United States, the WikiLeaks release of embarrassing US diplomatic cables enraged the Obama administration and set in motion a blockade by credit companies. In November 2011, a US judge ruled that Twitter must release details of the accounts of an Icelandic woman and two others linked to WikiLeaks. Evgeny Morozov points out that state security services use the internet and cybertools such as Twitter as effectively as do young dissenters, hacktivists, and would-be democratic revolutionaries.[38]

We now come to the fourth reason why the state continues to matter: the presence or absence of elite allies and coalitions with state entities and political parties can be critical to a movement's formation and growth. In the 1990s, government entities in the Netherlands, Sweden, and Denmark provided generous funding for transnational feminist networks (TFNs). In some cases, states have provided protest groups with needed leverage for their collective action. The GJM found an ally in the Brazilian government, as the Workers' Party and the city of Porto Alegre were crucial to the making of the WSF.[39] In a less salutary example, Islamist movements received funding and moral support from the United States, Pakistan, Saudi Arabia, Kuwait, Qatar, and other state entities in the 1980s and since. In 2011, Libyan rebels opposed to longtime strongman Muammar Ghaddafi received diplomatic and military assistance from several Western states, notably France, the United Kingdom, and the United States, as well as US ally Qatar. Following the Syrian government's repression of protests, Western powers and their regional allies (Turkey, Saudi Arabia, and Qatar) demanded regime change in Syria and extended support to the armed opposition. (China and Russia vetoed a UN Security Council resolution that would have legitimized regime change.) Destabilization of some states by other states is an old story that has not changed.

Nor has attachment to the nation-state disappeared. In Britain, the United Kingdom Independence Party (UKIP) and many "Eurosceptics" within the Conservative Party mobilized opposition to Britain's continued membership in the EU. The 2016 referendum on the matter was in favor of "Brexit," a tortuous process of a "Leave" agreement with the EU that continued through summer 2019. Not all forms of nationalism are reactionary. Nationalism remains strong in Scotland, Northern Ireland, the Spanish state of Catalonia, and among the Kurds of Turkey and Syria, which have progressive social programs.

In the Middle East, proponents of Islamic fundamentalism and supporters of revolutionary Iranian Islam initially saw their movements as supranational and railed against "artificial colonialist borders" that divided the *umma*, or the community of Muslim believers. After the death of Ayatollah Khomeini, the Islamic revolution's charismatic leader, Iran's Islamist rulers focused on what we may call "building Islamism in one country" and on reinforcing Iranian nationalism. The activities and objectives of many political movements have largely remained within national borders. Territorial state nationalism has deep roots in the region, as demonstrated all too vividly by the Iran-Iraq war of 1980–88, the overlong Israeli-Palestinian conflict, and the Kurdish struggle for autonomy or independence. On the other hand, the emergence of Osama bin Laden's al-Qaeda network in the 1990s and the later emergence of ISIS in Iraq and Syria would confirm that globalization facilitates the formation of loosely organized, deterritorialized transnational groups, such as al-Qaeda on the Arabian Peninsula, al-Qaeda in the Islamic Maghreb, extremists from across the globe joining ISIS in Syria and Iraq, and the Taliban of Afghanistan and Pakistan. Thus, attention needs to be directed toward sub- and supra-national processes, whether in terms of governance or resistance.

We may conclude that globalization has neither supplanted the international system of states nor relegated nationalism to the dustbin of history, even though it has generated powerful new global institutions that have weakened state sovereignty. States still matter, even though globalization has provided a new opportunity structure for social movements—one that enables them to take on a transnational form with a global reach or to draw on transnational networks to strengthen their cause at home.

GLOBALIZATION, EMPIRE, AND HEGEMONIC MASCULINITIES

Economic, political, and cultural aspects of globalization have promoted growing contacts between different cultures, leading partly to greater understanding and cooperation and partly to the emergence of transnational communities and hybrid identities. But globalization also has hardened the opposition of different identities. This is one way of understanding the emergence of reactive movements such as fundamentalism and communalism, which seek to recuperate traditional patterns, including patriarchal gender relations, in reaction to the "westernizing" trends of globalization. Various forms of identity politics are the paradoxical outgrowth of globalization, which Benjamin Barber aptly summarizes as "jihad vs. McWorld." He uses the term "jihad" as shorthand to describe religious fundamentalism, disintegrative tribalism, ethnic nationalisms, and similar kinds of identity politics carried out by local peoples "to sustain solidarity and tradition against the nation-state's legalistic and pluralistic abstractions as well as against the new commercial imperialism of McWorld." Jihad struggles against modernity and cultural imperialism alike and "answers the complaints of those mired in poverty and despair as a result of unregulated global markets and of capitalism uprooted from the humanizing constraints of the democratic nation-state."[40]

"Jihad" is perhaps best known for its struggle against "empire," also known as imperialism, colonialism, or neocolonialism. Technically speaking, empires no longer exist, though the term was revived in one sense through the writings of Antonio Negri and Michael Hardt, and in a different sense altogether in the wake of the US invasion of Afghanistan in 2001 and Iraq in 2003. Thus, "empire" has been used as shorthand for hegemonic militarism and expansion.[41] In particular, many Islamist groups look beyond the "near enemy" (their own rulers or states) and target the hegemonic behavior of the United States (the "far enemy"), even though they were once supported by the United States. In world-historical terms, the US-supported war in Afghanistan in the 1980s was especially significant. Its immediate outcomes were the collapse of the Soviet Union and world communism, the expansion of a militarized Islamist movement, and the emergence of a unipolar world and single economic system dominated by the United States.[42]

Although the United States had been the world-system's hegemon since the end of World War II, its power had been checked periodically by the Soviet Union.[43] The end of the Cold War and the collapse of the Soviet Union left the United States in a position of unparalleled military predominance. In the 1990s, the US ruling elite began using this strategic asset to redraw the imperial map of the world, first in the Gulf War and then in the Yugoslav wars. It should be noted that this development encompassed the administrations of President George H. W. Bush and President Bill Clinton, with the cooperation of both political parties. The new imperial design did not become fully realized, however, until the rise of the neoconservative wing of the ruling elite and the victory of George W. Bush in the presidential election of 2000. Even then, this scheme awaited the conditions in which it could be implemented. The attack on the World Trade Center in 2001 created those conditions.

For a while, following the invasion of Afghanistan in late 2001 and the routing of the Taliban, it appeared that the neoconservative "Project for the New American Century" was being successfully implemented. The invasion of Iraq in 2003 was doubtlessly intended to further US hegemony, but it served to underline the limits of US power. These limits had at least three sources. First, there was the relative economic weakness of the United States. Unlike during the golden age following World War II—when the dollar was supreme and the United States enjoyed economic growth, rising wages and prosperity, and high rates of employment—the rise of other advanced economies and the strength of the euro began to make the world-system a much more competitive environment. This reality propelled the Bush administration to rely on its military capacity to discipline both its allies and its competitors on the world stage. Second, the limits of US power came to be seen in the intense factionalism within the American ruling elite, including in the disagreements between and within Democrats and Republicans over the conduct, costs, and morality of the wars in Iraq and Afghanistan, and in the standoff, during the administration of President Barack Obama, over health care reform and government spending.[44] Third, there was the concerted resistance to the US government's designs in Iraq and Afghanistan—invasion, occupation, and privatization of the countries' resources and security apparatuses. The resistance was both homegrown and transnational, and it was fierce. It consisted of some nationalists but largely of Islamists with sophisticated weapons, a transnational reach, and patriarchal agendas. The resurgence of the Afghan Taliban was aided and abetted by Pakistani Taliban and by rogue elements of the Pakistani state security apparatus.

The NATO intervention in Libya—in which France and the United Kingdom took the lead and the United States "led from behind"—may be interpreted as a way of compensating for the foreign policy failures in Iraq and Afghanistan, maintaining a foothold in the Middle East and North Africa, and guaranteeing oil supplies. The "liberation" of Libya divided the country into military fiefdoms and created a conduit for illegal migration to Europe. The destabilization of the Syrian state from outside its borders, and the internationalization of its civil conflict, created the refugee crisis and made that country vulnerable to the growth of ISIS, which had its roots in Iraq. These developments served to complicate the initial US designs and expectations. Meanwhile, the Chinese economy continued to grow and prosper.

Here we must pause to consider competing hegemonic or hypermasculinities, such as those of al-Qaeda and the Bush administration, or of the Ghaddafi regime and the armed opposition, or the Syrian regime and its armed internal and external enemies. Hegemonic masculinity has become a key concept in gender analysis since R. W. Connell identified it as a particular culture's standards and ideal of real manhood, at a particular time in history.[45] In countries such as the United States and Australia, hegemonic masculinity is defined by physical strength and bravado, exclusive heterosexuality, suppression of "vulnerable" emotions such as remorse and uncertainty, economic independence, authority over women and other men, and intense interest in sexual "conquest." What Connell has defined as "emphasized femininity" is constructed around adaptation to male power. Its central feature is attractiveness to men, which includes physical appearance, ego massaging, suppression of "power" emotions such as anger, nurturance of children, exclusive heterosexuality, sexual availability without sexual assertiveness, and sociability. Both standards and ideals may be observed in many cultures, albeit with variations in the sexual element. In Muslim cultures, for example, female modesty is valued far more than sexual availability. And rather than intense interest in sexual conquest, hegemonic masculinity in, for example, a typical Middle Eastern context might consist of the capacity to protect family or personal honor by controlling the comportment of the women in the family, the community, or the nation. Hegemonic masculinity is reproduced in various social institutions, including the media, schools, the sports arena, the family, the military, the corporate sector, and sometimes religious institutions. In turn, it can be expressed at the level of an individual or a collective: a frat house, a military unit, a street gang, a movement, a political regime.

Lauren Langman and Douglas Morris advance a similar analysis in their discussion of "heroic masculinities." Civilizations and cultures based on conquest or expansion, societies where politics and militarism are fused, and countries where the military is a central and valorized institution all exhibit discourses, images, and practices of heroic masculinity. In considering American society and the role of its military in both economic growth and empire building, and in considering the foundational narratives of heroic masculinity in Islam, it is easy to imagine a "clash of heroic masculinities" (as Langman and Morris put it) between the American security state and a transnational Islamist network such as al-Qaeda or between Ghaddafi's forces and the armed rebels. But other hypermasculinities also are at play, in the contention between the Iraqi state and ISIS; among the Syrian state, the armed rebels, Turkey, and Israel; among the Saudis, Emiratis, and Houthi rebels in Yemen; or the standoff between the Trump administration, Iran, and Russia over the Middle East. In all these cases, men have died, but women have suffered specific losses and indignities. From a feminist perspective, hegemonic, heroic, or hypermasculinity is a causal factor in war, as well as in women's oppression. Anne Sisson Runyan has aptly noted that "[t]he world is awash with contending masculinities that vie to reduce women to symbols of either fundamentalism or Western hypermodernity."[46] To this I would add that women and girls are not saved by war; nor are they helped by economic sanctions.

In a way, contemporary rivalries in hypermasculinity mirror the intercapitalist rivalries of the early part of the twentieth century—which led to World Wars I and II. They underlie many of the factors that were attributed to the "new conflicts" of the post–Cold War era, such as the emergence of a global weapons market, the decreasing capacity of states to uphold the monopoly of violence, interethnic competition, and Barber's "jihad vs. McWorld."[47] Rival masculinities constitute a key factor in the conflicts that emerge over natural resources, such as oil or diamonds; in aggressive nationalism and ethnic rivalries; and in politicized religious projects. Hegemonic masculinity is a central ideological pillar of both empire and some forms of resistance, notably militant Islam, as well as in right-wing populisms.

Hypermasculinity similarly was in evidence during the financial meltdown of 2008. The crisis has been analyzed in many ways, but attention should be directed to the hypermasculinity that lies beneath capitalist relations of production and the behavior of the (predominantly male) transnational capitalist class. The masculinist institution par excellence may be the military, as feminist political scientist Cynthia Enloe has argued, but hypermasculinity is also a defining feature of the corporate domain—with its risk takers, rogue traders, reckless speculators, and manipulative financiers. In chapter 31 of volume 1 of *Capital*, Marx makes rather pithy comments about the emergence of the "modern bankocracy," along with the international credit system, the modern system of taxation, "stock-exchange gambling," and "the class of lazy annuitants thus created." In rereading those passages, I am struck by how insightful, prescient, and true they are. The economic crisis was the product at least in part of the overwrought masculinity of this "bankocracy" on trading floors and in bank boardrooms.[48]

Would the situation be better if there were a critical mass of women in the corporate world? Some argue that women in the corporate domain would be less likely to promote casino-style capitalism. Others retort that corporate women would have to conform to the corporate culture and imperatives. And yet, when we think of women like Sherron Watkins, who tried to blow the whistle on Enron; Sheila Bair of the FDIC, who tried unsuccessfully to rein in mortgage lenders; Brooksley Born of the Commodities Futures Trading Commission (CFTC) during the Clinton administration, who warned against deregulation and the emerging toxic assets until she was forced to resign; Gretchen Morgenson of the *New York Times*, with her sober and critical analyses of the financial crisis; and Harvard professor Elizabeth Warren (now a Massachusetts senator and in 2019 a presidential candidate), who led the Obama administration's credit card company oversight, chaired the Troubled Assets Relief Program (TARP) oversight panel, and then was overlooked by the Obama administration in its appointment of a head of the oversight agency that she had created, it would appear that there might indeed be less recklessness. There may be an argument for including more women on corporate boards, as first Norway did, with its law mandating a minimum 40 percent female share, followed more recently by France. Even so, having a critical mass of women on corporate boards might not save ordinary citizens from what is a crisis-prone system of capitalist economic governance. For that, alternatives and a new vision are needed.

ON GLOBAL SOCIAL MOVEMENTS AND TRANSNATIONAL COLLECTIVE ACTION

The capitalist world-system has often produced antisystemic movements that cross borders and boundaries, while national-level class conflicts and political contradictions similarly have generated forms of collective action and social protest, including social movements. Sociologists Susan Eckstein and Timothy Wickham-Crowley identified several arenas of rights that were at risk in Latin America as a result of the spread of neoliberal economic policies and categorized the attendant social movement: protests against cuts in urban services, strikes and labor struggles, gender-based movements, and rural movements.[49] Some of those movements came to be connected to the global justice movement (GJM) or to global feminism. In turn, the global feminist, justice, and Islamist and populist movements are products of globalization and target both states and the global order. They also reflect the growth of what has been called global civil society and the transnational public sphere.

The UN conferences of the 1990s were important to the making of global civil society and the growth of transnational social movements and their organizations/networks: the UN Conference on Environment and Development (UNCED), held in Rio de Janeiro in June 1992; the World Conference on Human Rights, held in Vienna in June 1993; the International Conference on Population and Development (ICPD), held in Cairo in September 1994; the World Summit on Social Development, held in Copenhagen in March 1995; and the Fourth World Conference on Women, held in Beijing in September 1995. As governments signed on to the international treaties associated with these and

Global Opportunity Structure
- Intergovernmental and governance structure
- Elite allies at international level
- International law
- Computer technologies

Cross-border Mobilizations
- Use of organizational infrastructure
- New networks, cells, associations
- Recruitment and financial drives

Cross-cultural Framings
- Shared identities
- Moral outrage
- Diffusion of tactics
- Website activism

Global Social Movement

Figure 2.1. The Making of a Global Social Movement

related conferences, their agreements created a conducive global opportunity structure for social movements and civil society actors. State integration into the world polity enabled cross-border networking and mobilizations and facilitated cross-cultural framings. The making of a global social movement is illustrated in figure 2.1.

It may be helpful to pause here to reiterate a working definition of transnational or global social movements. If a social movement is "a sustained campaign of claims-making, using repeated performances that advertise the claim, based on organizations, networks, traditions, and solidarities that sustain these activities," then transnational social movements are "socially mobilized groups with constituents in at least two states, engaged in sustained contentious interactions with power-holders in at least one state other than their own, or against an international institution, or a multinational economic actor."[50] As discussed in chapter 1, transnational social movements often consist of domestically based or transnational networks, including transnational advocacy networks. What makes transnational activists different from domestic activists is their ability to shift their activities among levels and across borders, connecting with groups outside their own countries, in part through the use of the new information and communication technologies.

What is it that transnational social movements do? Chadwick Alger's observations remain apt, at least with respect to the nonviolent transnational movements studied here: they create and activate global networks to mobilize pressure outside states, they participate in multilateral and intergovernmental political arenas, they act and agitate within states, and they enhance public awareness and participation—all of which has been easier to accomplish through the internet's time and space compression. Activists are thus able to organize structures above the national level, uniting adherents across borders with similar identities and goals around a common agenda. In the process, they contribute to the making of global civil society or a transnational public sphere: "Globalization has in fact brought social movements together across borders in a 'transnational public sphere,' a real as well as conceptual space in which movement organizations interact, contest each other, and learn from each other."[51]

In their study of the GJM, Mario Pianta and Raffaele Marchetti highlight the link between global civil society and global social movements. Global civil society is "the sphere of cross-border relationships and activities carried out by collective actors—social movements, networks, and civil society organizations—that are independent from governments and private firms and operate outside the international reach of states and markets." Global social movements are:

> cross-border, sustained, and collective social mobilizations on global issues, based on permanent and/or occasional groups, networks, and campaigns with a transnational organizational dimension moving from shared values and identities that challenge and protest economic or political power and campaign for change in global issues. They share a global frame of the problems to be addressed, have a global scope of action, and might target supranational or national targets.[52]

Are all transnational movements actors within global civil society? Here we must draw attention to the normative dimension of certain social science concepts and categories. Many scholars have viewed social movements and civil society (as well as revolutions and liberation movements) through a progressive lens. Mary Kaldor has noted that civil society tends to be defined as "the medium through which one or many social contracts between individuals, both women and men, and the political and economic centers of power are negotiated and reproduced." This is a "rights-based definition of civil society . . . about politics from below and about the possibility for human emancipation." However, the rise of nonstate movements, organizations, and networks that appear to eschew values of equality, democracy, and human rights has called such a view into question. Are all nonstate actors that engage in negotiated interactions with state actors, whether at the local or global level, constituent elements of civil society? What of a network such as al-Qaeda? Or the cells created by disaffected young Muslim men in Europe who planned and executed terrorist bombings? Or neo-Nazi groups in Europe? Kaldor concedes that some of the most vital forms of global civil society to emerge are found in religious and nationalist social movements, many of which are profoundly antidemocratic, and that this has tempered the initial enthusiasm for civil society among many activists. To avoid subjectivity, she and the other editors of the *Global Civil Society Yearbook* stated, "We believe that the normative content is too contested to be able to form the basis for any operationalization of the concept."[53]

Conversely, Rupert Taylor takes a strong position in favor of the normative content and offers a subjective as well as objective analysis of global civil society. There is little to be gained analytically, he argues, in including any and all nonstate actors in the definition of (global) civil society. Taylor maintains that "at an objective level" global civil society refers to "a multi-organizational field" encompassing organizations that work within the INGO and nation-state system, follow professionalized advocacy styles and agendas, and are involved in complex multilateralism." It also includes anti-neoliberal and anti-corporate movements "committed to street protest and other forms of direct action." At a subjective level, he continues, "the intent of global civil society activism is to confront neoliberal globalization and create a better world through advocating a fairer, freer, and more just global order." Global civil society, then, should be taken to be "a complex multi-organizational field that explicitly excludes reactionary—racist, fascist, or fundamentalist—organizations and movements."[54] This was the position of the transnational feminist network Women Living

under Muslim Laws (WLUML); it issued statements decrying violations of women's human rights by nonstate actors and published a
manual on the subject.

Viewed in normative terms, global civil society is the site of democratic, nonviolent, and emancipatory associational interaction. Viewed
in a strictly empirical way, however, (global) civil society is not a necessarily emancipatory sphere of action and identity, and not all (global)
social movements are progressive or democratic. Certainly, the segmentary, polycentric, and reticulate nature of social movements guarantees
the presence of different tendencies within a movement, including radical, militant, or even terrorist wings. We can thus distinguish between
progressive and reactionary social movements and civil society (or
nonstate) actors. Progressive social movements and civil society actors
seek to negotiate new relationships and arrangements with states and
institutions of global governance—including the building or deepening
of democratic practices and institutions—through popular support and
respect for human rights. Terrorist factions generally are not interested
in building or enhancing democracy; they neither work to cultivate
popular support nor respect human rights. Questions remain, as noted
previously, about Islamist and right-wing populist movements and parties. This book recognizes that globalization has enabled the formation
of all manner of nonstate organizing, contentious politics, and political
party formation, and that not all of these may be viewed as emancipatory or transformative. In much the same way that globalization itself is
complex and contradictory, the transnational social movements associated with it or resulting from it are similarly complex and contradictory. That is, globalization has enabled a continuum from life-affirming,
nonviolent, and democratic social movements to antidemocratic political and economic practices and finally to deadly rebellions, martyrdom
operations, and transnational networks of violent extremists.

All transnational collective action takes place within, and is shaped
by, the capitalist world-system and its current phase of globalization. In
turn, globalization has given rise to criticisms and grievances, as well as
opportunities for collective action. It has created a global opportunity
structure and enabled cross-border framings and mobilizations. These
framings and mobilizations may be driven by proximate causes but, as
was discussed in chapter 1, are rooted in preexisting discourses, collective memories, and organizational infrastructures. Islamist activism has

been motivated by corrupt, authoritarian, or pro-Western regimes in their own Muslim-majority countries; by solidarity with their confrères in Palestine, Iraq, and Afghanistan; and by opposition to secularizing and westernizing tendencies. The transnational Islamist movement consists of groups and networks ranging from moderate to extremist, using methods that range from participation in the political process to spectacular violence. Transnational feminist activism is motivated by concern for women's participation and rights in an era of neoliberal globalization, militarism, war, and patriarchal fundamentalisms. Transnational feminist networks—the principal mobilizing structure of global feminism—consist of women from three or more countries who mobilize for research, lobbying, advocacy, and civil disobedience to protest gender injustice and promote women's human rights, equality, and peace. At its heyday, the GJM consisted of loosely organized mobilized groups protesting the downside of globalization and calling for economic and social justice. More recently, it is part of the New Global Left, which opposes neoliberalism, climate change, racism, xenophobia, and fascism. Right-wing populism reflects the anger of people left behind by neoliberalism, concentrated power, and open borders.

The movements examined in this book are transnational, inasmuch as they target states and international institutions, and each is a coalition of local grassroots groups as well as transborder groups. But they differ in significant ways. Feminists are most closely aligned, ideologically, with the New Global Left and with global justice activists, emphasizing human rights and favoring a form of cosmopolitan social democracy or democratic socialism, the application of international conventions on women's human rights, and greater attention to feminist values. For Islamists, the solution to current problems is the widespread application of Islamic laws and norms; for right-wing populists, it is to reclaim their "own culture" in the face of external influences and the normative impositions of domestic elites. The similarities and differences, as well as the connections to globalization, are elucidated in the subsequent chapters.

CONCLUSION

A key characteristic of the era of late capitalism, or neoliberal globalization, is the proliferation of networks of activists within transnational social movements. Guidry, Kennedy, and Zald correctly regarded globalization as a new opportunity structure for social movements. Globalization brings important new resources to mobilization efforts, and movements can frame their claims in terms that resonate beyond territorial borders. I have noted the paradoxes of globalization: while its economic, political-military, and cultural aspects have engendered grievances and opposition, it has also provided the means for rapid cross-border communication, coordination, mobilization, and action. The next chapters explore in more detail how movements of Islamists, feminists, global justice activists, and populists address globalization. But first, we turn attention to the democratizing potential of social movements at both national and global levels.

CHAPTER 3

GLOBALIZATION AND SOCIAL MOVEMENTS

WHITHER DEMOCRACY?

The democratization of the world beyond the states has yet to begin.

—John Markoff

Western democracy is going through a mid-life crisis. Its prime is past.

—David Runciman[1]

The financial crisis that began with the mortgage meltdown in the United States, triggering financial crises and the Great Recession, generated a massive wave of protests, from labor protests in Egypt and Tunisia to the Arab Spring, anti-austerity protests in Europe, and Occupy movements across the globe. "Movement parties" emerged in Spain,

Greece, and Portugal, rekindling hopes that the Latin American pink tide could be replicated. At the same time, the first democratic elections in Egypt, Morocco, and Tunisia resulted in significant votes for Islamist parties. The 2015 refugee crisis—generated by the breakdown of state authority in Libya and Syria, and by poverty and unemployment in Sub-Saharan Africa—exacerbated existing tensions in Europe, strengthening right-wing populist (RWP) movements and their political parties. Donald Trump was elected president of the United States, and the widespread feminist protests against him the next year were followed by the MeToo and Time's Up campaigns against sexual harassment and violence against women. These are examples of diverse, grassroots, and popular movements, but what is their relationship to democracy? Are they all pro-democracy movements? If so, what model of democracy do they seem to support? And might they represent reactions to neoliberalized democracy?

This chapter shows how some social movements have the potential to bring about genuine democratization at societal and global levels, while others may use democracy to undermine it. It offers a brief survey of the literature on democracy, democracy waves, and democratic transitions, and shows how both internal and external factors and forces may affect the rise and demise of social movements. As argued in chapters 1 and 2, the premise is that social movements arise during certain world-systemic conjunctures, which also affects the movements' evolution. This chapter thus considers prospects for genuine democratization at different levels.

DEMOCRACY AND SOCIAL MOVEMENTS

Social movements are critical for advancing inclusion and democracy, but the literature examining the democratic nature of social movements is relatively sparse. John Guidry, Michael Kennedy, and Mayer Zald point out that, until relatively recently, most academic social movement theory was being developed in the United States. Analysis was dominated by an implicit metatheory of movements as a variation on the voluntary organization sector, and the mobilization of resources was the key to success or failure in movement activity. Social movements were theorized as alternative means of expressing a democratic pluralism or, as in the case of the US civil rights movement, helping to deepen democracy through full citizenship for a previously excluded and marginalized population. In recent years, scholars have more explicitly examined the contributions of social movements to democratic transitions in authoritarian settings or the deepening of democracy in mature democratic societies. Hank Johnston asserts that in democratic societies, social movements are part of regular politics; they derive from civil society organizations, draw on or create public opinion, and challenge elites using democratic expectations; their goals are to extend state openness or capacity for citizenship, equality, responsiveness, and protection. He is thus in agreement with the postulate of the "social movement society," as discussed by David Meyer and Sidney Tarrow, to the effect that social movements are a part of normal politics in a democratic society, with tactics such as e-petitioning, advocacy and lobbying, the spread of professional social movement organizations, and checkbook memberships.[2] Such a view may (inadvertently) dovetail with the Marxist perspective of civil society as co-opted by the state and an instrument for legitimation.

Early studies on democratic transitions in authoritarian contexts emerged from the experiences in southern Europe (Portugal, Greece, Spain) and Latin America (Argentina, Brazil, Chile), and they focused on "pacted negotiations" by elites.[3] Others, however, took a cue from Barrington Moore's classic 1966 study, *Social Origins of Dictatorship and Democracy*, to examine the role of social class. Where Moore emphasizes the role of the bourgeoisie, the study by Rueschemeyer, Stephens, and Stephens argues that the working class was behind the rise of democracy, as its historical struggles for universal suffrage, citizenship rights, and redress of economic grievances set the stage for subsequent broad political coalitions and claims.[4] Other studies have drawn attention to social movements or civil society in triggering the protest movements that result in democratic transitions, with some emphasizing the presence of political parties with left-wing or left-of-center programs at both local and national levels. Kenneth Roberts points out that the Workers' Party (PT) in Brazil, the Broad Front (FA) in Uruguay, and the Movement toward Socialism in Bolivia "had deep roots in social movements and civic associations, and both the PT and the FA used their experience in municipal administration—and the reputations for innovative and effective governance this provided—as springboards to national executive office."[5] Indeed, in much of the region, the post-adjustment turn to the left wing occurred outside and against established party systems, providing evidence of the crisis of representative institutions—much as the more recent turn to right-wing populism has done.

In South Africa, the antiapartheid movement and demands for full enfranchisement of the country's black majority brought about a democratic polity and one of the most egalitarian constitutions in the world. In the 1980s in South Korea, protest groups consisting of militant industrial workers, Christian groups, students, and intellectuals formed a pro-democracy movement that ended authoritarian military rule and, in 1987, ushered in a remarkable period of democratic consolidation that entailed a growing civil society with the capacity for considerable reform from below. Social movement organizations such as the Citizens' Coalition for Economic Justice and the Citizens' Coalition for Participatory Democratic Society actively promoted democratic practices and policy making. Argentina's democratic transition vastly expanded political spaces for workers, feminists, students, and other social groups, though it was not until after the economic crisis of 1998 that the full extent of citizen direct action could be seen. The practices of Argentina's trade unions changed, with more female participation and leadership and considerable internal discussion and debate on "women's issues" as well as on economic rights. Daniel Ozorow's study of Argentina's popular movements and practices following the financial crisis reveals the extent of cross-class mobilizations, including that of the "middle-class revolt."[6] The pro-democracy activists of the Arab Spring in Egypt, Morocco, and Tunisia, and especially the socialists among them, seemed to be calling for a robust social democracy that would provide for the health, education, and welfare of citizens; the equality of women and men in the family and society; workplace democracy through worker participation in decision making; protection of small business owners; and regional and global cooperation for peace and rights-based development.[7]

Social movements may help bring about democracy, but what conditions bring about pro-democracy social movements and enable democratic consolidation? Scholars have identified several causes or contributing factors: a society's wealth, socioeconomic development, capitalism, an educated population, a large middle class, civil society, civic culture, human empowerment and emancipative values, a homogeneous population, and foreign intervention. John Keane, for example, finds democracy and civility in public discourse dependent upon a vibrant civil society/public sphere. In classic democratic theory, socioeconomic development is key to the making of a democratic polity and culture; Kenneth Bollen finds "a positive relationship between economic development and political development."[8] In other words, structural conditions essential for the formation of a sustained pro-democracy movement include socioeconomic development, modern social classes, and resources for coalition building and mobilization. Whether a pro-democracy movement succeeds depends on a complex of factors, including the capacity of the state and its responses to the movement, the strength of the coalition, and the movement's ability to resonate with the population at large as well as with world society.

Sociologist Barbara Wejnert identifies two broad sets of factors that contribute to the making of democracy: *endogenous* or internal features—that is, socioeconomic development broadly defined—and *exogenous* variables that influence democratization via forces that work globally and within a region. This second set of factors may be referred to as diffusion processes, which may come through media, international organizations, and connections to transnational advocacy networks.[9] In an era of globalization, with its feature of "time-space compression," such diffusion processes are especially rapid and arguably more effective than in earlier periods or waves of democratization. Through diffusion processes, movements and processes in one country can inspire citizens in other countries. The Latin American pink tide reflected that process, when one country after another elected left-wing governments. Similarly, the Arab Spring of early 2011, which was launched in Tunisia, spread to Egypt, Morocco, Bahrain, and elsewhere. Diffusion processes need not occur simultaneously or immediately; the Arab Spring's earlier inspirations may have included the Kefaya (Enough) movement in Egypt in 2005 and the Green Protests in Iran in June 2009, the first time in the new century that Middle East and North Africa (MENA) citizens boldly took to the streets to challenge authoritarian rule. Diffusion also may be part of transnational learning; connections between the Egyptian April 6 Youth Movement and the Serbian youth organization Otpor, which had hoped to topple Slobodan Milošević, provide another example of diffusion as well as the salience of international linkages.[10]

Diffusion of frames and tactics includes the spread and adoption of notions of human rights, dignity, democracy, women's human rights, and environmental protection, as well as movement tactics such as the sit-in or the protest encampment. Echoing Keck and Sikkink, Mala Htun and Laurel Weldon show widespread norm diffusion regarding violence against women, and they make the same claim about family law reform. Understanding how norm diffusion works requires identifying the actors that facilitate diffusion, including institutions, organizations, and activist networks; how globalized diffusion may be localized; and the ways that diffusion might be resisted by powerful states or corporate actors.[11] Mainstream institutes such as the National Endowment for Democracy, National Democracy Institute, National Republican Institute, and Middle East Partnership Initiative (MEPI) in the United States; the European Commission and development agencies in Europe; and nonpartisan transnational advocacy agencies (e.g., the Open Society Institute, and International IDEA, based in Stockholm) all play a role in democracy promotion, although they also have come under criticism.[12] Social movements and activist networks construct and diffuse frames (e.g., anti-neoliberalism, against austerity, for climate justice), strategies (noncentralized and "horizontal" organizing and decision making), and repertoires of collective action (sit-ins, encampments, popular assemblies) within and across countries.

What kind of democracy do social movements advocate? Benjamin Barber notes that different types of democracies and their varied practices produce similarly varied effects. In a liberal democracy, a high degree of political legitimacy is necessary, as is an independent judiciary and a constitution that clearly sets out the relationship between state and society, as well as citizen rights and obligations. Written constitutions serve as a guarantee to citizens that the government is required to act in a certain way and to uphold certain rights. According to Guillermo O'Donnell and Philippe Schmitter, democracy's guiding principle is citizenship:

> This involves both the right to be treated by fellow human beings as equal with respect to the making of collective choices and the obligation of those implementing such choices to be equally accountable and accessible to all members of the polity. . . . Given the existence of certain prominent "models" and international diffusion, there is likely to exist a sort of "procedural minimum" which contemporary actors would agree upon as necessary elements of political democracy. Secret balloting,

universal adult suffrage, regular elections, partisan competition, association recognition and access, and executive accountability all seem to be
elements of such a consensus in the contemporary world.[13]

This definition, however, is not inclusive of notions of social and
economic rights. Indeed, democracy in the neoliberal era often is associated with competitive elections (political democracy) and free
markets (liberal capitalist democracy) and not with more expansive
decision making within workplaces (economic democracy) or within
the family, which many feminists have called for.[14] Schmitter and Terry
Lynn Karl explain that "the liberal conception of democracy advocates
circumscribing the public realm as narrowly as possible, while the socialist or social-democratic approach would extend that realm through
regulation, subsidization, and, in some cases, collective ownership of
property." This observation points to the difference between *formal* and
substantive democracy as well as the difference between formal political rights and the material means to enjoy or exercise them—or what
T. H. Marshall calls social and economic rights of citizenship.[15] It is
this expanded understanding of democracy that informed the claims,
aspirations, and practices of progressive social movements such as Occupy Wall Street, the World Social Forum (WSF), many transnational
feminist networks (TFNs), and the Gilets Jaunes movement in France.

OCCUPY WALL STREET AND
THE PRACTICE OF DEMOCRACY

The Universal Declaration of Human Rights asserts, "The will of the
people shall be the basis of the authority of government." There are,
however, serious problems with the realization of people's democratic
aspirations as well as with the models of democracy that are in place.
People have less and less control over decisions that affect their daily
lives, and they see far too much control in the hands of political and
economic elites. As discussed in chapter 2, globalization has altered
the capacity and sovereignty of national states, affecting national policy
making, the practice of democracy, and the ways that popular groups
can advance their interests. The growing wealth and power of economic
elites and the hegemony of the financial sector coincided with rising
unemployment and the cost of living. In Occupy Wall Street, as in the

European anti-austerity movement and the global justice movement (GJM) more generally, many became angry that globalization had taken decision making away from citizens and placed it in the hands of lobbyists and those in institutions of global governance, bringing into focus the deficiencies of a "representative" democracy that represented the interests of Wall Street and the transnational capitalist class rather than the basic needs and rights of citizens.

On September 17, 2011, in response to an appeal by Adbusters, a Canadian-based free-information group, several hundred people gathered in New York's Zuccotti Park located in the Wall Street financial district. In the days that followed, the demonstrators quickly grew in number as their message about social inequality, corporate greed, and corporate power in government and their slogan, "We are the 99%," resonated with a wider population. An initial media blackout was followed by news accounts that dismissed OWS as comprising hippies and naïfs, but as the movement grew and its main tactic, encampment, spread across the country, mainstream media began to take the movement more seriously. By October 2011, OWS encampments were seen in more than one hundred major cities and six hundred communities across the United States, and on October 15, a global day of solidarity with OWS took the form of demonstrations in hundreds of cities across more than forty-five countries. The Occupy protests spread across the world because the problems they railed against were global in scope.[16]

From its inception, and given the media blackout and negative media criticism, OWS relied heavily on cyberactivism and alternative media—Facebook, Twitter, Flickr, Buzz, Myspace, YouTube, and its own website—to mobilize supporters and disseminate information. OWS placed a high premium on democratic practices and deliberation, as was evident in both the way that decisions were made at the encampments (by consensus) and the features of their website. An examination of the OWS website in early 2012 found daily updates, meeting agendas, and video clips and media coverage. The OWS website's "Forum" link took users to a blog-style page where they could log in to post material for discussion or to comment on others' posts. However, access required that visitors register with the site and read the rules for posting. Not allowed were spamming, advertising, and posting of other people's personal information, election material, threats, or conspiracy theories. There was a place to report any of these activities;

when reported, such posts would be removed and the author barred from participating in the public online forum. Users were nonetheless encouraged to comment on the rules; the "Chat" tab took users to a site where they could register to post comments and take part in a live chat on the "LiveStream" page. Emphasis on democratic deficits in the United States and the need to deepen democracy was evident across the OWS website and in its framing devices.

OWS frames such as "We are the 99%," "Democracy not corporatocracy," and "This is what democracy looks like" were simple but effective. They drew attention to the concentration of wealth and the gaping income gap in the United States, the inordinate power of banks and corporations and their close ties to government, and the need for genuine democracy. The following is a representative expression of the movement's grievances and values:

> The participation of every person, and every organization, that has an interest in returning the U.S. back into the hands of its individual citizens is required. Our nation, our species and our world are in crisis. The U.S. has an important role to play in the solution, but we can no longer afford to let corporate greed and corrupt politics set the policies of our nation. We, the people of the United States of America, considering the crisis at hand, now reassert our sovereign control of our land. Solidarity Forever![17]

This passage is interesting for the way it bridges two American master frames—democracy and patriotism—in an enactment of frame alignment and frame resonance. But OWS was clear about its goals, aspirations, and sources of inspiration:

> #ows is fighting back against the corrosive power of major banks and multinational corporations over the democratic process, and the role of Wall Street in creating an economic collapse that has caused the greatest recession in generations. The movement is inspired by popular uprisings in Egypt and Tunisia, and aims to fight back against the richest 1% of people that are writing the rules of an unfair global economy that is foreclosing on our future.[18]

OWS's emergence and spread across the globe were significant in that the Occupy movement reinvigorated the GJM and reinforced the transnational movement for global democracy. Its call for economic justice for the 99 percent resonated with intellectuals and politicians, who went on to promote the movement in their writings or to concretize its demands in policy terms. But OWS came to face two challenges. Internally, its horizontal and leaderless model proved unable to sustain itself; as a repertoire of collective action, the encampment strategy could not continue indefinitely. Externally, OWS protesters faced intrusions and at times police action, with encampments having to be dismantled. Even in a democracy, there are structural and political limits to the so-called social movement society.

The role of mass media is relevant to the discussion of democracy and democratic movements. In the mature democracies, the media are typically outside of state influence and located within civil society, but their corporate ownership tends to make them favorable toward "business as usual" and against movements that might challenge the status quo. Drawing on both Gramsci and Althusser, we might observe that the media are part of the hegemonic culture and help reproduce it. As such, social movement events might face limited or no coverage at all. For example, the United States Social Forum in Atlanta in 2007 and Detroit in 2010, while attended by thousands, was ignored by the mass media. In contrast, the right-wing Tea Party Convention, which was much smaller, received extensive media coverage. In authoritarian settings, state ownership or control of media often has similar effects. The internet does afford rapid and extensive coverage and diffusion through alternative media, but in the United States, progressive media cannot compete with Fox News, CNN, or talk radio for cultural hegemony.

DEMOCRACY MOVEMENTS: WAVES, LOCATIONS, WOMEN'S RIGHTS

When communism collapsed and Eastern Europe transitioned away from socialism, Francis Fukuyama declared this "the end of history" and the triumph of liberal democracy and free market capitalism across the world. Samuel Huntington's response was to theorize waves of democratization and to argue that the history of democracy should be viewed as a succession of waves that have advanced and receded, then rolled in and crested again. Huntington's definition of democracy, democracy waves, and democratic transitions was limited to successful outcomes of liberal democracy.[19] Hence he left out many movements that aimed for popular sovereignty or more expansive concepts of democracy: populist, anarchist, socialist, communist, and nationalist.

In Huntington's account, the first wave occurred with the democratic revolutions of Europe and North America in the late eighteenth and early nineteenth centuries. Some of the democratic revolutions lost momentum in the period between World Wars I and II, when authoritarian and fascist regimes arose; Huntington cited the democratic breakdowns in Italy in the early 1920s and in Germany a decade later. The second wave occurred after World War II, encompassing Germany, Italy, and Japan, but it petered out in the 1960s, when authoritarian regimes arose again. The third wave began in the mid-1970s in southern Europe, with the democratic transitions in Greece, Portugal, and Spain, followed by South Korea, the Philippines, and Latin America in the latter part of the 1980s and the former communist countries of Eastern Europe in 1989 to 1990. Huntington had this wave ending in 1990, but the trend continued with transitions in South Africa (1990–94) and Indonesia (1998). Political liberalization occurred during this period in countries of the Middle East and North Africa, notably Algeria, Jordan, Morocco, Turkey, and Tunisia, though they were partial or aborted. But what of the movements of the twenty-first century, such as the wave of antiglobalization protests that took place in the early part of the new century and the emergence of the WSF? What of Latin America's pink tide, with the election of left-wing governments in Argentina, Brazil, Chile, Venezuela, Uruguay, Bolivia, and Ecuador? What of the wave of pro-democracy movements in Iran (2009), and in Tunisia, Egypt, and Morocco (2011)? Do they constitute a fourth wave, as some studies suggested?[20] And what of new forms of subnational radical democracy, such as the Kurdish-run autonomous Rojava region in northern Syria?[21]

Tables 3.1 and 3.2 illustrate the various waves of democratization. They draw on but go beyond the Huntington framework by including movements he missed, highlighting failures and imperialist interventions, identifying a fourth wave, and underscoring the salience of world-system dynamics. For example, research has found that the social transformations accompanying semiperipheral development, along with diffusion processes, have provided the conditions for democracy movements and transitions. Democratic transitions have been concentrated in semiperipheral countries—in Latin America, Eastern Europe,

Table 3.1. Four Waves of Democratization: Successes, Failures, and External Impositions

	First Wave: 1770s–1880s	Second Wave: 1900–post-WWII	Third Wave: 1968–1990	Fourth Wave: 1990–Present
Successes	American Revolution; French revolutions (1789 and 1848); Chartist movement (United Kingdom, 1838–1850)	Germany, Italy, Japan; India; US civil rights movement	Student revolts, 1968; Greece, Portugal, Spain; South Korea, Taiwan, Philippines; Chile, Argentina, Brazil; Eastern Europe	South Africa, 1990–1994; Ghana, 1993; Liberia, 2003; Northern Ireland, 1998, 2011; Latin American "pink tide," 2001–15; Morocco, 1998–present; Ukraine, 2004; Tunisia, 2011
Failures	Haiti (antislavery revolt, 1794)[a]	German uprising 1918[b]; Iran's Constitutional Revolution, 1906–11[c]; Iran's nationalist movement, 1951–53; Guatemala, 1954; Dominican Republic, 1963[d]	Burma, 1988; China, 1989; Algeria, 1990[e]	Haiti, 2004 (Jean-Bertrand Aristide and Fanmi Lavalas); Iran, 2009; Libya, Syria, Yemen, 2011; Egypt, 2013; Ukraine
External control or imposition				Serbia, Bosnia, Kosovo, 2000; Afghanistan, 2001; Iraq, 2003; Libya, 2011
Ongoing			Feminist movements; youth/student movements	Zapatista indigenous movement (Mexico, since 1994); World Social Forum (since 2001); Rojava (2014–19)[f]

[a]Led by Toussaint-Louverture, the revolt did not lead to democracy but did overthrow slavery and the plantation system.

[b]Revolutions in Mexico and Russia brought about progressive sociopolitical change but did not lead to democracy.

[c]Iran's Constitutional Revolution of 1906–11 introduced a constitution and brought down the Qajar dynasty but failed to bring about a democracy or a republic.

[d]The pro-democracy movements in Iran, Guatemala, and the Dominican Republic were defeated by U.S. intervention.

[e]The failure in Algeria was caused by the violent extremism of the Islamist opposition as well as by the ruling party's cancellation of the 1991 election results.

[f]Inspired by the writings of U.S. anarchist writer Murray Bookchin, left-wing Kurdish forces announced regional autonomy in northern Syria in early 2014, with elections, popular assemblies (co-led by a woman and a man), and a constitution. In October 2019, Turkish forces invaded and the fate of Rojava became uncertain.

Table 3.2. "Third Wave and Fourth Wave" Pro-Democracy Sociopolitical Movements in the Semiperiphery

Semiperiphery	Frames	Outcomes
1970s: Greece, Portugal, Spain	Against dictatorship; for democracy, constitutionalism, and/or socialism	Successful transition and consolidation; shift from socialism to social democracy in Portugal; entrance of all into EU in new century
1980s: Argentina, Brazil, Chile	Against dictatorship; for democracy, human rights, and women's rights	Successful transition and consolidation; "pink wave" in new century; women leaders in all three countries; setback in Brazil with right-wing populist Jair Bolsonaro elected in 2019
South Korea, Taiwan, the Philippines	Against dictatorship; for worker rights (South Korea), "people power" (Philippines)	Successful transitions and consolidation; setback in the Philippines with right-wing populist Rodrigo Duterte elected in 2016
Eastern Europe	Against communism; for liberal democracy and human rights	Successful transitions and consolidation; contention over women's rights; entry of various countries into EU in new century; right-wing populism in Hungary and Poland
1990s: South Africa	Against apartheid; for democracy, civil rights, and/or socialism	Black majority government; rights-based constitution and laws; truth and reconciliation process; shift to neoliberalism in new century; poverty, inequality, and violence against women persist
Mexico: Zapatistas	Against neoliberal globalization; for indigenous rights in Chiapas	Truce between state and Chiapas; autonomy; left-wing populist government in 2018
Indonesia	Against Suharto dictatorship and economic hardships	Multiparty elections; rise of Islamic parties and movements; marginalization of religious minorities

(continued)

Table 3.2. *Continued*

Semiperiphery	Frames	Outcomes
2001–19: Global Justice Movement and World Social Forum	Against neoliberal globalization; for democratic spaces and deliberation	Annual meetings held in semiperipheral sites; regional forums that include core countries; mobilization of democrats, feminists, socialists, youth, and labor, environmental, and indigenous rights activists; internal discussions as to way forward
2005: Egypt's Kefaya movement; 2011–13: from political revolution to military coup	Enough of Mubarak; for change, no to succession/ inheritance of power;	Charges of election fraud levied against presidential contender Ayman Nour; Hosni Mubarak's "election" to a fifth term; Tahrir Square uprising against Mubarak and his resignation; elections and brief Muslim Brotherhood governance; renewed protests, military intervention in July 2013 and authoritarian reversal
2009: Iran's Green Protests	"Where is my vote?"; against dictatorship; for genuine electoral democracy	State repression
2011: Tunisia, Morocco	Against personalist and authoritarian rule; for dignity and economic, civil, and political rights	Political revolution in Tunisia and democratic transition; constitutional amendments in Morocco, July 2011
2014–19: Kurdish-led Rojava, northern Syria	Radical democratic confederalism; women's emancipation	The Kurdish "self-defense" and anti-ISIS fighters declared autonomy and a new form of pro-feminist radical democracy. In October 2019, it was derailed by the Turkish invasion.
2018–19: Algerian protests	Against a fifth term for ailing President Abdelaziz Bouteflika; for democratization of *le pouvoir*	Ongoing; Bouteflika drops out of race

South Korea, and South Africa. But world-systemic processes could adversely affect democratization as well. The tables draw attention to what could be a key difference between the third and fourth waves; the latter includes transnational or global as well as national movements for democracy. Note the absence of right-wing populist movements from the fourth-wave category; at the time of writing (2019), it is clear that they pose a serious challenge to democracy, but whether they undermine it or (perhaps paradoxically) help revive a robust social or socialist democracy is as yet difficult to determine.

WOMEN'S MOVEMENTS AND DEMOCRATIZATION

It is well known that socialist revolutions opened political space for women and other historically marginalized or disadvantaged groups, as evidenced by state policies for women's emancipation in revolutionary Russia, China, Cuba, Vietnam, South Yemen (1967), and Afghanistan (1978).[22] But what of social movements?

Political philosopher Nancy Fraser has differentiated social movements that call for recognition and representation from those that focus on redistribution.[23] This is one way of distinguishing "old" class-based movements from "new" identity-based social movements, but arguably the women's movement entails redistribution of economic resources (across women and men more broadly), recognition of women's roles and contributions, and demands for representation in the political process as well as other domains. Many studies show that women's organizing tends to be inclusive, and women's movement activism often involves the explicit practice of democracy. As pro-democracy social movements, women's movements have contributed to democratic transitions and the deepening of democracy.[24]

Laurel Weldon has examined how women's movements in the United States brought to public and government attention women's policy issues related to the family, work, and violence, showing how women's movement organizations helped increase women's representation in the public sphere through their role as powerful policy advocates. Such action on behalf of marginalized groups, Weldon argues, deepens *representative democracy*. Yesim Arat shows how a vibrant feminist movement in Turkey contributed to *liberal democracy* in the country. Graciela Di Marco emphasizes the significance of social movements to *radical democracy*, such as in the case of Argentine workers who took over factories abandoned by their owners following the financial crisis of 1998. For Di Marco, Argentine democracy was deepened and radicalized as a result of the social movements of the period, including the coalitions of workers, students, intellectuals, and feminists that brought to power the left-wing populist government of Nestor Kirchner. In turn, this triggered a broader regional wave of anti-neoliberal popular mobilizations.[25] Women's movement activism and advocacy—whether in the form of social movements, transnational networks, or professional organizations—contribute to the making of vibrant civil societies and public spheres, which are themselves critical to sustaining and deepening democracy.

Democratic transitions can create a window of opportunity for legal and policy reforms for women's rights. In Portugal, the fall of the dictatorship was accompanied by the adoption of a socialist constitution and multiparty parliamentary system, with the strong presence of the Communist Party; this created an advantageous environment for feminists to organize a movement to legalize divorce, improve access to contraception, and decriminalize abortion. In the Philippines, women played important roles in the labor and liberation movements. The feminist coalition GABRIELA was formed in 1984 and challenged the 1985 presidential elections that Ferdinand Marcos won. Such groups, along with women in general, were a visible presence in the "people power" revolution that overthrew the Marcos regime.[26] In Latin America, women's movements and organizations played an important role in the opposition to authoritarianism and made a significant contribution to the "end of fear" and the inauguration of the transition. Women organized as feminists and as democrats, often allying themselves with left-wing parties.[27] Where women were not key actors in the negotiated ("pacted") transitions, they nonetheless received institutional rewards when democratic governments were set up and their presence in the new parliaments increased. In addition to the quotas that enhanced their parliamentary representation, women were rewarded with well-resourced policy agencies and legislation on violence against women. As Jane Jaquette observes,[28]

> Feminist issues were positively associated with democratization, human rights, and expanded notions of citizenship that included indigenous rights as well as women's rights. This positive association opened the way for electoral quotas and increased the credibility of women

candidates, who were considered more likely to care about welfare issues and less corrupt than their male counterparts.

In Tunisia, advantageous preconditions for democratization were a strong feminist movement, a relatively long tradition of secular republicanism, and a well-organized and well-coordinated civil society staffed by activists who had acquired strong civic skills. As I have argued elsewhere, these conditions were almost unique to Tunisia, although in Morocco, feminist organizations similarly were openly pro-democracy.[29]

These examples would confirm that women's rights movements are not "identity movements" but, rather, democratizing movements that entail redistribution as well as recognition and representation. However, if women are good for democracy, it does not hold that democracy is always good for women. Following the collapse of the communist bloc in 1989, scholars were surprised to discover that women's political representation declined dramatically with the new democratic elections, and women also lost jobs when the wave of privatizations and factory closures set in (men lost jobs as well).[30] The historical record reveals a cost to women's rights with a democratic process that is institutionally weak or is not founded on principles of equality and the rights of all citizens or lacks a well-organized civil society. Under such conditions, a political party bound by patriarchal norms may come to power and immediately institute laws relegating women to second-class citizenship and imposing controls over their mobility.

This was the Algerian feminist nightmare, which is why so many educated Algerian women opposed the Front Islamique du Salut (FIS) after its expansion in 1989. The quick transition unsupported by strong institutions did not serve women well. Algeria had long been ruled by a single-party system in the "Arab socialist" style. The death of President Houari Boumédiène in December 1978 brought about political and economic changes, including the growth of the Front Islamique du Salut (FIS), which intimidated unveiled or divorced women, and a new government intent on economic restructuring. Urban riots in 1988 were followed quickly by a new constitution and elections, without a longer period of democracy building. The electoral victory of the FIS—which promised (or threatened) to institute sharia law, enforce veiling, and end competitive elections—alarmed not only Algeria's educated female population but also the ruling party and the military, which stepped in to annul the election results. That the FIS went on to initiate an armed rebellion and a decade-long bloody civil conflict when it was not allowed to assume power only confirms the violent nature of that party. The even more extreme Groupe Islamique Armée committed numerous atrocities.[31] Tunisian and Moroccan feminists were well aware of this experience, which is why they mobilized quickly to protect their acquired rights in the face of empowered Islamic parties with the political opening of 2011.

Apart from their varied effects on women and gender equality, democratic transitions in some cases are unable to narrow social inequalities, unemployment, and income and wealth inequality, despite the adoption of procedural democratic practices and regular elections. South Africa and Brazil, for example, have high rates of poverty, income inequality, urban violence, and violence against women. The mass protests in Chile in 2019 were triggered by the high costs of health and education, as well as widening income inequality. In yet other cases, democracies may come to be captured by "the 1 percent," in terms of the economic and political benefits that accrue to the corporate sector and very wealthy citizens, or they are captured by populist demagogues. In its 2002 study of globalization and democracy, the United Nations Development Programme asserted that "economically, politically, and technologically, the world has never seemed more free—or more unjust."[32] Kenneth Roberts notes that, although the vast literature on transitions has emphasized the tentative and uncertain character of new democracies, the empirical record offers few cases of outright breakdowns or authoritarian reversals in third-wave democracies. (But see chapter 7, on the emergence of right-wing populisms, in this book.) He then cites Philippe Schmitter to the effect that the more recent democratization efforts have done little to bring about significant changes in power relations, property rights, policy entitlements, economic equality, and social status.[33] We refer to these as the paradoxes of democracy, or democracy's deficits, to which we now turn.

SETBACKS AND REVERSALS: DEMOCRACY PARADOXES AND DEFICITS

In the late 1990s and into the new century, European citizen groups as well as scholars used the term "democracy deficit" to refer to the displacement of local or national decision making onto the new bureaucratic centers in Brussels. With increased bureaucratization and the corporate capture of power, the deficits have only grown. Moreover, democracy setbacks and reversals have occurred. The Arab Spring, for example, showed that a promising case of a democratic transition such as Egypt's could revert to military authoritarianism. Tunisia is the one success story of the Arab Spring, but its democratic transition has struggled with economic difficulties and some political dysfunction. The democratic polities that were supposed to emerge in Afghanistan after the US invasion in late 2001, in Iraq after the US/UK invasion in 2003, and in Libya after the NATO bombing in 2011 all collapsed. Among the third-wave democracies examined by Huntington and the subject of many studies on democratic transitions, right-wing populist-nationalist parties and governments have been in power in Hungary and Poland, with setbacks to the rights of women and minorities. The Latin American pink tide has ended in the countries where left-wing governments were most robust. Right-wing populist movements have emerged in even the oldest and most mature democracies. Both the recognition of democracy's deficits and the fear of RWP have led to a spate of books with titles such as *How Democracy Ends*, *How Democracies Die*, *Democracy and Its Crisis*, *The People vs. Democracy*, *Kidnapped Democracy*, *Anti-Pluralism: The Populist Threat to Liberal Democracy*, *The Retreat from Western Liberalism*, and *Why Liberalism Failed*. In March 2014, the *Economist* magazine had a special section titled "What's Gone Wrong with Democracy."

COERCIVE DEMOCRACY

Political scientists point out that processes through which international actors bring pressure to bear for democratization include "contagion, consent, control, and conditionality."[34] Contagion—or what we have already discussed as diffusion—may occur in relation to tactics and frames, but norms, institutional models, and bureaucratic procedures also spread. Consent refers to the voluntary adoption of norms, models, or procedures. In contrast, control (or coercion) has come about through colonialism, neocolonialism, unequal terms of trade, conditionalities, or military intervention. The 2003 invasion of Iraq was justified in part as a means to replace Saddam Hussein's dictatorship with a democracy; elections and constitution writing were quickly organized. The effort failed spectacularly, as did the putative one in Libya in 2011.

If coercive democratization is flawed, control and conditionality on the part of the core have been the primary means of undermining democracy movements in the periphery, including movements that Huntington did not include in his framework of democratic waves. Conditionality commonly refers to terms set by lenders and creditors, or more powerful allies, for any assistance provided. As discussed in chapter 2, in the 1980s semiperipheral and peripheral countries facing large debts were forced to accept economic conditionalities—known as structural adjustment policies (SAPs)—in return for new loans or debt restructuring. In addition to austerity measures to bring down government spending, other policies included denationalization, contraction of the public-sector wage bill, privatization, flexibilization of labor markets, and liberalization of prices and trade. These were the principal means by which countries were forced to shift from state-led growth toward the neoliberal model advocated by the World Bank, the International Monetary Fund (IMF), and the US government.

Some scholars noted that SAPs in Africa coincided with a wave of democratization in the region in two ways: by diminishing the power and maneuverability of authoritarian regimes and by directly or indirectly broadening opposition to the regimes. Conversely, others argued that the adjustment regime was a critical factor in bringing down more benign regimes. Gambia's democratic regime "had a record of stability, respect for human rights, and the rule of law for nearly three decades. As a result of the 50 percent devaluation of the CFA franc in 1994, the Gambia's vital re-export trade was crippled. Essential imports plummeted, and economic hardship became widespread. These effects cost the Jawara regime much of its legitimacy, and paved the way for widespread public acceptance of the July 1994 military coup."[35] Civil society as promoted by outside agencies was less the site of associational groups to provide a buffer between citizens and the state and generate a public sphere than it was an organized alternative economy to meet basic needs. The imposition of SAPs, therefore, could be regarded as a form of de-democratization.

In very rare cases, countries manage to withstand core pressure and reject conditionalities. This was the position taken by Argentina, which chose in 2001 to default on its debt and came out in very good shape.

Most countries, however, are unable to do so. An example is Greece—the birthplace of democracy, a pioneer in democracy's third wave, and a member of the European Union (EU). Greece's experience echoed that of Third World countries in the 1980s and 1990s.

In 2011, the EU's monetary union, the Eurozone, faced a crisis due to high levels of debt and deficits on the part of the several southern European countries. Greece had to accept conditionalities similar to those that peripheral countries had endured in an earlier era, only this time the conditions were demanded by fellow Europeans in Berlin, Paris, and Brussels. Indeed, as became evident in the new century's second decade, the core has its own, internal periphery—countries more vulnerable to economic crisis and susceptible to outside control and conditionality. Like Spain and Portugal, Greece was hit hard by the Great Recession and Eurozone crisis, but it came to be even more subject to control and conditionality than the other countries, because its debts and deficits were perceived to be threatening to the EU's economic stability. Its elites chose to remain in the Eurozone and suffer punishing austerity in return for loans and grants. The austerity measures were accompanied by rising unemployment and loss of incomes, but they also generated massive protests in Syntagma (the central square in Athens opposite the parliament) and in public spaces in other major cities. Calling themselves the "outraged," Greek citizens attacked what they viewed as the pauperization of working people, the loss of sovereignty, and the destruction of democracy.[36] Greek protesters were especially vociferous in their denunciation of the EU's democracy deficit. They demanded a say in how their country's huge debt burden should be tackled, arguing against the conditionalities emanating from the EU's Brussels headquarters, Berlin, and Paris. They called the imposed conditions antidemocratic and, at times, fascistic. Between 2008 and 2013, some four hundred thousand Greeks emigrated, the third-largest mass migration since the start of the twentieth century.[37] The mass protests eventually forced the collapse of the government of Andreas Papandreou and the formation of the left-wing populist Syriza party, led by the young and charismatic Alexis Tsipras.

Greece's Syriza party came to power in January 2015 because of the cronyism and ineptitude of previous governments; the country's GDP crashed by 25 percent, and Greece saw five general elections between 2009 and 2015. Prime Minister Tsipras and his government initially took a strong anti-austerity stance; however, this changed, and the party morphed from radical left-wing to center-left, after the crushing EU fiscal regime that was imposed on the government. The EU was pleased with measures such as improvement of tax collection, allowing gay couples to foster children, and Greece's recognition of its northern neighbor under the compromise name North Macedonia (Tsipras visited there in late March 2019). But in 2019, Greece still had not recovered as well as Portugal and Spain.[38] Greece's elected government under Syriza found itself unable to carry out its promised policies in the face of pressure from the EU, the IMF, and international finance, leaving many Greeks fuming about a de facto takeover from international institutions. Tsipras angered citizens when he overturned a referendum in which voters backed Syriza's tough stance toward Europe. Tsipras rejected finance minister Yanis Varoufakis's proposal to adopt the drachma, and he implemented harsh fiscal measures imposed by Brussels and the IMF. Even the *Economist* magazine noted that "[t]he crisis caused profound damage to the economy in real terms. . . . A fifth of the workforce, and two-fifths of young people, are unemployed."[39] Tsipras resigned in June 2019 after his party lost heavily in the European parliament elections. The subsequent snap election was won by the previous ruling party, New Democracy. In their book on the Greek saga, Heiner Flassbeck and Costas Lapavitsas argue that Germany was largely responsible for the crisis, having caused acute imbalances within the Eurozone by persistently suppressing domestic demand and accumulating unhealthy surpluses. Rather than acquiesce to the pressure, they insist, the Greek government should have taken Greece out of the Eurozone.[40]

Tunisia is the sole success story of the Arab Spring, with elections, new institutions, a high proportion of women's political representation, and an enviable set of freedoms and rights set out in the 2014 constitution. But some years after its political revolution, political progress had not translated into improved livelihoods and a renewed sense of dignity, especially in Tunisia's interior and south.[41] Tunisia's democratic transition was affected by difficult economic conditions, including continued high unemployment and an austerity program that accompanied an IMF loan and generated protests in 2018. (In 2016, the government received an Extended Fund Facility of nearly $3 billion from the IMF.) Surveys showed that faith in democracy had declined. Egypt's democratic transition lasted just under two years; renewed protests, this time against the first democratically elected government and president, surged in early 2013, and by July, the military had taken over. In an interesting analysis that hints at the limitations of a thin version of electoral democracy, Nathan Brown argues that elections came about too quickly in post-Mubarak Egypt, that there were too many of them, and that turnout was low.[42] Two other examples of democratic setbacks may be cited, and these in Huntington's "third-wave democracies." Following nearly fifteen years of progressive government, Brazilians elected the extreme right-wing populist Jair Bolsonaro as president. The Philippines had famously enjoyed a "people's power" political revolution in 1986, but the 2016 presidential election saw the victory of right-wing president Rodrigo Duterte, who went on to authorize extrajudicial killings of drug users and criminals. Both Bolsonaro and Duterte have joined the global wave of right-wing populist movements, parties, and governments.

John Markoff has theorized the close relationship between democracy and social movements.[43] But social movements in the core have not been able to prevent conflicts, wars, or crippling sanctions initiated by democracies (e.g., the United States, United Kingdom, France, and Israel). As stated in chapter 2, the more powerful countries in the world-system, including the hegemon, have deflected the "justice cascade" that Kathryn Sikkink analyzed; the United States and United Kingdom have not had to answer for the devastating consequences of their invasion and occupation of Iraq, and US allies Israel and Saudi Arabia have avoided accountability for their actions in Palestine and Yemen, respectively. Such powerful countries impede development and democratic transition in poorer countries. The hard-liners in Iran's Islamic state consistently thwart the democratic aspirations of its citizens, but international sanctions, most notably those imposed by the United States during the Trump administration, reinforce rather than weaken Iran's authoritarian rule. Democratic countries may decline to wage war on each other (the "democratic peace" thesis), but they launch wars or help cause them in other countries. Social movements may need to do more to hold their governments to account for destructive foreign adventures.

Nearly two decades after its exciting launch in 2001, the WSF remained a site for dialogue and deliberation around neoliberalism, human rights, the climate crisis, and indigenous rights while continuing to eschew political strategizing, planning, coordination, and action. It was not able to contest "a consistent pattern of U.S. support for opposition politicians" to unseat democratically elected left-wing governments in Bolivia, Nicaragua, and Venezuela, the subject of Timothy Gill's analysis.[44] Occupy Wall Street fizzled out without any changes to the fortunes and power of the oligarchic 1 percent, although its legacy remains in its continued support for the Bernie Sanders campaign. In 2019, neoliberalism remained in place as the economic model of the capitalist world-system, although liberal democracy was being challenged by right-wing populist-nationalist movements and governments in core and semiperipheral countries alike.

The identification of a fourth wave and its rollback, setbacks in some of the third-wave democracies, and democracy deficits in the core confirms Huntington's observation about the uneven history of democracy, but it also shows the connection between social movements and world-system dynamics. A country's core, semiperipheral, or peripheral position in the world-system may shape the rate and quality of democratic growth, its possibilities and its vulnerabilities. Successful and sustained democratic movements or polities are less likely to be found in peripheral countries that are disadvantaged economically, unable to access global resources, and devoid of large middle classes, a modern working class, or a vibrant and influential feminist movement. External intervention or control may undermine efforts by social movements or their leaders to effect positive social change; this has occurred time and again in the semiperiphery and especially in peripheral countries.

CAN DEMOCRACY SURVIVE?

The third wave of democratization opened or expanded political systems and extended civil and political rights, but this took place during the emergence and growth of neoliberal capitalist globalization, which also saw the contraction of social/economic and labor rights. While not all models of democracy guarantee the material means for the enjoyment of civil and political rights, the "golden age of capitalism" had afforded citizens a modicum of social rights and economic prosperity, and with that, governments ruled with a high degree of legitimacy and consent. This began to change in the era of neoliberal globalization and especially with the onset of the world economic crisis. In the aftermath of the global economic crisis, governments in the core looked for ways to cut social spending. In a few countries, citizens revolted, but the rules of the game did not change. In 2018–19, France's Gilets Jaunes took umbrage with President Macron's neoliberal "reforms" and neglect of the basic needs of citizens in peripheral regions. Their protests may be seen not only as a reflection of the French political culture but also as the symbol of a more transnational disillusionment with (neo)liberal democracy.

The persistence or heightening of income inequality at the national level is one of democracy's paradoxes, but scholars have identified other aspects of democracy's dark side. In *Setting the People Free: The Story of Democracy*, John Dunn provides a sweeping history of the origins and evolution of democratic theory and governance. He maintains that as early as the late eighteenth and early nineteenth centuries, the ideals of democracy had been co-opted and distorted by advocates of a competitive market economy. This notion is echoed in a study by Adam Przeworski and colleagues: "Today, modernization means liberal democracy, consumption-oriented culture, and capitalism." It also points to concerns raised by Benjamin Barber and German political philosopher Jurgen Habermas, who maintain that the public sphere—so critical to the functioning of a democracy—has been taken over by private or market interests.[45] Perhaps nowhere is this more obvious than in the United States, with its array of paid lobbyists and the revolving door between government and business; the pervasive role of money in US politics is seen as corrupting and corrosive of democracy.[46] Such democracy deficits have been long criticized by left-wing scholars and activists, but in recent years, they have generated the wave of right-wing populist nationalism, with its "people vs. elites" grievances.

Since at least the 1980s, the democracy frame has been diffused throughout the world by movements and advocacy networks as well as by international organizations and governments in the core. In some cases, however, the democratic opening can have highly problematic consequences, bringing fringe elements to power, putting minorities in jeopardy, or unleashing violence. In *World on Fire*, Amy Chua argues that markets and elections often pull societies in opposite directions. Indonesia's democracy movement was accompanied by attacks on ethnic minorities, notably the Chinese, who had held a prominent position in the country's economy. Attacks on Christian churches followed. In 2019, Ethiopia's young prime minister and pro-democracy reformer, Abiy Ahmed, saw challenges to his democratizing and decentralizing efforts in the form of dreadful ethnic violence. John Lukacs, in *Democracy and Populism: Fear and Hatred*, maintains that unchecked popular sovereignty often unleashes a host of evils, targeting minorities but also degrading democracy itself.[47] This echoes Huntington's observation that democracy can rise and fall, as it did with the collapse of the Weimar Republic and the coming to power of the Nazi Party, which then set about targeting critics, communists, Jews, and other "undesirables." The recent rise of right-wing populist movements and governments may not have reached such depths, but their nativist and anti-immigrant rhetoric and policies are both a reflection of the political and economic contradictions of neoliberal globalization and a challenge to democracy, human rights, and decency.

ON GLOBAL DEMOCRACY

If democracy at the national level is difficult to sustain and is subject to reversals and setbacks, how does it operate at the global or regional level? The EU, like the United Nations (UN), has its origins in the post–World War II determination by major powers to end wars and create conditions for economic cooperation and development. The European Economic Community was the initial iteration of the vision, which then expanded its remit to encompass an array of political and social policies, regulations, and institutions. After the collapse of communism, EU membership grew to include former Soviet bloc countries. The European Parliament has been an interesting experiment in regional deliberative democracy, though it lacks authority. Even so, it has not been immune to the neoliberal trend, as it voted to consider the Trade in Services Agreement, which would liberalize trade in banking, transport, and even services. Discussed in private, it was made publicly available by WikiLeaks and immediately faced public criticism for its pro-business bias.[48] Sylvia Walby posits that the EU is characterized by the tension between social democracy and neoliberalism, but Wolfgang Streek insists that the EU has become thoroughly neoliberalized and may be beyond repair.[49] Many European feminists appreciate the EU directives and initiatives on gender equality, ending violence against women, and human rights. But those directives, and especially ones pertaining to the distribution of migrants and refugees across member states, came to be resented by citizens, governments, or political parties of several EU member states. As the chorus of populist criticism of EU policies grew louder, right-wing populists in power began to defy some of the regulations and directives in the name of national sovereignty and local democracy. At the same time, left-wing critics condemned the EU for its shift away from social democracy and embrace of neoliberalism, as well as for its treatment of Greece. Critics outside the EU would point to other deficits in the EU's democratic governance model, such as sanctions against Iran and Syria but large arms deals with Saudi Arabia and the United Arab Emirates; a provocative stance toward Russia by enabling the enlargement of NATO; and tepid or declining financial support for certain UN agencies.

What of the UN? In her 2008 book *Social Movements for Global Democracy*, Jackie Smith identifies two contending global networks. The neoliberal globalization network includes agents and institutions such as the World Bank, the IMF, the World Trade Organization (WTO), transnational corporations and banks, and the transnational capitalist class (see also table 2.2 in this book). The pro-democracy or democratic globalization network includes the WSF, nonhegemonic international organizations, and various civil society and social movement organizations. The pro-democracy network, Smith argues, has real and potential allies in the world of multilateral organizations. Drawing on Robert O'Brien and colleagues, Smith identifies "complex multilateralism" as constituting possibilities for different actors to articulate and advance their interests, build transnational alliances, and so on. Smith identifies the UN as providing "ideals and principles for organizing a transnational state that can challenge the neoliberal globalization project."[50] She contrasts the UN Charter—with its references to peace and human rights—with the financial and interstate system, which breeds war and violations of civil, political, and social/economic rights. Neoliberal globalizers, Smith writes, have sought to redefine the functions of national governments and transform the welfare state into a garrison state; marginalize international organizations oriented toward social welfare, such as the UN and specific agencies within it; advance international organizations that support neoliberal economic policies; and promote a culture/ideology that advances consumerist practices worldwide, justifies the activities of business, and delegitimizes opponents of neoliberalism. In contrast, "democratic globalizers" have advanced the cause of global democracy, Smith writes, "by expanding global agendas, promoting multilateral initiatives, encouraging national implementation of international law, reconciling competing visions of globalization, and generating alternatives to the programs of governments and corporations."

Much as many Europeans seek to reform and reclaim the EU, Smith stresses the need to "reclaim the UN and other global institutions for all the world's people."[51] Smith's democratic globalizers are located in civil society, social movements, and alternative media; they operate through dense horizontal webs, linked by shared values even though they represent a "diversity of identities, structures, and organizational logics." The shared values are an anticapitalist orientation and concern about social and economic destruction wrought by market processes. She points to the WSF, the gathering of activists and progressive intellectuals and a key site for amplifying the values of democracy, cooperation, and community over the neoliberal values of profit, competition, and individualism. In calling the WSF an "incubator" or "laboratory" for global democracy, Smith echoes Donatella della Porta's assertion that democracy functioned as a unifying theme and shared value for many in the GJM.[52]

Can the UN be saved? The UN has been the target of reform by both neoliberal and pro-democracy networks, though in different ways and for divergent ends. Whereas the neoliberal network has sought financial reform, management changes, and streamlining, the pro-democracy network has focused on democratizing decision making, updating the Security Council from its post–World War II configuration to make it more reflective of contemporary international politics, increasing financing for rights-based development, and shifting power from the Bretton Woods institutions to something like an Economic and Social Council. As I have argued in a paper with Dilek Elveren, the era of globalization has seen a hierarchy among the major international organizations such that the international financial institutions and the WTO have much more power, influence, and enforceability than do UN agencies such as the International Labour Organization (ILO), United Nations Children's Fund (UNICEF), United Nations Educational, Scientific and Cultural Organization (UNESCO), United Nations Conference on Trade and Development (UNCTAD), or the United Nations High Commissioner for Refugees (UNHCR).[53] It is true that the UN continues to exert normative influence, but inasmuch as it is an intergovernmental organization dependent on contributions from member states, it lacks the power to prevent unilateral action by the hegemon and its allies.[54] Moreover, because financial contributions are voluntary and not always delivered on time, the UN has become increasingly reliant on the private sector to fund programs.

Liberal democracy refers to a system of government in which those who hold public political office are chosen through regularly held competitive elections in which all adult citizens possessing legal capacity may freely participate by casting equally weighted votes. The strength of this model of democracy is that citizens are constitutionally guaranteed their rights to acquire and disseminate information, organize for lawful purposes, express their views, receive due process of law, and participate in the political process. But this form of democracy does not require that the state be proactive in ensuring the participation and rights of citizens, providing economic rights, or guaranteeing social equality. The entrenchment of this model has allowed neoliberal globalization to shift the balance of power and oversight from citizens to financiers, corporate heads, and lobbyists—to whom elected representatives have become increasingly beholden. Moreover, "faceless bureaucrats" in institutions of global governance make many decisions with significant implications for the living standards and welfare of citizens. This has created frustration and resentment not just among leftists with a propensity for critical thinking and activism but also citizens who are increasingly showing their anger by voting for right-wing populist parties and leaders.

CONCLUSIONS: THIS IS WHAT DEMOCRACY LOOKS LIKE

In *How Democracy Ends*, political scientist David Runciman engages in a thought experiment, proposing three sets of circumstances under which Western democracies are likely to end: coup, nuclear or environmental catastrophe, and technological takeover. His analysis raises questions about how social movements might be able to push governments and institutions of global governance alike in a more sustainable and democratic direction. Can democracy be saved? And what would democracy look like at a global or regional level? What follows is a vision of my own, but one shared by many within pro-democracy social movements.

Apart from the restructuring of the UN and redistribution of power and budgets across multilateral organizations, national economies would be realigned to favor local producers and service providers. The global economy would see the reining in, and regulation of, transnational corporations and banks, a cap on CEO earnings, and implementation of the Tobin tax on financial transactions. Redistribution would enable a global social policy regime predicated on full employment, decent work, decent wages, paid maternity leave, child and elder care, and universal health care.[55] There would be full adoption of the UN convention on the rights of migrant workers and their families, along with the development of a culture of human rights, peace, and international solidarity. One feasible idea consists in tax increases for cross-border corporations such as Facebook and Google, regardless of their physical presence or measured profits in a country; at the June 2019 meeting in Japan of G20 finance ministers, a communiqué was issued for new global tax rules "by 2020," although the United States opposed the idea.[56] This form of "global Keynesianism" would entail initiatives at regional, national, and local levels, with full citizen participation in the making of a more expansive and robust democracy. The EU would need to shift away from its embrace of neoliberalism (and arms exports) and promote more social spending on health, education, and social welfare. In the United States, the Green New Deal would be enacted and financed by tax increases for the top 1 percent, gun sales and ownership would be brought under control, and resources would shift from militarism to green-powered industries and the upgrading of the country's deteriorating social and physical infrastructure.[57] Such policies echo the call for "industrial policy" by Felix Rohatyn in the 1980s and 1990s, and even further back in American history, to the developmental model of Alexander Hamilton. Such a turn in economic policy would help weaken the base of right-wing populism by strengthening confidence in government and democracy.

In the 1990s and into the new century, scholar-activists within the GJM began to identify another site for democratic practices and economic citizenship: the burgeoning "solidarity economy," constituted by forms of cooperative and nonprofit economic relations and enterprises found in Spain, Brazil, Quebec, Bolivia, and some parts of the United States. Walden Bello, a key figure in the WSF who has advocated for deglobalization, emphasized "democratic forms of economic decision-making" in place of market governance (or what some have called free market fundamentalism and economic totalitarianism). Philosopher William McBride has written of the workers' self-management model in the former Yugoslavia as an appropriate alternative to neoliberal capitalist control. A similar model was found in Porto Alegre, Brazil, where participatory and gender-responsive budgeting was predicated on citizen participation in preparing municipal budgets; this helped reallocate spending toward human-development priorities. During the first seven years of the experiment, the share of households with access to water services increased, moving from 80 to 98 percent, and the percentage of the population with access to sanitation almost doubled, moving from 46 to 85 percent.[58]

Such experiments have encouraged scholar-activists to explore more locally based initiatives for sustainable development and participatory democracy. Ideas for the revival of democracy include the new "municipalism," with emphasis on the principle of subsidiarity and local decision making. Benjamin Barber argues that nation-states had become dysfunctional and that cities were doing a better job of tackling complex problems. Jackie Smith refers to "place-based efforts to realize human rights in localized settings" and describes efforts in Pittsburgh, Pennsylvania, to realize "the right to the city" on the part of low-paid workers and racial minorities. The so-called Cleveland model entails green and worker-owned cooperatives that were formed in response to economic distress; in Preston, a northern city in England that was hit by both de-industrialization and austerity, the Centre for Local Economic Strategies identified 12 large institutions anchored to the city—including the city and the county council, the university, the police, and the hospital—to redirect the £1.2 billion total annual spending power of these anchors to local businesses. Barcelona was a victim of the 2008 mortgage and financial crisis and suffered the subsequent austerity measures, but in 2015, it elected a former activist, Ana Colau, as mayor; priorities are affordable housing, the regulation of tourism, and direct democracy. In northern Syria, and in the midst of a brutal internationalized civil conflict with the intervention of legions of jihadists from around the world, a Kurdish community created an experimental autonomous region, Rojava. Inspired by the writings of US anarchist and social ecologist Murray Bookchin, Rojava was based on concepts of democratic confederalism, women's liberation and participation, and the social economy.[59] These are inspiring examples of progressive local initiatives. We know, however, that right-wing populists similarly call for local (as well as national) sovereignty, and the risk of reactionary and exclusionary localism is always present in such experiments. Local democracy, therefore, needs to be part of a broader national democratic polity, which in turn is best sustained through a more democratized global environment.

In the perspective of this chapter, real democracy should be seen as a multifaceted and ongoing process at different levels of social existence: in the family, community, workplace, economy, civil society, and polity. In turn, global democracy reinforces national and local democracy through the efficacy of multilateralism, democratic decision making at the global level, and wealth redistribution. Certainly an infrastructure exists for a global democracy in the form of international nongovernmental organizations (NGOs), transnational advocacy networks, transnational feminist networks (TFNs), global civil society, transnational social movements, and peace movements, all of which are carriers of a deliberative, participatory democracy. Social movement organizations in particular have a historic role to play in changing the status quo and deepening democracy at all levels. Markoff has aptly stated that democracy has never been a finished thing but has been continually renewed, redefined, and reinvented. It is past time to bring about a more robust social, if not socialist, democracy. We now turn to our case studies to examine the extent to which social movements may contribute to this goal or undermine it.

CHAPTER 4

ISLAMIST MOVEMENTS

The crisis exists precisely in the fact that the old is dying and
the new is not yet born; in the interregnum a great variety of
morbid symptoms appear.

—Antonio Gramsci, *Prison Notebooks*[1]

Like the women's movement and the global justice movement (see
chapters 5 and 6), Islamism may be seen as a "movement of movements" with an overarching common goal of the establishment or
reinforcement of Islamic laws and norms as the solution to economic,
political, and cultural problems. Islamist movements are heterogeneous
and diverse, evincing different tactics and strategies in achieving goals.
This organizational feature is in keeping with the segmentary, polycentric, and reticulate character of social movements, as discussed in
chapters 1 and 2. Distinctions have been made between "moderate" and

"extremist" Islamists. Generally, moderates engage in nonviolent organizing and advocacy in civil society, forming or joining political parties and fielding candidates in parliamentary elections, and include the Muslim Brotherhood of Egypt and Jordan, Islah of Yemen, the Justice and Development Party (AKP) of Turkey, the Parti de la Justice et du Développement (PJD) of Morocco, and Tunisia's an-Nahda (Ennahda in the Tunisian spelling). Such parties often engage in populist rhetoric about "the people," "the Muslim people," "justice," and "dignity."

Extremists call for the violent overthrow of political systems they regard as anti-Islamic, westernized, or dictatorial, branding as un-Islamic any participation in electoral politics. They operate clandestinely, form networks and cells across countries, and may engage in spectacular forms of violence. Also known as jihadists (or Salafi jihadists), they may or may not have links to the transnational network of al-Qaeda, with its satellites in South Asia, North Africa, and Iraq, or with the so-called Islamic State of Iraq and the Levant (ISIL or ISIS), which briefly formed a "caliphate" in parts of Iraq and Syria. Salafists—influenced by Saudi Arabia's Wahhabi dogmatism—argue that Islam is at once political, economic, cultural, social, and religious. This view is shared by radical Islamists, who promote Islamization of their societies and often engage in fiery rhetoric (e.g., calling for executions of apostates or infidels, jihad against oppressors, and so on), though they may not themselves engage in violent acts. Such groups include the United Kingdom–based Hizb ul-Tahrir and al-Muhajiroun.[2] Yet other radical Islamists, such as Palestine's Hamas, Lebanon's Hezbollah, and Iraq's Mahdi Army have large social bases of support and are widely seen as patriots and national heroes engaged in legitimate resistance against foreign intervention.

This chapter examines the relationship between Islamism and globalization and identifies the political opportunities—both national and global, including state complicity—that enabled Islamist growth, mobilizing structures, recruitment patterns, and grievances. It distinguishes parliamentary and moderate Islamist movements from radical and jihadist, and draws attention to the more promising liberal, democratic, and pro-feminist tendency. The chapter begins by identifying the different types of Islamist movements and organizations, their origins, diverse activities, and cultural frames.

THE CONTINUUM OF ISLAMISM

There is no single Islamist movement but varied types, although all are rooted in, and draw on, Islamic history. Radical and jihadist movements, for example, use modern methods, but their grievances and objectives are rooted in the past. Hugh Roberts shows how Algeria's Front Islamique du Salut (FIS) was part of the legacy of orthodox, urban-based Islamic reformists associated with the Salafists of the early decades of the twentieth century. Islamic fundamentalism in Egypt and the Sudan, John Voll explains, had links with eighteenth- and nineteenth-century Wahhabist and Mahdist movements. Contemporary radical Islamists are inspired by the rigid and puritanical legacies of Ibn Taymiyyah, a medieval Hanbali jurist, and Ibn Abd-al-Wahhab, an eighteenth-century theologian who formed an alliance with Muhammad Ibn Saud and built a religio-political movement that was defeated by the Ottomans but in the twentieth century formed the foundation of the new state of Saudi Arabia. Other sources of inspiration and guidance are the writings of Abul Ala Mawdudi (who founded the Jamiat-e Islami in India in 1941), the Egyptians Rashid Rida and Hassan al-Banna (who founded the Muslim Brotherhood in 1929), and Sayyid Qutb of Egypt; all these men took issue with modernity as it was proceeding in their countries and called for a return to strict implementation of sharia law. Sayyid Qutb's 1948–50 stay in the United States convinced him that the *jahiliyya*—the so-called age of darkness that characterized pre-Islamic Arabia—had returned and needed to be combated. Today's radical Islamists use the term "*jahiliyya*" to describe the state of the world and justify their aggressive tactics. From Ibn Taymiyyah they adopted the duty to wage jihad against apostates and unbelievers.[3]

Fawaz Gerges conducted interviews with scores of jihadists during 1999 and 2000, stressing the importance of distinguishing between national jihad and transnational jihad and arguing that the latter arose from the "failure" of the former. Quintan Wiktorowicz shows how Salafi reformist and militant networks alike developed, changed, and helped drive political crises from Algeria to Afghanistan over three decades. Jordan's Salafists, he explains, focused on spreading their ideas through study circles and publishing, and he concludes that "radicals respond rationally and strategically to structures of opportunity." Mohammed Hafez argues that Islamic radicals turn to violence when the state forecloses opportunities for participation and inclusion in the public sphere and resorts to repression.[4] The rise of ISIS generated a new wave of Islamist studies, focused on its relationship to the destabilization of states in the Middle East, its ideology and recruitment patterns, and its transnational appeal, including its growth in Sub-Saharan Africa. Abrahms and Glaser argue convincingly that rather than the "grievance model" of movement radicalization, the rise of ISIS could be better understood through the "opportunities model," whereby the destabilization of first Iraq and then Syria, and especially external support of Syrian rebels by Turkey, Gulf states countries, and other US allies, fed the growth of ISIS.[5]

Scholars also have studied the activities and goals of "moderate" Islamist movements and political parties, using ethnographic research methods as well as a close reading of Islamist literature. Jillian Schwedler and Janine Clark examined Islamist parties in Jordan and Yemen and their role in the political process, while Jenny White, Carrie Rosefsky Wickham, and Malika Zeghal studied Islamists in Turkey, Egypt, and Morocco, respectively. They described the social-service and charity activities of Islamist groups, as well as the role of Islamist women as charity workers, voters, and recruiters.[6] Such Islamist groups were conservative in their cultural and social worldviews, though in this respect the groups were not so different from the general population. In general, moderate Islamists who accept and join the parliamentary process are distinguished not only from jihadists at one end of the Islamist continuum (see figure 4.1) but also from a tendency that other scholars call liberal or democratic Islam, a tendency that has been associated with both individual scholars and collective groups. The late Pakistani scholar Fazlur Rahman was one such scholar and proponent of liberal Islam. Others have included Iranian scholars Seyyid Hossein Nasr and Abdolkarim Soroush and Egyptians Hassan Hanafi and Nasr Hamed Abou Zeyd.[7] (Egyptian philosophy professor Abu Zeyd was harassed in Egypt between 1992 and 1995 because of his historical and

←——————————————————————————————————→

Moderate	Radical	Jihadist / Extremist
An-Nahda/Ennahda (Tunisia)	Hamas (Gaza Strip)	Taliban (Afghanistan, Pakistan); ISIS

Figure 4.1. The Islamist Continuum: Moderate to Jihadist

hermeneutical approach to the Qur'an. When an Egyptian family court charged him with apostasy and ordered him divorced from his wife, the couple left for the Netherlands, where he held a professorship at Leiden University until his untimely death in 2010.) In the Islamic Republic of Iran, a generation of lay advocates and dissident clerics known as the "new religious intellectuals" emerged in the 1990s (e.g., Abdolkarim Soroush, Mohsen Saidzadeh, Mohsen Kadivar, Hasan Yousefi Eshkevari, and Mohammad Mojtahed Shabestari), calling for human rights and civil liberties informed by an emancipatory interpretation of Islam, along with the separation of the clerical establishment and religious law from the state apparatus.[8]

In the United States, a number of liberal Muslim groups and institutions exist, including Muslim Wake-Up; the Free Muslims Coalition; the Center for the Study of Islam and Democracy, based in Washington, DC; the Ahmadiyya Muslim Community USA, which offers a strong message of peace and nonviolence; and the American Society for Muslim Advancement (ASMA), led by Imam Feisal Abdul Rauf and his wife, Daisy Khan, a Muslim feminist.[9] In a manner very different from the radical Islamist use of the concept of "jihad," moderate and liberal Muslims emphasize the "inner struggle" that Muslims are called on to perform in order to strengthen their faith. They also stress *ijtihad*, or rational reasoning and reinterpretation to address a problem, such as women's roles, slavery, age at first marriage, and so on. For example, applying a historical perspective, they note that in early Islam, apostasy was equivalent to the modern concept of treason; hence, in an era of modern nation-states, changing one's religion cannot be considered a treasonous, capital offense.

Another version of liberal and democratic Islam is found in the global network of Islamic feminists who have taken issue with patriarchal and violent interpretations of Islam, seek legal reforms, and call for women's rights through their own rereadings of the Qur'an and early Islamic history. Among the most organized, vocal, and visible are Malaysia's Sisters in Islam (SIS), who work with feminist groups across the globe and are associated with the transnational feminist network Women Living under Muslim Laws (WLUML). They helped found Musawah ("equality"), a transnational network of Muslim women from different countries and organizations advocating for equality in the family on the basis of Islamic *ijtihad*. Established in 2009 at a global conference of 250 activists and scholars from more than fifty countries, the network embarked on research, advocacy, and knowledge dissemination for legal and policy change. Its "framework for action" states that reform is needed in the following areas: Islamic sources, international human rights standards, national laws, and lived realities of men and women. Musawah is linked to women's groups in a number of countries, including Morocco's Association Démocratique des Femmes du Maroc (ADFM), and was inspired by Morocco's landmark 2004 family law reform, the result of years of feminist advocacy as well as public debates and marches. Musawah holds it up as an example of the kind of change that is possible through an engagement with Islamic jurisprudence and works with Muslim women around the world for similar reform in their countries.[10] The Muslim groups or scholars with liberal views on cultural and social issues should not be deemed "Islamist," but they also may not be highly representative of populations in the Muslim world, especially on such issues as homosexuality, gender equality in religious and family matters, and the equal legal status of all citizens.

How might we define Islamism? Let us begin first with "Islamic fundamentalism," which motivated much research in the 1980s and 1990s, including the grand Fundamentalism Project. Syrian Marxist political philosopher Sadik al-Azm identified fundamentalism, whether Christian or Islamic, as the notion of inerrancy or infallibility of holy texts. Thus, "the Koran [or Bible or Torah] is absolutely infallible, without error in all matters pertaining to faith and practice, as well as in areas such as geography, science, history, etc." As such, fundamentalism may be found in Christianity and Judaism as well as Islam. Political Islam refers to movements and ideas predicated on the spread of Islamic laws and norms, whether through parliamentary or violent means. Wiktorowicz prefers the term "Islamic activism," which he defines as "the mobilization of contention to support Muslim causes." His definition would include both moderate and radical tendencies of political Islam. Wiktorowicz maintains that "Islamists are Muslims who feel compelled to act on the belief that Islam demands social and political activism, either to establish an Islamic state, to proselytize to reinvigorate the faithful, or to create a separate union for Muslim communities." He argues, as does Mohammed Hafez, that Islamist rebellions arise from state repression.[11] Sadik al-Azm provides a rather less sympathetic definition of Islamism:

Islamism is a highly militant mobilizing ideology selectively developed out of Islam's scriptures, texts, legends, historical precedents, organizations, and present-day grievances, all as a defensive reaction against the long-term erosion of Islam's primacy over the public, institutional, economic, social, and cultural life of Muslim societies in the twentieth century. The ideology is put in practice by resurrecting the early concept of Islamic jihad in its most violent and aggressive forms against an environing world of paganism, polytheism, idolatry, godlessness, infidelity, atheism, apostasy, and unbelief known to that ideology as the Jahiliyya of the twentieth century.[12]

Similarly, Egyptian political economist Samir Amin (died 2018), a key figure in the global justice movement (GJM) and a longtime activist in Third World, anti-imperialist, and socialist movements, penned harsh criticisms of Islamism, including an essay titled "Political Islam in the Service of Imperialism." He maintained that Islamist movements should be understood as politically and culturally right-wing, pointing out that the Muslim Brotherhood members of the Egyptian parliament "reinforce[d] the rights of property owners to the detriment of the rights of tenant farmers (the majority of the small peasantry)."[13] (See table 4.1 for examples of Islamist movements across countries.)

Table 4.1. Types of Islamist or Muslim Movements, Organizations, or Tendencies, 1980s–Present

Parliamentary	Muslim Brotherhood (Egypt); an-Nahda (Tunisia); PJD (Morocco); Islamic Action Front (Jordan); Hezbollah (Lebanon); AKP (Turkey); Islah (Yemen)
Liberal/ Democratic	"New religious intellectuals" (Iran); Sisters in Islam (Malaysia); Musawah (transnational); Gulen movement (Turkey); American Society for Muslim Advancement, and Women's Islamic Initiative in Spirituality and Equality, Center for the Study of Islam and Democracy (United States)
Radical	Front Islamique du Salut (Algeria); Nour Party (Egypt); Mahdi Party (Iraq); Jamaat-I Islam (Pakistan); Hamas (Palestine); Hezbollah (Lebanon); Tablighi Jamaat, Hizb Tahrir (United Kingdom)
Jihadist	Mujahideen, Taliban, Haqqani network (Afghanistan); Armed Islamic Group (Algeria); Islamic Jihad, Gama'a Islamiyya (Egypt); Jemaah Islamiah (Indonesia); Islamic State (Iraq and Syria); Salafiyya movement and Jaish Muhammad (Jordan); Boko Haram (Nigeria); Tahrik-I Taliban, Lashkar-I Taiba (Pakistan); al-Shabab (Somalia); Islamic Jihad, Farah al-Islam (Palestine); al-Muhajiroun (United Kingdom); al-Qaeda (transnational); ISIS (transnational)

My own understanding of Islamism combines elements of the perspectives mentioned here but moves beyond them. Like Wiktorowicz and Hafez, I believe that the concepts and categories of social movement theory can be applied to elucidate the dynamics of Islamist activism. However, the evidence does not confirm that Islamists are motivated exclusively by state repression; as discussed in chapters 1 and 2, sociopsychological and gendered explanations, including the role of masculine identities and religiously informed heroic masculinities, are pertinent. The violence perpetrated over Salman Rushdie's *The Satanic Verses* in 1989 and the Danish cartoons caricaturing the Prophet Muhammad in 2006 was not related to state repression. Here my approach to Islamist politics is similar to that of Amin: it is firmly on the right wing and often on the Far Right. My definition of Islamism is more consistent with that of al-Azm: I see it as a politicized movement, network, or ideology selectively based on Islamic theology and history but motivated by contemporary developments and opportunities. My analysis situates the rise and expansion of contemporary Islamism in world-systemic and globalization processes while also recognizing the gendered nature of Islamist politics and practices.

ORIGINS AND POLITICAL OPPORTUNITIES

Contemporary Islamist movements have their origins in the history and theology of Islam, which are also inscribed in the movements' cultural frames. Salafists and jihadists emphasize the doctrinal obligation of Muslims to defend the faith when Islam is deemed to be under threat. They point out that the Prophet Muhammad and his companions engaged in battle to defend themselves and spread the faith, and they interpret Quranic verses in particular ways to justify attacks on "apostates" and "infidels." (Islam did not spread by the sword alone. Trade, empire, and settlement by Muslims helped the community to grow, while the decency of Muslim neighbors encouraged others to convert.) Most Islamists have been inspired by Sayyid Qutb's writings, but transnational jihadists take special inspiration from his book *Jahiliyyat al-Qarn al-Ishrin* (the *jahiliyya* of the twentieth century), which implies that now that Western modernity has come full circle to the *jahili* condition, Arabs and the Muslims should lead humanity once more out of the *jahiliyya* created by Europe and defended by the West in general.

STATES, THE COLD WAR, AND ISLAMIST GROWTH

Islamist movements became prominent in the 1980s, but Islam had been a mobilizing frame in the decades before. Both Islamic and nationalist frames were used in anticolonial struggles, but Islamist groups often opposed progressive nationalist leaders, not to mention communist movements and parties. The Cold War and fervent US anti-communism led to sustained efforts to eliminate left-wing movements and governments, as well as nationalist governments perceived to be soft on communism. Seminal events are the 1953 coup d'état against Iranian prime minister Mohammad Mossadegh; the 1965 coup in Indonesia that eliminated the Communist Party and brought the military dictator Suharto to power; the support for military dictatorships in Pakistan and Bangladesh in the 1980s; and aid to Islamist rebels fighting a Soviet-supported left-wing government in Afghanistan in the 1980s. Many Muslim intellectuals and clerical leaders had long been opposed to the secularism and perceived atheism of communist movements. In this they converged with repressive regimes as well as with various US governments.

The growth of left-wing movements in the 1960s and 1970s led some regimes in Muslim-majority states to encourage the Islamic tide in hopes of neutralizing the Left. Egypt's President Anwar Sadat released Muslim Brotherhood prisoners to counter the Egyptian Left in his campaign of de-Nasserization. Iran's Shah Mohammad Reza Pahlavi followed the same strategy in the early 1970s, as did the Turkish authorities after the 1980 military coup. Indeed, in the latter case, as the generals' overriding objective was to rid Turkish society of Marxist ideology and parties, they encouraged Islamic ideas and education as an antidote. Thus, in 1982 the military regime made the teaching of Islam compulsory in schools; since 1967, it had been optional. When Islamists in Iran were able to seize control of what had been a cross-class populist revolution against the shah in 1978–79, the victory of the "Islamic revolution" inspired and encouraged Muslims and Islamists throughout the world.[14]

In Indonesia, after Muslim militants helped track down and kill communists during the mass murders that accompanied the 1965 coup d'état, elements of the Indonesian state and military covertly funded and promoted Muslim groups, a policy that facilitated the growth of more extremist Islamist networks; further funding came from Saudi Arabia and other foreign sources. Throughout this period, the United States was in close alliance with Saudi Arabia for its oil, arms purchases, and anticommunism, turning a blind eye to Saudi use of oil wealth to help build Islamic institutions and networks across the globe. Thomas Hegghammer has described how the Saudi state and its many religious institutions not only funded jihadist activities but were instrumental in igniting the jihadist movement—at least until al-Qaeda formed in the Arabian Peninsula and began to attack Saudi targets. Afghan specialist Barnett Rubin refers to the 1980s "arms pipeline" to the Afghan mujahideen and other militant Islamist groups, made possible by Saudi and Kuwaiti money; in 1992, the US-supported Afghan mujahideen toppled the modernizing government of President Mohammad Najibullah. In Yemen, when the northern regime fought the southern socialists in a short civil war in 1994, the Islamists fought alongside them to defeat the socialists. By this time, Islamist networks existed across the globe, and they proliferated steadily. The collapse of the Soviet Union may have been celebrated by some, notably conservative political theorist Francis Fukuyama, as the harbinger of the worldwide expansion of liberal democracy. But in the Muslim world, it meant the end of the reigning alternative ideology of socialism/communism and the expansion of Islamism.

In his 1999 study of the "unholy wars," John Cooley refers to the "strange love affair which went disastrously wrong: the alliance, during the second half of the twentieth century, between the United States of America and some of the most conservative and fanatical followers of Islam." In his book *Secret Affairs*, Mark Curtis has written of what he calls "Britain's collusion with radical Islam," tracking that country's role in the overthrow of Iranian premier Mohammad Mossadegh in 1953; its alliance with Saudi Arabia as a hedge against Egyptian president Gamal Abdel Nasser's secular pan-Arab vision; Margaret Thatcher's support for the anticommunist mujahideen of Afghanistan and her stated hope that Muslims would not "succumb to the fraudulent appeal of imported Marxism"; the creation of "Londonistan," where Islamist groups from Algeria, Libya, Egypt, and elsewhere were based; and the fallout from the British roles in Iraq and Afghanistan.[15] Saudi Arabia's role is critical in this regard. In his 2009 book, Emile Nakhleh, who had a long career with the US State Department, writes, "I have visited numerous

Qur'anic *madrasas* and other Islamic schools throughout the Muslim world financed by Saudi NGOs" and adds that some officials expressed to him "their concern about the pervasive Wahhabi-Salafi influence."[16] All may be considered political opportunities for the growth of Islamism, especially its militant incarnation.

Elites, state agencies, and state-managed media all played a role in the diffusion of Islamist action and frames. In some cases, Muslim elites become involved in or encouraged Islamist contention to enhance their own credentials, undermine the organized Left, or distract the public from pressing socioeconomic issues. Geopolitical rivalries furthered the process.

The 1990s saw transition on a world scale, defined by the consolidation of neoliberal capitalism. It also saw the growth of radical and jihadist Islam. The Afghan mujahideen came to power in Afghanistan in 1992, though they quickly turned on each other. Events in the 1990s include the attacks on US marines in Lebanon and the withdrawal of American troops; the breakup of formerly socialist Yugoslavia; the Islamist revolt in Chechnya; spectacular terrorist assaults in various parts of the world, including Tanzania and Kenya; and the emergence of the Taliban in Afghanistan following its 1996 overthrow of the mujahideen. Islamism became globalized in the context of the post–Cold War world order; geographic reordering and collapsed states allowed for the distribution of arms and militants across porous borders.

In Pakistan, state and media complicity against the Left enabled the gradual radicalization of Pakistani society and the growing power of Islamists. By 2011, a leading politician could be assassinated—by an Islamist policeman, no less—because he had defended an impoverished Christian woman falsely accused of insulting Islam. The murder of Salmaan Taseer followed a campaign of vilification by the clergy and sections of the press, and the assassin's cause received support in Pakistan, with lawyers outside the court showering him with rose petals. As one report stated, "The Pakistani state has given succor to violent, extremist organizations."[17] A group of young Pakistani men, groomed by Islamist jihadists, carried out the assault on the Taj Hotel in Mumbai, India, in 2008.

Our analysis is not complete without reference to sociodemographics and social psychology, including issues of urbanization, anomie, class background, and education. As early research by Saad Eddin Ibrahim and John Entelis reveals, recruits to Islamist movements in the 1980s were often first-generation educated urbanites from the lower middle classes and conservative family backgrounds. Such sociodemographic and class features have been widely theorized to evince status anxiety and cultural discomfort, in a pattern that suggests parallels with recruits to right-wing populist as well as fascistic movements. At the same time, feminist research has shown that women's growing social visibility and participation challenged men's dominance in public spaces, rendering recent migrants and men of the lower middle classes and conservative backgrounds alienated and angry. As the late Moroccan feminist sociologist Fatima Mernissi wrote, "If men are calling for the return of the veil, it must be because women have been taking off the veil." The conditions made some men highly vulnerable to an ideology whose grievances and solutions resonated because it was anchored in religion. In the case of Islamic fundamentalism and political Islam, therefore, a linkage between structural strain and movement contention at a national level could plausibly be made. In turn, global processes of which Muslim societies were a part exacerbated structural strain. Whether in Europe or in Muslim-majority countries, the Islamist message came to resonate largely with young men confronting socioeconomic difficulties and cultural changes that provoked feelings of anxiety, alienation, and anger. Islam became the source of a mobilizing ideology and organizational resources used to combat domestic injustices, cultural imperialism, and changes to traditional notions of the family.[18] Islamism was further helped along by geopolitical rivalries and the wreckage of the Left.

GRIEVANCES AND CULTURAL FRAMES

Muslim grievances were diffused across the Muslim world via the internet and Arabic-language media. Grievances were tied to national and local effects of the reordering of the global economy, from the structural adjustment policies of the 1980s and the gradual withdrawal of the state from an array of services and subsidies, to the growing inequalities of the turn of the century and the loss of job opportunities for the growing pool of university graduates. These conditions generated grievances as well as opportunities for protest, recruitment, and mobilization, and they culminated in the Arab Spring of 2011 as well as rebellions in Libya, Yemen, and Syria.

This broad world-systemic perspective is critical to an understanding of Islamist movements because it contextualizes the periodic protests that had arisen over structural adjustments and unemployment since the 1980s; the spread of Islamic nongovernmental organizations (NGOs) and their social-welfare activities; the political openings that allowed the "Islamic alternative" to present itself, in some cases as moderate and parliamentarian and in others as radical and jihadist; and the successful electoral outcomes of Tunisia's an-Nahda, Egypt's Muslim Brotherhood, and Morocco's Parti de la Justice et du Développement (PJD) in the countries' first elections in late 2011, following the Arab Spring revolts.

Islamists blamed the spread of Western values and practices for a wide range of social and economic ills, including rising unemployment, stagnant development, soaring debt, housing shortages, dwindling public social and welfare expenditures, and what Islamists see as the breakdown of the traditional Muslim family. Blaming Western influence for such developments is, as Wiktorowicz notes, "an important component of most Islamic movement diagnostic frames."[19] It follows that the solution is the return to or strengthening of Islamic values, norms, and laws.

For the moderate Islamist, the answer is peaceful "regime change" within the Muslim world through parliamentary means and the gradual Islamization of key social institutions, such as charities, schools, clinics, and professional associations. This includes a call for adherence to Muslim family laws and the sharia as the guide to personal and public behavior. This was the strategy of the Muslim Brotherhood in Egypt during the 1990s.

For the radical Islamist, it is a short step from viewing Islam as endangered by the West to taking up arms against Western targets and their domestic allies. Such is the motivation behind, inter alia, the Islamist revolution against the shah in Iran (and later against the Left in that country), the assassination of Egyptian president Anwar Sadat, the targeting of secular intellectuals in Egypt and Turkey, the violent revolt in Algeria in the 1990s, the Red Mosque affair in Pakistan in 2007, the resurgence of the Afghan Taliban in 2006, and terrorist acts in Europe, the United States, and elsewhere. The view of Islam as under threat was behind the rise of transnational networks of militant Islamists, notably al-Qaeda in the early part of this century and ISIS after the Arab Spring. In these cases, violence becomes the principal form of contention.

GLOBALIZING ISLAMISM: THE JIHADIST TURN

Aspects of globalization, including changing borders, ease of travel, and the new information and computer technologies (ICTs), helped diffuse Islamist frames and recruit adherents, thus globalizing Islam. The worldwide distribution of the fatwa, or religious edict, that was issued against Indian-British writer Salman Rushdie in early 1989 by Ayatollah Khomeini, leader of Iran's Islamic revolution, mobilized militants across the world to protest what Khomeini claimed was an affront to the Qur'an and the Prophet. Another example is the 2006 Danish cartoons conflict, and Thomas Olesen argues that elites and media were the prime movers in the transnational escalation of the controversy. Demonstrations and riots took place first in Palestine and Kuwait, then in Yemen, Indonesia, Turkey, Syria, Lebanon, Afghanistan, Iran, Egypt, and the Philippines. Danish embassies in Damascus and Beirut were set on fire. Egyptian state-owned newspapers called for a boycott of Danish goods, decrying the cartoons as "a crime against the Muslim world."[20]

In analyzing the rise of transnational Islamism, Fawaz Gerges writes that Islamists—steeped in Sayyid Qutb's revisions of the classical doctrine of jihad—aimed to target "apostate" Muslim rulers who were not enforcing sharia; these were the "near enemy." In the 1980s and early 1990s, the national jihad in Afghanistan took a global turn when thousands of young Muslims poured into Afghanistan to join it; they were allowed to do so by governments that either wished to rid themselves of unruly young men or genuinely desired the downfall of a left-wing state in a Muslim-majority country. When the "Afghan Arabs" returned home—for example, to Algeria, Egypt, and Jordan—they triggered bloody confrontations with the state. Al-Qaeda was formed in the years following Iraqi ruler Saddam Hussein's invasion of Kuwait in 1990 and the subsequent events. Osama bin Laden, a Saudi citizen from a rich family, was angry that the Saudi government had selected the US Army rather than his own militia to rout Saddam Hussein in Kuwait, and he was especially provoked by the presence of US troops on Saudi soil. Expelled in 1991, he went to Sudan until 1996, then to Afghanistan to be harbored by the Taliban, which by that time had replaced the US-supported mujahideen. In Afghanistan, bin Laden and Ayman al-Zawahiri, his Egyptian-born deputy, shifted attention to the "far enemy": the United States. In 1998, they publicly declared the creation of a transnational network called the International Front for Jihad against Jews and Crusaders. The September 11, 2001, attacks on the United States were carried out by nineteen young men, fifteen of them Saudis. The repercussions for the United States of its support for the Afghan jihad in the 1980s have been termed "blowback."[21]

Migration helped globalize Islamism. The migration of large populations of Muslims to the West, largely for economic reasons, has created both an existential burden and an opportunity structure. One aspect of the burden is trying to live a meaningful life in the new countries of residence, which are secularized and hold values and practices deemed contrary to Muslim values. This has led to difficulties in integration and to antipathy on the part of the native population. In Europe, therefore, there has been much discussion of what is often framed as the problem of Muslim integration and sometimes as "Islamophobia." The opportunity structure of Western liberalism, tolerance, and pluralism, as well as explicit policies of multiculturalism in Europe, has meant that Muslim immigrants have been able to practice their faith openly, in highly visible ways, such as by building mosques and faith-based schools, wearing veils, spilling out onto the streets during prayers, establishing halal meat stores, building Islamic charities and other associations, demanding prayer rooms at universities, and proselytizing and seeking converts for the Islamic faith. In some countries, "Islamic courts" have provided informal rulings. Such practices, as noted, have not always been well received by natives or by liberal or secular Muslim immigrants, and this has created or reinforced a collective identity among a certain section of the immigrant population as self-defined "Muslims" or even as "fighters for Islam." (In the United Kingdom, the category "British Muslim" was assumed by many citizens originally from South Asia but eschewed by Iranian-born Britons who left Iran because of Islamism.)

The presence of radical youth who engaged in terrorist actions on European soil eventually led to many debates about multiculturalism, self-segregation, discrimination, and social exclusion. More typically, the spread of veiling, the growth of mosques and other Muslim institutions in Europe, and the ability of radical preachers to recruit young people were blamed on "misguided multicultural policies" in Britain, the Netherlands, Finland, Germany, and elsewhere, countries that now reject those policies and insist on assimilation. In Catalonia, a Salafist-run Islamic court allegedly kidnapped a North African woman charged with adultery and sentenced her to death. She fled, and her captors were arrested, but not before moderate Muslim groups criticized the Catalan government for giving "a free rein to the most radical forms of Islam." Discomfort with Islamist growth led to the Swiss vote in 2009 to disallow construction of any more tall minarets alongside mosques. Heavy veiling was banned in France, Belgium, and Austria, and after terrorist attacks in London, British prime minister David Cameron ended the local council funding to Islamic groups that he said had bred extremism and "home-grown terror."[22]

STATE REPRESSION AND VIOLENT CONTENTION

The literature on social movements suggests that state repression could have a preemptive or dampening effect on collective action. Conversely, state repression could force contenders to turn to violent methods. John Entelis, a scholar of North African politics, saw the Algerian regime as conforming to a widespread practice of confrontation that "unleashed a much more virulent form of Islamic radicalism." In their joint work and separate writings on Islamic activism and Muslim rebellions, Wiktorowicz and Hafez argue that the use of violence by the Armed Islamic Group (GIA) in Algeria "was, to a large extent, a tactical response to shifting opportunity structures and emerged under particular conditions and circumstances." The GIA, Hafez maintains, moved toward "a growing belief in total war" when the Islamist movement was excluded from institutional politics and suffered state repression. Here he refers to the events of 1991, in which Algeria's ruling party, supported by the military, annulled the results of elections that favored the FIS and subsequently banned it. Hafez and Wiktorowicz likewise maintain that "the cycle of violence in Egypt [by Gama'a Islamiyya] began largely in response to a broad crackdown on the Islamic movement that targeted moderates, radicals, and a number of tangential bystanders." There and elsewhere, it is argued, Islamist insurgencies are provoked by state-sponsored exclusion, marginalization, and repression.[23]

State repression, however, is not the only trigger, or even the main one. Islamist grievances resonate with many Muslims across the globe, and some are shared by non-Muslims. These include repression and corruption of ruling elites; the dire effects of the United Nations (UN) sanctions against Iraq following Saddam Hussein's invasion of Kuwait; the presence of US troops in Muslim lands (Kuwait, Saudi Arabia, Lebanon); the continuing injustices suffered by Palestinians at the hands of Israel; the killing of Chechens, Bosnians, and Kosovars; the US bombing of what turned out to be a pharmaceutical factory in Khartoum, conducted during the search for bin Laden; and the US/ UK invasion and occupation of Iraq in 2003. Those grievances did not result in violent contention on the part of all Muslims. Violent contention erupted or escalated on the part of those already influenced by radical or jihadist frames.

Between 1992 and 1997, Egypt's Gama'a Islamiyya was responsible for 1,442 deaths and 1,799 injuries, which came about through vicious attacks on government representatives, Egyptian civilians, and foreign tourists.[24] During Algeria's "black decade," scores of Algerians were killed in what became a battle between jihadists and the military. Violence became the tactic of choice of what had become transnational jihadist Islamism.

Efforts by political elites to incorporate or co-opt Islamist institutions between the 1960s and 1980s were only partially or temporarily successful, for radical elements that saw the society or state as insufficiently Islamic would periodically assert themselves. Islamists in Algeria, after all, had been encouraged by their experience in Afghanistan and were allowed to operate openly in the 1980s. Algerian feminists were alarmed when Islamists began to bully unveiled women in the districts where they predominated. When the new government of Chadli Bendjedid acquiesced to Islamist pressure and pushed through a patriarchal family law, feminists mobilized to protest the proposed family law. Even Hafez admits that the Algerian GIA—whose revolt against the state in the 1990s featured wanton and breathtaking brutality against civilians and foreigners—did not resort to violence because of the cancellation of the election results and the banning of the FIS. "On the contrary, it viewed its 'jihad' as a broader struggle to rid the Muslim world of un-Islamic rulers and establish the 'rule of God.'" In the GIA's own words, expressed in a 1993 communiqué, "Our struggle is with infidelism and its supporters beginning with France and ending with the leader of international terrorism, 'the United States of Terrorism,' its ally Israel, and among them the apostate ruling regime in our land." Four years later, the group expressed the following views in a London-based Islamist paper:

> The infidelism and apostasy of this hypocrite nation that turned away from backing and supporting the mujahideen will not bend our determination and will not hurt us at all, God willing. . . . All the killing and slaughter, the massacres, the displacement [of people], the burnings, the kidnappings . . . are an offering to God.[25]

Algerian state repression may have played a role in exacerbating societal strains and political grievances, but the GIA's extreme violence, including sexual violence against women, suggests a pathology and misogyny that is rather far removed from rational, cost-benefit calculations, much less a justified defense. Similarly, Egyptian Islamists not only targeted symbols of the state, such as financial centers and the tourism industry; they also killed tourists, Egyptian Christians (Copts), and secular intellectuals. In the new millennium, nineteen young Arab men plotted to attack symbols of American power in the United States. After the launch of the American "war on terror" and the invasion of Iraq, the cycle of violent contention continued, with bombings of commuters in London and Madrid. In Indonesia, bombings by extremist Muslim groups affiliated with al-Qaeda struck a Bali nightclub, the Marriott hotel in Jakarta, the Australian embassy, Christian churches, and gatherings of religious minorities such as the Ahmadiyya sect. Mobilizing structures developed from nationally based to transnational and often coordinated networks. And in the years after 2003, an Iraqi named Abu Bakr al-Baghdadi created ISIS, which grew in the chaos caused by the destabilization of Libya and Syria.

Sociologist Jeff Goodwin identifies "categorical terrorism," or forms of extreme violence that deliberately target civilians, as a strategy taken up in a context of "indiscriminate state repression" and "civilian complicity." Terrorism thus becomes a way of punishing mass passivity or complicity with the state. Goodwin applies this framework to the actions of militants in French Algeria, the West

Bank and Gaza, and Chechnya. Also, to a certain extent, he employs this conceptual lens in looking at al-Qaeda's September 11 attacks. While persuasive on one level, Goodwin's thesis basically posits that extremists—like repressive states or occupying powers—can and do engage in collective punishment to achieve their goals and assert their authority. Abrahms makes a more convincing argument, highlighting the difference between centralized and decentralized Salafi jihadists, whereby the latter are more likely to engage in "lone wolf" forms of indiscriminate violence.[26] A tragic example is the April 2019 wanton killing by Islamist terrorists of some 250 Sri Lankan Christians celebrating Easter mass in three churches.

It is true that many liberation movements and social revolutions have entailed armed struggle and other forms of violent contention as a key tactic. And yet the hyperaggressive language and actions of the GIA, al-Qaeda, ISIS, and similar groups should help analysts and progressives alike clarify the distinction between the legitimate actions of a liberation movement and the illegitimate actions of terrorists. There is a world of difference between the ideology and actions of the Nicaraguan Sandinistas or, before them, the Viet Cong, on the one hand, and the actions and ideology of violent jihadists (and before them and in another place, the Khmer Rouge).

MODERATE AND PARLIAMENTARY ISLAMIST MOVEMENTS: WHAT OF THE GRAY ZONES?

Frame alignment among moderate Islamists is distinctive and diverges from that of militant Islamists as the two groupings address different audiences, whether domestic or international. In general, moderate Islamists eschew violence as a tactic to gain political or state power; they take part in electoral politics and field candidates, whether openly or through independents; and they take an active part in civil society associations or build new ones. In Turkey, moderate Islamists claimed to accept the secular and republican ideals of modern Turkey's founder Kemal Ataturk, and in Egypt, the Muslim Brotherhood maintained that it favored democracy and civil rights for all citizens. Rachid Ghannouchi, head of Tunisia's an-Nahda party and its spiritual guide, stated, "We want an-Nahda as an open space: open to religious people, non-religious, male, female, open to all Tunisians."[27] Some scholars

have therefore pondered the possibility that moderate, reformist Islam evinces similarities either to Christian liberation theology or to
the Christian-democratic (conservative) political parties of Europe.
Examining the now defunct Refah (Welfare Party) that made electoral
headway in the 1990s before it was banned by the Turkish military,
Turkish sociologist Haldun Gulalp writes:

> While liberation theology constitutes a novel interpretation of Chris-
> tianity from a socialist perspective, Welfare's Islamism focused on the
> question of cultural superiority or inferiority. . . . Turkey's political
> Islam . . . was concerned with a cultural project and attempted to mo-
> bilize people by addressing their class interests in order to effect that
> project. . . . Welfare used class-related issues as a vehicle to promote
> a project of change in lifestyle and to establish its own version of an
> "Islam" society.[28]

As we shall see, such Islamist concerns and claims mirror those of
right-wing populists in Europe. Gulalp goes on to argue that moderate Islamist movements are part of the phenomenon of postmodernist
"new social movements" in that they are focused on issues of culture,
identity, and lifestyle rather than class and ideology. In discussing the
social bases of Turkey's Islamism, Gulalp links mobilization and recruitment to broad structural changes. He notes, correctly, that the rise of
Islamism coincided with the decline of the Keynesian economic project, Fordist industrialization, and the welfare state, with its attendant
focus on the working class. Islamism gained prominence concurrently
with the economic trends of privatization, subcontracting, and entre-
preneurship, which favor property owners and small businesspeople.
In Turkey, while political power remained in the hands of bureaucratic,
military, and political elites, economic power was shifting to the growing private sector. The Islamist movement claimed to be the voice of
the owners of small and medium-sized businesses, who complained of
inadequate financial support by the state.

Gradually this movement nudged its way from the fringes to the
centers of political power. Thus, in contrast to Latin American–style
liberation theology, with its focus on the poor and its demand for redistribution, Turkey's Islamists created a new capitalist culture. Their
vision prioritized both business and Islamic lifestyle norms such as
veiling for women, the prohibition against alcohol, and attention to

religious schooling. Gulalp notes that the Islamist party's discourse of "justice" appealed to working-class voters, even though the party was in reality an extension of the neoliberal project.[29] Written from a left-wing perspective, Gulalp's analysis elucidates the compatibility of Islamism with neoliberalism, even if Islamists may oppose cultural aspects of globalization or engage in populist rhetoric.

Gulalp's analysis of Turkey can be extended to Tunisia and Morocco. Giulia Cimini finds that Islamic parties' economic agendas are "trapped between ideology and actual constraints." Tunisia's an-Nahda had "an ambitious platform" that included an economic growth rate of 5 percent, reducing the state budget to 3 percent, and reducing unemployment from 19 percent in 2011 to 15 percent by the end of 2013; it called for "a social market economy" based on "fair competition and social balance." In fact, the party continued previous narratives about the causes of unemployment ("education-employment mismatch") and—as was mentioned in chapter 3—it joined its coalition partner in turning to the International Monetary Fund (IMF) for loans. Mathieu Rousselin has argued that much like the AKP and Egypt's Muslim Brotherhood, an-Nahda "was able to skillfully combine Islamic ideology with a liberal free-market ideology." In Morocco, the PJD platform was launched with the slogan "For a new Morocco of freedom, dignity, development, and justice," and in July 2015, it did increase the minimum wage slightly. But as Cimini shows, the PJD explained youth unemployment the same way as in Tunisia, and incurred citizen ire by "selling state-owned lands at very cheap prices to former ministers, high-ranking diplomats and other state officials." What emerged in both Morocco and Tunisia are "forms of mixed economies that seem to reflect more international constraints, neoclassical and neoliberal stances and the imperatives of electoral politics, rather than explicit attempts to address socio-economic grievances."[30]

The fate of Egypt's Muslim Brotherhood (MB), or Ikhwan—once the world's largest, oldest, and most influential Islamist organization—is worth considering. Founded by Hassan al-Banna, the MB was for decades a radical movement bent on overthrowing the secular Egyptian regime and replacing it with an Islamic state. An early leading figure, Sayyid Qutb, became an arch opponent of the Nasser regime. For his role in fomenting violent resistance, the government of Gamal Abdel Nasser executed him; the MB was banned from 1954 until the political revolution of 2011, although supporters ran as "independents." Sympathizers have portrayed Egypt's Muslim groups as pressure groups oriented toward specific political interests and operating within and upon a regime whose mix of repression, acculturation, and semi-toleration effectively limited their room for maneuver. Others point out that the MB maintained its societal and political presence through a sympathetic judiciary, Al-Azhar University and theological seminary, adherents in professional syndicates, and parliamentary candidates running as independents. The MB eventually forged influential branches around the world and, in Egypt, had an estimated membership ranging from one hundred thousand to four hundred thousand.[31]

The metamorphosis of the Egyptian Muslim Brotherhood from a religious mass movement into a modern political party has its roots in the changing political economy of the 1980s, with the deterioration of public services, declining real wages, and rising unemployment. Although the brotherhood distanced itself from some of the more rigid doctrines of its founder, it continued to proffer the slogan "Islam is the solution" and to call for adherence to the sharia. Shrewd political maneuvers, including extensive participation in local councils, grassroots associations, and syndicates, assured electoral gains by moderate Islamists associated with the Muslim Brotherhood. The MB shocked the ruling National Democratic Party and Western observers in 2005 by winning one-fifth of the seats in the Egyptian parliament through independent proxies. Its association with Al-Azhar, a site of fundamentalist Islam as well as a university, provided the movement with both legitimacy and an important mobilizing structure.

But the gray zones persisted, leading Brown, Hamzawy, and Ottaway to identify ambiguities and inconsistencies in the group's positions on the application of Islamic law, the use of violence, political pluralism, civil and political rights, the equality and rights of women, and the equality and rights of religious minorities. In 2007, the supreme guide of Egypt's Muslim Brotherhood, Mohamed Mahdi Akef, was responsible for the drafting of the MB's first political platform. Among other things, it advocated banning women as well as Coptic Egyptians, who make up one-tenth of Egypt's population, from election to the presidency and raised the specter of an Iran-style religious council. Akef and his associates viewed globalization as naked US ambition and regarded Western democracy as "subservient to whims of the masses, without moral absolutes."[32]

The Egyptian Center for Women's Rights (ECWR) has monitored the social realities of women's lives—most notably, lobbying against the widespread problem of sexual harassment of women—while also integrating itself into the larger civil society movement for clean elections, human rights, and democratization. In August 2010, the ECWR issued a statement criticizing the MB's Youth Forum for denying, during its mock presidential elections, a request by the forum's Muslim Sisters' Group to be included as potential nominees. The following November, the ECWR issued another press release protesting the parliament's overwhelming vote against the appointment of women judges. In March 2011, the ECWR decried the absence of women from the committee drafting Egypt's new constitution.[33] Apart from vague references to social justice, the Muslim Brotherhood did not evince interest in economic issues or develop a critique of Egypt's neoliberal economic strategy. Egyptian voters may have expected the MB to improve their economic conditions, but scholars attribute the general lack of interest in economic need and the focus on social and political change to the fact that most MB members are from the educated, professional middle classes. The MB's 2011 election platform stated that it would support international human rights conventions "so long as they are not contrary to the principles of Islamic law."[34] According to Mona El-Ghobashy, "They still grant culture and identity issues pride of place in their platform." According to Alison Pargeter, the Muslim Brotherhood is in essence a reactionary movement unable to break from its past.[35] Its notion of human rights was conditional on compliance with sharia law. For those reasons, perhaps, the MB was not able to expand its social base of support after it won parliamentary and presidential elections in 2011. By 2013, widespread protests against the MB-led government led to a military coup.

Rachid Ghannouchi, leader of Tunisia's an-Nahda party, is often hailed as an exemplar of a reformist, democratic Islam. Many Tunisian feminists, leftists, and secularists would dispute that, as I have found in numerous conversations, interviews, and Facebook postings since at least 2011. A look at Ghannouchi's 1993 essay "The Participation of Islamists in Non-Islamic Government" is instructive. He writes that "it is the religious duty of Muslims, both individuals and groups, to work for the establishment of Islamic government" so that "the believers remain in close contact with the fundamentals of the Shari'ah . . . in the situations of both strength and weakness." He defines Islamic government as follows: "(1) Supreme legislative authority is for the Shari'ah, that is the revealed law of Islam, which transcends all laws. . . . [and] (2) Political power belongs to the community (*ummah*)." At the same time, he encourages Muslims to "enter into alliances with secular democratic groups" toward a government "which will respect human rights, ensuring security and freedom of expression and belief—essential requirements of mankind that Islam has come to fulfil." He also approves of helping to transform *darul harb* (the land of war) to a land of peace that may "guarantee the freedom to worship and belief." He ends by noting that any alliance "must not include provisions that would in any way undermine Islam, or impose restrictions on those who work for Islam and who seek to establish its system in the land."[36] Ghannouchi's preference for democracy appears to be motivated by a strategic interest in enhancing the religious rights of Muslims and paving the way for sharia law. His essay makes no mention of socioeconomic matters, or of the need to enhance the rights of non-Muslim minorities in Muslim-majority countries.

In Europe, many Muslims draw on human rights and antidiscrimination frames to claim the right to veil and to build mosques. And yet, in Muslim-majority countries such as Egypt, Christian citizens cannot build churches without arduous approval processes, and those churches often are the target of Islamist violence. In countries such as Pakistan, where extremist views hold sway, individual Christians may be prosecuted for "blasphemy" against Islam, and they may be the target of extrajudicial violence. The case of Asia Bibi, a poor Christian woman, is a case in point; after several years in prison, the country's Supreme Court ordered her release, but massive protests erupted, organized by the Tehreek-e Labbaik—a group proudly responsible for the assassination of two politicians who had dared to defend her. Asia Bibi was offered asylum in Canada.[37] Muslim human rights appeals in Europe and the United States need to be extended to the rights of secularists and non-Muslims in Muslim-majority countries.

In a penetrating review of Tariq Ramadan's 2009 book *Radical Reform: Islamic Ethics and Liberation*, Mona Siddiqui, a professor of Islamic studies and public understanding at the University of Glasgow, writes that the real challenge is "how reformers can liberate themselves from the shackles of the law when their goals . . . are still conceptualized within medieval legal frameworks." She concludes that Ramadan's "is a pertinent voice, but in the end, it is just not bold enough."[38] Boldness certainly is needed to help change certain hard-line religious attitudes in the Muslim world. A 2010 Pew Research Center survey of attitudes toward sharia-derived punishments in Egypt, Pakistan, Jordan, Nigeria, Indonesia, Lebanon, and Turkey found that an astonishing 82 percent of Jordanians and Egyptians, 78 percent of Pakistanis, and 50 percent of Nigerians favored the death penalty for people who leave Islam. More than 80 percent of Egyptians and Pakistanis, 70 percent of Jordanians, 58 percent of Nigerians, and 40 percent of Indonesians favored stoning for adultery. Almost 80 percent of Egyptians and Pakistanis and 60 to 62 percent of Jordanians and Nigerians endorsed whippings and cutting off of hands for theft. Conversely, very few Muslims in Lebanon and even fewer in Turkey favored any of these punishments. The survey suggested the extent to which radical Islamist frames could resonate in Egypt, Pakistan, Jordan, and Nigeria.[39] On a more positive note, and in his analysis of World Values Survey (WVS) results between 2010 and 2015 in Egypt, Iraq, Lebanon, Pakistan, Saudi Arabia, Tunisia, and Turkey, sociologist Mansoor Moaddel finds that on nearly all measures, Lebanon, Turkey, and Tunisia are the most liberal. The majority of respondents were opposed to polygamy, but 50 percent of Saudis supported polygamy; there, too, nearly 70 percent find that sharia law implementation is important or very important. Everywhere, those with university education are most liberal except for Saudi Arabia. In all countries, women are more liberal than men, except in Egypt, where their views on gender equality are the same as men's and far less egalitarian than in Tunisia, Turkey, or Lebanon. Christian citizens everywhere are the most liberal; Shia citizens also are more liberal than Sunni, except in Iraq.[40]

MOBILIZING STRUCTURES AND STRATEGIES

Social movement theorizing has identified the importance of informal ties and social networks to recruitment and movement formation and has focused much attention on the role and formation of organizations, networks, informal groups, and other mobilizing structures. With respect to Islamist movements, recruitment occurs through kinship connection as well as through informal organizations or networks. Wiktorowicz writes that potential recruits are usually contacted by activists in preexisting social environments—family, peer groups, mosques, workplaces—or at public demonstrations. During the initial contacts, he writes, the recruiters try "to shake certitude in previously held beliefs and generate a sense of crisis and urgency."[41] The principal vehicles for recruiting adherents and attracting supporters are mosques, madrassas (religious schools), *nadwas* (Quranic study groups), and charities. In some cases, the bazaar or souk has played a role, mainly through partnership with a mosque. In turn, these institutions constitute an "organizational infrastructure" for Islamist movements both local and transnational. In some countries, Islamists also recruit university graduates and have influence in professional associations. In her 2002 book, Carrie Rosefsky Wickham found that the Muslim Brotherhood recruited from student unions and professional syndicates; bin Laden's coterie included engineers and physicians, and the nineteen hijackers of September 11, 2001, were almost all university educated.

In much the same way that churches have played a role in mobilizing people and framing protest in the United States, Eastern Europe, and South Africa, mosques have been both places of worship and sites of religio-political mobilization in the Muslim world. The mosque was a key institution for the mobilization of protest in the years that led up to the 1979 Iranian revolution and was used by the Islamist state for the distribution of ration coupons during the war with Iraq in the 1980s. Cihan Tugal's ethnographic study of the Islamist movement in Turkey, conducted between 2000 and 2002, underscores the movement's mobilization strategy of "transforming everyday practices" while also seeking to reshape the state, which was eventually accomplished under the AKP. The transformation strategy occurred through mosques, teahouses, religious high schools, and municipalities.[42] Across the Muslim world, the mosque and its attendant institutions, such as the madrassa, the *nadwa*, and charitable foundations, connect communities of believers in peaceful (if politically strategic) ways. However, they also provide a base from which to organize and mobilize, whether peacefully or for violent purposes, as in the Red Mosque affair in Pakistan.[43]

Other religious institutions provide assistance, build community, and foster collective identity. Judith Harik describes how Lebanon's Hezbollah, which is both a political party and a militant Islamist organization, built a network of charities and how that investment in welfare organizations translated into electoral gains at the grassroots level, especially in the southern suburb of Beirut. Janine Clark's study of Islamist charities and social welfare organizations in Egypt, Jordan, and Yemen demonstrates their success with poor and middle-class citizens alike, though she reports that the beneficiaries of Islamic charity often receive such a pittance that they seek benefits from non-Islamic charities as well. Sarah Roy describes the active role of Hamas in Palestinian civil society, showing how its social work empowered the organization and enhanced its legitimacy and popularity. Providing assistance with marriage, health care, and schooling, these and other "Islamic social institutions" have proved critical in offering marginalized and disaffected citizens both symbolic and material rewards, thus ensuring steady recruitment to the Islamist cause.[44] Charities and *nadwas* are especially successful at mobilizing women and providing them with roles to play within the Islamist movement or party, such as fund-raising for the poor during Ramadan and carrying out *da'wa*, or preaching. In some countries, Islamist influence extended to professional and student associations that are able to build transnational ties of solidarity with confrères.

Islamists have mobilized support, disseminated their messages, and influenced public policy through traditional institutions as well as the political process. Thus, even before the 2011 mass movements for political change, Islamists had managed to forge large networks of faith-based social service agencies, clinics, schools, charities, youth clubs, worship centers, banks, and businesses in countries such as Egypt, Jordan, Turkey, and Yemen. As a number of scholars have noted, Islamic movements emerged as a dominant opposition in the Muslim world because they command more societal institutions and resources than other movements and because of their ability to tap religious resources.[45]

The more radical and jihadist Islamists similarly recruit members and supporters and raise funds through mosques, madrassas, religious study groups, and charities, as well as through social and family ties. In Europe, radical mosques and imams with fiery messages appealed to disaffected young men, who went on to join cells or engaged in militant activism to defend what they felt were slurs or attacks on Islam. Increasingly porous borders in Europe facilitated interactions between contacts, some of whom were able to engage in bombings and other violent acts. Failed or fragile states elsewhere—in Afghanistan, Iraq, Libya, Syria, Niger—enabled Islamist militants to travel for purposes of recruitment, training, or militant action.

The internet is another mobilizing vehicle as well as a framing tool. Islamists have made effective use of ICTs and social media for purposes of information exchange, dissemination of their message, and projection of desired symbols and images. Local as well as transnational Islamists control numerous websites, enabling a kind of virtual activism. Al-Qaeda had a media wing called al-Sahib, while ISIS used Twitter and other social media extensively and effectively. Ayman al-Zawahiri, Osama bin Laden's deputy, emphasized the importance of "jihadi information media," saying they were "waging an extremely critical battle against the Crusader-Zionist enemy."[46] The many Islamist websites function as loci of self-advertisement, recruitment, and communication; in this they are sometimes helped by some Arab media. In broadcasting Islamist messages and images, Al Jazeera and Al Arabiyya helped disseminate the idea that Islam and Muslims are in danger and need to fight back. As Manfred Steger notes, Arab satellite media are part of a "chain of global interdependencies and interconnections" that make possible the instant broadcast of messages and images, including those of militant Islamists. Similarly, Gary Blunt's study of English- and Arabic-language Islamic blogs and militaristic websites from across the globe shows how they create online Muslim identities or reinforce existing ones. The Islamic blogosphere, he argues, fosters new forms of Muslim networking, as "iMuslim netizens" use blogs to impact society both locally and globally via dialogue and debate or protest, information gathering and dissemination, or propagation of Islamic beliefs and values. He also elucidates the operations of e-jihad, whereby the internet is used as a logistic device for funding, information sharing, and planning. Another report shows that across the Muslim world, many privately financed religious and lifestyle channels promote Salafism and broadcast a strident, aggressive tone against Shia and Christian minorities.[47]

Technology and political allies alike have been useful to jihadists. In 2014, the BBC reported that a web-based data mining software found a large number of pro-ISIS tweets originating in Saudi Arabia, Kuwait, and other Gulf countries. In his lengthy report in *Wired*, Brendan Koerner draws attention to *Dabiq*, the English-language magazine that ISIS regularly publishes as a PDF and distributes through various social media sites.[48]

Thus over and above the effective use and creation of mobilizing structures, Islamists have taken advantage of the opportunities afforded by globalization—specifically, the internet, global media, shifting geographies, and funding sources—to organize, build networks, coordinate activities, disseminate their message, and otherwise engage in collective action. Social media have broadened the range of contemporary global Muslim discourses, even those that are locally grounded, creating transnational Islamic identities.

Millions of Muslims worldwide practice Islam in peace and with quiet dignity. Those who turn to violent contention, however, can justify their actions by selective recourse to Islamic scriptures regarding the imperative to defend Islam against its enemies. As sociologist Farhad Khosrokhavar has explained, Islamic martyrdom differs from Christian martyrdom in that it is an offensive tactic (rather than a passive response) to ward off challenges to the religion and thereby protect what is cherished and valued.[49] Concerns about cultural invasion, or the Israeli occupation of Palestinian land, or the presence of "infidel" soldiers and "crusaders" in Saudi Arabia, Afghanistan, and Iraq, or even a relatively minor event such as the awarding of a British Medal of Honor to the writer Salman Rushdie—all these can trigger intense emotions and strong beliefs about insults to Islam, a war against Islam, and the religiously mandated imperative to defend the faith in a militant fashion. In this way, Muslim militants can draw on a ready-made cultural frame while also utilizing the existing organizational infrastructure.

REPERTOIRES OF VIOLENT CONTENTION: ISLAMIST VERSUS LEFT-WING TERRORISTS

At the time of writing (August 2019), the US public sphere was consumed by discussions around homegrown white supremacist violence in the wake of assaults in Ohio and Texas. Can we better understand contemporary militant Islamism by way of comparison with other militant groups? Could Islamist terrorism represent not a growing worldwide movement but a futile attempt at power? Syrian political philosopher Sadik al-Azm compared Islamist terror networks to those of the extreme Left in Europe in the 1970s. The latter's acts included the abduction and murder of the German industrialist Hanns Martin Schleyer by the Baader-Meinhof Gang in summer 1977 and the similar abduction and assassination, a year later, of Aldo Moro, dean of Italy's senior political leaders after World War II, by the Italian Red Brigades. Carlos the Jackal, the Red Army Faction in West Germany, the Japanese Red Army, and other extreme leftist groups and individuals dominated the European scene at the time. The left-wing terrorism of the 1970s in Europe, al-Azm maintains, was a "desperate attempt to break out of the historical impasse and terminal structural crisis reached by communism, radical labor movements, Third Worldism, and revolutionary trends everywhere, by resorting to violent *action directe* of the most extraordinary and phenomenal kind." The terrorism of that period, he argues, was "(a) the then barely viable manifestation of that impasse and crisis, and (b) the prelude to the final demise of all those movements and trends including world communism itself."[50]

Similarly, "the *action directes* Islamists have also given up on contemporary Muslim society, its socio-political movements, the spontaneous religiosity of the masses, their endemic false consciousness, mainstream Islamic organizations, [and] the attention of the original and traditional Society of Muslim Brothers (from which they generally hail in the same way the original *action directes* hailed from European communism)." They have rejected all this, he writes, in favor of "their own brand of blind and spectacular activism, also heedless and contemptuous of consequences, long-term calculations of the chances of success or failure and so on." This kind of politics takes the form of "local attacks, intermittent skirmishes, guerrilla raids, random insurrections, senseless resistances, impatient outbursts, anarchistic assaults, and sudden uprisings." Al-Azm refers to "an Islamist impatient rejection of and contempt for politics in almost any form: conventional, radical, agitational and/or revolutionary in favor of the violent tactics of nihilism and despair. For them, the only other alternatives available are either cooptation or plain withdrawal or an admission of defeat." The *action directe* Islamists, like their European counterparts, "evince a sense of entrapment within an alien and alienating monolithic sociopolitical reality."[51] Al-Azm continues:

With maximalist Islamism we get *action directe* terrorism on a global scale where the only kind of politics permitted is direct and immediate armed attack against the enemy. The assumption in all this is that such apocalyptic Islamist self-assertion will (a) explode the obstacles blocking the way to the global triumph of Islam, (b) overcome the structural impasse in which the Islamist project finds itself at present, (c) develop better objective conditions for the success of that project, (d) catalyze the Muslim people's energies in its favor, and (e) create poles of attraction around which the Muslims of the world could immediately rally, for example the Al-Qaeda set of networks, organizations, training camps, etc., and the Taliban model of the supposedly first authentic Muslim society and government in modern times.[52]

The analogy is useful in showing how repertoires of violent contention can travel from one geocultural space to another, but the scale of European extremist left-wing violence was far smaller, and its time span shorter, than that of contemporary Islamism. This may be because the European extremists were more isolated, less networked, and less popular than contemporary Islamists; they also had fewer resources, including culturally resonant frames, at their disposal. Militant Islamist radicals have more in common with violent American white supremacists as well as with European neo-Nazi and neo-fascist groups. Islamist political parties, on the other hand, have more in common with right-wing populist parties, as we shall see in chapter 7.

CONCLUSION

Political Islam appeared on the international stage in the late 1970s and grew in the 1980s and 1990s in the context of national and global opportunities, and it includes an array of locally based groups and transnationally active networks. Some groups have attempted the overthrow of local regimes; others have long been entrenched in cooperative relations with them; yet others have sought to bring about social, political, and legal reforms by "bypassing the state" and building strong grassroots institutions. Moderate Islamists take part in the electoral process and promote democracy to widen their social base and advance their interests; radicals rail against national and international injustices and call for strict adherence to Islam; extremists spread their message and assert themselves through violence. Many jihadists around the world enjoy sufficient "street credibility" to sway younger hearts and minds. Political Islam is cross-generational. The older militants won their spurs as fighters in the US-backed campaign against the Soviet intervention in Afghanistan; another generation emerged after the 2003 invasion and occupation of Iraq.

Since the late 1970s, Islamists of different orientations have come to power in Iran, Pakistan, Bangladesh, Sudan, Afghanistan, and Turkey, as well as in parts of Nigeria, Malaysia, and Indonesia. As self-described Muslim states have expanded, members of Islamist movements, as well-educated members of their societies, have become employees of state bureaucracies, giving rise to questions about the compatibility of Islamism with democracy, women's rights, and human rights. To date, no Islamist movement or party has been instrumental in the transition from authoritarianism to democracy, equality, and civil liberties. They appear to have no concrete plans for socioeconomic development and rights, even as Islamic parties are in power in Kuwait, Jordan, Morocco, and Tunisia. Young people are increasingly disillusioned and express their desire to emigrate.[53]

In an early essay, Graham Fuller identifies three obstacles to the liberal evolution of political Islam. Among them are the role of international politics, which often pushes Islamist parties and movements, including Muslim national liberation movements, in a militant direction. Another "comes from the Islamists' own long list of grievances against the forces and policies perceived to be holding Muslims back in the contemporary world, many of them associated with liberalism's supposed avatar, the United States."[54] These points may also pertain to the hard-line stance of the Islamic Republic of Iran as it reacts to continued US and European pressures.

The radical Islamist focus on the West as the source of all ills—economic, political, and cultural—is of course the mirror image of Samuel Huntington's thesis of "the clash of civilizations" whereby the most profound clash is that between Islam and the West.[55] In both cases, cultural values and norms are emphasized as preeminent and seen to be at stake. In the Huntington perspective, the world of Islam is at odds with Western notions of democracy, tolerance, and pluralism. The solution is to keep a distance, close ranks, and protect Western values. In the Islamist perspective, the West is responsible—through such ills as secularism, feminism, gay liberation, and support for repressive regimes—for undermining Muslim societies and exerting control over them. The solution is to reject Western values and institutions and adhere strictly to Islamic laws, norms, and institutions. Both arguments essentialize religion and culture and cast the religio-cultural differences between Islam and the West into sharp relief. In the perspective taken in this book, analysis should be directed not at a clash of civilizations, cultures, or religions but, rather, at broad macro-level (economic and political) processes and forms of masculinity that engender violent contention, as well as the organizational and cultural resources available to challengers. With respect to moderate Islamist political parties and governments, their democratizing, developmentalist, and welfarist potential remains unrealized and elusive.

CHAPTER 5

FEMINISM ON A WORLD SCALE

> The world will not change without feminism; and feminists cannot change women's lives unless we change the world.
>
> —World March of Women, 2002

> Capitalism is incompatible with real democracy and peace. Our answer is feminist internationalism.
>
> —Notes for a Feminist Manifesto, 2018[1]

The women's rights movement has been the subject of considerable scholarly analysis. Feminist theorizing has focused on national-level factors such as the growth of the population of educated women with grievances about their second-class citizenship, the evolution of women's movements and campaigns, varieties of feminism, and cross-regional similarities and differences in mobilizing structures and strategies. Research also distinguishes "feminist movement" as a social movement guided by feminist ideas and "women's movement" as defined by a demographic group or constituency, with the former being a subset of the latter.[2]

Since the 1990s, a growing literature has connected women's movements and organizations to global processes such as the role of international organizations or the global women's rights agenda of the United Nations (UN), and it has examined the ways that women's organizations engage with the world of public policy. While not all feminists agree on the matter, many argue that the "women's movement" is a global phenomenon and that—despite cultural differences, country specificities, and organizational priorities—there are observed similarities in the ways women's rights activists frame their grievances and demands, form networks and organizations, and engage with state and intergovernmental institutions.[3] Some of the similarities include adoption of discourses of women's human rights and gender equality; references to international agreements such as the Convention on the Elimination of All Forms of Discrimination against Women (CEDAW) and the Beijing Platform for Action; campaigns for legal and policy reforms to ensure women's civil, political, and social rights; solidarity and networking across borders; and coalitions with other civil society groups. Action by feminist groups and allies on violence against women and workplace sexual harassment has now permeated the globe. Another observation is that women's rights activists—whether in South Asia, Latin America, the Middle East, or North Africa—are opposed to "fundamentalist" discourses and agendas and espouse feminist discourses and goals, whether explicitly or implicitly. Scholars have defined "feminist action" as "that in which the participants explicitly place value on challenging gender hierarchy and changing women's social status, whether they adopt or reject the feminist label," and described "global feminist activism" as international feminist mobilizations involving women in more than one country or region "who seek to forge a collective identity among women and to improve the condition of women." I have identified such mobilizations as "transnational feminist networks" that advocate for women's participation and rights while also engaging critically with policy and legal issues and with states, international organizations, and institutions of global governance.[4]

Like the Islamist movement studied in the previous chapter and the global justice movement (GJM) in the next, the women's movement is transnational and diverse, exhibiting the segmentary, polycentric, and reticulate features that Luther Gerlach identifies as common to many social movements (see chapter 1). Those features of the global women's movement were especially evident during the Fourth World Conference on Women, which took place in Beijing, China, in September 1995. For three weeks, women's groups from across the world met to take part in the massive nongovernmental forum that preceded but also overlapped with the official, intergovernmental conference. (The purpose was to discuss, finalize, and adopt the draft Beijing Platform for Action, which identified twelve "critical areas of concern," including education, health, employment, poverty, the girl-child, and decision making.) At the latter, women's groups with UN accreditation were able to enter conference halls, lobby delegates, disseminate their literature, and hold rallies. This was hardly a movement with a center or a bureaucracy or hierarchy. It was a movement of movements, albeit internetworked. And although the women's groups at Beijing had something to say about an array of issues, they also had common grievances concerning war, peace, fundamentalisms, and the new economic order.

This chapter examines the relationship between globalization and the global women's movement, with a focus on three types of transnational feminist networks (TFNs) that emerged in the 1980s and continue to be active to this day. I do not delve into recent academic feminist debates around imperial, neoliberal, governance, or decolonial feminism, although the second quote at the beginning of this chapter does echo those recent debates.[5] Discussed in this chapter are activist networks that target the neoliberal economic policy agenda; those that focus on fundamentalism and insist on women's human rights, especially in the Muslim world; and women's peace groups that target conflict, war, and empire. I discuss their activities, the strategies they pursue, and their framings. The chapter begins with a discussion of the global context and the opportunity structure(s) within which transnational feminism emerged.

THE ROAD TO TRANSNATIONAL FEMINISM

Chapter 1 described the precursors to the contemporary women's movement, including international women's organizations and campaigns of the early twentieth century. At mid-century, the women's movement began to diverge, grouping itself within national boundaries or economic zones, emphasizing different priorities, and aligning with divergent ideological currents. In particular, North-South differences became pronounced as feminists in the core countries and those in the developing world expressed radically different grievances and formed divergent strategies.

The women's movement of the second wave, which began in North America and Europe in the 1960s, consisted of feminist groups that emerged within national borders and addressed themselves to their own nation-states, governments, employers, male colleagues, and kin. As women's groups expanded across the globe, they remained largely nationally based and oriented. Feminist groups encompassed liberal, radical, Marxist, and socialist ideologies, and those political differences constituted one form of division within feminism. The Cold War cast a shadow on feminist solidarity, in the form of the East-West divide; there was, for the most part, antipathy between women's groups aligned with the communist movement and liberal feminist groups aligned with the so-called Free World. The Women's International Democratic Federation (WIDF), founded in 1945 in France and later headquartered in East Berlin, was affiliated to the communist movement. Francisca de Haan, who studied the organization, writes that WIDF representatives attending a meeting of the UN's Commission on the Status of Women (CSW) proposed that the UN declare International Women's Year in 1975. WIDF's main areas of concern were world peace, antifascism, child welfare, and improving the status of women. It enjoyed consultative status with the UN's Economic and Social Committee (ECOSOC), but there was hardly any connection between WIDF and noncommunist Western women's groups, although links with the Women's International League for Peace and Freedom (WILPF) did exist.[6]

Another division took the form of North-South, or First World–Third World, differences in terms of prioritizing feminist issues; many First World feminists saw legal equality and reproductive rights as key feminist demands and goals, while many Third World feminists emphasized underdevelopment, colonialism, and imperialism as obstacles to women's advancement. Disagreements over what constituted top-priority feminist issues came to the fore at the beginning of the UN Decade for Women, especially at its First and Second World Conferences on Women, which took place in Mexico City in 1975 and in Copenhagen in 1980. The disagreements at the Mexico City and Copenhagen conferences pitted women activists from the North and South against each other and revolved around prioritizing issues of legal equality and personal choice versus those pertaining to global economic and political hierarchies.[7]

A shift in the nature and orientation of international feminism began to take root in the mid-1980s, during preparations for the UN's Third World Conference on Women, held in Nairobi, Kenya, in 1985. The shift took the form of bridge-building and consensus across regional and ideological divides and the emergence of a women's organization of a new type. Three critical economic and political developments within states and regions and at the level of the world-system enabled the shift: (1) the transition from Keynesian to neoliberal economics, along with a new international division of labor that relied heavily on (cheap) female labor; (2) the decline of the welfare state in the core countries and the developmental state in the Third World; and (3) the emergence of various forms of fundamentalist movements. These changes led to new thinking, ways of organizing, frame alignments, and collective action repertoires on the part of activist women in developing and developed countries. Let us examine the issues in more detail.

GLOBAL RESTRUCTURING AND THE FEMINIZATION OF LABOR

Beginning in the late 1970s, cross-national research, including studies by those working in the field of women-in-development or women-and-development (WID/WAD), showed that an ever-growing proportion of the world's women was being incorporated as cheap labor into what was variously called the capitalist world-economy, the new international division of labor, or the global assembly line. Maquiladoras along the US-Mexico border and export-processing zones in the Caribbean and Southeast Asia relied heavily on female labor, while garment factories geared to the world market employed women in North Africa and Bangladesh. Studies showed that women were gaining an increasing share of many kinds of jobs, but this was occurring in a context of growing unemployment, a decline in the social power of labor, and an increase in temporary, part-time, casual, and home-based work—that is, in the context of the shift in the capitalist world-system from Keynesian to neoliberal economic policy. Disproportionately involved in irregular forms of employment increasingly used to maximize profits, women also remained responsible for reproductive work and domestic labor. In addition, women were disadvantaged in the new labor markets in terms of wages, training, and occupational segregation. In the late 1980s, International Labour Organization (ILO) economist Guy Standing termed this phenomenon the "feminization of labor." He argued that the increasing globalization of production and the pursuit of flexible forms of labor to retain or increase competitiveness, as well as changing job structures in industrial enterprises, favored the "feminization of employment" in the dual sense of an increase in the numbers of women in the labor force and a deterioration of work conditions (labor standards, income, and employment status).[8] By the 1990s, women comprised nearly half of the world's labor force, though most working women experienced poor working conditions, low wages, and minimal benefits. A large number of publications emanating from the feminist women-in-development (WID) community analyzed the global changes and their effects on working and poor women.[9]

WELFARE AND DEVELOPMENT CUTS

The new labor markets enabled employers to offer more jobs with part-time or temporary ("flexible") contracts. Privatization and denationalization meant the contraction of the public sector, which historically entailed good benefits and stable employment, if not the highest wages, and tended to be the preferred employer for women in many countries. At the urging of the World Bank, the old social contracts guaranteed by the "developmental state" in the Global South were replaced by the introduction of "user fees" for purposes of "cost recovery" in the sectors of health and education, while generous social-welfare programs were whittled away. As a result, women's growing labor-market participation was not accompanied by a redistribution of domestic, household, and child-care responsibilities; rather, women's burdens increased. The changing nature of the state vis-à-vis the public sector entailed the withdrawal, deterioration, or privatization of many public services used by working- and middle-class women and their families. In the United States, President Reagan's pro-business bias ("government isn't the solution; it's the problem") was accompanied by attacks on unions and welfare policies, as well as deregulation and even more leeway for business—all of which adversely affected many women's work conditions and options. In the United Kingdom,

Prime Minister Margaret Thatcher's policies, which began with an attack on the miners' union, began the slow move toward what was later called "zero-hours" work contracts.

As global restructuring expanded to encompass the former communist bloc, studies showed that women in Eastern Europe and the former Soviet Union experienced unemployment and the loss of income and benefits that accompanied privatization. A body of research also emerged to address another new global phenomenon: the "feminization of poverty," or the growing female share of the population living under the poverty line. Much of this research was carried out by scholar-activists with links to the women's movement, and this academic involvement helped shape new and often coordinated feminist strategies across the globe.[10]

FUNDAMENTALISMS

Another important development that led to the narrowing of the political and ideological divide between First and Third World feminists was the rise of Islamic fundamentalism in Muslim countries and Hindu communalism in India. As discussed in chapter 4, the movements sought to recuperate traditional norms and codes, including patriarchal laws and family roles for women; they put pressure on states to enforce public morality, increase religious observance, and tighten controls over women—ostensibly to protect the nation or culture from alien influences and conspiracies. In many cases, there was collusion between states and the religio-political movements, usually to the detriment of women's rights. Such movements alarmed feminists in the peripheral and semiperipheral countries where the movements emerged. At the same time, feminists in the United States began to take notice of the increasing influence of the Christian Right.[11]

Divergences, therefore, began to narrow in the mid-1980s as a result of the changing environments in both the North and the South, notably with the rise of neoliberalism and the growth of fundamentalist movements. The new economic and political realities gradually led to a convergence of feminist perspectives across the globe: for many First World feminists, economic issues and development policy became increasingly important, and Third World feminists began to direct greater attention toward women's legal status, autonomy, and rights. Regionally, too, changes came about. In Latin America, divisions among participants of the *encuentros feministas*, or feminist gatherings—which first took place in Bogotá, Colombia, in 1981 and in Lima, Peru, in 1983, and where women identified themselves as either "feminists" or "politicos/militants"—were eventually eclipsed by common concerns and frames.[12]

New framings—women's empowerment, human rights, gender equality—were accompanied by new mobilizing structures, notably the formation of TFNs that brought together women from developed and developing countries alike to respond to economic pressures and patriarchal movements. They included Development Alternatives with Women for a New Era (DAWN), Network Women in Development Europe (WIDE), the Women's Environment and Development Organization (WEDO), Women Living under Muslim Laws (WLUML), and the Sisterhood Is Global Institute (SIGI). Others formed in the 1990s, joining older groups such as the Women's International League for Peace and Freedom (WILPF). They engaged in policy-oriented research, advocacy, and lobbying around issues pertaining to women and development and women's human rights. Many of the women who formed or joined the TFNs were scholar-activists who had been involved in the WID/gender-and-development (GAD) research community. With the formation of these networks and other women's activist groups, a global social movement of women was in the making (see table 5.1).

During this period, however, international feminism paid surprisingly little attention to one important issue: the conflict in Afghanistan and the implications for Afghan women of Western support for the Islamic-tribal alliance of the mujahideen ("holy warriors"). The Afghan revolution and change in regime had taken place in April 1978, one year before the Iranian revolution and the victory of the Sandinistas in Nicaragua. The new Democratic Republic of Afghanistan set about legislating land reform, legal equality for the ethnic groups, and rights for women and girls in the family and society. Almost immediately, the United States, Saudi Arabia, Pakistan, Egypt, and other countries formed a coalition in opposition to the pro-Soviet Afghan government. When the Islamist rebellion, backed by the Central Intelligence Agency (CIA) since summer 1978, came to threaten the viability of the new republic, the Soviet Union agreed to the Afghan government's request for troops to help stabilize the situation. Shortly thereafter, the United States beefed up its covert operation to support the mujahideen and end communism in both Afghanistan and the Soviet Union. (See also chapter 4.) That women and girls would forfeit schooling, the right

Table 5.1.   Types of Transnational Feminist Networks (as of 2019)

	Website and Mission	*Location/HQ*
Critique of Economic Policy		
Development Alternatives with Women for a New Era (DAWN)	http://www.dawnnet.org: Feminists from the South working for gender, economic, and ecological justice, as well as sustainable and democratic development.	Fiji
Marche Mondiale des Femmes	http://www.marchemondiale.org: An international feminist action movement connecting grassroots groups and organizations working to eliminate the causes at the root of poverty and violence against women.	Quebec
Network Women in Development Europe (WIDE+)	http://www.wide-network .org: A European network of associations and activists that fights for women's rights, as part of a larger struggle for social justice, sustainable livelihoods, and human rights.	Brussels
Women's Environment and Development Organization (WEDO)	http://www.wedo.org: A global women's advocacy organization for a just world that promotes and protects human rights, gender equality, and the integrity of the environment.	New York
Advocacy for Women's Human Rights		
Arab Women's Solidarity Association (AWSA)	http://www.awsa.be: An association of men and women of Arab, Belgian, and other origin. AWSA-Be is a mixed secular association that promotes the rights of Arab women, whether they are living in their country of origin or elsewhere. The association has no national, political, or religious affiliation.	Belgium (originally founded and based in Egypt)
Association for Women's Rights in Development (AWID)	http://www.awid.org: A global, feminist, membership, movement-support organization working to achieve gender justice and women's human rights worldwide.	Canada

(*continued*)

Table 5.1. *Continued*

	Website and Mission	*Location/HQ*
Equality Now	http://www.equalitynow.org: "Since 1992, our international network of lawyers, activists, and supporters have held governments responsible for ending legal inequality, sex trafficking, sexual violence & harmful practices, such as female genital mutilation (FGM) & child marriage."	New York, Nairobi, London, Beirut
International Women's Tribune Center (IWTC)	http://www.iwtc.org: Provides communication, information, education, and organizing support services to women's organizations and community groups working to improve the lives of women, particularly low-income women, in Africa, Asia and the Pacific, Latin America and the Caribbean, Eastern Europe, and Western Asia.	United States
MADRE	http://www.madre.org: "Our grassroots partners are women leaders who protect and provide for communities facing war and disaster. Together, we build skills, strengthen local organizations and advance progressive movements. And we bring women's demands to policymakers and advocate for rights, resources and results."	United States
Women for Women International (WWI)	http://www.womenforwomen .org: "We work to ensure the women in conflict-affected countries have the ability to proudly stand on their own two feet. Through our program, women learn economic and social empowerment skills . . . and resources to build self-confidence, understand their rights, earn an income, and gain the respect of their family and community."	United States

	Website and Mission	Location/HQ
Women Living under Muslim Laws (WLUML)	http://www.wluml.org: An international solidarity network that provides information, support, and a collective space for women whose lives are shaped, conditioned, or governed by laws and customs said to derive from Islam.	United Kingdom, Nigeria, Pakistan
Women's Caucus for Gender Justice	http://www.iccwomen.org: Works globally to ensure justice for women and communities affected by armed conflict and an independent and effective international Criminal Court.	The Netherlands
Women's Learning Partnership (WLP)	http://www.learningpartnership .org: A partnership of twenty autonomous women's rights organizations in the Global South that promote women's leadership and human rights.	United States
Peace, Antimilitarism, and Conflict Resolution		
Code Pink	http://www.codepink4peace .org: "A women-led grassroots organization working to end US wars and militarism, support peace and human rights initiatives, and redirect our tax dollars into health care, education, green jobs and other life-affirming programs."	United States
MADRE	http://www.madre.org: Provides humanitarian aid to women in conflict zones; opposes militarism and patriarchy; calls for a new US foreign policy.	United States
Marche Mondiale des Femmes	http://www.marchemondiale.org: Regards the interconnection of capitalism, militarism, and patriarchy as the source of poverty and violence against women.	Quebec

(continued)

Table 5.1. *Continued*

	Website and Mission	Location/HQ
Medica Mondiale	http://www.medicamondiale.org: "The Grants Program funds women-led organisations in war and conflict zones. Medica Mondiale provides support to women's organisations working at the local, regional or national level to protect and promote the rights of women and girls affected by sexualized and gender based violence."	Germany
Nobel Women's Initiative	https://nobelwomensinitiative.org: "As women recipients of the Nobel peace prize [we] work together to use the visibility and prestige of the Nobel prize to spotlight, amplify and promote the work of grassroots women's organizations and movements around the world. We work to strengthen and expand feminist efforts to promote nonviolent solutions to war, violence and militarism."	Ottawa, Canada
Women for Women International (WWI)	http://www.womenforwomen.org: "We work to ensure the women in conflict-affected countries have the ability to proudly stand on their own two feet."	United States
Women in Black	http://www.womeninblack.org: A world-wide network of women committed to peace with justice and actively opposed to injustice, war, militarism, and other forms of violence.	Seventeen countries
Women's Initiatives for Gender Justice	http://www.iccwomen.org: Works globally to ensure justice for women and communities affected by armed conflict and an independent and effective international criminal court.	The Netherlands
Women's International League for Peace and Freedom (WILPF)	http://www.wilpf.org: "We see patriarchy, militarism, and neoliberalism as three inter-related causes that push us all towards more conflict. . . . The antidote is feminism."	Global; Geneva and New York

to work, and rights in the family under an Islamist regime was of no consequence to US policy makers.[13] Surprisingly, it was of no apparent consequence to international women's groups other than those affiliated to the socialist bloc, such as WIDF. Feminists in the United States and Europe were silent; they extended no support to Afghan women and did not express any concerns about the implications of American support for Islamists. The silence and confusion of the 1980s may have been due to the anticommunism of liberal feminist groups, to an idealization of "Islamic guerrillas," to a misplaced cultural relativism, or to ignorance about Afghanistan. The left-wing government was defeated in late April 1992, and the mujahideen came to power—only to turn on each other and introduce a reign of lawlessness and warlordism. It was not until the mid-1990s, after the Taliban had removed the mujahideen from power and instituted a draconian gender regime, that Western feminists took notice and responded to appeals from Afghan and Pakistani feminists for solidarity and support. By this time, TFNs were more vocal and visible. Thus began the highly effective international feminist campaign against diplomatic recognition of the Taliban. In the United States, the Feminist Majority led the campaign against "gender apartheid" in Afghanistan.

UN CONFERENCES AND THE ICTs REVOLUTION

The UN Decade for Women (1976–85) began what I have called the global women's rights agenda, reinforced through the UN conferences of the 1990s along with the proliferation of TFNs. The earlier North-South and East-West divides were replaced by a broader feminist agenda that included a critique of neoliberalism and structural adjustment policies (SAPs) as well as an insistence on women's full citizenship, reproductive rights, bodily integrity, and autonomy, no matter what the cultural context. Eventually, that common agenda took the form of the 1995 Beijing Declaration and Platform for Action, but along the road to Beijing, there were other UN venues: the United Nations Conference on Environment and Development (UNCED) in Rio de Janeiro in 1992, the Human Rights Conference in Vienna in 1993, the International Conference on Population and Development (ICPD) in Cairo in 1994, and the World Summit for Social Development (the Social Summit) in Copenhagen in 1995. (For details, see table 6.1 in chapter 6.) The UN conferences constituted a global opportunity structure for transnational feminist mobilizing and for the crafting of common frames. There, women declared that environmental issues were women's issues, that women's rights were human rights, that governments were expected to guarantee women's reproductive health and rights, and that women's access to productive employment and social protection needed to be expanded. Slowly, new frames emerged that resonated globally and came to be adopted by women's groups throughout the world: women's human rights, gender justice, gender equality, ending the feminization of poverty, and ending violence against women. Feminists from countries in the Middle East and North Africa (MENA) had been attending the conferences, and in examining their documents and attending their meetings, I identified the following priorities for women: Muslim family law reform, ending domestic and family violence against women and girls, equal nationality rights, and enhanced political and economic participation.[14]

In the 1990s, TFNs worked with various UN agencies, notably the United Nations Development Fund for Women (UNIFEM) and United Nations Population Fund (UNFPA), but they also were consulted by various multilateral organizations. They attended the annual CSW meetings and helped write CEDAW shadow reports. As a result, TFN activities and partnerships with other advocacy networks resulted in some successes at the UN conferences of the 1990s and afterward. TFN lobbying led to the insertion of important items in the final Vienna Declaration of the 1993 Conference on Human Rights, such as the assertion that violence against women was an abuse of human rights and the demand for attention to the harmful effects of certain traditional or customary practices, cultural prejudices, and religious extremisms. The declaration also stated that human rights abuses of women in situations of armed conflict—including systematic rape, sexual slavery, and forced pregnancy—are violations of the fundamental principles of international human rights and humanitarian law. TFNs were influential in lobbying delegates for a favorable outcome document at the 1994 ICPD, such as references to women's rights to reproductive health and services. They were active at the March 1995 Social Summit, where they drew attention to structural adjustment's adverse effects on women and the poor, and, as noted, they were especially prominent at the September 1995 Beijing conference. TFNs endorsed and helped secure support for the establishment of "national machinery for women"—or women's policy agencies—as well as gender budgets in a number of countries. As such, TFNs influenced institution building, policy dialogues, and norm diffusion in connection with women's participation and rights.

These and other activities were boosted by the computer revolution. The new information and computer technologies (ICTs) helped women connect and share information, plan and coordinate activities more rapidly, and mobilize more extensively. Two feminist networks focusing on communications came to serve as conduits for activist materials: the International Women's Tribune Center (IWTC), based in New York, and ISIS International Women's Information and Communication Service, with one center in Quezon City, Philippines, and another in Santiago, Chile. Many TFNs developed informative and increasingly sophisticated websites.

Some scholars have differentiated professionalized women's lobbying groups (NGOs or international NGOs) from "grassroots" women's groups. The former are said to be elitist while the latter are more movement oriented. Yet many of the professionalized TFNs are led and staffed by feminist activists with strong commitments to gender equality, women's empowerment, and social transformation. Moreover, the women's movement is diffuse and diverse, with different types of mobilizing structures, discourses, and action repertoires. The overarching frame is that of achieving gender equality and human rights for women and girls. Across the different types of feminist organizations, strategies vary and include research and analysis, lobbying efforts, coalition building, feminist humanitarianism, and public protests (see table 5.2). All of these means, therefore, are movement oriented.

Table 5.2.　Strategies Deployed by Transnational Feminist Networks

	Code Pink	DAWN	MADRE	Marche Mondiale	WILPF	WIDE+	WLP	WLUML
Grassroots organizing	X			X	X	X		
Research and analysis	X	X	X	X	X	X	X	X
Lobbying		X			X	X	X	
Public advocacy and education	X		X	X	X	X	X	X
Coalition building	X	X	X	X	X	X	X	X
Humanitarian action	X		X		X			
International solidarity	X	X	X	X	X	X	X	X
Public protests	X			X	X			

NEOLIBERALISM AND THE WOMAN QUESTION

"The woman question" was the phrase used by socialist, communist, and nationalist movements in the nineteenth and early twentieth centuries to describe both the oppression that women faced in societies and the alternative vision that the movements offered. I use it here to refer to more recent feminist contentious politics concerning the effects of neoliberal economic policies on women and the preferred alternatives.

The latter part of the 1990s saw feminists addressing issues of globalization and the new global trade agenda. As noted, feminist scholar-activists had been critical of SAPs—with their conditionalities of privatization and liberalization—and were now alarmed by the global reach of neoliberalism. A wave of workshops was organized and publications produced to increase knowledge about the technical details of trade liberalization and its gender dynamics. Of concern was that neoliberal policies—with the attendant features of flexible labor markets, privatization of public goods, commercialization of all manner of services, and "free trade"—threatened the economic security of workers, small producers, and local industries; placed a heavy burden on women to compensate for social cutbacks and deteriorating household incomes; and led to increased vulnerability and poverty. TFNs and other advocacy networks argued that the new rules of global free trade undermined existing national laws that protected workers, the environment, and animals and that World Trade Organization (WTO) intellectual property provisions allowed large corporations to appropriate (through patents) the knowledge and products of Third World countries and their local communities. Additionally, transnational feminists argued that the employment losses and dislocations brought about by the new international trade agreements would be disproportionately borne by women.[15]

TFNs such as DAWN, WIDE, and WEDO prepared documents analyzing the policies and activities of multinational corporations, the World Bank, the International Monetary Fund (IMF), and the WTO, as well as the policy stances of the US government. They criticized the World Bank and IMF for their corporate bias and for policies that undermined the well-being of workers and the poor, while the WTO was charged with conducting its deliberations in secret and not subjecting them to rules of transparency and accountability. TFNs joined broad coalitions such as Jubilee 2000 for Third World debt cancellation, which involved challenges to corporate capitalism and global inequalities by labor, religious, environmental, and human rights groups. As such, transnational feminist groups were allied with, and indeed became part of, the global justice movement (GJM) as it took shape in the late 1990s and into the new millennium. It is important to note, however, that the global feminist agenda on neoliberalism preceded that of the GJM by roughly a decade.[16]

An example of transnational mobilizing around neoliberalism was the World March of Women (WMW) 2000. The initiative, launched two years earlier in Montreal, Canada, by the Fédération des Femmes du Québec, culminated in a series of coordinated marches and other actions held around the world to protest poverty and violence against women. Nearly six thousand organizations from 159 countries and territories were represented in the rallies and marches held. It is noteworthy that MENA women activists, not usually visible in transnational feminist organizing and mobilizing around economic justice, were involved in the planning and execution of the march, in part because of the shared knowledge of French. Women trade unionists, too, were involved; in April 2000, some three thousand trade unionists, including many women workers, marched in Durban, South Africa, in an event organized jointly by the International Confederation of Free Trade Unions (ICFTU) and its South African affiliates. The demands included affordable and accessible housing and transportation, protection against all forms of violence, equal rights for women in the workplace and throughout society, an end to SAPs and cutbacks in social budgets and public services, cancellation of the debt of all Third World countries, making gender issues central to labor policies and programs, and treatment and protection for people with HIV/AIDS.[17] The WMW initiative's *Advocacy Guide to Women's World Demands* described the world as governed by two forces, neoliberal capitalism and patriarchy, which were singled out as the structural causes of poverty and forms of violence against women. The WMW proposed concrete measures to combat poverty and incidents of violence against women: an end to SAPs and to cutbacks in social budgets and public services, implementation of the Tobin tax on speculative transactions and for financial justice, changes to global governance including democratization of the UN (including the Security Council), and the establishment of a World

Council for Economic and Financial Security. These demands were presented to the president of the World Bank on October 15, 2000.[18]

The WMW remained an important actor within the GJM and the World Social Forum (WSF), participating in the WSF in Porto Alegre, Brazil, in 2001; the People's Summit in Quebec in April 2001; and the anti-G8 demonstrations in Genoa, Italy, in July 2001. In 2002, in Porto Alegre it organized a seminar on feminism and globalization. In 2005, the network launched another global mobilization, centered on the Women's Global Charter for Humanity. As described by Pascale Dufour and Isabelle Giraud, the run-up to the mobilization entailed compromises on the network's agenda (e.g., on language pertaining to abortion and homosexuality) but had the effect of including many more women's groups, especially African and Indian ones. While painful to some members, the decision was important to the goal of building a global social movement with a collective identity.[19] Highly dedicated despite its shoestring budget, WMW attended the WSF in Tunis in 2013 and 2015, with a visible presence at the opening ceremony and leadership of many workshops.[20] It has widened its praxis to include campaigns against mining and other forms of extraction, in a way to build solidarity and coalitions around the interests and needs of rural, poor, and indigenous women.

The WIDE network was formed in 1990 and quickly became one of the principal TFNs focused on economic development and social rights. Its argument was that recent global economic processes—trade and investment liberalization; financialization of the economy; SAPs; and deep cuts in social policy budgets—were undermining gender equality and women's human rights. Identifying neoliberalism as the root cause of these adverse global processes and their social/gender effects, WIDE called for "changes in currently unjust economic policies and shifts in social mindsets in Europe and globally" in order to contribute to "gender equality and social, economic, and ecological justice globally; and women's empowerment and women's power to claim their human rights, for building participative democracy and shaping a just economy." To this end, WIDE engaged in coalition building with other feminist groups and progressive groups, helped to strengthen women's organizations, and extended international solidarity. Throughout the years, it undertook research, produced reports on gender and economic processes, and lobbied EU agencies.[21] WIDE's economic justice frame allowed for bridge building with other progressive organizations, including those associated with the WSF, while its feminist frames enabled coalitions with an array of women's rights groups.

In the wake of a decline in funding and the loss of some paid positions, WIDE reorganized itself as WIDE+, continuing to hold meetings, issue newsletters, and prepare position papers on the Sustainable Development Goals (SDGs). The report of its June 2015 meeting in Barcelona included a sober assessment of the EU and global environment and a set of recommendations for renewed feminist strategies.[22] As with DAWN and other TFNs, WIDE members or supporters attended the 2016 meetings of the UN's Commission on the Status of Women, which focused on "women's economic empowerment in the changing world of work."

FUNDAMENTALISM AND THE WOMAN QUESTION

Part of the collective action repertoire and framing strategy of Islamist movements was to demand the reinforcement and strengthening of existing Islamic laws and norms or their introduction and strict application. In addition to the prohibition against alcohol and usury and the insistence that women veil in public, Islamists demanded an orthodox interpretation and implementation of Muslim family laws, which regulate marriage, divorce, child custody, inheritance, and other aspects of family relations. In particular, Muslim family laws—which date from the Middle Ages, reflect one or another of the four Sunni schools or the Shia school of jurisprudence, and were codified in the modern period of state building—place females under the authority of male kin and wives under the control of husbands. Although notions of Islamic "complementarity" of sex roles may once have been considered equitable and natural, the rise of second-wave feminism and subsequently of "global feminism" put feminism and fundamentalism on a collision course.

This is the global context in which the international solidarity network Women Living under Muslim Laws was formed. In July 1984, nine women—from Algeria, Sudan, Morocco, Pakistan, Bangladesh, Iran, Mauritius, and Tanzania—set up a WLUML action committee in response to "the application of Muslim laws in India, Algeria, and Abu Dhabi that resulted in the violation of women's human rights."[23]

By early 1985, the committee had evolved into an international network of information, solidarity, and support, with such key figures as Marieme Hélie-Lucas of Algeria and France, Salma Sobhan of Bangladesh, Ayesha Imam of Nigeria, and Khawar Mumtaz and Farida Shaheed of Pakistan. These and other feminists were concerned about changes in family laws in their countries, the rise of fundamentalism and Islamist movements, and threats to the legal status and social positions of women in Muslim-majority societies. Tasks for the network were established at the first planning meeting in April 1986, involving ten women from Algeria, Morocco, Tunisia, Egypt, Sudan, Nigeria, India, Pakistan, and Sri Lanka. Subsequent meetings and action plans took place in Dhaka, Bangladesh, in 1997 and in Dakar, Senegal, in January 2006. WLUML became a well-known network of women who were active in their local and national movements but met periodically to reach a strategic consensus.

As a fluid group rather than a membership-based organization, WLUML gave priority to creating strong networks and ties of solidarity among women across countries rather than seeking to influence national or global policy through interaction with governments or intergovernmental bodies.[24] Nonetheless, it was present at the UN's 1993 human rights conference and sponsored the participation of Khalida Messaoudi, an Algerian feminist leader who faced an Islamist death threat. WLUML also attended the 1994 UN Conference on Population and Development, where it joined other feminist networks in criticizing efforts by the Vatican, conservative states, and Christian and Muslim fundamentalists to remove references to women's reproductive rights in the conference declaration. The conferences helped WLUML expand its collaborations and alliances with transnational feminist networks such as WIDE and DAWN, in addition to its links with the Center for Women's Global Leadership at Rutgers University; Shirkat Gah in Lahore, Pakistan; and Baobab in Lagos, Nigeria.[25]

As early as 1990, WLUML warned of an "Islamist international" with the organizational, human, financial, and military means to threaten secularists, feminists, and democrats. Prominent members were critical of European governments granting political asylum to radical Islamists. After the Taliban took control of Afghanistan in September 1996 and instituted a harsh gender regime, WLUML helped disseminate appeals from expatriate Afghan women in Pakistan for international solidarity and support. As a result, feminists brought pressure to bear on their governments not to recognize the Taliban; thus, only three states—Pakistan, Saudi Arabia, and the United Arab Emirates—came to recognize the Taliban regime. In the new century, WLUML pointed to the Front Islamique du Salut's and Armed Islamic Group's record of terrorism, including harassment, kidnapping, rape, and murder of Algerian women, to oppose any legalization of these groups without prosecution of those responsible for crimes.[26] At the same time, WLUML was critical of the US bombing raids in Afghanistan, which were conducted to bring down the perpetrators of September 11, identified as Osama bin Laden, his al-Qaeda network, and their Taliban hosts. WLUML was concerned that the raids brought devastation to ordinary Afghans. And the network accused Western countries of having turned a blind eye to Islamists—and in the case of the United States, having actively supported them.[27]

Exemplifying the fluid and flexible nature of contemporary transnational social movements and their organizations, WLUML's work was maintained through the activities of "networkers" who communicated largely via the internet but met occasionally to agree on plans. The January 2006 action plan meeting in Dakar was attended by fifty networkers from twenty-two countries, but affiliates sent their input via e-mail. This double strategy of real and virtual communication enabled the network to agree on four priority issues: "peace-building and resisting the impact of militarization; preserving multiple identities and exposing fundamentalisms; widening debate about women's bodily autonomy; and promoting and protecting women's equality under laws."[28]

From the outset, WLUML's collective action repertoire included gathering and disseminating information on formal and customary laws in the Muslim world and on women's struggles and strategies. A ten-year project on reinterpreting the Qur'an, led by the Malaysian group Sisters in Islam, culminated in a book and increased awareness of the religious women involved in the misapplication of Islamic law in the Muslim world. Eschewing lobbying, the network's central activity was its solidarity and support work. WLUML received appeals and responded to as well as initiated campaigns around violations of human rights, including women's human rights. After 2003, the network issued countless appeals on behalf of Iraqi women.[29] It issued numerous action alerts, produced occasional journals ("dossiers"), and published an informative news sheet. WLUML was the prime vehicle through which information was distributed worldwide in 2005 concerning the planned establishment of a sharia court in Ontario, Canada; and it initiated or disseminated numerous petitions to protest violations of women's rights. WLUML worked with other feminist networks and web-based projects—such as the Women's Human Rights Net, a project of the Canada-based Association for Women's Rights in Development—to highlight women's human rights violations as well as examples of feminist collective action. In 2008, its website listed seventy-five linked networks, many of them in Middle Eastern or Muslim countries. In all these ways, WLUML linked dispersed communities, creating a new cyberculture and reinforcing a collective identity. Mobilization to protest gender injustices occurred rapidly and often effectively.

The Women's Learning Partnership for Rights, Development, and Peace (WLP) was formed in 2000 by veteran Iranian women's rights activist Mahnaz Afkhami. WLP defines itself as "a builder of networks, working with eighteen autonomous and independent partner organizations in the Global South, particularly in Muslim-majority societies, to empower women to transform their families, communities, and societies." The goals are to "improve the effectiveness of feminist movements in Muslim-majority societies and globally" and to help women secure human rights, contribute to the development of their communities, and "ultimately create a more peaceful world."[30] This is done in part through the production and circulation of curricular and training manuals such as *Leading to Choices*, and through the training of trainers in a long-term, bottom-up, participatory process. The materials were developed in a protracted and deliberative process, with consultation and testing across the partnership; as such, WLP evinces the democratic practices and internal democratic culture emphasized by many feminist organizations.

For WLP, the goals of building capacity (strengthening women's organizations) and building democracy (strengthening civil society and the public sphere) are carried out in both virtual and physical spaces. Through its own website and links to partner websites, WLP creates a virtual community for women's human rights and a transnational and collective identity via websites, blogs, and e-communications. WLP is an exceptionally tech-savvy TFN, with such internet-related features as Facebook, Twitter, Flickr, and YouTube accounts; the Our Vision & Our Voices blog; and an information technology manual titled

Making IT Our Own. WLP also holds face-to-face meetings—through seminars, conferences, trainings, and regional institutes—to enhance community, identity, and solidarity.[31] As with WLUML, solidarity is emphasized. Since at least 2007, when the government of Mahmoud Ahmadinejad clamped down on Iran's burgeoning civil society and especially on feminist activists, WLP has been active in mobilizing international support for Iranian feminists subjected to harassment, imprisonment, or prosecution.

Through their virtual activism, therefore, WLP and WLUML (as well as Musawah, discussed in chapter 4) exemplify at least two key characteristics of social movement networks in an era of globalization: creating or actively participating in the transnational public sphere and creating and maintaining a collective identity as networkers for women's human rights.

CONFLICT, WAR, AND EMPIRE: FEMINIST RESPONSES

Chapter 1 mentioned one of the oldest transnational feminist networks (TFNs) and, indeed, one of the world's oldest peace organizations. The Women's International League for Peace and Freedom (WILPF) was founded in 1915 by thirteen hundred women activists from Europe and North America opposed to what became known as World War I. Feminists and women's groups have long been involved in peace work, with analyses of the causes and consequences of conflict, methods of conflict resolution and peace building, and conditions necessary for human security. Antimilitarist and human rights groups such as WILPF, Women Strike for Peace (United States), the Women of Greenham Common (United Kingdom), the Raging Grannies (Canada and the United States), and the Mothers and Grandmothers of the Plaza de Mayo (Argentina) are well known, and their legacy lies in ongoing efforts to "feminize" or "engender" peace, nuclear disarmament, and human rights. Women's peace activism has been long associated with world affairs.[32]

At the 1985 Nairobi conference, organized by the United Nations, the themes of equality, development, and peace were addressed by attendees in various ways. The Nairobi conference took place in the midst of the crisis of Third World indebtedness and the implementation of austerity policies recommended by the World Bank and the IMF. Feminists were quick to see the links among economic distress, political instability, and violence against women. As the Jamaican scholar-activist Lucille Mathurin Mair noted after Nairobi,

> This [economic] distress exists in a climate of mounting violence and militarism. . . . Violence follows an ideological continuum, starting from the domestic sphere where it is tolerated, if not positively accepted. It then moves to the public political arena where it is glamorized and even celebrated. . . . Women and children are the prime victims of this cult of aggression.[33]

The era of globalization and a new wave of conflicts brought even more urgency to the matter. The 1990s saw conflicts in Afghanistan, Algeria, Bosnia, Rwanda, Burundi, Sierra Leone, and Liberia—all of which were marked by serious violations of women's human rights. Women's groups responded by underscoring the specific vulnerability of women and girls during wartime, the pervasive nature of sexual abuse, and the need to include women's groups in peace negotiations. Joining WILPF in its antiwar actions were newly formed feminist peace, human rights, and humanitarian organizations and networks such as Women in Black, Medica Mondiale, Women Waging Peace, and Women for Women International. Advocacy networks and scholar-activists produced research to show that women's groups had been effective in peace building in Northern Ireland as well as in Bosnia, Burundi, and Liberia.

In response to such research, lobbying, and advocacy initiatives, the UN Security Council in March 2000 issued a resolution that was embraced by women's groups, if not by all governments, and in October, it passed Resolution 1325, calling on governments—and the Security Council itself—to include women in negotiations and settlements with respect to conflict resolution and peace building.[34] Key points of the resolution are

- increasing the representation of women at all decision-making levels;
- integrating a gender perspective into peacekeeping missions;
- appointing more women as special representatives and envoys of the secretary-general;

- supporting women's grassroots organizations in their peace initiatives;
- involving women as participants in peace negotiations and agreements;
- ensuring protection of and respect for the human rights of women and girls;
- protecting women and girls from gender-based violence; and
- integrating a gender perspective into disarmament, demobilization, and reintegration of former combatants.

While Security Council Resolution (SCR) 1325 was widely hailed as a historic achievement in a domain usually considered off-limits to women and the preserve of men, its impact was muted not long afterward, when new conflicts erupted that would sideline the resolution in the name of the "global war on terror."

The aftermath of September 11, 2001, and the invasion of Iraq prompted many women to join existing peace organizations or build new ones. In India, women's groups joined a coalition called Jang Roko Abhiyan (Antiwar Campaign), which condemned the massacre of American civilians on September 11 but called on the United States to accept responsibility for the fallout from past foreign policies and to refrain from military retaliation in Afghanistan that would very likely cause considerable civilian death and suffering.[35] In Pakistan, women's groups held a protest rally on September 25, 2001, against terrorism, religious fundamentalism, and war. The US-based Feminist Majority issued a courageous statement on September 11 that noted the US role in the 1980s in supplying "billions of dollars to fund, train, and arm the mujahideen, which gave rise to the Taliban" and calling on the United States to refrain from blaming Afghans, Arabs, or Muslims.[36] An appeal from the Medica Mondiale Kosovo women's center was both pertinent and poignant:

> We have lived through war. We know what it is like to be attacked, to grieve, and to feel anger. We understand the urge for revenge is strong . . . [but] a violent response can only bring more violence not justice. [I]t kills more innocent victims and gives birth to new holy avengers. It begins a new cycle and perpetuates more hate, more insecurity, more fear and ultimately more death amongst civilians. We therefore urge

the U.S. and its allies to temper their anger and to refrain from the folly of sweeping military solutions. Terrorists are not nations. And nations must not act like terrorists.[37]

The invasion of Iraq was preceded by massive antiwar protests across the globe. In the United States, progressive women's groups and feminist activists refused to side with the George W. Bush administration and took part in street and media protests. The radical feminist magazine *Off Our Backs* carried an article by veteran activist Starhawk, who wrote, "Oppression of women is real, in Muslim societies and non-Muslim societies around the globe. But women cannot be liberated by the tanks and bombs of those who are continuing centuries-old policies of exploitation, commandeering resources for themselves, and fomenting prejudice against the culture and heritage which is also a deep part of a woman's being."[38] An audacious group of women who wanted to draw attention to the hypermasculinity of war called themselves the Missile Dick Chicks.[39] A press release issued on March 28, 2003, by the US-based feminist humanitarian group MADRE described a meeting of women's organizations worldwide (including itself) that gathered at the UN and urged the General Assembly to "unite for peace." It added, "This action follows a recent call in New Delhi made by women's organizations from over thirty-five countries condemning the Bush administration's war against Iraq and urging the General Assembly to challenge U.S. aggression."[40] The spring 2003 issue of *Ms. Magazine* carried a special action alert titled "No Time for Despair: Women Take Action Worldwide," signed by American feminists Robin Morgan, Ellie Smeal, and Gloria Steinem. Its authors referred to "an elective war launched against Iraq, where 50 percent of the population is under age fifteen. Yes, they are oppressed by a brutal dictatorship, but it's also clear—from polls showing that some 70 percent of Americans oppose Bush's unilateral action against Iraq—that a majority of us don't trust the judgment of our leader." At the bottom of the statement was a listing of women's organizations and progressive groups that *Ms. Magazine* readers could contact. Also included was a "National Council of Women's Organizations Statement on War with Iraq," stating in part that "U.S. foreign policy should be driven by human rights, justice, and equality—values that will decrease the threat of terrorism—and not by corporate interests or the desire to secure natural resources for U.S. consumption."

The issue of *Ms. Magazine* also carried a statement by author and poet Grace Paley titled "Why Peace Is (More Than Ever) a Feminist Issue."[41]

The invasion of Iraq produced another women-led peace and antiwar organization—Code Pink—which grew in numbers and notoriety (among the Right) and fame (among the Left) throughout the decade. Code Pink was formed in 2002 by a group of women who had worked with each other as well as in other networks. Medea Benjamin cofounded Global Exchange in 1988 with Kevin Danaher; Jodie Evans had worked for former California governor Jerry Brown; and Gael Murphy was a longtime public health advisor in Africa and the Caribbean. The group's name is a play on the national security color codes established by the Bush administration in the aftermath of September 11, and Code Pink activists have shown their creativity and innovative style of protest in various ways. Wearing pink costumes and engaging in daring acts of public protest, they have become known for infiltrating congressional meetings, unfurling antiwar banners, shouting antiwar slogans, and badgering members of Congress about their stand on the war, military spending, health care for veterans, and support for Iraqi civilians. One of their innovations is the issuance of "pink slips" to political culprits. In one daring act, a Code Pink activist, her hands painted red, approached US secretary of state Condoleezza Rice on Capitol Hill and accused her of having the blood of the Iraqi people on her hands.[42]

While almost all TFNs may be regarded as internationalist and solidaristic—inasmuch as they are concerned about the plight of "sisters" across borders and boundaries of nationality, religion, and class—not all engage in feminist humanitarianism. I define feminist humanitarianism as operational work, carried out by women's groups to alleviate suffering or to meet basic needs while being informed by the strategic goal of achieving women's human rights and gender equality. This understanding is very different from the "humanitarian intervention" that was conceptualized in the 1990s to justify bombing Serbia and later invading Iraq.

Code Pink's repertoire includes feminist humanitarianism and international solidarity, as evidenced by visits to Baghdad to demonstrate opposition to war and solidarity with the Iraqi people. Medea Benjamin, Jodie Evans, and Sand Brim traveled to Iraq in February and December 2003. In December 2004, Code Pink coordinated the historic

Families for Peace delegation to Amman, Jordan, involving the three Code Pink founders and a member of the antiwar group United for Peace and Justice (UFPJ), along with several relatives of fallen American soldiers and families of September 11 victims. According to one report, "In an inspiring act of humanity and generosity, they brought with them $650,000 in medical supplies and other aid for the Fallujah refugees who were forced from their homes when the Americans destroyed their city. Although the American press failed to cover this unprecedented visit, the mission garnered enormous attention from Al Jazeera, Al Arabiyya, and Dubai and Iranian television, who witnessed firsthand the depths of American compassion."[43] Code Pink's website literature presents its activities and goals as "bringing our war dollars home; holding our leaders accountable for war crimes; boycotting war profiteers; defending the truth tellers and changing the game; demilitarizing our society; countering corporate corruption; building bridges, not bombs; cultivating vibrant communities and a healthy planet; and declaring (loudly and proudly) that war is insane."[44]

Code Pink has been involved in coalitions with other feminist and social justice networks, including WILPF, the National Organization for Women, and UFPJ, and it has taken part in the WSF. In 2007, six women Nobel Peace Prize winners formed the Nobel Women's Initiative, and its first international conference focused on women, conflict, peace, and security in the Middle East.[45] These and other feminist networks engage in research, advocacy, and solidarity work to uncover human rights violations and war crimes, ensure that local women's peace groups are recognized, and promote the International Criminal Court (established in 1999 as the first international war crimes court) and SCR 1325. Of the peace-oriented TFNs, Code Pink is politically closest to WILPF as well as to the group Peace Action in the United States, and it works with them to support the Iran Nuclear Deal, to oppose the nearly $1 trillion US military budget under President Trump, and to call for an end to arms sales to Saudi Arabia and similar countries that engaged in armed conflict. One of Medea Benjamin's books is *Kingdom of the Unjust: Behind the U.S.-Saudi Connection*, published in 2016.

MADRE began its work during the US-sponsored Contra war in Nicaragua in 1983 and initially devoted itself to that issue. Its work in Iraq dates back to the 1991 Gulf War, when it began collecting an assortment of needed supplies for Iraqi families, including milk and medicine. It continued this work throughout the 1990s and frequently decried the detrimental effects on women and children of the sanctions regime. After the 2003 invasion and occupation of Iraq, MADRE partnered with UNICEF-Iraq and provided twenty-five thousand citizens with supplies and emergency aid, including essential drugs and medical supplies for those in need. It also worked in Cuba, Nicaragua, El Salvador, Palestine, and Haiti, partnering with sister organizations.[46] In 2005, MADRE worked with Zenab for Women in Development to provide emergency aid to displaced women and families in Darfur, sending $500,000 worth of clothing and bedding to small refugee camps for use during harsh weather and in combating illnesses such as malaria and meningitis.[47] In another example of its feminist humanitarian work, MADRE partnered with UNICEF to provide supplies in Iraq and worked with the Organization of Women's Freedom in Iraq (OWFI) to support the creation of women's shelters for victims of domestic and community violence in the Iraqi cities of Baghdad, Kirkuk, Erbil, and Nasariyeh. The OWFI-MADRE campaign against "honor killings" gave rise to a web of shelters and an escape route for Iraqi women, which came to be known as the Underground Railroad for Iraqi Women.[48]

Although SCR 1325 was followed by additional resolutions, these have no enforcement mechanisms. The Security Council itself has been unable or unwilling to change or enact policies that would end conflicts, much less honor SCR 1325, because of its internal divisions and disagreements over geopolitics, especially among the five permanent members with veto powers. The contrast with the dedication and commitment of TFNs, often working in coalition with broad peace groups, is striking. WILPF-International, with its secretariat in Geneva and an office in New York across from the UN, continues to promote SCR 1325 and its disarmament program, "Reaching Critical Will," and seeks to enhance transparency and accountability for the number and cost of weapons production and the number of deaths caused by such weapons. In the wake of the Arab Spring, WILPF organized a series of consultations in Geneva that resulted in a report titled "Ending Discrimination and Reinforcing Women's Peace and Security in the MENA Region." The US section produces a biannual magazine, *Peace and Freedom*, and works closely with Code Pink and Peace Action.

In addition to the collective efforts spearheaded by TFNs, scholar-activists have penned numerous op-ed pieces, journal articles, and books on wars in Afghanistan and Iraq, tying these to capitalism, militarism, and empire. Zillah Eisenstein's *Against Empire*, for example, is a powerful indictment of neoliberal globalization, imperial arrogance, and racism and a clarion call for a polyversal feminism and humanism. Cynthia Enloe's *Globalization and Militarism* offers a trenchant critique of masculinist international relations, especially in the context of the war against Iraq, while also noting the contributions of women peace builders across the globe.[49] Global peace action is a key strategy of transnational feminist activism.

GLOBAL FEMINISM AND GLOBAL JUSTICE

The global women's movement and the global justice movement (GJM) are internetworked social movements. Many TFNs have participated regularly in the WSF, although for several years, some activists felt that feminist issues were not present outside the Feminist Dialogues and sessions. In the first forum (2001), women made up 54 percent of participants but less than 15 percent of the most important panelists in the official forum program. By the third forum (2003), two major feminist groups—the World March of Women (WMW) and Latin America's Mercosur Feminist Articulation—were responsible for two of the five thematic areas. At the Fourth WSF in Mumbai, feminists were placed in charge of the development of several of the self-organized panels, and in 2005, more than six thousand women's groups participated in the WSF. The Feminist Dialogues that took place at the Fifth WSF focused on three key problems: neoliberal globalization, militarism and war, and fundamentalisms.[50]

According to Jane Conway, "The 2004 WSF in Mumbai and the Americas Social Forum in Quito merit special attention as historical high points in making the forum feminist." She highlights the role of the WMW on the WSF International Council and notes that its slogan, "The world will not change without feminism, and feminists cannot change women's lives unless we change the world," met with roars of approval at the closing ceremonies at the 2002 WSF. What was distinct about the Mumbai WSF, she wrote, was that its political vocabulary was expanded to include struggles against patriarchy, militarism and war, racism, casteism, and religious communalism alongside neoliberalism. The Feminist Dialogues that have taken place during the WSF frame feminism as "an ideology [that] attempts to understand the oppression and agency of women within a patriarchal structure and in the present neoliberal economic, social and political systems[; . . .] that is against fundamentalism, global capitalism, and imperialism[; . . .] which allies itself with the marginalized, dalit and indigenous peoples [; and . . .] which unfolds its practice every day in our lives and continues the quest for collective and democratic functioning."[51] In its April 2011 newsletter about the Dakar WSF, WIDE reported on the presence of representatives of the WMW, the Feminist Dialoguers, and La Via Campesina, who led many of the women's assemblies. The WMW international coordinator, Miriam Nobre, served as co-coordinator in the Assembly of Social Movements (the plenary bringing together around three thousand people). This was an important acknowledgment, the WIDE report continued, of women's struggles as common social struggles.[52] At the WSF in Tunis in 2013, feminism was vocal and visible everywhere. The local organizing committee included the long-standing feminist groups *Femmes Démocrates* and AFTURD, the large trade union UGTT, the Tunisian League of Human Rights, the National Bar Association, and student groups. The WSF opened with a Women's Assembly, and the venue—the Amphitheatre of the Law Faculty—was filled to capacity, with perhaps one-third of the audience being men. Later, the Women's March—led by the widow of an assassinated leftist leader—proceeded through the city center and ended at the Olympic Stadium, where the famed Brazilian singer and former minister of culture Gilberto Gil spoke and performed.[53]

Global feminism shares with the GJM a common opposition to neoliberalism and militarism but also emphasizes an antifundamentalist action frame. In this respect, differences may be observed. Whereas feminists associated with WLUML or WLP would insist on the right of Muslims not only to leave their religion but to criticize it, others might view such a stance, or a position in favor of a ban on the all-enveloping *niqab*, as a form of "Islamophobia." At the 2013 Tunis WSF, a woman at an informal group discussion said, "I cannot understand the Western fascination with Islamist parties or moderate Islam; the agenda is the monopolization of political power and the fusion of religion and politics."[54] This sentiment echoed a 2005 complaint by WLUML about accommodations of Islamists in the name of a broad anti-imperialist front. WLUML was also exercised by an invitation to speak at the WSF that had been extended to the European Muslim intellectual Tariq Ramadan, who had earlier made statements defending the veil as integral to Islamic identity.[55] Similarly, WLUML considered French feminist Christine Delphy's defense of Muslim women's "right to veil" incoherent in the absence of an analysis of the complex context in which (re)veiling occurs.

STRATEGIES, COLLECTIVE IDENTITIES, AND CULTURAL FRAMES

Earlier, this chapter referred to tactics and strategies that transnational feminist networks (TFNs) deploy to achieve their goals: research, outreach, and advocacy; lobbying and engaging with domestic and global policy makers; organizing and coalition building; and public protests and direct action. Here we revisit Chadwick Alger's framework (see chapter 2) to examine more closely the strategies pursued. First, like other transnational social movement groups, they create, activate, or join global networks to mobilize pressure outside states. TFNs build or take part in coalitions and have been active in the WSF. Working alone or in coalitions, they mobilize pressure outside states via e-petitions, action alerts, and appeals; acts of civil disobedience; other forms of public protest; and sometimes direct action. Second, TFNs participate in multilateral arenas and meetings of intergovernmental organizations (IGOs). They observe and address UN departments such as ECOSOC and bodies such as CSW, and they consult for UN agencies, including UN Women (formed in 2010) and regional commissions. By taking part in IGOs meetings and preparing background papers, briefing papers, and reports, they help set agendas and increase expertise on issues. By lobbying delegates, they raise awareness and cultivate supporters. A number of TFN members and founders have been recruited by multilateral organizations, including the World Bank and UN Women. The purpose of such interaction (or employment) with IGOs is to raise new issues—such as gender and trade, women's human rights, violence against women in war zones, and the need for more precise gender (in)equality measurement tools—and to influence policy.

Third, TFNs act and agitate within states to enhance public awareness and participation. They work with labor and progressive religious groups, the media, and human rights groups on social policy and humanitarian, development, and militarization issues. They link with and support local partners, take part in local coalitions, and provoke or take part in public protests. In the context of the Arab Spring, TFNs extended solidarity to Arab women while also disseminating the concerns raised by Arab feminist organizations about the place of women's participation and rights in the new polities. In May 2019, DAWN held a meeting in Addis Ababa on public-private partnerships and corporate accountability, with a focus on African countries. In recent years, TFNs have joined or supported coalitions to challenge the growth of right-wing populism. Fourth, TFNs network with each other, in a sustained process of internetworking and internet-working. Many take part in the biannual meetings of the Association for Women's Rights in Development (AWID) or of the International Association for Feminist Economics (IAFFE). A coalition of women's groups—including WIDE, AWID, the Center for Women's Global Leadership, and the Feminist Alliance for International Action—issued a joint statement in March 2011 asking that UN Women "design its policy and program on women's economic empowerment from an economic, cultural, and social rights framework." More recently, WIDE+ sponsored a session on the trade agenda at the IAFFE meeting that took place in Glasgow, Scotland, in June 2019.[56]

In all these ways, feminist activism spans local, national, regional, and global terrains. The ultimate goal of the strategies deployed by TFNs is not just to set agenda for policy reform but to contribute to normative cultural change and broader societal transformation. As such, TFNs reflect the possibilities inherent within global civil society.

The internet has allowed TFNs (and other advocacy and activist networks) to retain flexibility, adaptability, and nonhierarchical features while also ensuring efficiency in their operations. That is, TFNs have been able to perform optimally without having to become formal or bureaucratic organizations. Avoiding bureaucratization is particularly important to feminists, who prioritize process, inclusion, and participation. The network form of feminist organizing suggests a mode of cooperation that may be more conducive to the era of globalization, as well as more consistent with feminist goals of democratic, inclusive, participatory, decentralized, and nonhierarchical structures and processes. And the "gift" of the internet has allowed them to transcend borders, boundaries, and barriers in their collective action against neoliberalism, militarism, and fundamentalisms.

What leads women from across the globe to common mobilizing structures and frames? The chapter earlier identified three processes at the global level that had led women's rights activists to overcome North-South differences and form TFNs with such resonant frames as women's empowerment, women's human rights, gender equality, and gender justice. Here we identify material conditions at macro and micro levels that influence feminist activism. At a macro level, neoliberal capitalism, war, and patriarchal fundamentalisms—all aspects of contemporary globalization—affect and disadvantage women in distinct ways. These can have a galvanizing effect, especially when political opportunities and resources are available. A second macro-level influence is the global women's rights agenda, which includes norm and policy diffusion through international conventions and declarations such as CEDAW, ILO conventions on nondiscrimination and on maternal employment, the Beijing Declaration and Platform for Action, SCR 1325, and Millennium Development Goal 3. Promoted by the UN and advocated by TFNs, the global women's rights agenda is especially resonant cross-culturally with working women across the globe and can inspire, motivate, and mobilize women. The repertoire of conventions and declarations constitutes an important set of tools that can legitimate women's rights activism in difficult cultural or political circumstances.

At a micro level, women's lived experiences within the family and society—including experiences of marginalization in the labor market and the polity, the largely unacknowledged importance of women's role in social reproduction, violence against women, and workplace sexual harassment—can set the stage for receptivity to mobilizing processes. Such common material conditions and lived experiences can help create collective identities that are then fostered through sustained activism, whether in the virtual public sphere, on the streets, or at conferences. Similarly, framing strategies across movements or networks can create or reinforce collective identities.

We have seen that transnational feminism can be in disagreement on some issues, such as sexuality, which may have distinct resonances in specific cultural contexts; there also could be disagreement on foreign policy issues and "humanitarian intervention." Peruvian feminist and WSF veteran Virginia Vargas makes a point of referring to "the diverse and plural feminisms that exist."[57] She notes that feminists, although they are all opposed to fundamentalism, differ on abortion and sexual rights. Transnational feminists also have differed on who has been re-sponsible for the over-long Syrian conflict. Still, given the formidable structural and institutional constraints of the contemporary capitalist world-system, TFN achievements are all the more remarkable.

CONCLUSION

This chapter has discussed the women's rights movement as a global social movement—albeit one with segmentary, reticulate, and polycentric characteristics—and identified key social movement organizations and transnational feminist networks (TFNs) focused on issues of neo-liberalism, antifundamentalism, women's human rights, and peace. I have drawn attention to the range of global feminist activism: research, advocacy, and lobbying; conferences, seminars, and meetings; solidarity and international networking; progressive humanitarian work; and protest and direct action. Transnational feminist frames such as wom-en's human rights, empowerment, gender equality, and gender justice derive from analyses and critiques of the sexual division of labor and hypermasculinity and of institutions of global governance, US milita-rism, and specific actions by states and nonstate actors; solidarity with women across the globe; and recommendations for a women-friendly democratic polity and set of social and economic policies. These have been presented at such global venues as UN conferences, meetings of multilateral organizations, and the WSF. Cognizant of the strategic importance of securing allies at local, national, and global levels, TFNs also have celebrated the WSF as an autonomous space for the conver-gence of social movement and civil society organizations, including feminist ones, and a critical venue for deliberative democracy. Clearly, transnational feminist politics is goal directed and focused on solidarity rather than being identity based.

Chapter 6

The Global Justice Movement

We don't want violence. . . . Our fight is to recover a right which is the right to education.

> —Camila Vallejo, student protest leader, 2011, Chile[1]

We are the 99%!

> —Occupy Wall Street slogan, 2011

Formed in the late 1990s, the global justice movement (GJM) became the subject of many new studies, analyzed as a reaction to neoliberal globalization, an expression of "globalization-from-below," a key element of global civil society, and an exemplar of the transnationalization of collective action. Composed of nongovernmental organizations (NGOs), social movement and civil society organizations, transnational advocacy networks, unions, religious groups, and individual activists opposed to neoliberalism and war, the GJM has existed, to varying degrees of coordination and activism, across regions, although some have argued that it was most active in Europe.[2] Since 2001, the GJM has convened at the annual World Social Forum (WSF), regional forums, and on the web, planning and coordinating activities, and taking part in various forms of public engagement and protest activity to spread its ideas and recruit new supporters. Its campaigns included debt relief or cancellation as well as ending poverty in developing countries, taxing of financial speculations and movements, fair trade and labor rights, environmental protection, and reform or transformation of institutions of global governance.

One offshoot was the Occupy movement of 2011, which gained global fame through its encampments and its cry of "We are the 99%!" More recently, scholar-activists have used the term "New Global Left" to describe not only the community of anti- or other-globalization activists around the WSF but also progressive political parties and politicians, the growing climate justice movement, and new groups in the United States such as Black Lives Matter, the MeToo and Time's Up campaigns against the sexual harassment of women, and youth groups for gun control and for climate justice. At the same time, debates have emerged as to how to confront the continued hegemony of corporations, banks, and powerful states in what remains an unequal and hierarchical capitalist world-system, and—perhaps most important—how to craft a common, collective identity and set of strategies across diverse movements, campaigns, and identities. The ebb of the Latin American pink tide, the Arab Spring's modest harvest and the ongoing regional crisis, and the rise and spread of right-wing populisms certainly are sobering developments, but the story of the GJM, like that of global feminism, is an important and instructive one, filled with possibilities.

The rise of the GJM, known as the "movement of movements," confirms that issues of class, inequality, and redistribution do not belong to a bygone era. Some theorists had counterposed the so-called old social movements of class-based mobilizations and economic demands with the more recent "new social movements," which focused on identity, self-expression, and lifestyle. In fact, the GJM is the inevitable result of the capitalistic features of the contemporary world-system and its attendant globalization processes. And while advocacy and public policy engagement certainly are part of the collective action repertoire of the movement, many activists are also likely to engage in direct action against what they see as the symbols of neoliberal capitalism. Examples include the encampments and acts of civil disobedience by participants in the Occupy Wall Street (OWS) movement in the United States; the street protests against austerity measures and cuts in social spending in Athens, Madrid, Lisbon, London, Santiago, and elsewhere; the anti-fascist street battles with the rise of right-wing populism and especially its fringe elements; and the angry protests of France's Gilets Jaunes, which began in late 2018 (see chapter 7).

This chapter describes the participants of the GJM and their organizations, leading figures, grievances and critiques, actions and strategies, and proposed alternatives. But first it examines origins and antecedents. The Battle of Seattle in late 1999 is usually cited as the movement's "takeoff," and much of the literature notes the cycle of protests against neoliberalism that ensued in subsequent years throughout Europe and, to a lesser degree, North America. However, the movement's origins lie in an earlier cycle of protests that took place in the Third World against structural adjustment policies (SAPs). The literature on globalization and its discontents sometimes overlooks the structural adjustment episode and anti–International Monetary Fund (IMF) protests, but it should be noted that the SAPs of the 1980s and the trade agenda of the 1990s were part and parcel of the same global trend toward neoliberal capitalist globalization. Indeed, many of the older participants of the GJM had been involved in protests against SAPs in the 1980s or active in solidarity movements for Central America, South Africa, and Palestine. Thus, in analyzing the relationship between globalization and transnational collective action, we should recognize the links between the earlier SAPs and the later consolidation of neoliberal financialization and trade, noting also the two cycles of collective action, the first of which took place in the Global South. In the present century's first decade, media reports tended to focus on dramatic protests in Europe and North America, but we should acknowledge the genuinely global nature of the movement for economic justice and its strong roots in the developing world. One Global South country in particular—Brazil—was pivotal in the formation of the WSF, which became a key institution of the GJM.

FROM STRUCTURAL ADJUSTMENTS AND ANTI-IMF PROTESTS TO THE GLOBAL TRADE AGENDA AND PROTESTS AGAINST THE WORLD TRADE ORGANIZATION

SAPs were first implemented in some African and Latin American countries as a result of the debt crisis in the 1970s and early 1980s. As conditions for receiving new loans from the IMF or World Bank or for acquiring lower interest rates on existing loans, SAPs aimed to balance budgets and increase competitiveness through trade and price liberalization. Debt servicing and balanced budgets required austerity measures that led governments to halt development planning, cut back on social spending, or seek "cost recovery" through the implementation of "user fees" in sectors such as health and education, as well as through the elimination of subsidies for utilities and basic foodstuffs. Currency devaluation, foreign exchange restructuring, and contraction of the public-sector wage bill resulted in a reduction of real wages, rising unemployment, and deteriorating living standards, as found by studies commissioned by United Nations (UN) agencies such as the United Nations Children's Fund (UNICEF) and the International Labour Organization (ILO). By the late 1980s, some seventy countries of the Global South had submitted to the World Bank and IMF programs. Economist Lance Taylor and his associates, among others, documented the difficulties of such "economic reform."[3]

SAPs came to be criticized by activists for halting development, exacerbating poverty, and creating new categories of the poor. (As discussed in chapter 5, feminists also were highly critical.) One activist noted, "Ghana is supposed to be one of the Bank's success stories, but in the 1990s, the Bank itself calculated that it would take the average Ghanaian forty years to regain the standard of living she had had in the 1970s." Walden Bello of the Philippines interpreted structural adjustment as a way of not only instituting market discipline but also disciplining the Third World and imposing a single economic model, that of global neoliberal capitalism. Among the milestones in the process of institutionalizing neoliberalism that he identified were "the IMF's new role as the watchdog of the Third World countries' external economic relations in the 1970s; the universalization of structural adjustment in the 1980s; and the unilateralist trade campaign waged against the Asian 'tiger economies' by Washington beginning in the early 1980s."⁴ Writing about Uganda's experience, Mahmood Mamdani explains that "by the late 1980s, the IMF had taken charge of the Ugandan treasury, and the World Bank was running [the president's] planning." Both international financial institutions (IFIs) also encouraged the privatization of higher education, and even produced a formula for fees, with the result that "[t]he Bank had managed, very effectively, to starve the central administration of funds."⁵

When highly indebted Third World countries followed the policy advice of traveling World Bank and IMF economists without consulting trade unions or civil society organizations, and when households began to feel the financial pinch, popular protest was inevitable. A cycle of protests—at the time called food riots or anti-IMF riots—enveloped the Third World from the latter part of the 1970s, when the first SAPs were introduced, to the early 1990s. In their documentation of protests against SAPs in some 40 countries between 1976 and 1992, John Walton and David Seddon counted two-digit protests in Peru, Ecuador, Argentina, Brazil, and Panama. Multiple protests also took place in the Philippines, Zaire, Chile, Bolivia, Haiti, Zambia, Poland, and Venezuela.⁶ Other countries had between one and four protests in a particular month during that period of anti-IMF protests.

Walton and Seddon's listing shows that Mexico experienced two such riots in February 1986. Some years later, Mexico entered into discussions with the United States and Canada to form a regional free trade agreement that would ostensibly improve economic relations through the freer flow of capital and goods. Thus was born the North American Free Trade Agreement (NAFTA). Very quickly it came to be seen as a joint corporate-state strategy that had eschewed consultation with unions and civil society groups. Activists viewed it as a plan that would best serve the interests of American corporations rather than workers, and therefore, protests arose from left-wing citizens in all three countries. The critique of NAFTA coincided with the emergence of the Zapatista movement. Its dramatic appearance in early 1994—on the day that Mexico officially adopted NAFTA—captured the imagination of leftists and globalization critics everywhere. With the charismatic Subcomandante Marcos as its chief spokesperson, the Zapatista Army of National Liberation (its Spanish acronym is EZLN) arose from the long-standing indigenous movement but was also a direct response and reaction to Mexico's adoption of NAFTA. As Marcos observed in an interview, the "dialogue" proposed by the government of Vicente Fox would not include a rethinking of the country's neoliberal economic policy path. As a result, the Zapatistas crafted a dual movement strategy that entailed dialogue with the government and forming an armed force.[7]

The decade also saw powerful international campaigns to cancel the Third World debt, establish fair trade with developing countries, and oppose the spread of genetically modified food by major corporations. These initiatives were framed in the language of development, morality, ethics, and justice, and they brought to international prominence advocacy groups such as Food First, Oxfam, and Greenpeace. Indeed, Greenpeace was one of the founding members of a transnational network that launched a campaign in 1994 calling for an end to the World Bank and the IMF (the "50 Years Is Enough" campaign) on the basis of their failed policies in the developing world. Other groups involved in the network were the Development Group for Alternative Policies (D-Gap), the International Rivers Network, Global Exchange, Friends of the Earth, the Maryknoll Office for Global Concerns, and the United Methodist Women's Division.[8] A number of transnational feminist networks (TFNs), notably Development Alternatives with Women for a New Era (DAWN) and Network Women in Development Europe (WIDE), also were involved.

In the latter part of the 1990s, the anti-debt campaign collected millions of signatures and held successful mass actions involving tens of thousands of people. Called Jubilee 2000, the campaign took its name from the biblical notion of the Jubilee, or periodic forgiveness of debts, attracting many progressive religious persons and ultimately a powerful coalition of left-wing and religious groups to mobilize for the elimination of Third World debt. In 1998, when leaders of the core countries met in Birmingham, England, at the invitation of British prime minister Tony Blair, some seventy thousand activists congregated to form a human chain ("make a chain to break the chains of debt") to tell the G7 summit that it had to act on debt cancellation. The campaign proved influential and effective, and politicians agreed to cancel billions of dollars' worth of debt for forty-two developing countries.[9]

In the United States, activists for labor rights launched campaigns to draw national and international attention to sweatshop conditions in the global commodity chains that were producing cheap goods for retail enterprises like Nike, the Gap, and Walmart. The campaign drew students on college campuses, with protest actions in front of local Walmart stores becoming a staple of college towns. In Europe, Asia, and Canada, concern began to grow over the new rules and regulations attached to the emerging world trade regime. Activists were alarmed by the creeping commercialization—through privatization and patents—of all manner of services, natural resources, and traditional knowledge. Other concerns were the future of biodiversity and the safety of genetically modified foods, which were being promoted by multinational agribusinesses and some governments.

The worldwide opposition to the Multilateral Agreement on Investment (MAI) began after the MAI was being negotiated in secret in 1995 at the Organisation for Economic Co-operation and Development (OECD) in Paris and was tied to what activists later would call the "new global trade agenda" led by the World Trade Organization (WTO). The MAI would have enabled governments to hasten trade agreements while also giving huge advantages to transnational corporations, allowing them the right to sue governments for introducing measures that might limit their present or even future profits.[10] The Bill Clinton administration was in favor of such a fast-track negotiating authority, but activists in the Global South raised the alarm, and in the United States, leading roles in the anti-MAI coalition were played by Ralph Nader, Lori Wallach, and others within the Washington-based advocacy association Public Citizen. After the details of the secret agreement became public across Europe and North America, the bad publicity came to worry politicians in France, whose ruling coalition of socialists, communists, and greens decided to withdraw from the MAI negotiations. This disruption effectively killed the MAI, which was considered a major victory for the emerging GJM.

In the Global South, the SAPs were inaugurating a full transition from the former model of state-directed economic development with large public sectors, high government spending, and protection of domestic industries to a neoliberal model of denationalization, privatization, and liberalization of prices and trade. The shift to free markets, however, was not smooth, as market volatility created regional macroeconomic and financial crises in Latin America and Southeast Asia (see also chapter 2). Concern over global developments and the social implications of the neoliberal economic policy turn set the stage for the now famous Battle of Seattle, which became a watershed event in the GJM's history. In late November 1999, the WTO's Ministerial Conference was scheduled to hold a "millennial" round of world trade negotiations in Seattle, a coastal city in the US state of Washington that was home to the Boeing Corporation and Microsoft. There, some thirty thousand militants blocked the delegates' entry to the conference. The act was followed by a cycle of protests against the WTO, the World Bank, the IMF, and the G8. (The G7 became the G8 with the inclusion of Russia, until Russia's suspension and its own withdrawal in 2017.) Although there was a brief lull in the protests following the attacks of September 11, 2001, the actions against neoliberal capitalism continued and expanded into work against the invasion and occupation of Iraq and US plans for the privatization and sale of Iraqi economic assets and natural resources, including its oil industry. The mobilizations assumed an increasingly coordinated nature, culminating in the creation of a new global activist institution, the World Social Forum (WSF), which first convened in Porto Alegre, Brazil, a stronghold of the left-wing Workers' Party (PT), in 2001.

TRANSNATIONAL OPPORTUNITIES

The preceding narrative of movement activity and emphases—from sporadic, nationally based anti-IMF protests and "food riots" to coordinated trade and antiglobalization demonstrations—helps us understand the links between global economic restructuring and collective action, or how globalization-from-above engendered globalization-from-below. To better explain the rise of the GJM and the WSF, we return to social movement theory and examine the political opportunities that were available to movement activists. In particular, we identify three transnational opportunities that were conducive to the emergence and expansion of the new mobilizing structures: the UN conferences of the 1990s, the spread and increasing use of the internet, and the coming to power of the Workers' Party in Brazil. That these events should have occurred at the same time as neoconservative intellectuals were touting the "end of history" and a world future of liberal democracy and capitalism captures the ironies and paradoxes of history.

The UN held a series of world conferences in the 1990s, beginning with its Conference on Environment and Development (UNCED) in

1991, and activist groups were able to network at the parallel NGO forums (see table 6.1). The UN meetings in particular offered political space for the discussion of proposals such as the Tobin tax, while the many conventions, standards, and norms associated with UN conferences provided moral legitimacy to the movement's call for the globalization of rights. As we saw with the discussion of TFNs (chapter 5), the UN meetings in the 1990s constituted a transnational political opportunity structure conducive to the growth of all manner of NGOs,

Table 6.1. United Nations Conferences of the 1990s: Transnational Opportunities for Mobilizations and Framings

UN Conference	Intergovernmental Conference Themes	NGO/Activist Frames
Conference on Environment and Development (Rio de Janeiro, June 1992)	Environmental protection; poverty and environmental degradation; sustainable development	The "plunder of nature and knowledge"; protecting biodiversity; ending privatization and commercialization of "the commons"; reducing pollution, CO_2 emissions, and waste
World Conference on Human Rights (Vienna, June 1993)	Status of human rights conventions and practices in the world	Human rights; indigenous people's rights; "women's rights are human rights"
International Conference on Population and Development (Cairo, September 1994)	Population growth; family planning	Reproductive health and rights for women
World Summit on Social Development (Copenhagen, March 1995)	Poverty alleviation; employment generation; tackling social exclusion	Promoting welfare; financing development through the Tobin tax; combatting structural adjustment and Third World debt
Fourth World Conference on Women (Beijing, September 1995)	Addressing twelve critical areas of concern regarding women and girls	Political and economic empowerment; gender equality; human rights for women and girls
Conference on Human Settlements (Habitat II; Istanbul, 1996)	Promoting socially and environmentally sustainable human settlements and adequate shelter for all	Empowering the urban poor; transforming cities into safer, healthier, greener places; reversing or preventing privatization of public utilities

activist groups, and transnational advocacy networks. At the UN conferences, activists could lobby delegates and policy makers, disseminate their publications, and interact with each other.

The spread of new information and communications technologies (ICTs) and the end of the Cold War offered opportunities for increased interaction, cross-border meetings, organizing, and mobilizing. Travel across borders once difficult to traverse became easier and cheaper, while the internet made communications faster and more expansive. Personal computers were now cheaper to buy, and e-mail became an increasingly common form of communication. The internet allowed for the formation of numerous websites that became increasingly interactive; they were important sources of information and exchange as well as highly effective mobilizing tools for planning "global days of action." Movement media such as Indymedia captured various protests on film, issuing videos that were shown on campuses and at community meetings in North America, helping recruit more people to the emerging GJM. In the new century, scholars studied the implications of internet-based mobilizations, or "cyberactivism," in terms of not only recruitment but also the creation of a "virtual civil society," a "transnational public sphere," and, indeed, "cyberdemocracy."[11]

Both symbolic and material resources became available to groups critical of the growing power of multinational corporations, international financial institutions, and the neoliberal economic policy agenda. Scholar-activists not only in Europe and North America but also in India, the Philippines, Malaysia, Brazil, and Sub-Saharan Africa mobilized their own resources to form or join antiglobalization networks such as Focus on the Global South, Environnement et Développement du Tiers Monde (ENDA), and the Third World Network, formed by activists from the Philippines, Malaysia, Thailand, Senegal, and India. In some regions, opposition to the presence of the US military was also on the agenda, and Southeast Asian activism helped shut down American military bases in the Philippines in the early 1990s.[12]

A third important opportunity came in the form of the October 2002 Brazilian elections that saw the formation of a left-wing government headed by President Luiz Ignacio "Lula" da Silva of the Workers' Party (PT). The city of Porto Alegre had become the stronghold of the PT, and movement activists were invited there to strategize and plan activities. In 2001, the city played host to the First WSF, planned explicitly as a counter-conference to the World Economic Forum, held in Davos, Switzerland, and attended by world politicians, policy makers, and corporate heads. As Bello observes, "What the Brazilians were proposing was a safe space where people in the movement could come together to affirm their solidarity."[13] The election of Lula da Silva proved especially fortuitous to the GJM's resource mobilization and to the WSF: the PT continued to lend moral and financial support to this important transnational institution.

THE GLOBAL JUSTICE MOVEMENT'S CYCLE OF PROTESTS

Documenting the growth of mobilizations across the globe is a key research strategy of scholars of transnational social movements. Italian scholars Mario Pianta and Raffaele Marchetti, among others, tracked the growth of global civil society events and showed a steady and rapid increase after 1998. These included protests against the US war in Iraq held on February 15, 2003, March 20, 2004, March 19, 2005, and March 18, 2006.[14] US sociologist Bruce Podobnik carried out events analysis to examine the global spread and sustained nature of protests between 1998 and 2004, as well as the number of protesters at each event. He also grouped the protests into five categories of "summit events": WTO ministerials, IMF/World Bank annual meetings, G8 summits, World Economic Forums, and World Social Forums.[15] Faculty and students of world-system theory from the University of California–Riverside distributed surveys at the World Social Forum (WSF) to capture some key characteristics of movement participants.

In short, the next major mobilizations after the Battle of Seattle took place in Bangkok in February 2000, when a thousand activists marched on a UN trade conference calling for radical changes to the global financial system, which they claimed kept a majority of the world in poverty. This event was followed by the UN Millennium Forum of NGOs in New York in May 2000, with 1,350 representatives of more than one thousand NGOs. The cycle of protests continued through most of 2000 and 2001 and included the anticapitalist protests in London on May Day 2000, the antiglobalization protests in Melbourne and Prague in September 2000 and in Montreal the following month, and protests in Zurich in January 2001. When the World Economic Forum met at

Davos in February 2001, protests took place there, too. The cycle of protests continued in Quebec City, Canada, in April 2001, in Goteborg, Sweden, in June during the European Union (EU) summit, and the following month in Genoa, Italy, where the G8 were meeting. The demonstrators in Genoa numbered three hundred thousand. In Genoa, the police turned nasty; one protester was killed, and dozens were hospitalized, while many activists were taken into custody after the police raids. The tragedy of September 11 put a temporary halt to the antiglobalization protests, especially in the United States, but they resumed in early 2002. In February 2002, the World Economic Forum met in New York, and roughly one thousand antiglobalization protesters appeared. That same month in Italy, fully 3 million people came out to protest a new labor law. In March, as the EU summit took place in Spain, around five hundred thousand people held an anticapitalist protest in Barcelona.[16]

The year 2002 saw increasing activism on war and peace issues, which intensified after the decision by the administrations of US president George W. Bush and British prime minister Tony Blair to invade Iraq. Activists in Barcelona gathered in March to denounce US plans to invade Iraq and Israeli actions in Palestine. The antiglobalization movement joined forces with the growing antiwar movement, culminating in a huge demonstration in Florence, Italy, in November 2002, where more than half a million people from all over Europe gathered to protest capitalism and impending war. The start of 2003 saw demonstrations across the globe against the impending invasion of Iraq. On February 15, millions of people around the world joined in huge protests against the imminent war. Antiwar demonstrations in London and Washington, DC, also took place, led in part by activists from the GJM. After the 2003 invasion and occupation of Iraq by US and UK forces, global protests increasingly took on an antiwar frame. When the leaders of the main core countries, the G8, met in Evian, France, in early June 2003, an alternative summit, along with protests, took place in nearby Geneva, Switzerland.[17] In November 2007, activists from the No Bases Initiative in the Czech Republic staged protests against the plans of the Czech government to host the radar for a US antimissile system. Throughout this period, participation at the WSF grew significantly after its first meeting in 2001.

As Pianta and Marchetti aptly observe, "At the turn of the millennium, a structural scale shift occurred in the nature, identities, repertoires of actions, and strategies of global social movements."[18] The scope and scale of transnationalization increased dramatically, with activists sharing information and coordinating actions across borders and continents, made possible—as noted earlier—by the convergence of the UN conferences, the new ICTs, and Brazilian support. By the time OWS emerged, it was possible to launch a Global Day of Action in solidarity with OWS on October 15, 2011. Solidarity rallies took place in nearly every European country, some fifteen countries in Latin America and around eleven in Asia, four countries in the Middle East (Egypt, Israel, Tunisia, and Turkey), and in South Africa, Canada, Australia, and New Zealand. In total, more than nine hundred cities across the world took part in the action day. Leading figures from various movements traveled across borders to forge alliances. Chilean student leader Camila Vallejo was quoted as saying, "This is a world battle that transcends all frontiers."[19] While targets of protesters' anger differed from place to place, they revealed a common grievance against social and economic injustices.[20]

MOBILIZING STRUCTURES

The global justice movement (GJM) is understood to be a "movement of movements," but it is possible to identify mobilizing structures, key institutions, and public intellectuals. Virginia Vargas writes that the World Social Forum (WSF) "harbors a multiplicity of movements whose common denominator is the struggle against the catastrophic consequences of neoliberalism. That struggle is their common ground."[21] The GJM is highly networked, but according to one survey, the overall structure "shows a multicentric network organized around four main movements that serve as bridges that link other movements to one another: peace, global justice, human rights, and environmental."[22] Participants include activists, policy experts, students, intellectuals, journalists, and artists. Campaigns have focused on ending poverty in developing countries, the taxing of capital movements, debt relief or cancellation, fair trade, global human rights, and reform of international intergovernmental organizations.

Italian sociologist Donatella della Porta drew attention to the crucial role played by transnational networks in the making of the GJM, defining a transnational network as "a permanent coordination among different civil society organizations (and sometimes individuals such as experts), located in several countries, based on a shared frame on at least one specific global issue, and developing joint campaigns and social mobilizations against common targets at the national or supranational levels."[23] As we saw in the previous chapter, this would be an apt definition of TFNs and their sustained and coordinated activities. It also describes Global South networks such as the Third World Network, Focus on the Global South, and ENDA. Europe and North America had the Council of Canadians; Association for the Taxation of Financial Transactions and for Citizens' Action (ATTAC), with networks in France, Germany, Sweden, Norway, Italy, and other countries; Christian Aid and Globalize Resistance (United Kingdom); Movimiento de Resistancia Global (Spain); and the Center of Concern and Global Exchange (United States). In North America, the movement also included university-based student groups and left-wing community organizations.[24] (See table 6.2 for issues and types of movements and networks in the GJM.)

For reasons having to do with the more social democratic nature of its political culture, Europe had an especially strong presence in the GJM, involving unions, progressive religious groups, the Old and New Lefts, farmers, environmentalists, and representatives of some political parties (notably greens and communists). A brief diversion on ATTAC is instructive. Founded in France in 1998, l'Association pour la Taxation des Transactions Financière et l'Aide aux Citoyens defines itself as "an international movement working towards social, environmental and democratic alternatives in the globalisation process." According to its website:

> ATTAC is an international organization involved in the alter-globalization movement. We oppose neo-liberal globalization and develop social, ecological, and democratic alternatives so as to guarantee fundamental rights for all. Specifically, we fight for the regulation of financial markets, the closure of tax havens, the introduction of global taxes to finance global public goods, the cancellation of the debt of developing countries, fair trade, and the implementation of limits to free trade and capital flows.[25]

At the height of the GJM at the start of the new century, ATTAC's website received around 4 million hits from 130 countries per month,

Table 6.2. The Global Justice Movement: Issues and Types of Movements and Networks

Type of Movement or Network	Name	Activities and Frames
Anticorporate governance	50 Years Is Enough; ATTAC; Public Citizen; Occupy Wall Street	Democratize global governance; tax financial markets; "We are the 99%!"
Antipoverty	Oxfam; Jubilee South; Make Poverty History	Against neoliberalism; for sustainable development; end Third World debt
Environmental	Greenpeace; Earth First!; Friends of the Earth International; 350.org	Environmental protection and sustainable development
Feminist	DAWN; Marche Mondiale des Femmes; WLUML; WIDE; Mercosur Feminist Articulation	Feminist Dialogues; gender justice; women's human rights
Human Rights	Amnesty International; Fédération International de Droits Humains; Students against Sweatshops; Global Exchange	For civil, political, and socioeconomic rights of citizens and immigrants
Indigenous Rights	Congresso Nacional Indígena de México; Confederación de Nacionalidades Indígenas del Ecuador; Zapatistas	For cultural and land rights
Labor	Australian Council of Trade Unions; Canadian Labour Congress; COSATU; Korean Confederation of Trade Unions	Worker and trade union rights; against job loss and outsourcing; worker solidarity
Peace	Peace Boat; Code Pink; WILPF; Stop the War Coalition; United for Peace and Justice	Against militarism and war; for creating sustainable peace
Religious	Christian Aid; World Council of Churches; Catholic Agency for Overseas Development; American Friends Service Committee	Support for the poor; abolish the debt; critique of neoliberalism
Third Worldist	Focus on the Global South; Third World Network; Third World Forum	Against neoliberalism and imperialism; for deglobalization and local/regional solutions

Note: Some of the organizations and networks served terms on the International Council of the World Social Forum, and many were involved in two or more movements.

roughly thirty-nine thousand documents were downloaded every day, and more than eighty thousand people were subscribed to ATTAC's weekly e-mail newsletter.[26] Public intellectuals associated with ATTAC were prominent in the GJM as a whole as well as in the WSF. As of 2019, ATTAC was present in forty countries across four continents, and its website was available in four languages: English, French, German, and Spanish.[27] Other public intellectuals associated with both the GJM and WSF have included Samir Amin, Arundhati Roy, Vandana Shiva, Naomi Klein, Medea Benjamin, Virginia Vargas, Tariq Ali, Walden Bello, Martin Khor, Immanuel Wallerstein, José Bové, Kevin Danaher, George Monbiot, and Teivo Teivainen.

THE WORLD SOCIAL FORUM

Organized as the popular alternative to the World Economic Forum, which brings together elites to develop global economic policies, the World Social Forum (WSF) was initially supported by the Brazilian Workers' Party (PT) and the Brazilian Sem Terre (landless peasant movement). Intended as a forum for grassroots movements from all over the world, the WSF was most frequently held in Porto Alegre, Brazil, a traditional stronghold of the PT. The first meeting of the WSF in 2001 reportedly drew 5,000 registered participants from 117 countries, but by the 2005 meeting, there were 155,000 registered participants from 135 countries.[28] The first three meetings took place in Porto Alegre, and in 2004, the venue shifted to Mumbai, India. It reverted to Porto Alegre in 2005, but in 2006, a "polycentric" WSF took place at three main venues: Bamako, Mali; Caracas, Venezuela; and Karachi, Pakistan. The meetings in 2007 and 2011 took place in Nairobi, Kenya, and Dakar, Senegal, respectively, in an effort to involve more Africans. In solidarity with the 2011 Arab Spring protests and especially Tunisia's democratic transition, the WSF was held in Tunis in 2013 and again in 2015. It convened in Montreal in 2016 and in Salvador, Brazil, in 2018. In between, there have been numerous regional and local forums. Local forums have been slower to develop within the United States, although they did take place in Boston, Massachusetts; Milwaukee, Wisconsin; Austin, Texas; and Raleigh, North Carolina. In June 2007, the first US social forum took place in Atlanta, Georgia, and the second convened in Detroit, Michigan, in

June 2010, with a large number of attendees. It was not able to repeat its success; a sobering analysis of the reasons why is offered by sociologists Rose Brewer, Wanda Katz-Fishman, and Jerome Scott.[29]

At its heyday, the size and scale of networks within the GJM/WSF was considerable. As Tom Mertes explained, the Brazilian Sem Terre itself counted in its ranks more than a one-third of a million landless families—"and this is not a passive, card-carrying membership but one defined by taking action: risking the wrath of *latifundários* and the state by occupying land. Within this layer there are, again, around twenty thousand activists."[30] Mertes went on to compare the massive size of the landless peasant movement to the far smaller scale of individual North Atlantic networks. On the other hand, there were numerous, and very active, North Atlantic networks—unions, progressive religious groups, feminist groups, and an array of left-wing and social justice activists—with the human, organizational, and financial resources to attend meetings, conferences, and protest events in their own countries and elsewhere.

While the WSF may be described as an institution, with a mission and vision and a structure that includes a coordinating group (the International Council), it has been regarded by its adherents as an "open space" where activists from around the world can meet, exchange ideas, participate in cultural events, and coordinate actions. The events and the opportunity for democratic deliberation have been open to all those opposed to neoliberal globalization and militarism but "exclude groups advocating armed resistance."[31] Research conducted by scholar-activists such as Donatella della Porta, Christopher Chase-Dunn, Boaventura de Sousa Santos, Jackie Smith, Marina Karides, and others shows that participants have been connected with different movements and types of organizations, including local or national groups. Some participants are longtime veterans of transnational organizations and the Left. What has connected them all, in addition to a shared antipathy toward neoliberal globalization, is attachment and commitment to an expanded and inclusive form of democracy that encompasses civil, political, and social rights, enables active participation, and encourages civil dialogue and discussion. For this reason, I have identified the WSF, as well as the GJM past and present, as part of democracy's fourth wave (as seen in table 3.2).

In addition to democratic practices, on display at the social forums have been alternative values, diverse cultures, and an emphasis on supporting local products. At the forums, fair trade, organic farming, environmental protection, and diversity (bio and cultural) were promoted, along with concepts of equality, justice, and human rights. The products of neoliberalism were opposed: genetically modified foods, sweatshop labor, commercialization, and global capitalist structures. Opposition was mounted through publications, meetings, boycotts, marches, and (at times) direct action. Protest marches were often accompanied by a carnivalesque atmosphere and evidence of individual and collective creativity, including massive puppets, whistles, drums, and costumes. The GJM may have expressed hostility toward neoliberal globalization, but it also demonstrated creativity, parody, playfulness, and joy.

Who participated in the WSF? A team from the University of California–Riverside led by Christopher Chase-Dunn launched a research project on the characteristics, political views, and political activity of WSF participants by surveying individuals attending the meetings. It found that most participants came from the country or region in which the WSF convened. Thus, from 2001 to 2005, most participants were from Brazil and the larger Latin American region, followed distantly by participants from Europe and North America. Another survey similarly reported a preponderance of participants from Brazil and elsewhere in Latin America: Santos found that, at the 2003 WSF, fully 86 percent of participants were Brazilians, but this proportion decreased to 80 percent at the 2005 WSF. At the 2005 WSF, the next largest group came from Argentina (13 percent), followed by the United States (9.5 percent). A significant proportion of participants have been youth (fifteen to twenty-four years of age)—42 percent in 2005, most of whom declared themselves to be students. Most WSF participants also have been highly educated, with at least some years of university education. Still, 22 percent had between zero and twelve years of schooling only. This is suggestive of the cross-class as well as cross-cultural nature of WSF participants. At the 2005 WSF in Porto Alegre, the Riverside research team found that more than one-fifth of their respondents were affiliated with a union. While many were members of professional or artists' unions, this finding does suggest an affinity with the labor movement and the possibility for more coordinated action between sectors represented within the GJM.[32] A study by Peter Smith and Elizabeth Smythe showed that WSF attendance increased dramatically after 2001, when twenty thousand individuals attended the First WSF. In 2003, the number was one hundred thousand, and in 2009 it was 115,000. The 2015 WSF in Tunis, held for the second time at the El Manar campus of the University of Tunis, was attended by around seventy thousand participants, representing more than four thousand mass-based movements and organizations from 130 countries.[33]

Within the International Council of the WSF, geographic and organizational representation increased. In 2006, out of 136 members, 33 percent were from Europe; 28 percent from Latin America and the Caribbean; 12.5 percent from North America; 9.6 percent from Africa; 6.6 percent from Asia; and 2.9 percent from the Middle East (that is, four members). The council included representation by a large number of major trade unions, regional associations, feminist groups, progressive religious groups, progressive media, and an array of civil society organizations. Feminist groups with representation on the International Council have included Mercosur Feminist Articulation, DAWN, Forum des Femmes Africaines pour un Monde de l'Économie Solidaire, Fédération Démocratique Internationale des Femmes, International Gender and Trade Network, National Network of Autonomous Women's Groups, Rede Mulher e Habitat (Women and Shelter Network), Women's Global Network for Reproductive Rights, and Marche Mondiale des Femmes/World March of Women.[34] In November 2011, most of the feminist organizations were still on the council. At least five Arab organizations were on the council as well. By reaching out to even small civil society organizations and including them in decision making and leadership, the International Council has been an incubator and transmitter of the democracy frame and practice.

WOMEN, FEMINISM, AND THE WSF

Among the women-led groups active in the World Social Forum (WSF) has been the Mothers and Grandmothers of the Plaza de Mayo. Initiated as a human rights group led by Argentinian women who had lost children to the military junta's "dirty war" of the 1970s, it aimed to gain information on the whereabouts of grandchildren born during their parents' incarceration and to achieve an end to dictatorship and the military's impunity. Famous throughout the world, it became one of the most studied women's movements in Latin America. Elizabeth Borland describes how the group's discourses and activism expanded to encompass neoliberalism, external debt, hunger, unemployment, and corruption.[35] This kind of frame alignment reflects the capacity of social movement organizations to resonate with diverse audiences, and it shows their recognition that new political realities require new repertoires of collective action.

As demonstrated in chapter 5, global feminism and global justice share a common frame of challenging neoliberalism and militarism and calling for democratic decision making at all levels. At the 2002 WSF, the International Gender and Trade Network (IGTN) produced a statement pointing out that "in the current trading system, women have been turned into producers and consumers of traded commodities and are even traded themselves." The document continued:

> In solidarity with our sisters across the globe, we acknowledge that another world will be possible when systems of inequitable power among governments, among institutions, among peoples, and between women and men have been changed to represent the needs of the majority of people and not the market. . . .
>
> IGTN representatives from Africa, Asia, Latin America, the Caribbean and North America here in Porto Alegre are calling for a halt to WTO, FTAA, the Cotonou Agreement and other regional negotiations that are inherently flawed and demand an alternative multilateral trading system that will include the incorporation of a democratic process, corporate accountability, gender and social impact assessments and a commitment to put human rights and social development at the core of all negotiations. Women have much to lose! Today, we women celebrate our power, our partnership and our vision for peace and social justice, and we will continue in the struggle because—another world is possible![36]

Initially the WSF was criticized for the underrepresentation of women and biased selection process for invited guests. Santos cites critiques from the Mothers and Grandmothers of the Plaza de Mayo, Flora Tristan Feminist Centre of Peru, and the Mercosur Feminist Articulation, but DAWN and WIDE also aired criticisms. At the Third WSF (2003), just 26 percent of the plenary speakers were women (ten women and twenty-eight men).[37] This marked an improvement in women's representation, but sadly there were cases of violence against women in the Youth Camp, where thirty-five thousand young people stayed. As a result, a security force was organized, the Brigadas Lilas, and this too became an issue.[38] Hegemonic masculinity seemed to be operating at two levels: that of representation of women and feminist issues and that of the security of young women. The potential crisis was resolved through dialogue and mechanisms to improve both safety and representation. At the Fourth and Fifth WSFs, feminist groups were put in charge of a number of key sessions. Women's attendance at the WSF grew; women have comprised about half of all participants, and prominent spokespersons include Arundhati Roy, Vandana Shiva, Virginia Vargas, Naomi Klein, Susan George, and Medea Benjamin. Scholar-activists noted women's growing presence and influence within La Via Campesina, a transnational peasant movement that has had an active presence in the WSF. The growing influence of feminist and women's groups at the WSF eventually led to an integration of women's rights issues into WSF declarations and objectives. For example, the Declaration of the Social Movements Assembly at both the 2011 WSF in Dakar and the 2012 WSF in Porto Alegre included the following frames:

Fight against transnational corporations
Fight for climate justice and food sovereignty
Fight against violence against women
Fight for peace and against war, colonialism, occupations and militarization of our territories[39]

Preparations for the 2013 WSF in Tunis were coordinated in part by the country's two long-standing feminist organizations, the Femmes Démocrates and the Association des Femmes Tunisiennes pour la Recherche et le Développement (AFTURD). They helped organize feminist workshops with titles such as "Roundtable on Secularism: A Guarantee for Tunis2013"; "No to Political Violence against Women in the Arab World"; "Women in Revolutions in Arab Countries"; "The Struggles of Unionist Women in Industry: How to Build North-South Solidarities"; "No! To Women Genocide / Stop! Stoning"; "World March of Women: Building a Feminist and Anti-Capitalist Movement"; "Rural Women and Development: Issues and Challenges"; "Maghreb Experience in the Struggle against Violence"; "Women's Resistances to Debt in the South and the North"; "A Progressive Approach to Women's Rights."[40]

DEMOCRATIC DELIBERATION AT THE WSF

Boaventura de Sousa Santos is a Portuguese scholar and former member of the WSF Secretariat. In his book on the WSF, he describes the institution as "a set of forums—world, thematic, regional, sub-regional, national, municipal and local—that are organized according to the Charter of Principles." The fourteen-point Charter of Principles, drawn up and adopted in 2001, emphasizes the free flow of ideas and exchanges. It begins with the following statement:

> The World Social Forum is an open meeting place for reflective thinking, democratic debate of ideas, formulation of proposals, free exchange of experiences and interlinking for effective action, by groups and movements of civil society that are opposed to neoliberalism and to domination of the world by capital and any form of imperialism, and are committed to building a planetary society directed towards fruitful relationships among Humankind and between it and the Earth.[41]

Apart from agreeing with the Charter of Principles, what do participants understand about globalization and its alternatives? A survey at the 2003 WSF found that, for participants, globalization meant the following: a concentration of wealth that makes the rich richer and the poor poorer (81 percent); dominion of the world by capital, commanded by the big corporations (75 percent); and a new name for imperialism (68 percent). On the question of "the possibility of societies connecting on the planetary scale," responses were polarized: 47 percent totally or partially agreed, 34 percent totally or partially disagreed, and 20 percent were indifferent. Fully 78 percent disagreed with the statement that globalization meant "more opportunities for all, rich and poor." Participants had strong feelings about the means by which "another possible world" could be achieved: through the strengthening of civil society (94 percent), democratization of governments (78 percent), or democratization of multilateral organizations (63 percent). As for whether direct action with use of force could help achieve another world, fully 84 percent of respondents totally or partially disagreed.[42]

Many participants have regarded the WSF as an important instrument for achieving cohesiveness and more effective strategizing within the GJM. Movements are more likely to be cohesive when participants share political goals and beliefs, use similar strategies, and are culturally or socially alike. However, the diversity within the WSF has generated a number of polarizing debates. A difference of opinion divided those who preferred that the WSF remain broad, inclusive, horizontal, and fluid, primarily a site for democratic dialogue, and those who urged more deliberate action and a more unified, cohesive, and strategically oriented movement. Other sites of disagreement included the issue of socialism or social emancipation (sometimes also framed as reform or revolution); whether to regard the state as enemy or potential ally; whether to focus on local, national, or global struggles; whether to engage in direct action, institutional action, or civil disobedience; and whether to place greater emphasis on the principle of equality or on the principle of respect for difference.[43] Those in favor of more deliberate and strategic action issued the Manifesto of Porto Alegre, which is discussed later in the chapter. In 2007, Ellen Reese, Chase-Dunn, and their team identified five general debates:

- whether to reform existing social structures and global governance institutions or to fundamentally transform them;
- whether to create more economic growth in order to meet workers' demands for employment and goods or to reduce growth in order to protect the environment;
- whether upholding international social and labor standards will protect human rights or simply protect Northern workers' interests at the expense of Southern workers' interests;
- whether to uphold Western values as universal goals, to respect cultural diversity, or to reconstruct universal values in order to acknowledge the experiences of the marginalized; and
- whether to prioritize democratic initiatives at the local, national, or global levels.[44]

This diversity of perspectives was perhaps inevitable, given that WSF participants encompassed indigenous groups, trade unionists, leftists, feminists, and social justice Catholics. Such diversity parallels the different strands of the GJM identified by Pianta and Marchetti: (1) reformists with the aim of humanizing or civilizing globalization, (2) radical critics with a different project for global issues, (3) alternatives who self-organize activities outside the mainstream of the state and market spheres, and (4) resisters of neoliberal globalization who

strive for a return to local and national spheres of action. These categories—which may be extended to describe those who participated in the
Occupy encampments and their numerous outside supporters—may
be seen as dividing lines or as reflections of healthy debate around the
common theme of opposition to neoliberal capitalism, imperialism, and
war. For Kevin Danaher of Global Exchange, "Inside, outside, we're all
on the same side."[45] In other words, opposition to neoliberalism is its
master frame and the basis for its collective action. There is less consensus, however, on how to achieve progressive social change.

FRAMING THE PROBLEM
AND PROPOSING SOLUTIONS

We have seen how the critique of neoliberalism evolved from the earlier critique of SAPs and from the global shift away from Keynesian
economics. Neoliberalism was behind the onerous Third World debt,
the 2007–8 financial crisis, deteriorating standards of living, and competition, conflict, and war. It was imposed by "globalizers" such as the
World Bank, the IMF, multinational corporations, the WTO, Western
banks, and an emerging transnational capitalist class. But whereas
Margaret Thatcher declared, "There is no alternative" to neoliberal globalization, the OWS frame of "We are the 99%!" drew attention to the
gross inequality and unsustainability of neoliberalism's preference for
the top 1 percent, while participants of the social forums could confi-
dently proclaim, "Another world is possible." Such messages, and the
organizations behind them, had tremendous narrative capacity.

What are the key elements of this "other world," or of the "other
globalization" (*altermondialisation*)? First and perhaps foremost is the
concept of international solidarity and identity construction of global
citizenship. While many participants retain national attachments and
remain rooted in local and national struggles, they are also highly
vested in broader planetary and human rights concerns. Thus they
expressed strong opposition to the war in Iraq, sympathy with Palestinians and Lebanese victims of Israeli bombings, and concerns about
environmental degradation and global climate change. "Another world"
would be one without invasions, occupations, or wars; without hunger,
poverty, exploitation, or pollution. A second feature is the GJM's focus
on the world's policy environment, which has been captured by politi-

cal and corporate elites, or what some refer to as an oligarchy (the 1 percent identified by the OWS movement). "Another world" would be one in which the resources captured and monopolized by the 1% would be redistributed far more broadly. Echoing the (re)construction of a robust democracy as was discussed at the end of chapter 2, proposed alternatives may be summarized as follows:

- For economic justice, environmental justice, and gender justice
- For economic, social, and cultural rights, including rights of indigenous peoples and the landless
- For people-oriented sustainable development
- For local and global democracy
- For global solidarities
- For multilateralism and reform of institutions of global governance
- For a new worldwide program of taxation and redistribution[46]

Is another world, then, possible? In a book written in 2004, Susan George offers a set of ten guidelines for how to achieve it. First, activists need to know "what we're talking about." Globalization is not a harmless process of integrating states and markets, she observes, but rather the latest stage of world capitalism and the political framework that it helps to thrive, replete with inequalities. Second, the planet needs to be salvaged from the climate-changing practices of corporations and states. Third, the actors need to be identified: the World Bank and IMF (which George called "the Terrible Twins") and the WTO, which was seeking to commercialize services as well as goods. In stating that the system's shift to the primacy of financial markets portended instability and crisis, George anticipated the 2008 financial crisis. Her fourth guideline is about targeting the right adversaries: public and private actors on national, regional, and international levels. Fifth, Europe should "win the war within the West." George is clearly among those who viewed the EU and the European social model as an alternative to the American model of neoliberal capitalism and war making. But she warns about the neoliberal route that the EU was taking and calls for resistance against it. Sixth, the movement needed to be inclusive and forge alliances. Her book goes on to discuss, in nuts-and-bolts terms, how to attract, recruit, and retain activists and how to forge alliances with progressive faith-based groups, peace groups, and political parties.

Her seventh and eighth guidelines pertain to knowledge and politics. She cites the example of the anti-MAI campaign, noting that the highly technical aspects of the secretive agreement had to be understood by activists and disseminated in ways that could resonate with a broader public. Scholar-activists, or the many academics and "professional knowledge workers" involved in the GJM would play an important role in advancing "critical globalization studies." Ninth, George argues for the abandonment of cherished illusions, warning NGOs against accepting corporate-initiated "dialogues" without setting clear objectives and conditions, and she notes the limits of individual lifestyle and consumption changes when compared with larger, sustained collective action repertoires such as boycotts. Finally, she insists that the movement should continue to practice nonviolence, as it distinguished the GJM from "the violence of the strong, the powerful, and the state," and violent tactics could be used by the media to eclipse other aspects of the movement or campaign.[47]

Another set of proposals for creating an alternative world was the Manifesto of Porto Alegre, produced and signed by a number of prominent scholar-activists at the 2005 WSF. It called for economic measures such as cancelling all debts in the Global South, establishing a tax on financial transactions, removing tax and bank account havens, ensuring that all citizens enjoy social security and pensions, promoting fair trade, ensuring food security and sovereignty, and prohibiting every form of patenting knowledge. Other recommendations promoted "cooperative life" in peace and justice, combating all forms of discrimination and xenophobia, ending the destruction of the environment, and closing down military bases in foreign countries. Recommendations for local and global democracy called for the free flow of communication and information and for reforming and democratizing international organizations. (The 2006 Bamako Appeal made a similar set of proposals.)[48]

Some activists and prominent figures within the GJM prefer "deglobalization" and a focus on local communities. In 2001, the International Forum on Globalization issued a statement titled "Alternatives to Economic Globalization" and proposed eight principles, summarized here: (1) a new democracy and popular sovereignty; (2) subsidiarity, or favoring the local; (3) ecological sustainability; (4) human rights; (5) jobs, livelihood, and employment; (6) food security and food safety; (7) equity; and (8) cultural, biological, economic, and social diversity.[49]

Two of the signatories were the well-known scholar-activists Walden Bello of the Philippines and Vandana Shiva of India. Bello is a prominent advocate of deglobalization, by which he means the removal of all the new rules and regulations of trade, along with the attendant institutions of global governance. The new structures, he argues, constitute an "iron cage" that can only encourage "oligarchic decision-making" and an entrenchment of existing inequalities. The solution, he asserts, lies in "a fluid international system, where there are multiple zones of ambiguity that the less powerful can exploit in order to protect their interests." Vandana Shiva, an eco-socialist-feminist and member of the International Forum on Globalization, argues,

> We want a new millennium based on economic democracy, not economic totalitarianism. The future is possible for humans and other species only if the principles of competition, organized greed, commodification of all life, monocultures and monopolies, and centralized global corporate control of our daily lives enshrined in the WTO are replaced by the principles of protection of people and nature, the obligation of giving and sharing diversity, and the decentralization and self-organization enshrined in our diverse cultures and national constitutions.[50]

In the years before the financial crisis and Great Recession, challenges and alternatives to neoliberal capitalist globalization included the GJM, the World Social Forum (WSF), and the Latin American pink tide. Left-wing governments in Latin America enacted new policies including nationalization of key sectors of the economy, land reform, and major investments in education, literacy, and health care. The governments of Venezuela, Costa Rica, Argentina, Uruguay, and Bolivia announced that they would no longer send students to the School of the Americas (now called the Western Hemisphere Institute for Security Cooperation), the police and military training center in Fort Benning, Georgia, that had become infamous for graduating future torturers. In Brazil, the farmers of the Landless Workers' Movement (MST) formed hundreds of cooperatives to reclaim unused land. In Argentina, the movement of "recovered companies" was led by workers who resuscitated two hundred bankrupt businesses and turned them into democratically run cooperatives. Venezuelan president Hugo Chávez made the cooperatives in his own country a top political priority, giving them first refusal on government contracts and offering them economic incentives to trade with one another. Naomi Klein, a key figure in the GJM, described the Bolivian Alternative for the Americas (ALBA) as "the continent's retort to the Free Trade Area of the Americas, the now-buried corporatist dream of a free-trade zone stretching from Alaska to Tierra del Fuego." In this fair-trade plan, Bolivia would provide gas at stable, discounted prices; Venezuela would offer heavily subsidized oil to poorer countries and share expertise in developing reserves; and Cuba would send thousands of doctors to deliver free health care all over the continent, while training students from other countries at its medical schools. Last but not least, a Bank of the South, planned as a regional alternative to current international financial institutions, would make loans to member countries and promote economic integration among them. Naomi Klein, David Graeber, and others suggested that such initiatives augured a crisis of credibility for the World Bank, IMF, and WTO.[51]

Another developing alternative to the hegemony of neoliberalism and the capitalist crisis has been the solidarity economy, also known as the social economy. It refers to collective practices of sustainable development that are meant to contribute to building a more just and egalitarian world. Such forms of social enterprises—characterized by cooperatives or collectives under worker control or partnerships between groups of private citizens and (progressive) government geared toward the common good and citizen empowerment—were found in Quebec (Canada), Brazil, Spain, Bolivia, and Ecuador, among other countries. Workshops on the solidarity economy were plentiful at the United States Social Forum (USSF) in Detroit in June 2010, drawing interested crowds, especially from among young Americans who knew less about this alternative form of economic production and distribution. The US Solidarity Economy Network (SEN), founded at the Atlanta social forum in 2007, organized many of the workshops, and representatives took part in the International Forum on Social and Solidarity Economy, which convened in Montreal in October 2011. As an alternative to corporate capitalism and state capitalism alike, the solidarity economy could be the pathway to the kind of economic citizenship that has eluded citizens throughout the world.[52]

The proposals and initiatives outlined here could not be implemented or expanded, in part because the three political opportunities described at the start of this chapter could not be sustained. The UN conferences of the 1990s ended. Although the Sustainable Development Goals (2015–30) are considered an improvement over the Millennium Development Goals (2000–2015), the UN's recent reliance on private-sector partnerships and the bullying tactics of some of its wealthier member states are not conducive to supporting an alternative world. Brazil is no longer run by a progressive government and political party. As for the internet, Zeynep Tufekci describes its "power and fragility." It enables networked global movements to grow dramatically and rapidly, and to obtain and exchange information without having to go through state-owned media or self-censored corporate media. But by relying on what we may call inter/net/working, movements lacking prior experience in building formal or informal organizations and other collective capacities are at a disadvantage when faced with the inevitable challenges or the opportunity to respond to what comes next. In particular, leaderless networked movements lack the capacity for decision making or negotiating with officials—as had occurred with the Gezi Park protests in Turkey in 2013.[53] At the same time, terrorist groups like ISIS and white supremacists in the United States have used digital technologies to gather, organize, and amplify their narratives.

As of 2019, many of the protest movements of this century's first decade appear to be in retreat or dispersal. In the United States, the Occupy movement did not make political or economic demands, propose legislation, or even involve itself in the political process (although members did support the Bernie Sanders presidential campaign). New movements and campaigns have appeared, including Black Lives Matter, Moral Mondays, Standing Rock, Time's Up, 350.org, Extinction Rebellion, and Sunrise. From time to time, Black Bloc and anti-fascist groups engage in street fights with far right groups; but as Susan George predicted, it is their violence that receives media attention rather than their overall grievances and objectives. All movements need a certain resilience to survive and to be sustainable. As social-movement scholarship has established, "tactical innovation" is crucial for movements in the long run. What will be the next innovative tactic, not to mention broad strategy, of peace and justice movements in the United States? More to the point, what will be the next steps for the New Global Left?[54]

CONCLUSION

We have seen how the "movement of movements" created a dynamic transnational public sphere replete with discussions, debates, research, and collaborative action. Like the transnational feminist movement, the global justice movement (GJM) has been an integral part of global civil society and a democratic space beyond the spheres of the state and the market.

If contemporary globalization's origins lie in the changes to the world-economy that began in the 1970s and took off in the 1980s, then opposition to neoliberal capitalist globalization can be regarded as almost continuous. Nevertheless, it has been useful to distinguish two cycles of collective action as well as to establish their connections to each other and to globalization. Santos correctly notes that the WSF was born in the Latin American South and represents "an epistemology of the South." Although much of the literature on the GJM has focused on activities in Europe and North America, I have sought to show that its roots lie in the Global South, principally in the anti-IMF and anti-SAP protests of the 1980s. These points confirm the argument that the semiperiphery of the world-system is the locus of much social movement activism. Certainly a connection exists between the activities, institutions, and intellectuals of the contemporary GJM and those involved in earlier cycles of mobilizations and protest in the Third World. Such observations and affirmations, moreover, help globalize social movement theory.

The study of the GJM shows the fallacy of previous hypotheses and claims regarding the evolution of social movements. In the 1980s and 1990s, some scholars were too quick to argue that the "new social movements" privileged identity, lifestyle, and values (in contradistinction to the "old social movement" issues of class, inequality, and power); that single-issue campaigns were more effective than broad politics; and that lobbying was now the preferred strategy. These hypotheses were premature even in the 1980s, when TFNs emerged and addressed major global issues.[55] The Battle of Seattle, the World Social Forum (WSF), the Arab Spring, and OWS showed that a broad-based politics against economic injustice, inequality, and exploitation could feature as prominently in the twenty-first century as it did in centuries past. A weakness of social movement theorizing has been inattention to both political economy and class. The post-structural turn has emphasized agency, identity, and culture to the neglect of the larger socioeconomic environment(s) that shape the causes, dynamics, and consequences of social movements. Understanding why the Latin American pink tide receded, why the Occupy movement dissipated, why the Arab Spring protests did not have robust social-democratic outcomes, and why the GJM seems to have lost momentum calls for a world-system perspective complemented by a Marxist class analysis. That is, the capitalist world-system, led by the hegemon with the cooperation of a transnational capitalist class, constitutes the ultimate structural constraint on the capacity of movements to effect social transformation. At the same time, Marxist approaches generally maintain a robust role for agency, both collectively and individually, as does social movement analysis. The difference, however, is that inscribed in the Marxist approach is a *political* agenda, one that calls for more strategic organizing, mobilization, coordinating, and leadership than has been the case with the GJM or the WSF. It remains to be seen whether the transition can be made from democratic forums and disparate campaigns and movements to more centralized movement organizations with clear political platforms connected to each other.

CHAPTER 7

POPULISMS IN THE WORLD-SYSTEM

History repeats itself, the first time as tragedy, the second time as farce.

—adapted from Karl Marx,
The Eighteenth Brumaire of Louis Napoleon[1]

A bas les priviliégés!

—Gilets Jaunes slogan, 2019

Right-wing populism has become a global phenomenon, inspiring an ever-growing literature. Populism is not new, however, given its long history in Russia and the United States, as well as the deployment of populist rhetoric and policies of various ideological hues in Latin America and Europe. Marx's *Eighteenth Brumaire of Louis Napoleon* was a political and class analysis of what later would be called a populist coup. Late eighteenth- and early twentieth-century populism, often tinged with nativism, emerged from the contradictions of the transition from traditional, agrarian-based society to modern, industrializing society, with its features of displacements, exploitation, and anomie. Many studies of the contemporary wave describe it as a backlash against the contradictions of globalization, including economic difficulties, cultural changes, and democracy deficits. Some studies emphasize social-psychological causal conditions, including emotions like fear, insecurity, anger, cultural grievances, or *ressentiment*. This chapter does not deny the salience of emotions but gives primacy to world-systemic processes; cultural and attitudinal backlashes are the symptoms of the dual crises of neoliberal capitalism and liberal democracy.

Although it is still difficult to classify varieties of right-wing populism (RWP), this chapter attempts to do so, while also elucidating its gendered nature and differences across cases. Much of the commentary on contemporary populism focuses on Europe and the United States; Armin Schafer states that "right-wing parties mobilize 'angry white men' who believe the elites do not care about them and who deeply mistrust establishment parties."[2] However, RWP has been afflicting non-Western democracies as well, encompassing the anti-Arab religious Right in Israel, the Hindu Right in India, the Islamist Justice and Development Party (AKP) in Turkey, and Islamist parties and movements in the Middle East and North Africa (MENA).[3] As noted by the late Samir Amin and argued in chapter 4, Islamist parties are right-wing parties, and many deploy a populist rhetoric about "justice," though without a clear economic program. Some but not all have charismatic or authoritarian leaders, and most are concerned about "alien" Western cultural influences in their societies. Islamist parties won the first free elections in post–Arab Spring Egypt, Morocco, and Tunisia, and in Morocco they swept aside long-standing liberal and socialist parties allied with the feminist movement. RWP parties or leaders have won elections and gained control of government in European countries as well as in Brazil, Turkey, India, the Philippines, Israel, Poland, Hungary, and the United States. These countries include democratic polities in all three economic zones (core, periphery, and semiperiphery) with cultural legacies of Islam, Christianity, Hinduism, Judaism, secularism, and communism. As such, RWP parties and movements mobilize "angry brown men" (and women as well) across world-regions (see table 7.1).

Table 7.1. Right-Wing Populist Parties: Year Established and Election Results

Country	Party	Year Founded	Comments
Australia	One Nation	1997	One Nation wins seats in upper and lower houses in 2016 elections.
Austria	Austrian Freedom Party (OVP)	1956	OVP joins coalition government in 2017 and takes control of three ministries.
Denmark	Danish People's Party (DPP)	1996	DPP comes in second in 2015 parliamentary elections.
Finland	Finns Party	1995	In the 2011 elections, Finns Party wins 39 parliamentary seats.
France	Front National (FN)/Rassemblement National (RN)	1972	In the 2017 elections, FN/RN earns 34% of votes (compared to 66% for Macron's En Marche!), mostly in the north, southwest Bordeaux, south in Marseille, and south of Montpellier.
Germany	Pegida Movement	2014	In the 2017 parliamentary elections, AfD gains nearly 13% of seats, working with Pegida.
	Alternative for Germany (AfD)	2013	
Hungary	Fidesz	1988	Fidesz wins two-thirds majority in parliament in 2014. Jobbik wins 19% of votes in 2018 parliamentary elections.
	Jobbik	2003	
India	BJP	1980	BJP takes 54.4% of votes in 2014 and wins again in 2019.
Israel	Likud	1973	In 2015, Netanyahu's Likud party again wins parliamentary elections and formed coalition government with five religio-nationalist and anti-Arab parties. Likud wins again in 2019.
Italy	League (formerly the Northern League)	1991	Center-right coalition including League and Five Star Movement wins in March 2018 elections; falls apart in 2019.
	Five Star Movement	2009	
Netherlands	Party for Freedom (PVV)	2006	In 2012, PVV wins 10% of the national vote, and Geert Wilders secures fifteen parliamentary seats.
Poland	Law and Justice Party (PiS)	2001	PiS becomes majority party in 2015.
Sweden	Swedish Democrats	1988	Passing the 4% parliamentary threshold in 2010, they take 17.5% of votes in 2018, winning 62 seats.
Turkey	AKP	2001	In November 1, 2015, elections, AKP gains 49.5% of votes and MHP 11.9%; the two parties have close relations. AKP wins 2019 elections and successfully contests key mayoral losses but loses re-run in Istanbul in June.
	MHP	1969	
United Kingdom	UKIP	1993	In 2001, UKIP wins 1.5% of votes but 2.3% in 2005 and 3.2% in 2010. Brexit Party runs for seats in European Parliament, May 2019.
	Brexit Party	2019	
United States	Tea Party Caucus	2010	The Tea Party Caucus was a faction of the Republican Party. Alternative Right was formed by white nationalists but later associated with Steve Bannon and Trump presidency.
	"Alt-Right"	2016	

Sources: Various, including the *Economist* magazine and Wikipedia.

This chapter highlights RWP's economic, political, and cultural roots and dimensions, echoing arguments made in previous chapters. It identifies commonalities and differences across cases, including class and gender dynamics and cultural frames. It ends by drawing attention to left-wing populist movements and parties and possible alternatives, showing how new mobilizing structures and resonant frames could check the growth of right-wing populism.

DEFINITIONS AND DISTINCTIONS

Definitions and analyses of populism vary, and in some accounts, a populist uprising or movement may consist of "the people" in a broad cross-class coalition against elites. Such an approach appears in some analyses of the 1978–79 Iranian revolution against the shah and his regime.[4] Others note the rise of populist movements during periods of political polarization, leading to an "us versus them" approach to grievances and mobilizations.[5] Populist leaders appeal to "the people," "the real people," "the silent majority," and similar terms. In one overview of the literature, populism appears as an ideology, a discursive style, and a political strategy.[6] For Margaret Canovan, populism is "an appeal to the people against both the established structure and the dominant ideas and values of the society." For Archibugi and Cellini, populism expresses the popular will for a more participatory democracy. Ionescu and Gellner discuss cases from Russia and the United States (farmers' movements in the late nineteenth century), Latin America (e.g., Peronism), Eastern Europe, and Africa. Recent populist movements and parties may be left wing (e.g., the Latin American "pink tide" of the first decade of the twenty-first century) or right wing (the anti-immigrant movements and parties in contemporary Europe). Aytac and Öniş compare the left-wing populism of the Kirchners in Argentina with the right-wing populism of Erdoğan in Turkey. Dorraj and Dodson apply the term "neopopulism" in their account of the social and economic policies of Iranian former president Mahmoud Ahmadinejad and the late Venezuelan leader Hugo Chávez. In an account that focuses on Turkey, populism arises as "an alternative movement that may become a remedy to [people's] unfulfilled demands during times of crisis. . . . Populist politicians [then] set up an imaginary unity among the people and present institutional inability as a scapegoat to be blamed for the unmet demands of the people."[7]

In their recent book, Norris and Inglehart define populism as "a rhetorical style of communication claiming that (i) the only legitimate democratic authority flows directly from the people, and (ii) established power-holders are deeply corrupt and self-interested, betraying the public trust." They further argue that "populist narratives can be reduced to these—and only these—twin components."[8] Cas Mudde similarly refers to populism as a thin-centered ideology that is "people-centered" and inveighs "the people against the elites."[9] What this implies is that populism can take different forms and have different meanings—and policy solutions—beyond the "people versus elites" frame, and that there will inevitably be varieties of populism. These will be explored later in the chapter.

Common features of populism identified in the literature include dissatisfaction with the status quo, establishment parties, the media, and elites (in Europe, "Euroscepticism"); a suspicion of external influences and preference for the nation-state; antipathy toward minorities, immigrants, and refugees; and promotion of a presumed common cultural identity and values that are in some cases traditional, conservative, and rooted in religion but, in other cases, may be socially liberal. A propensity for nativism and authoritarianism is another feature.

The use of "the people" in populism ties it to some extent to the deployment of "the people" and "the nation" in nationalist movements and parties. Both populist and nationalist rhetoric tend to be nativist and exclusionary, reflected in what Muis and Immerzeel call the frame of "own people first." Norris and Inglehart point out that the "nativist component of authoritarian populism is sharply at odds with cosmopolitan values, which favor open borders, international engagement, and global cooperation." Authoritarian impulses also feature in many, though not all, populist leadership. Norris and Inglehart emphasize the "hybrid democratic/authoritarian regimes" that have produced right-wing populist leaders—Hungary, Poland, Turkey, the Philippines, and Venezuela. The authors seem to place Venezuela's late president Hugo Chávez as well as Bernie Sanders and Spain's Pablo Iglesias in the same category as right-wing European populists and Donald Trump (see especially the book's introduction). Without distinguishing left-wing and right-wing populism, they associate "authoritarian values" with populism and then highlight three components: conformity and social conservatism, loyalty, and security. Norris and Inglehart add: "Among those holding authoritarian values, cultural change can activate deep feelings of social intolerance and resentment directed toward those blamed for change."[10]

As discussed in this book's earlier chapters, the global shift to the radical Right is not new; the world saw a sharp rightward turn in the 1980s, with the rise and spread of the Religious Right in the United States, the Middle East, Afghanistan, India, and Israel, which had distinctive gender dynamics. The later consolidation of neoliberal capitalist globalization disadvantaged certain categories of the working class and lower middle class while favoring banks, corporations, and certain professionalized elites. The 2008 financial crisis may have been the historic turning point, whereby mainstream political parties and elites were blamed for the crisis and had to face new challengers: right-wing populist movements, parties, and leaders. If the earliest critiques of globalization had come from the Left, now it was the Right joining the chorus.

As a thin-centered ideology, populism is complex and variegated, and some distinctions are in order:

- Populist political parties and governments in power, which typically present a clear agenda, should be distinguished from populist protest movements, whose grievances and frames may be more fluid and ambiguous. Later in this chapter, I discuss the Gilets Jaunes (yellow vests) movement in France, as well as protests that have erupted in the Middle East and North Africa.
- While Islamist populism does place a high premium on loyalty, conformity, and social conservatism (as in Norris and Inglehart's conceptualization), security is less emphasized than is the retention of religio-cultural norms and laws.
- Authoritarian impulses appear strongest in new or transitional democracies, where political institutions are not as fully established and resilient as they may be in the mature democracies. Hence the authoritarian orientation of right-wing leaders such as Turkey's Recep Tayyip Erdoğan, Hungary's Viktor Orbán, India's Narendra Modi, Israel's Benjamin Netanyahu, the Philippines's Rodrigo Duterte, and Brazil's Jair Bolsonaro.
- Gender dynamics are not the same across all right-wing populisms. In some cases, the traditional sexual division of labor,

conservative gender norms, and pro-family values are stressed. In some European cases, right-wing populists promote liberal values and norms, which they claim are threatened by immigrants, migrants, and asylum seekers.

- Populism should not be conflated with either conservatism or fascism.
- Despite some common ground, left-wing and right-wing populisms can and should be differentiated.

This chapter will address all the issues just mentioned, but what follows is an elaboration of the last two points. Populism is not the same as conservatism; nor should it be conflated with fascism. In France, Marion Maréchal is a traditional conservative, attuned to the France of church spires, rural roots, and family values, which taps into a seam of Catholic nationalism. In contrast, her aunt, Marine Le Pen, who leads the RWP Rassemblement National, is more exercised by unfettered capitalism and "savage globalization," in line with her courtship of the working-class vote in France's rustbelt. According to one account, Le Pen's "is a classic anti-elite populism," as her slogan for May 2019 elections to the European Parliament was "Let's give power to the people."[11] In Germany, Annegret Kramp-Karrenbauer succeeded Angela Merkel as leader of the ruling Christian Democratic Union (CDU) party. One account attributes her "social market" philosophy to her experiences in a state (Saarland) ravaged by deindustrialization: she backs minimum wages and does not share the tax-cutting zeal of some in the CDU. She has a Catholic's view of matters like gay marriage and gene-editing, and might be tougher than Merkel on immigration and security, but she is arguably more a conservative than a populist.[12]

RWP, whether of the Western or Islamic varieties, should not be conflated with violent white nationalism or with jihadism; neither Ukrainian neo-fascism nor the various extremist Islamists identified in chapter 4 should be regarded as part of the global RWP panoply.[13] The rhetoric of the AKP's Erdoğan in Turkey, Likud's Netanyahu in Israel, and Narendra Modi of the Bharatiya Janata Party (BJP) in India includes the valorization of religion, nation, and culture. In the United States, President Trump's rhetoric includes attacks against immigrants, asylum seekers, and Iran. Such rhetoric does resonate with extremists, such as Turkey's Grey Wolves, Israel's Kahane supporters, India's

Rashtriya Swayamsevak Sangh (RSS), and white nationalists in the United States. Still, although neo-fascists do lurk on the margins of RWP movements, they are not in the majority or at the center. Finally, despite what certain authors—such as former US secretary of state Madeleine Albright—may declaim, fascism is not at the doorstep of the mature, liberal democracies of Europe and the United States. Runciman (and others) may have underscored the crisis of confidence in the liberal, representative form of democracy that has prevailed since at least the Great Recession, but the analogy to the 1930s is vastly exaggerated, as Runciman himself has argued.[14]

As populism's language frames politics as a battle between the will of ordinary people and corrupt or self-serving elites, populism can exist on the Left or Right. However, although Left and Right populisms may share some common ground, the two have different worldviews and agendas. Left-wing critics have emphasized unemployment, austerity, and income inequalities, and many have disparaged free trade agreements that give away too much to capital and very little to labor, as seen in the opposition to the Trans-Pacific Partnership (TPP) that was promoted by the Obama presidency. Right-wing populist nationalists similarly decry free trade and open borders for having led to precarious employment contracts and low wages, but they are also unsettled by "unbridled" immigration, multicultural policies, refugees, and liberal values, which have generated culture clashes. For most such right-wing populists, the answer lies in a retreat to nationalism, protectionism, secure borders, and traditional values, sometimes rooted in a religious frame. For left-wing populists, the solution lies in solidarity at home and across borders against corporate capitalism and neoliberalized states.

GRIEVANCES: ECONOMIC, POLITICAL, AND CULTURAL

The economic, political, and cultural grievances that underpin the shift to right-wing populism are rooted in structural processes and the actors that have enabled them (refer again to table 2.2). Economic grievances are tied to lowered wages, austerity policies, unemployment or precarious employment, and rising income inequality. Political grievances include perceived loss of local or national sovereignty to elites or external institutions, along with anger over external interventions—military or otherwise—in domestic matters. Cultural grievances emphasize liberal or Western or otherwise "alien" values seemingly imposed on communities or countries, whether through elite decision making or the influx of immigrants and refugees or interstate obligations.

With a focus on Britain, Goodhart argues that populism is an understandable reaction to liberal overreach. In contrast to the "anywheres" with their portable identities and wealth, the "somewheres" have been left behind by global capitalism, economically but mainly in terms of respect for the things they cherish. With the tightening of social housing and competition for social services, many working-class citizens feel that the political elites care more about migrants or transgender persons, a sentiment that Arlie Hochschild found in the US communities she observed. Doerschler and Jackson find that radical right-wing populist parties draw majority group members' votes through their stance against immigration and multiculturalism, their socioeconomic appeals and ideological signals, and by stoking citizens' sense of personal grievance as members of a group that is discriminated against.[15] In a 2011 speech, Marine Le Pen called such citizens "the forgotten ones . . . triple nothings." Personal grievances led to opposition to multiculturalism as a source of crime as well as discrimination against natives.

Right-wing populisms in both the West and the Middle East, along with protests that erupted in 2018–19 in France, Morocco, Iraq, Lebanon, and Chile, reveal the economic, political, and cultural biases and flaws of capitalist development and global governance since the 1970s. In Europe, the United States, and Australia, galvanizing issues are economic deprivation, immigration, refugees, integration, law and order, terrorism, and the perceived loss of culture. Sociologist Arlie Hochschild writes of American voters who feel dispossessed and are angry about how mainstream politicians have ignored them or ridiculed their culture and religiosity. Many also see their economic woes and the end of the "American dream" tied to free trade agreements, immigration, and security concerns.[16]

In the MENA region, Islamist parties were strengthened by regional revulsion at the 2003 invasion of Iraq, the rise in food prices as markets were liberalized and subsidies removed, and the Great Recession, which seemed only to exacerbate the long-standing unemployment problem when European investment declined. As with European RWPs, however, cultural issues loom large, and for Islamists, these include fear of the spread of liberal ideas and the perceived threats to family and religion; Western intrusions and their effects on youth, women, and government policy; and the long-standing Palestinian question (see also chapter 4). In the same way that Germany's Alternative for Deutschland (AfD) voters cited threats to "the German language and culture," many Muslims vote for Islamist parties in order to protect and preserve their culture and religion. And in the same way that many Muslims feel that Islam is under threat, right-wing populists in Poland and Hungary argue that "Christian Europe" is in danger of being overrun by Muslim immigrants and refugees who cannot or will not assimilate.[17]

The political-economy thread across all the cases is the collapse of the post–World War II world order and the failures of neoliberal capitalist globalization, generating conflicts and wars, the financial crisis and Great Recession, economic migrants, and refugees. In turn, these have heightened status anxieties among citizens, along with frustration and anger directed at the established, mainstream parties.

ECONOMIC GRIEVANCES

Over the past forty years, the main beneficiaries of global trade flows, financial flows, and foreign direct investment have been corporate heads, bankers, lawyers, professional managers, and politicians. In Denmark, the leader of the Social Democrats—which is not a right-wing populist party—was quoted as saying that "the price of unregulated globalization, mass immigration, and the free movement of labor is paid for by the lower classes."[18]

Governments have cut back on job creation and social welfare, claiming there is not enough in the public budget, while at the same time taking in economic migrants, refugees, and asylum seekers. These economic realities have stoked the right-wing populist revolt, which in many cases is directed at wealthy elites. Jeremy Harding, who observed the Gilets Jaunes (yellow vest) protesters in France, writes that "ultra-egalitarian sentiments" were widespread among them, and that *"A bas les priviliégés!"* (Down with the privileged!) was one of several anti-wealth slogans he saw. He describes meeting protesters from rural and small-town France who had seen their work contracts and salaries deteriorate. For example, a volunteer medic tending demonstrators injured by police told Harding that she earned around 1,100 euros a month from her job as a care-worker for the elderly. Harding writes: "Quite a few *gilets jaunes* work in the care sector, and as the state opts for outsourced labour, or simply lets recruitment dwindle, they can find themselves on reduced earnings in the private sector, selling their skills via agencies, which take a cut from their wages."[19] He also mentions criticism of the European Union (EU) for the rules on budget deficits laid down in the Stability and Growth Pact, suggesting the presence of some "Frexiteers" among the yellow vest protesters.

Several of the European right-wing parties recruit working-class supporters by criticizing or offering alternatives to economic policies that have affected workers and low-income rural citizens. In the Netherlands, Geert Wilders's Party for Freedom (PVV) lambasted the government over cuts to health care. The right-wing Alternative for Germany exploits anger over unequal pensions in the country's east and west. Marine Le Pen of France's National Front criticized President Emmanuel Macron's plans for flexible labor markets. And in Hungary, Orbán launched public works programs. Such parties in Europe "call for a welfare state for their 'own people' first."[20]

RWP governments decrying excessive competition from rivals in the global economy and trade regime institute protectionism and a certain degree of deglobalization. US president Donald Trump is most associated with such a position, whereby he targets China in particular. But the position has been assumed elsewhere: in December 2018, India passed rules targeting Amazon and Walmart, which dominate commerce there, preventing them from owning inventory; the objective was to protect local and traditional retailers.[21]

POLITICAL GRIEVANCES

In Europe, RWP parties are in revolt against the perceived loss of national sovereignty because of EU rules on economic policy, banking, and migrants.[22] There also is anger toward what is seen to be a tendency toward oligarchy. As John Judis notes, technocratic elites lost much of their credibility in the global financial crisis of 2008. In many Western states, established elites—along with their organized lobbies and institutions—have ignored the democratic will of the majority, and people's frustration with the limits of liberal democracy has been exacerbated by economic difficulties. Those sentiments, and what the *Financial Times* called "fear of migration, economic insecurity, and cultural conservatism," were behind the lengthy debates in Britain over the outcome of the 2016 referendum on EU membership ("Brexit"), in which a majority voted to leave.[23] At this writing, those debates continued.

In Italy, political and economic grievances initially led to the rise of the Five Star Movement (M5), a hard-to-define movement and party that combines elements of both Left and Right populism. The RWP party led by Matteo Salvini, the League, was bolstered by anger over the EU's failed MENA policy, including the destabilization of Libya and Syria that generated the massive refugee crisis of 2015. Grievances against the EU include its economic/fiscal policy and directives on treatment of economic migrants, refugees, and asylum seekers; Salvini stated in 2019 that he would not allow more migrants to come to Italy.[24] Resentment toward EU meddling led the Italian government, in early 2019 and at the insistence of the M5 coalition partner, not to join ten other EU members in recognizing Juan Guaidó, opposition leader in Venezuela, as the legitimate president of Venezuela. Opposition to EU directives is shared with France's Rassemblement National, led by Marine Le Pen.

As Judis has noted, Left and Right populists alike are suspicious of traditional institutions, on the grounds that they have been either corrupted by elites or left behind by technological change. As discussed in chapter 3, this suggests not only that neoliberal globalization has produced a critical mass of disaffected voters and politicians but that representative democracy itself is in crisis, inasmuch as it has been unwilling or unable to tackle the policies that have given rise to the problems and the backlash.

CULTURAL GRIEVANCES

Cultural grievances loom large in right-wing populism. In Europe, mainstream politicians in 2010 declared that "multiculturalism had utterly failed" because so many immigrant communities had been unable or unwilling to integrate, and because of homegrown jihadism.[25] The social exclusion or self-segregation or "parallel societies" of certain Muslim communities had led right-wing politicians in the Netherlands, a country that had long had a policy of sexual rights and the equality of same-sex partnerships, to decry the lack of tolerance among Muslim populations. The late Dutch politician Pim Fortuyn was an early critic of multiculturalism and what he called the intolerance of Muslim immigrants; the same may be said of the Party for Freedom (PVV), led by Geert Wilders. In France, a spate of anti-Semitic actions by African and Arab Muslim men, and the murderous 2015 attack on the satirical newspaper *Charlie Hebdo*, not only alarmed liberal and left-wing French citizens but also was appropriated by the right-wing National Front party as another sign of Muslim rejection of French values. The Nordic right-wing populist parties, too, focused on the rising tide of refugees and immigrants, their capacity for integration, and the fiscal effects on the welfare state.[26] Danish members of Parliament (MPs) passed a law in June 2018 banning the burka and imposing a penalty of 10,000 kroner ($1,600) for repeat offenders. In a type of frame alignment to appeal to more voters, the Danish Social Democrats, led by Mette Frederiksen (a former trade union official who became prime minister in June 2019), adopted an antiglobalization and anti-immigrant stance. Many Danes complain that some Muslims "do not respect the Danish judicial system," that some Muslim women refused to work for religious reasons, and that Muslim girls were subject to "massive social control"—issues also raised by Ms. Frederiksen. (Prime Minister Frederiksen is credited with calling US president Trump's offer to buy Greenland "absurd" in August 2019.)[27]

The MENA counterpart to this combustible mix was anger over continued US military domination of the region, the presence of Western troops in Afghanistan, the invasion and occupation of Iraq, and the nonresolution of the Palestinian question. There also was frustration with rulers allied with the United States who engaged in cronyism and could not improve the people's living conditions, as well as concerns over Western cultural intrusion. Muslim citizens of Denmark were angry over Danish troops' involvement in the NATO-led invasion of Afghanistan in 2001; the antagonism grew with the invasion of Iraq in 2003, and in 2005, it was fueled by reaction to published cartoons of Prophet Muhammad. With the destabilization of Syria, roughly 150 Danish citizens went to fight in Syria with ISIS. This precipitated a rightward turn on Islam and immigration even within Denmark's left-wing Social Democrat party, as noted earlier.

In the West, RWP antipathy is directed not only at Muslims but also at "identity politics" and diversity policies, which have alienated many voters who self-identify as conservative or religious. In Canada, some voters from the Conservative Party defected to the new People's Party of Canada, created in September 2018 by Maxime Bernier, who opposed what he called Prime Minister Trudeau's "cult of diversity" and "extreme multiculturalism." In traditionally social-democratic Quebec, the sweeping victory of the right-leaning Coalition Avenir Québec in the provincial elections of October 2018 suggested that "there is plenty of support for a harder line on immigration. The coalition wants a 20% decrease in immigrants to the French-speaking province and the expulsion of immigrants who fail new language and value tests."[28]

GENDER DYNAMICS

Right-wing populist movements are gendered, in that their leaders and founders are mostly men and their discourses and tactics often evince a problematical form of hypermasculinity. Typically, their notions of femininity and of women and the family are traditional and would strike feminists as dangerous, but such notions do resonate with a certain section of the female population. Indeed, conservative and right-wing parties and movements have not been devoid of women supporters. A brief look at the feminist scholarship of the 1980s and 1990s on nationalism elucidates the centrality of women, gender, and the female body to the implementation of nationalist goals of modernity or secularism or anticolonialism.[29] Such studies showed that the centrality of "woman" to the nation had been alternately positive and negative for women's participation and rights, and for their full citizenship.[30] Jayawardena described the compatibility of and synergy between nationalist movements and feminist aspirations in the nineteenth and early twentieth centuries, with a focus on Asia. Indeed, the term "the woman question" was coined in reference to struggles for women's rights in the context of socialist, independence, and nationalist movements in the first half of the twentieth century. Subsequently, I argued that tensions between feminism and nationalism arose later in the twentieth century and into the new millennium, the result of the new religio-nationalist movements that saw the nation as "the family writ large" and women's roles as reproducers and socializers of "ideal" citizens.[31] This was evident in the rise of fundamentalist Islamist movements and parties in MENA, which associated "woman" with family and morality, sought to strengthen or introduce sharia laws and norms, and regarded feminism and socialism as alien ideologies.[32] A series of studies on Christian, Hindu, and Jewish fundamentalisms—by Rebecca Klatch, Sucheta Mazumdar, Debra Kaufman, and Madeleine Tress—similarly drew attention to social conservatism, right-wing politics, or ethnic exclusivism in the United States, Israel, and India, along with the apparent paradox of female support.[33] In her study of the US-supported 1973 military coup in Chile, Margaret Power reveals its origins in the 5,000-strong women's march in Santiago in December 1971, which produced an anti-Allende organization called "Feminine Power." Nicola Pratt's analysis of the Cairo conferences of 2002–8 (a series of meetings growing out of opposition to the US war in Iraq) shows that members of Egypt's Muslim Brotherhood at one session she attended railed against a form of cultural globalization—whereby the West exported "feminist" concerns such as domestic violence, gay rights, and the eradication of female genital mutilation—rather than the impacts of neoliberal economic policies on Egypt's working people. The consensus at that session, she writes, was that Western moral and cultural values were corrupting "Egyptian womanhood."[34] This is the counterpart to the European right-wing claim that Muslim immigrants are a threat to liberal or Christian values or to women's freedoms.

The studies just mentioned are relevant to the present discussion of RWP and its gender dynamics because they reveal a history of women's attraction to and involvement in right-wing politics and some underlying reasons: economic displacement or anxieties, disillusionment with the cultural politics of secularism and liberal feminism, support for and comfort with the traditional sexual division of labor, and effective political manipulation. The studies are important for situating both the deep roots of right-wing populism across the world and its complicated gender dynamics. For some deeply conservative women, political power rightly lies with men. At the same time, an interesting aspect of the 1990s studies of women and fundamentalisms was the recognition of complexity, paradoxes, and contradictions, points expressly made in Kaufman's study of Orthodox Jewish women, Klatch's and Stacey's discussions of right-wing women's political activism, and Manning's discussion of Catholic, Protestant, and Jewish women.[35] This, too, aligns with the apparent contradiction of a typical contemporary Muslim Brotherhood party casting women as wives and mothers and men as breadwinners and fighters but also urging female supporters to vote and to run for parliamentary seats. For both Islamist and European right-wing populist parties, the presence of women parliamentarians is an important recruiting tool that expands the parties' constituencies.

More recently, two feminist political scientists have observed that women "are not a homogenous but a heterogeneous group," thus necessitating presentation of "complementary, competing and conflicting views on what women, and their interests and needs, are."[36] Women who support right-wing populist or nationalist movements and parties—such as the 53 percent of white American women voters who cast their ballots for Trump in the 2016 presidential election or the 54 percent of Turkish women who voted for Erdoğan in 2011—may subscribe to the narratives of culture or religion in danger, but they also may be homemakers who find security in the traditional sexual division of labor and do not support gender equality.[37]

European research finds a gender gap in votes and supporters, but women figure prominently as voters, supporters, members, activists—and sometimes leaders. One European variety has women leaders who can connect with and recruit conservative women voters; this has been called "men's parties with women leaders."[38] Women are vocal and visible in certain Islamist parties as well, taking seats in parliament and resisting aspects of feminist agendas in their countries.[39] There is as yet no Islamist party with a woman leader, although an-Nahda's Meherriz Laabidi in Tunisia plays a very prominent role, and the new mayor of Tunis, elected in 2018, is a woman who ran as an independent but is associated with an-Nahda. RWP parties in Poland, Hungary, Turkey, Morocco, and India promote conservative gender roles, but this is not the case in the French, Dutch, or the Nordic parties. Instead, that European variety invokes gender equality and sexual rights to demarcate its "own cultural values" from those of immigrants and refugees. A recurring theme is that Muslim refugees and immigrants threaten the open, tolerant, and emancipatory values of such societies. The degree of patriarchal entrenchment varies, therefore, across RWP movements, parties, and governments.

Melissa Deckman, a political scientist at Washington College in Chestertown, Maryland, who has written about women in the Tea Party, surveyed likely female voters in the midterms in June 2018 and found that Democratic women ranked gender equality among their top political priorities, whereas Republican women ranked it among the lowest, far behind terrorism, immigration, and education.[40] In the wake of Donald Trump's election to the US presidency, Hillary Clinton's loss of many women voters "showed that issues of culture and class mattered more to many American women than their gender," as fully 62 percent of white women without a college degree voted for Trump. Such women might identify with white ethno-nationalism and some could be part of the American Alt-Right. The right-wing populists of the Republican Party had been signaling to their adherents "that rejecting feminist positions is part of what it means to be a Republican." And yet, the existence of self-defined empowered right-wing women cannot be denied. A segment of the right-wing female population may consider it a form of feminist self-empowerment to carry guns. Another segment may push for seats in Congress in order to defend a conservative agenda or support "family values," including opposition to abortion on demand.[41]

On the part of liberal and left-wing women, the response to the Trump victory was a series of powerful women's marches in January 2017. Planning for the Women's March originated in the United States but quickly spread, so that the numerous US cities with demonstrations by hundreds of thousands of women were replicated around the world. The frames of the global march, as inscribed in signs and banners, seemed to target Donald Trump's cultural position as a stand-in for the rise of a patriarchal and xenophobic global Right while also calling for a defense and expansion of feminist goals.[42]

Beyond the observations about the varied gender dynamics of right-wing populism, it is worth noting the important role that women can play in launching populist protest movements. France's Gilets Jaunes movement began with online complaints by two Frenchwomen. As Jeremy Harding explains, in summer 2018, "Priscilla Ludosky, a young entrepreneur with a small-scale cosmetics business, launched a petition on change.org calling for a reduction in petrol prices. Ludosky works in a built-up, peri-urban landscape (beyond the capital and the banlieues), where car travel is a necessity." Ironically, Harding adds, she is a "perfect fit for [French president] Macron's vision of a new, striving France," as she is a "thirty-something black Frenchwoman." In October 2018, Jacline Mouraud, "a talkative, eccentric figure from Brittany

. . . posted a video on Facebook in which she denounced the tax burden on motorists, along with speeding fines, as systematic pillage. . . . [T]he number of visits to Mouraud's Facebook page reached six million and signatures on Ludosky's petition passed the one million mark."[43] Before long, scores of women and men in Paris and across France took to the streets, and continued their demonstrations against Macron's neoliberal reforms well into 2019.

In their overview of gender and European RWP, Krizsán and Siim state that gender and family issues are front and center in the East, Central, and Southern European countries, as well as in Germany.[44] European populists rail against immigrant communities where women wear burkas or eschew employment, or where families do not allow their daughters to attend swimming classes.[45] In the same way that Islamist parties throughout the Muslim world have drawn on anxieties about liberal Western values and a perceived threat to Islam and Muslims by Western policies as well as wars and occupations, the right-wing populist-nationalist parties and movements of Europe and the United States bank on their members' and supporters' anxieties about perceived threats to Christian, European, or American values and to security by foreigners, mainly Muslims. Among them, one strand of right-wing women finds solace in religion, family, and the nation and finds feminism and foreigners inimical to their sense of identity. Hence the female votes for the AKP, Law and Justice Party (PiS), Fidesz, and Trump's Republican Party.

In the May 2019 elections for the European Parliament, populist parties secured almost one in three votes. Who votes for RWP parties? Inglehart and Norris created a model to compare the predictive power of the economic insecurity and cultural backlash explanations of the rise of populism. Their study looked at preferences of all voters in 31 European countries (EU member states plus Norway, Switzerland, and Turkey) and support for 268 parties. Among other things, they found that religiosity and age increase the likelihood of support for right-wing populist parties; this was true in Turkey and East-Central Europe. Another study, however, found the opposite, arguing that a longer tradition of liberal democracy could help explain that religiosity and age actually *decrease* the likelihood of support for right-wing populism.[46] Class, occupation, and geographic location seem to matter. Gregor Gysi, a founder of the left-wing Die Linke party, which has been kept out of German coalitions, explained the surge of RWP in the east as former East Germans viewing themselves as the "losers of history" and then "like second-class Germans" after reunification.[47] While in the German federal election in September 2017 the right-populist AfD took 12.6 percent of the vote, it was 19 percent among workers (and 15 percent among union members). In eastern Germany, AfD won 22 percent of the vote, largely from among blue-collar and unemployed voters.[48] Similarly, the United States was successful in gaining above-average support from working-class voters, if one uses education as a proxy. According to exit polls at the presidential election of November 2016, Trump was voted in by 52 percent of Americans without a college degree (Clinton, 44 percent) but an overwhelming 67 percent of *whites* without a college degree (Clinton, 28 percent).[49]

A study of who voted for Brexit in 2016 showed how Britain was divided along economic, educational, and social lines. Goodwin and Heath found that the poorest households, with incomes of less than £20,000 per year, were much more likely than the wealthiest households to support leaving the EU, as were the unemployed, people in low-skilled and manual occupations, people who felt that their financial situation had worsened, and those with no qualifications. Groups vulnerable to poverty were more likely to support Brexit. The strongest driver, Goodwin and Heath found, was educational inequality. "Groups in Britain who have been 'left behind' by rapid economic change and feel cut adrift from the mainstream consensus were the most likely to support Brexit."[50] Material and cultural interests alike galvanized such voters, who resonated with the RWP parties and leaders calling for a welfare state for their "own people" first.

A study organized by the *Guardian*, a British newspaper, found outcomes of populist governance that surprised the research team, composed of academics as well as journalists: populist parties reduced poverty and income inequality. The *Guardian*'s "Team Populism" created a database of populist discourses and policies and found that populists across the political spectrum tended to narrow the gap between rich and poor, describing the correlation between populism and greater equality as "a fairly large effect." The impact on inequality appeared largely to have been driven by left-wing Latin American populist presidents, such as Bolivia's Evo Morales, Ecuador's former president Rafael Correa, and the late Venezuelan leader Hugo Chávez. "However the statistical analysis controlled for ideological differences between leaders, and also holds, although to a lesser extent, for centrist and right-wing populists."[51] There were also several examples of non-populist leaders who presided over major reductions in inequality, such as Jens Stoltenberg, who was twice prime minister of Norway, and Luiz Inácio Lula da Silva, Brazil's president between 2003 and 2010. One of the academic team members offered tentative explanations for the reduction in inequality; one was that the China-fueled commodity boom had increased living standards in the mid-2000s, during which a number of populists happened to come to power in oil- and gas-producing countries with previously high levels of inequality. Another was that populist governments funneled money into state entities and state companies, providing fiscal stimulus and boosting wages through minimum wages, formalization of the labor force, or limits on income generation of the very wealthy. The study found that populist governments were associated with higher rates of voter turnout, but also with a decline in the quality of elections and press freedom, as well as a concentration of power in the hands of the executive, often at the expense of constitutional checks and balances.

Could Islamist parties in power produce similar outcomes? As we saw in the chapter on Islamism, Islamist political parties include social justice and equity frames in their platforms. In Egypt, the Muslim Brotherhood–led government of Mohamed Morsi declared its intention to institute social justice policies but, in its short time in office, managed only to raise non-Islamist citizen ire by strengthening the power of the executive. Ibrahim Saif and Muhammad Abu Rumman explain that, for the most part, Islamist political parties

> do not call for nationalization of industries or renationalization of privatized state-owned enterprises and demonstrate respect for private property rights. All of the parties welcome partnerships with the private sector to implement their proposed projects, particularly when it comes to public utilities and infrastructure. They consistently agree on the need to combat corruption, strengthen the foundations of good governance, eliminate financial and economic waste, and enact socially just policies. And all demonstrate a commitment to international economic agreements, with Morocco and Tunisia in particular focusing on relations with Europe.[52]

Islamists have been in power in Tunisia and Morocco, but research has yet to focus on poverty and inequality outcomes. In Iran, the former populist president Mahmoud Ahmadinejad instituted a cash transfer program that helped reduce poverty; some policies of Turkey's AKP have reduced poverty as well. In both countries, however, income inequality has increased.

VARIETIES OF POPULISM: COUNTRY VIGNETTES

Right-wing populism reflects the contradictions of neoliberal capitalist globalization and the crisis of liberal democracy, but frames may differ across cases of RWP parties and governments. Some political parties take umbrage with the excesses of globalization, but this is not necessarily the case in Turkey, Israel, or India, where frustration with neoliberalism plays less of a role than does a certain religio-nationalism that resonates with citizens disaffected by established secular parties. European RWP leaders may call for the defense of "their own" tolerant and liberal cultural values, but in the Philippines and Brazil, Duterte and Bolsonaro, respectively, call for an iron fist against crime and corruption and the defense of family values. What follows are some examples of RWP, starting with parties in power in Turkey, Hungary, Poland, Israel, and the United States. Later the chapter offers vignettes of populist protests. Finally, the chapter examines the rise of *left-wing* populist movements and political parties, and it contrasts their discourses and policy agendas with those on the right.

RIGHT-WING POPULISM IN TURKEY

Neoliberalism in Turkey began after 1983, when the military rulers left the political arena to civilians and Turgut Özal became first prime minister and, in 1989, president. Özal introduced capital account liberalization, an export-oriented growth strategy, and preferential interest rates for small investors. With the gradual erosion of social rights and public services and aggravation of unemployment and inequality, Islam became the refuge of neoliberalism's losers, and Refah (Welfare Party) gained momentum after the two big 1990s economic crises. In the March 1994 municipal elections, Refah captured the mayorships of Istanbul and Ankara, with Recep Tayyip Erdoğan becoming Istanbul's mayor. Political Islam became the main power in the 1990s because it created "specific and concrete anti-poverty projects designed to improve the material conditions of the disadvantaged."[53] The growing popularity of Refah and its leader, Necmettin Erbakan, was unsettling to the military establishment, and it closed down the party in 2001, but Refah had already made its mark on Turkish society and politics. It was succeeded by a new Islamic party, Justice and Development (AKP), under Erdoğan's leadership, and it has been ruling Turkey ever since.

The 1999 earthquake and 2001 economic crisis boosted the AKP's electoral chances, as voters expressed disillusionment with the establishment parties; they favored the pro-market and pro-EU AKP as well as the party's consultative meetings with a wide variety of civil society organizations. Such outreach "pleased public opinion as a first step in the direction of a more inclusive and open government"; the AKP rose because it "made a populist call for economic equality."[54] At this time, the AKP appeared to support ascension to the EU, dialogue with Kurdish leaders, and women's rights. In 2002 and 2004, and with the help of the women's organizations, the Penal Law and the Civil Law were amended to abolish men's privileged position as the head of the household, substitute the legal category "spouses" for "husband-wife," and allow the equal division of property acquired during marriage upon divorce, unless the couple chose a different marital property regime.[55]

Gradually, the party "became 'Islamic authoritarian' by utilizing populist and pragmatic policies to maintain and strengthen its vote base."[56] Credit was made even more available for small- and medium-sized enterprises and export-oriented firms, and some subsidies continued.[57] Revising the university entrance exam was aimed "to clear the way for graduates of religious 'preacher schools' (*imam hatip okulları*) to enter any university department."[58] The 2007 presidential election of Abdullah Gül opened a debate about removing the headscarf ban (his wife wore a headscarf). A constitutional amendment permitted a second term for a president. The AKP then began prosecuting members of the Kemalist and secular elites, including "retired generals, judges, prosecutors, journalists, professors, party and NGO leaders."[59] Police cracked down on the Gezi Park protesters, who in 2013 tried to save one of the few parks left in central Istanbul. Nationalist groups took an anti-EU stance.

The attempted military coup in July 2016 was "a gift"—Erdoğan's own words—as it enabled the president to deepen his power and accelerate the merger of Islamic piety and Turkish nationalism through school curricular reforms. The Diyanet, a body charged with monitoring political Islam, began to promote it, with one Turkish mufti quoted as saying that the Diyanet now had "a more Islamist, more Arab worldview."[60] The AKP backed away from women's issues in parallel with its fading interest in meeting EU standards,[61] shifting its political discourse from gender equality to celebrating women's complementary roles as mothers and wives, calling on women to have at least three children. Feminist economist Ipek Ilkkaracan argues that Erdoğan's AKP has instituted a "highly familialized care regime"; coupled with continued low female labor force participation and a masculinized and highly gender-segregated labor market regime, this leaves the male breadwinner family norm unchallenged. As Adem Elveren has noted, among the most prominent supporters of the president and the AKP are housewives and poor women. Ayşe Ayata and Fatma Tütüncü show that, despite increased roles for women in the political sphere, the AKP has not advocated for more gender-friendly policies.[62]

For years, the Turkish government's approach to refugees was distinctly different from that of most European countries. It hosted some 3 million refugees from Syria, in part with funds from the EU, but in 2019, resentment began to show "amid deepening economic malaise, frustration with the government's policy and resentment toward the refugees." According to one account, during the 2019 parliamentary elections, at least one of the candidates pledged to send the Syrians back home, and President Erdoğan suggested resettling Syrians in a border zone in northern Syria. A 2018 survey found that "86% of all Turks wanted the government to send the refugees back to Syria." In the city of Mersin, where Syrians make up more than one-tenth of the population, locals complained that they undercut wages, drove up rents, and avoided paying taxes.[63] As such, Turkish anti-immigrant and anti-refugee sentiment has converged with that of European RWP.

POLAND AND HUNGARY: "WELFARE FOR OWN PEOPLE FIRST"

Leaders in both Poland and Hungary have defied EU directives on the settlement of refugees and illegal migrants, and they have emphasized

Christian moral and religious values. How did it come to this? Developments in both countries reflect broader trends across the capitalist world-system over the past three decades rooted in neoliberalism and expressed in ethno-nationalism.[64]

The collapse of communism in 1990 paved the way for a market economy and ascension to the EU. In the new century, however, the Great Recession and disagreements with the EU over its refugee policy helped bolster the credentials and electability of nationalist parties. Populist leaders in Poland and Hungary boasted that they favored the "regular guy" over the elites and defied the "neocolonial attitudes" toward eastern Europe from Brussels.[65] In Szabo's account of developments in Hungary, Fidesz (the Hungarian Civic Union) had emerged in the 1980s as "a radical, anticommunist student movement" and then became "the leading and unifying force of the center right"; its main enemy was the reformed Socialist Party. After gaining and losing in many elections, Fidesz understood the importance of grassroots mobilization and organized a Hungarian Citizens' Alliance, in which "national and religious symbols play a role, establishing hegemony beyond the sphere of politics and society with cultural and social community building." Fidesz won the 2010 election under its leader, Viktor Orbán, and sought to balance populist mobilization with crisis management and EU membership requirements. The political culture of Fidesz thereafter included "fighting communist crime, emancipating the country from the past, being radical populists, and searching for an alternative third way for fiscal policy."[66] Fidesz and its supporters attempted to restrict women's reproductive rights by promoting the rights of the fetus, but that effort failed. Reflecting the government's ideology as well as the country's low birthrate and aging population, a series of financial incentives to encourage larger families was announced. As Wilkin argues, the postcommunist Hungarian state adopted neoliberalism as a criterion for joining the EU, but austerities and other aspects of the new policy framework angered many ordinary citizens, who preferred more rather than less social spending.[67]

Turning to Poland, in the new century, prominent political parties include the League of Polish Families (LPR), Self-Defense, and the Law and Justice Party (PiS). For the Self-Defense Party, "the most important issue is the economic fate of ordinary people," while PiS emphasizes "the need to nourish a national community based on shared values and traditions, with the principles of social solidarity as the basis for public policy."[68] As with Hungary, how this came about goes back to the steady march toward neoliberalism in Poland, with its concomitant emphasis on individualism, individual rights, and competition. This shift paradoxically alienated the very population base of workers and labor unions that had helped win Poland's democratic transition, engendering feelings of betrayal and suspicion toward liberal policies by working-class Poles. The government's globalized, liberal economic policies and their social repercussions became grievances for struggling Polish workers to reframe and organize their national identity. According to one account, "[m]any in Poland's small towns and villages felt that the previous government, led by the liberal Civic Platform party, looked down on them. Over the past two decades, the economy grew rapidly but inequality also rose, with poverty more common in rural areas. This is partly why Poles voted for PiS."[69]

As early as 2007, PiS adopted changes in the tax law to double the amount of tax exemption allowed for each child in the family.[70] In 2016, the new PiS government launched the "Family 500Plus" program, which pays a monthly stipend of 500 zlotys ($148) per child, starting with the second. Indigent parents qualify for their first child, which has cut the rate of extreme child poverty from nearly 12 percent to just 2.8 percent, according to a World Bank study. Child welfare programs are common in other European countries, but it is notable that in Poland the right-wing populist party "has seized the mantle of the party of welfare." The 500Plus program "has been a political boon for PiS, which continues to lead in opinion polls, ahead of the centrist opposition." In February 2019, PiS announced expansion of the popular program, equivalent to $132 per month after the first child.[71]

The pro-natalist policy has been driven by Poland's very low fertility rate, so that women could be encouraged to have more children. (At 1.4 in 2019, Poland's Total Fertility Rate is lower than the EU's 1.6.) In Poland as in Hungary, women's issues have been gradually replaced by family issues, while institutions responsible for gender equality are being replaced by ones dealing with family and demography.[72] Poland's government tried in 2016 to ban the already heavily restrictive abortion law, but the bill generated demonstrations throughout the country, notably the huge "Black Monday" march of October 2016, leading to its defeat. Polish feminists feared the possible repeal of advances in women's rights made since Poland's ascension to the EU.[73]

RELIGIOUS RIGHT-WING POPULISM IN ISRAEL

Israel's adoption of neoliberalism steadily increased income inequality during the 1990s and into the new century, and this helped precipitate Israel's version of Occupy Wall Street in Tel Aviv in summer 2011. (As of 2018, among MENA countries, Israel's Gini index of 41.1—the same as that of the United States—was second only to Turkey's 41.9. Other MENA countries with high income inequality were Morocco at 40 and Iran at 38.8.)[74] The year 2011 saw "Occupy Rothschild," named for the Tel Aviv boulevard where citizens camped out to protest rising prices and unaffordable housing. But after Prime Minister Netanyahu promised new construction, the protest movement dissipated.

What continued was the consolidation of the extreme Right under Netanyahu and virulent anti-Arabism within Israel's political elites, who stoked anti-Palestinian sentiments after each militant attack. As Micheline Ishay explains, the Israeli government discursively constructed a "Jewish state" identity along with restoration of nationalist pride and yearning for both security and religious purity. Following elections in 2015, Likud formed a coalition with a number of small extremist political parties, which include Jewish Home, United Torah Judaism, Shas, and Kulanu. Ishay writes that such parties knew how to galvanize the frustrations of the marginalized, and they channeled popular insecurities against Palestinians and others. They "call on Israelis to follow higher Jewish religious (Halakic) laws and to secure the de facto expansion of the Jewish community to the post-1967 borders." Anti-Arab racism is widespread in Israel; Ishay writes of how "ultra-orthodox fans of the Beitar Jerusalem football club, calling themselves La Familia, sing racist chants and are frequently involved in gratuitous violence against Arabs."[75] In recent years, there have been many efforts to expel African refugees and migrant workers. In fall 2018, the marriage of a Jewish Israeli actor to an Arab Israeli TV anchor and journalist sparked a public and online furor over intermarriage and assimilation. The language echoed that of xenophobes and racists in Europe.[76] As with "Christian" state identity in Poland and Hungary, and "Muslim" in Turkey, Netanyahu's proposal for Israel's "Jewish state" identity reflects a right-wing nationalist pride and yearning for religious purity. The Israeli case of right-wing populism, like that of Turkey, Poland, and

Hungary (also India), is an example of how democracies can become illiberal even while retaining some democratic processes.

Israel's xenophobic right-wing turn can be tied to the waning of the socialist-Zionist ideology of previous decades and the shrinking ranks of the leftist parties such as Labor and Meretz. Voices do exist in Israel that decry the sharp turn to the Right, especially after the February 2019 elections, which alarmed many liberals and leftists. According to the liberal newspaper *Haaretz*, "Trump's unabashed populism and ugly ethnocentrism paved Netanyahu's way on a similar trajectory. Trump's blatantly blind eye enabled the legislation of Netanyahu's landmark, Jews-only nation state law."[77] However, as of summer 2019, there was no effective alliance of the Left to counter the steady march of right-wing populist nationalism.

POPULISM AND TRUMP IN THE UNITED STATES

The right-wing populism represented by the 2016 Trump presidential victory has some similarities with the previous examples, such as hostility toward trade globalization and immigration, a religious surge, and antifeminism. But it is also part of a long history of populism in America that includes the Midwest farmers, the People's Party, William Jennings Bryan, and others who railed against the Gilded Age, to Huey Long of Louisiana. The architect of the Trump electoral victory, Steve Bannon, was the theoretician of the economic nationalism and populist policies promised during the presidential campaign. According to one account, Bannon said: "This whole movement has a certain global aspect to it. People want more control of their country. They're very proud of their countries. They want borders. They want sovereignty. It's not just a thing that's happening in any one geographic space." Trump's victory was hailed by the likes of Nigel Farage of Britain's UK Independence Party (UKIP) and the Brexit movement, Marine Le Pen in France, the AfD in Germany, Geert Wilders in the Netherlands, the Greek Neo-Nazi party, and Israel's right-wing Jewish Home party. Florian Philippot, Le Pen's chief strategist until his resignation, tweeted: "Their world is crumbling. Ours is being built."[78]

The populist backlash and rise of the American "Alt-Right" has its roots in the establishment's neglect over at least three decades of the "angry white men"—but also women—who have watched their communities decline and resent having their values ridiculed. The deterioration of once vibrant manufacturing towns and the export of jobs were blamed on global trade deals made by economic and political elites whose own wealth has increased exponentially, and by the entry of numerous illegal migrants from Mexico and Central America.[79] During the 2016 presidential campaign, Trump promised to help build those deteriorating towns, in part through a vague but effective "America first" framing device. Trump established tariffs against steel imports, but he also cut taxes for the rich. Müller notes the irony of Trump's wealth and concentration of wealth and power in his own family, despite his populist rhetoric.[80] Still, Trump's tweets are an effective form of speaking directly to "the people."

Trump's election came as a shock to many American liberals, but it could have been foreseen, in light of decades of neoliberal globalization led by the United States and of the effects of the 2007–8 mortgage meltdown and financial crisis. In *Death of the Liberal Class*, Chris Hedges points to the establishment's embrace of the "corporate power elite" and its effects on the working class and the poor. Joe Bageant's 2007 book, *Deer Hunting with Jesus*, is probably the most prescient in understanding the resentment of the white working class and rural poor against the values of the liberal elites, but more than a decade earlier, Christopher Lasch had argued that America's elites were engaged in a concerted revolt against the religious and patriotic values that so many Americans held dear; for years, Lasch also excoriated the growing power of corporate elites.[81]

In a largely social-psychological vein, Lauren Langman explains the votes for Trump as expressions of emotions of alienation and resentment, and rejection of cosmopolitanism. Combining Marx's concept of *alienation*—whereby capitalism denies the worker freedom, agency, self-creation, realization, as well as community—with Nietzsche's concept of *ressentiment*, Langman writes of "an intense loathing based on revenge toward the elites." He also refers to an "American tough, phallic aggressive masculinity," which he associates exclusively with white males.[82] This is the "white nationalism" that is behind not only much of the support for Trump but also the violence and aggression of its fringe actors. Curiously, however, and unlike European populism, American RWP and anti-immigrant sentiment does not extend to "welfare for our own people first." This may be because the American Right has always opposed welfare policies. Instead, "looking after our people" (and others) is the frame offered by left-wing Democratic politicians and their supporters.

POPULIST PROTEST MOVEMENTS

FRANCE

When France's President Macron, a former investment banker who already had done away with the popular wealth tax, announced plans in late 2018 to increase the fuel tax, this seemed to be the proverbial straw breaking the camel's back. Rural citizens who depend on cars to get to their jobs or to medical establishments spontaneously amassed to express their anger. They wore yellow vests, which French law requires all motorists to have in their automobiles, to symbolize both the danger they were in and their demand to be visible to the elite decision makers. According to Diana Johnstone, "the message was this: we can't make ends meet. The cost of living keeps going up, and our incomes keep going down. We just can't take it anymore. The government must stop, think and change course." Polls showed that an astonishing 70–80 percent of the French public supported them. Even when the Black Bloc and other anarchists joined and the Arc de Triomphe was vandalized, the support stayed high. But the minister of the interior, Christophe Castaner, decided to bear down hard on public disorder, hitting back on any and all demonstrators in central Paris. As a result, their Saturday protests began to take place at the Place de la Republique. But they had paid quite a price; police brutality inflicted "289 head injuries to protesters, 24 eyes shot out, 5 hands blown off, and 2 deaths."[83]

In his account of the protests, Jeremy Harding discusses the work of French geographer Christophe Guilluy, who studied the widening gap between the large metropoles and the periphery, or what Guilluy calls "the forgotten land of small and medium-sized cities and rural areas, home to most of the working class."[84] Criticizing what he calls "multi-cultural blather," Guilluy sees "anti-fascism as a bogus distraction from inequality," and he mistrusts "immigration for bringing down wages and best benefiting restaurant-goers." Poverty in France—defined as a standard of living that falls below 50–60 percent of the national average—is largely found in remote, rural areas (around a 24 percent poverty rate), but it also exists in city centers, such as Seine-St Denis, with its large numbers of migrants (around a 27 percent poverty rate). Harding writes that in France's second-most expensive city, Bordeaux, people cannot afford to buy or rent, with a shortage of social housing and property prices increasing by 40 percent in the last ten years. Here it is worth quoting from Harding's article, as it summarizes the feelings of economic insecurity that drive protests against the elites and votes for RWP parties:

> Europe has superb codes of practice, charters, laws proscribing insults levelled at minorities, but there is no code that protects the low-paid against the endless taunting to which they're subjected by news of lunatic salaries and bankers' bonuses. . . . They feel outcast, and though their numbers are high, they see themselves as a new minority with no recourse against economic discrimination. . . . The protests symbolize the standoff between ultra-liberal capitalism and its self-described losers.[85]

Diana Johnstone and others have described the Gilets Jaunes movement as nonideological, given support from across the political spectrum, including right-wing populists, communists, and trade unionists.[86] As both Johnstone and Harding explained, few of the protesters were unemployed; most were in low-paid jobs on precarious contracts, many in the care sector; there also were exasperated pensioners and small-scale entrepreneurs. Such citizens constitute the social base of populism almost everywhere. Their demands came to encompass a broad agenda: "zero homelessness," wealth redistribution, and a "popular referendum" mechanism that would allow laws to be proposed by citizens. Other demands were protecting French industry, caring for the elderly, bolstering rent controls, raising the minimum wage and the minimum pension, and capping monthly salaries at 15,000 euros.[87]

The Gilets Jaunes populist protest movement may be uniquely French in many ways, but it does call to mind the European anti-austerity protests of summer 2011 as well as the antiglobalization protests of the previous decade. What it also has in common with the earlier protest movements is a leaderless and horizontal structure, a feature that has come in for some criticism, inasmuch as it seems unable to sustain itself.

POPULAR DISCONTENT IN THE MENA REGION

Between 2017 and 2019, a series of protests erupted in Morocco, Iran, Tunisia, Algeria, Iraq, and Lebanon. For the most part, the protests were leaderless and horizontal movements with populist frames drawing on economic, political, and cultural grievances. In 2017, protests broke out in Morocco's Rif region, following news of the death of a fishmonger who was crushed to death in a rubbish truck after he jumped in to retrieve swordfish that had been confiscated because it had been caught out of season. The Rif region is predominantly Amazigh (Berber), and despite cultural recognition in the new 2011 constitution following the February 20 Movement, many Amazigh remain dissatisfied with their economic conditions. The Rif protests resonated with many Moroccans and came to be known as al-Hirak al-Shaabi, or the People's Movement.[88] This protest movement was followed in February 2019 with a nationwide general strike, rallies, and sit-ins, predominantly by public service employees protesting precarious employment conditions and medical students protesting privatization of public health. As Zakia Salime explains, the strike took place exactly eight years after the launch of the Mouvement 20 février during the Arab Spring, whose emotional appeal remains a mobilizing force. Angry at changes in training requirements and employment contracts that offer only fixed-term work arrangements and arduous terms, teachers joined the long-protesting unemployed university graduates (*les diplomés chomeurs*) "who have been claiming the right to public sector jobs" and carried placards such as "the contract is the grave of public education."[89] That a government led by the Islamist Justice and Development Party (PJD) should have developed such work arrangements for teachers confirms the argument in chapter 4 about the right-wing nature of Islamist political parties, their social justice rhetoric notwithstanding.

From December 2017 to January 2018, Iran was consumed by the most widespread protests since the 1978–79 revolution. Sociologists Kadivar and Sotoudeh analyzed the counties (*shahrestan*) where protests took place and showed that those counties that had voted for reformist president Hassan Rouhani had the largest and most sustained protests, precisely because of unmet expectations for improved economic conditions. Later that year, in October, protests launched by teachers—including many women teachers—demanded higher pay, improved pensions and health insurance, and more government support for schools in the private sector.[90] All told, the protests revolved around economic issues, service provision, ecological concerns, and political repression.[91] At around the same time, in January 2018, unmet expectations in Tunisia generated widespread protests and strikes, although strikes have been occurring sporadically for several years, and continued throughout 2018, mainly because of austerity measures instituted by the government in accordance with a large loan from the International Monetary Fund (IMF). (See also chapter 4.)

In early 2019, Algerians took to the streets to express frustration with a political class and system that kept reproducing itself without accountability or transparency, although long-standing youth unemployment was a major theme. What triggered the protests was the candidacy of the infirm President Bouteflika for a fifth term. He eventually withdrew his candidacy and in fact resigned, but protests against *le pouvoir* continued well into summer 2019. The protesters drew on familiar cultural frames that harked back to the national liberation struggle but also novel ones, such as calls for a civilian, not military, state and the unity of Algerian Berbers and Arabs.[92] Later that year, mass protests erupted in Iraq and Lebanon, reflecting people's anger over their governments' complacency or ineptitude over unemployment, income inequality, and poor public services.

The examples here are indicative of the capacity for popular mobilizations even in nondemocratic, semidemocratic, or newly democratizing contexts; of the capacity for peaceful cross-class mobilizations around common grievances like youth unemployment, the cost of living, and elites' corruption; of how protest movements cluster geographically and seem to come in waves; and of how their economic and political grievances echo other protest movements, perhaps through some diffusion processes.

LEFT-WING POPULISMS

When they erupted in the late 1990s, the protests and mobilizations that came to be known as the global justice movement (GJM) were not identified as populist. Yet in retrospect, they may be regarded as a left-wing populist protest movement, albeit one without a guiding ideology, leadership, or centralized authority. "Another world is possible," the slogan of the antiglobalization movement; "The people want the end of the regime," the slogan of the Arab Spring; and Occupy Wall Street's "We are the 99%!"—these may be seen as quintessential left-wing populist mobilizing frames. The Chilean protests of 2019 echo many of those frames: dignity, social equality, and a change of government. Images of more than a million people demonstrating in the capital city of Santiago, along with the proliferation of "*cabildos ciudadanos*," or self-organized participatory meetings of citizens that have gathered to discuss problems and solutions for their country, also echo the practices of the GJM and the WSF.[93] Left-wing populism is at least as potent as right-wing populism, and it too comes in the form of political parties.

Although the charter of the World Social Forum (WSF) eschewed party politics and privileged civil society organizations, left-wing populists created their own parties (see table 7.2). In the United States, where third parties struggle for recognition and inclusion, left-wing populists may be found in the Green Party but are more visible within factions of the Democratic Party, such as Democratic Socialists of America (DSA) or new entities such as the Working Families Party, Progressive Democrats, and Justice Democrats. In the 2016 presidential election, many American leftists who had supported Bernie Sanders's nomination preferred to vote for Jill Stein of the Green Party rather than Hillary Clinton, whom they regarded as a foreign policy hawk. Elsewhere, such disillusionment with or rejection of mainstream parties or politicians has meant votes for left-wing populists, including Juan Iglesias of Spain's Podemos, Jeremy Corbyn of the United Kingdom's Labour Party, Jean-Luc Mélenchon of France's Parti de Gauche and France Insoumise, Gregor Gysi and Sahra Wagenknecht of Germany's Die Linke, Selahattin Demirtaş of Turkey's People's Democratic Party (HDP), and Andrés Manuel López Obrador of Mexico's National Regeneration Movement (voted president in 2018).

In a world where capital has been able to shop around the globe for the cheapest labor and the lowest taxes, many working people have been left behind. For populist voters, including members of the working class, decision makers and mainstream parties care little about their interests and needs; as Schafer notes, "their anger is neither misinformed nor irrational and corresponds to a growing body of political science research, which documents how democracy is biased in favor of the better-off or even the wealthiest."[94] For some, this means disillusionment with or rejection of mainstream parties, with votes for the left-wing populist leaders and parties. Piñeiro and his colleagues show how in

Table 7.2. Left-Wing Populist Parties and Movements: Some Contemporary Examples (circa mid-2019)

Country	Party/Movement and Leaders/Spokespersons	Agenda/Objectives
France	Parti de Gauche; France Insoumise: Jean-Luc Mélenchon, Eric Coquerel, Danielle Simmonet	*Altermondialisation*; eco-socialism; "democratic refounding" of EU; reduce executive power; repeal of 2016 labor law reform; protection of common goods; raising minimum wage; peaceful foreign policy
Germany	Die Linke: Gregor Gysi, Sahra Wagenknecht	Eurosceptic; anticapitalist; democratic and eco-socialist; antimilitarist; international disarmament and peaceful foreign policy; strengthen anti-trust laws; empower cooperatives
Greece	Syriza (Coalition of the Radical Left): Alex Tsipras, Panos Skourletis	Eco-socialist democracy; feminism; against neoliberalism and privatization; for peace and diplomacy; review the role of the EU and Greece's role in it; economic nationalism
Mexico	National Regeneration Movement (Morena): Andrés Manuel López Obrador	Anticorruption; rein in war on drugs; rule for the poor; develop the south and create jobs via public tree-planting project
Spain	Podemos: Juan Iglesias, Íñigo Errejón, Irene Montero	*Altermondialisation*; anticapitalist democratic eco-socialist; poverty reduction through basic income; economic recovery with public control and promotion of small enterprises; reining in tax avoidance; withdrawing from free trade agreements
Tunisia	Front Populaire: Hamma Hammami, Mbarka Aouinia Brahmi	Socialism; secularism; Arab nationalism; workers' rights; women's rights
Turkey	People's Democratic Party (HDP): Selahattin Demirtaş, Figen Yüksekdağ, Pervin Buldan	Recognition and equality of minorities; participatory democracy; women's rights; political pluralism
United Kingdom	Labour Party/Momentum: Jeremy Corbyn, John McDonnell, Seumas Milne, Diane Abbott	A more equal society; affordable housing for all; increased funding for social care and mental health services; public investments for high-quality child care, schools, jobs; worker rights and security
United States	Our Revolution: Bernie Sanders; Left Democrats: Elizabeth Warren, Alexandria Ocasio-Cortez; Green Party USA: Jill Stein	Health care for all; free college tuition; higher minimum wage; increasing taxes on the rich; peaceful foreign policy; Green New Deal

Latin America populist leaders could activate popular latent grievances against socioeconomic exclusion and inequality.[95] In Mexico, left-wing populist Andrés Manuel López Obrador announced plans to cancel the overly generous retirement packages accorded to former presidents; he reduced his own pay to 40 percent of the previous salary and declined to live in the presidential palace, instead opening it up to the general public as a new museum.[96]

In advance of the 2016 presidential election in the United States, large numbers of citizens supported the democratic-socialist Bernie Sanders. Two years later, and in reaction to the Trump presidency, an unprecedented number of left-leaning women and minorities campaigned for congressional seats and other political offices; fully 125 won, of which 102 were Democrats (allowing that party to regain control of the House of Representatives), and "the Squad" came to prominence.[97]

In Spain, Podemos was one of the new parties that emerged from the wreckage of Europe's economic crisis. Its agenda includes nationalizing industries, hiking business taxes, raising the minimum wage, imposing a maximum salary, limiting the working week to 35 hours, and reducing the retirement age to 60. It also suggests nonpayment of illegitimate parts of public debt, and a referendum on leaving NATO. Its smart, telegenic leader, Pablo Iglesias, is a university lecturer. In Scotland, the pro-independence Scottish National Party pursues social-democratic policies, and members often criticize the "more than 35 years of neoliberal economic policy and directives from London."[98] In July 2019, DiEm25 (Democracy in Europe Movement 2025), the new pan-European movement formed by former Greek finance minister Yanis Varoufakis, forged an alliance with Britain's Labour Party to seek changes to EU policies, and DiEM25 planned further alliances through a new initiative called the Progressive International. Potential allies could be the Green parties in the EU, many of which—from the Netherlands, Germany, and Belgium—won additional seats in the European Parliament after the May 2019 elections. Earlier, a coalition including the Greens had taken power in Luxembourg in November 2017 and promptly abolished fares on public transport.[99] Some Green parties expanded their platform beyond environmental issues; in the Netherlands, tax avoidance by multinational corporations is a signature issue. In the United States, the Green Party opposes militarism and war. An alternative to the rise and spread of RWP would require coalition building within and across countries, as well as a common platform that would be attuned to national specificities. Something akin to a job-creating green social-welfarist model arguably could attract citizens previously drawn to Right populists.

CONCLUSIONS

For some pundits, contemporary right-wing populism has echoes of the 1930s (the tragedy and crimes of fascism). But in the same way that Marx analyzed the 18th Brumaire, there is also something farcical about many of the leaders of RWP parties and governments. If history is any guide, RWP parties and governments may serve only to reinforce the capitalist world-system, as appears to be the case in the United States. This is why genuinely democratic alternatives are needed.

Far from creating an expansive sense of global citizenship, the era of globalization has hardened identities due to its intrinsic contradictions: a tendency toward periodic crisis, economic inequality, democracy deficits, and precarious employment conditions. Right-wing populist parties reflect people's grievances related to economic conditions, institutions of global or regional governance, democracy deficits, and cultural changes. Immanuel Wallerstein has noted that the chaos and uncertainty of the contemporary capitalist world-system

> pushes popular opinion both to make demands for protection and protectionism and to search for scapegoats as well as true profiteers. Popular unrest determines the behavior of the political actors, veering them into so-called extremist positions. The rise of extremism ("The center cannot hold") pushes both national and world political situations toward gridlock.[100]

Although right-wing populism's appeal appears strong, it lacks an institution that the GJM, transnational feminist networks (TFNs), and others that make up the New Global Left have enjoyed—something akin to the World Social Forum (WSF), with its mobilizing capacity, democratic practices, and sense of unity and purpose amid celebration of diversity. This provides an opportunity for the New Global Left to coalesce around a more strategic program. Wallerstein writes that crisis "increases the viability of agency," and Chantal Mouffe makes a similar point, calling on the Left to "seize the populist moment" for a new agenda.[101] Coalitions with progressive political parties and local initiatives could harness the "popular will" toward a more inclusive, sustainable, and egalitarian model of democratic development. If past movements and party politics were dominated by men, the votes cast for Erdoğan and Trump, as well as the November 2018 midterm elections in the United States, showed that women are key constituents and voters. Today's social realities—women's presence across professions and occupations; involvement in all manner of movements, organizations, networks, and political parties; and leadership and creativity in their own organizations, movements, and networks—mean that women will be major players in the making of a broad progressive coalition for socio-political transformation. What is clear is that in the twenty-first century, women are everywhere in movements and protests, and often instigate them, as occurred with the Gilets Jaunes protests in France.

The *Economist* magazine, which tends either to ignore the left wing of Britain's Labour Party or ridicule its leader Jeremy Corbyn, invited him to write a commentary in its "The World in 2019" issue:

> A decade on, we are still living in the shadow of the great economic crash. But while there is widespread recognition that something fundamental changed in 2008, there is also denial about the necessary political response. The determination of powerful interests to cling to a failed economic orthodoxy has in many countries opened up a chasm between people's hopes and needs and the outdated prescriptions of the political class. Into that chasm have moved the fake populists of the far right, ready to rip up the fabric of our communities without real solutions to the crises facing our societies. . . .
>
> It is against this economic backdrop that a majority voted to leave the European Union in 2016. . . .
>
> Labour has shown that there is a popular alternative to austerity at home and conflict abroad. Beyond Brexit, a Labour government will champion our best internationalist traditions, putting negotiations before confrontation, supporting the Paris climate-change accord and Iran nuclear deal, and promising trade, not trade wars.[102]

CHAPTER 8

CONCLUSIONS AND PROGNOSTICATION

The philosophers have only interpreted the world, in various ways; the point, however, is to change it.

—Karl Marx, *Theses on Feuerbach*[1]

This book has examined transnational social movements, their relationship to globalization processes, and their similarities and differences. It has put the spotlight on the challenge of right-wing populisms as well as projects for more robust democratic alternatives. Drawing on social movement theorizing, we have looked at how social movements respond to political opportunities on a global scale, frame grievances and alternatives, and create new mobilizing structures. From Marxism and world-system theory, we have situated such grievances and mobilizations—as well as the recourse to war—in systemic and class terms. From feminism, we have unpacked the gender dynamics of both globalization and movements. And from world society theory, we have understood the global diffusion of norms, values, and policies. In the course of our study, we have drawn attention to national- and global-level opportunities and resources available for movement building, the salience of masculinities in global processes, and the use of violence by some networks as the main repertoire of contention. We also considered how social movements and revolutions alike have contributed to democratization, how neoliberal capitalism has impoverished democracy, and what the reactive and progressive challenges have been and could be.

This book began by posing a number of questions: What is the connection between globalization and social movements? How have people collectively responded to globalization? Have social movements changed to better confront globalization's economic, political, and cultural manifestations and challenges? And how are contemporary social movements and networks affecting the progression of globalization?

Globalization became a buzzword in the early 1990s, but the process had begun roughly two decades earlier, at the tail end of the golden ages of both Western capitalism and Third World development. Structural adjustments, Reaganomics, and Thatcherism were signs of what was to come in the capitalist world-economy. Capitalism had had other internationalizing stages, and collective action certainly had a long history. But contemporary globalization's economic, political, and cultural dimensions were distinct; they also had distinct effects on local communities, state capacities, and the labor-capital relationship. The collapse of communism, the consolidation of neoliberal capitalism, the global commodity chains, the worldwide spread of consumerism, the power of the international financial institutions, the new trade agreements being negotiated in secret, and the invasion of Iraq—all of these events were associated with globalization. And they all resulted in new and powerful forms of collective action, such as transnational feminist networks (TFNs), the global justice movement (GJM), the World Social Forum (WSF), and Islamist resistance.

The 2007–8 mortgage meltdown in the United States, the financial crisis, and the ensuing Great Recession were met with astonishing responses by the political elites in the ostensibly democratic core countries: governments bailed out banks and corporations while households were left to fend for themselves. In the United States, the financial institutions that had been responsible for the crisis were allowed to carry on as usual, and pay their CEOs the same enormous salaries and bonuses, but citizens lost homes, livelihoods, and assets. Vermont senator Bernie Sanders demanded to know exactly how much the George W. Bush administration allocated to the Wall Street banks, and it turned out to be $700 billion—on top of "trillions and trillions of dollars in near-zero interest loans and other financial arrangements the Federal Reserve doles out to every major financial institution in this country."[2]

In Europe, governments imposed austerity measures, which citizens had to endure on top of already existing precarious work conditions. In Arab countries, food and fuel prices had been increasing for some years, part of the steady privatization and liberalization processes encouraged by the international financial institutions and their own elites. Such injustices triggered tremendous anger and frustration, culminating in political eruptions across the globe: the Arab Spring protests, the anti-austerity protests in Europe, and Occupy Wall Street in the United States. Emotions and grievances were harnessed in both preexisting and new forms of organizing and mobilizing, and they found expression in both resonant and radical frames. In the United States, words like "capitalism," "socialism," and "inequality" returned to the public sphere after an absence of decades.

Indeed, globalization enabled forms of collective action rather broader in scale and scope than those that prevailed in the nineteenth or early twentieth centuries, albeit in a different organizational form. The communist movement of the twentieth century certainly was transnational and global in scope, but it was more centralized (and "vertical") than the transnational social movements found today. As noted in chapter 1, Gerlach's characterization of social movements as segmentary, polycentric, and reticulate is relevant to contemporary global social movements. The leaderless and "horizontal" movements that made up the GJM and especially the WSF were meant to be "prefigurative" of a more direct form of democracy. This form of collective action has its advantages; leaders are less likely to be coopted or arrested or assassinated, and the practice of participatory democracy can be inspirational as an ideal. Certainly the radical frames of the Occupy movement—"we are the 99%!"—resonated widely and had enormous emotional appeal. As the political theorist Benjamin Barber wrote some years earlier, there was great demand for "more democracy"—more democracy in politics; more democracy in the economy; more democracy in civil society. And he found such demands for more democracy to be radical and revolutionary.[3]

Collective action in the new century found a technological ally—the new information and computer technologies (ICTs)—that enabled it to organize at local, national, and transnational levels in fluid and flexible ways. Because of the internet, frames and tactics could be widely transmitted and diffused more rapidly than before, enabling networks to intersect and interact both virtually and physically.

ON THE MOBILIZING ROLE OF THE INTERNET

Social movement research has shown that recruitment into networks often occurs because of involvement in other networks. Activist networks not only ensure that a person is a member of a larger community but also frame issues and offer particular understandings. There is a large body of research on recruitment through formal networks, such as professional associations or organizations, what Mark Granovetter famously has called "the strength of weak ties," or through informal networks, also known as the friend-of-a-friend phenomenon. Our analysis has shown that ICTs have expanded the scope and rapidity of recruitment and mobilization, whether through formal or informal ties, and that the internet helps create and maintain new networks. Lauren Langman has written that the internet provides a variety of "virtual public spheres" where people can find information and "undistorted communication" that highlights adversity and offers frames for understanding that adversity. Virtual public spheres help foster the embrace of what Manuel Castells calls "project identities."[4] Such identities enable mobilizations that could articulate a vision of what a better policy or law—or, indeed, another, better world—might look like. Transnational movements, therefore, can be regarded as internet/networked movements. That is, much of their activist work takes place on the internet, and they are networked with each other both virtually and physically.

Global interconnectedness through "world society" or "network society" suggests a world full of movement and a complex mix of virtual and physical interactions. The "global" stimulates the creation of a transnational identity in a new "virtual" space that transcends borders. This new transnational social space is also a subject-supporting field in that it can provide solidarity and resources for individuals and groups at the local level. In this way, the "virtual" is a tool of empowerment. Virtuality does not replace normal communication; nor does it replace existing identities. It does, however, add new identities (e.g., world citizen, transnational feminist activist, international partner). Virtual networks extend social capital through the internet, allowing participants to build a sense of belonging that was previously difficult because of distance.

The internet has become a principal site for the formation of political and cultural communities and for the meeting and linking of movement networks. Enabling virtual and transnational public spheres and rapid communication of frames, the internet allows many movements to connect, thus facilitating the mobilization of "internetworked" social movements. Solidarities and collective action across borders are of long-standing existence, but the virtual public sphere allows for more rapid dissemination of political expressions and coordination of protest actions—including alerts, appeals, information exchange, petitions, and announcements of public rallies. The internet enables members of some networks to learn about and join other networks. Its capacity to foster the creation and maintenance of collective identities was evident in all the social movements and mobilizations of 2011 and thereafter.

Transnational collective action does not take place exclusively in the virtual sphere, of course. The preceding chapters have shown the importance of recruitment in madrassas, charities, and mosques (Islamist movements); of mobilizations at international conferences (feminist and global justice movements); and of recruitment by local and national political parties (right-wing but also left-wing populisms). The internet has become a prime vehicle for the transmission of information about movement strategies, the mobilization of resources, and the exchange of ideas across borders, boundaries, and barriers. This has been especially true of the international solidarity work of TFNs for Muslim women's human rights (e.g., Women Living under Muslim Laws [WLUML] and Women's Learning Partnership [WLP]) and for peace and antimilitarism (e.g., Women's International League for Peace and Freedom [WILPF], Code Pink, and Women in Black). In 2007 and 2008, for instance, TFNs such as WLUML, WLP, Development Alternatives with Women for a New Era (DAWN), and Equality Now—along with individual Iranian feminist expatriates—

disseminated information, transmitted petitions, and mobilized media interest around the One Million Signatures Campaign inside Iran (for law reform and women's rights) and the closure of a prominent Iranian women's magazine, *Zanan*. These examples make clear that the communications revolution associated with globalization enables actors to participate in collective action, in transnational advocacy networks, and in global social movements via cyberspace, while also helping to build a kind of cyberdemocracy. The local and the global are now linked in virtual public spheres, allowing activists to communicate, coordinate, exchange information, learn from each other, and build their collective identities and action repertoires across borders and, indeed, continents. In an era of globalization, mobilization processes have not replaced the traditional sites of family, neighborhood, religious groups, trade unions, and political organizations, but they now extend to the virtual public sphere. As such, the internet not only augments mobilization processes but also sometimes allows activists to circumvent obstacles and barriers created by repressive states. And in democratic polities where movement activity might be ignored by commercialized media, the internet can provide alternative sources of information about movement strategies and achievements.

The internet is not, however, the source of democratic activism; nor is it entirely a democratic space, or even a salutary one, as various untoward elements find it useful for violent, misogynist, or criminal activities, not to mention state surveillance and banking malfeasance. The big tech companies can no longer be trusted with users' data, and various states—the United States, China, Russia, Iran, Israel, and others—routinely use the internet to spy on their citizens or to recruit other citizens for purposes of destabilization. Evgeny Morozov has argued that the internet often constricts rather than expands freedom, and he argues against "digital Orientalism," the idea that in authoritarian societies, the internet can be a positive force for regime change. Morozov's criticism of the internet's encouragement of "slacktivism," or political nonengagement, is echoed in Zeynep Tufekci's analysis of the limits of cyberactivism. The excess reliance on Twitter and similar social media sites, along with the horizontal model of organizing, can hinder movements, especially when they are "unable to engage in the tactical and decision-making maneuvers all movements must master to survive." She contrasts the Gezi Park protests with the painstaking work of planning, coordinating, and recruiting that went into the US civil rights movement of the mid-twentieth century.[5]

THE POPULIST CHALLENGE AND DEMOCRATIC ALTERNATIVES

Neoliberalism, war, terrorist acts, and migration converged in Europe to generate right-wing populist responses. In the eastern part of Germany, citizens of the former socialist society who were never adequately integrated into the larger liberal capitalist society became resentful of immigrants and refugees as well as the governing elites who had welcomed them. Similar attitudes were found in other European countries. Populist parties old and new mobilized such angry citizens and won elections. At the same time that European leaders declared multiculturalism to have been a failure, Dutch urban studies specialist Paul Scheffer wrote a book asking difficult questions about immigration, including the gulf between European elites who regarded themselves as world citizens and the masses who remained emotionally tied to specific places.[6] The "populist moment" may be a temporary phenomenon, but its main benefit may be to jolt mainstream parties and governments to attend to citizen needs and demands, increase development assistance, stop destabilizing states, rein in the corporations, and regulate and tax financial transactions in order to avoid a repeat of the 2008 financial crisis and ensuing Great Recession.

The response from some governments thus far has been to move toward protectionism. This was the basic strategy of the Trump administration in the United States, but it has been deployed by other governments as well, with the result of a decline in world trade, leading some scholars to ask if a process of deglobalization is occurring (see chapter 1). But deglobalization has been a demand of certain scholar-activists from the Global South, as well as US and European opponents of the secretive fast-track trade deals that thus far have not been implemented. How to ensure the economic security and well-being of citizens while also extending solidarity and assistance internationally remains a dilemma facing many progressives. A clearer and more strategic vision and set of policies is needed.

SIMILARITIES AND DIFFERENCES

For ease of exposition in the comparisons that follow, I will refer to the global Left (which includes the TFNs, the civil society organizations that gather at the WSF, newer movements, and progressive political parties) and the global Right (which includes Islamist parties and right-wing populist parties in the Global North and Global South). The movements are counterhegemonic, but they differ on cultural frames, the use of violence, and their democratizing potential.

The worldwide spread of Western cultural products, discourses, values, and norms has been rejected *tout court* by militant Islamists but more selectively by global Left activists. That is, transnational feminists and global justice activists embrace the discourses and values of human rights, women's rights, climate justice, and a welcome mat for refugees, and they reject the dominant values of consumerism, commercialization, and privatization. Islamists are not preoccupied with neoliberal capitalist globalization; rather, the problem is framed as Western imperialism or cultural invasion or Islam in danger. Such concerns about culture, identity, and place are shared by anti-immigrant right-wing populists. Looking out for fellow Muslims exclusively and claiming that "Islam is the solution" is the mirror image of the call for "welfare for our own citizens first" and the argument that borders need to be closed. In contrast, the global Left tends to have a more internationalist and solidaristic approach toward "the Other," and toward marginalized groups in particular. It also views the main problem as the current model of neoliberal capitalism, and it has a common commitment to deliberative democratic processes, whether within their own organizations, in intergroup and coalition politics, in their countries, or across the world-system at large ("system change, not climate change").

Nonviolence has been a key principle of the broad global Left. Conferences, activist research, lobbying efforts, cyberactivism, protest rallies, and civil disobedience constitute the collective action repertoire of feminist and global Left movements. Militants do exist within the global Left, such as the Black Bloc anarchists and the anti-fascist warriors, who express moral outrage through *unarmed* violent protest such as destruction of property. Islamist extremists, on the other hand, may see *armed* violence as *the* strategy to attain territory or power. Many Islamists deploy militant and violent tactics not only against state repression but also in response to what they perceive as insults to their religion and culture. As for right-wing populists, the fringe elements among them have similarly shown a propensity for the use of violent tactics directed at opposing citizens or immigrants.[7]

The democratizing nature of feminist, global justice, and the broad Left movements is self-evident. I have raised questions, however, about the democratic potential of Islamist movements. The Arab Spring and the coming to power of Islamist parties in Egypt, Morocco, and Tunisia were a good test of two opposing propositions: that moderate Islamist parties could adopt democratic practices and work in coalitions with non-Islamist parties to build institutions enabling citizens to enjoy civil, political, and social rights; and that moderate Islamist parties would remain fixated on cultural and identity issues, unwilling to share power and unable to build stable, democratic, and prosperous societies. In Egypt, the Muslim Brotherhood's monopolization of power generated popular protests that, in turn, precipitated a military coup. In Morocco, the ruling Justice and Development Party (PJD) has faced protests over privatization of public services, despite its populist social justice rhetoric, and has cracked down on protesters in the Rif. In Tunisia, an-Nahda has governed in coalition, but it, too, has not delivered on citizens' socioeconomic needs and rights, although the rights of protest and association are far more respected in democratizing Tunisia than in most Middle East and North Africa (MENA) countries. The ruling party in Turkey took an authoritarian turn after 2011 and has jailed thousands of Turkish citizens as well as Kurdish dissidents. Even moderate Islamist parties, therefore, appear wanting in commitments to human rights, women's equality, and a deliberative and participatory democracy that would also prioritize the social and economic rights of citizens. They engage with elections, the media, professional associations, and other societal institutions to extend their influence, but they have not satisfied skeptics who raise questions about Islamist commitment to democratic processes, civil liberties, and inclusive citizenship. As for European right-wing populist parties, their electoral victories may be tied to the deficits of (neo)liberal capitalist democracy, but they do not offer coherent programs for a return to a more egalitarian and robust social democracy. In the United States, Trump's populist policies and rhetoric are likely to reenact what Marx analyzed (and in parts satirized) in the

Eighteenth Brumaire of Louis Bonaparte: reinforcement of the "bourgeois republic"—despite Bonaparte's petty-bourgeois and rural social base—with frames such as "property, family, religion, order."[8]

Paradoxically, then, globalization processes have given rise to both nonviolent democratic movements and violent antidemocratic ones. Recall Benjamin Barber's argument that "McWorld" had engendered jihad. But globalization also has been confronted by democratic movements such as feminism, global justice, youth for climate justice, Black Lives Matter, and other life-affirming and forward-looking movements.

Thus far I have considered the positive attributes of global Left movements. There are shortcomings, however, that need to be addressed. Social movements and transnational networks have helped build both vibrant civil societies in their own countries and a global civil society in which actors consciously communicate, cooperate, and organize across national boundaries, and promote democratic practices and values. Clearly, a well-developed infrastructure exists for the making of an alternative to the status quo, to "business as usual," and, specifically, to the logic of neoliberal capitalist globalization. What is required, however, is more deliberate strategizing across movements—labor, feminist, progressive religious, environmental, peace, global justice—toward a common vision and plan of action.

Social movement activism is neither a matter of individual rational choice nor an example of collective irrationality. It involves people coming together around common grievances, goals, and identities and creating meaning, forging alliances, building coalitions, and maintaining institutions. Such work is not easy. Constituting, sustaining, or participating in social movements is a difficult enterprise; it is even more so at the transnational level. Despite the longevity of certain TFNs, the WSF, and other global civil society organizations, movements face funding, staffing, and communication difficulties. Not everyone has the means to travel to global or even regional social forums.

The question of language and communication is central to the ability to participate meaningfully. Within the world of international diplomacy, simultaneous interpretation and rapid translation of documents are common, but the GJM, for example, has lacked the financial resources for such services. Much of the work of communicating across language groups other than English, French, and Spanish—for example, at the various meetings of the WSF—is done voluntarily by bilingual or multilingual activists. Multilingual websites are certainly helpful, and these are maintained by the WSF as well as by a number of TFNs, but they do not exhaust the languages of large parts of the global community that remain excluded from the deliberative processes of democratic transnational activism. Some activists, therefore, could find the financial burdens and linguistic barriers, and at times the cultural or political misunderstandings, tiring or frustrating or incomprehensible.

Another shortcoming that has been raised concerns the lack of meaningful change in "the system" and the apparent inability or unwillingness of global left movements to coalesce. TFNs played a key role in the 1990s at the United Nations (UN) conferences and in helping diffuse concepts of women's human rights, the care economy, and—especially at a time when globalization was being celebrated—the adverse effects of privatization and liberalization on women's working conditions and household burdens. In the new century, their participation in the WSF helped feminize and, indeed, legitimize the institution. The WSF itself should have become the place not only for deliberations and dialogues but also for planning and strategizing. The many disparate movements that exist at local, national, regional, and global levels require more formal connections, and those require con-certed bridge building and "translations" across those levels by move-ment intellectuals or activists tasked with that role, by party officials, and by media workers. Various calls were made for action around the Bamako Appeal and the Porto Alegre Manifesto (see chapter 6), or the formation of a Progressive International, or a World Political Party. All are worthy of consideration if the current model of neoliberal capital-ist globalization and the deficits of (neo)liberal democracy are to be replaced by a model of global governance that is genuinely democratic and oriented to the needs and interests of working people rather than tied to corporations, banks, and elites. Concerted action toward the construction of such a model might also help recruit people away from right-wing populisms and Islamisms.

FIVE PROPOSITIONS

This book also has offered a theoretical framework for the analysis of globalization, drawing primarily on world-system and Marxist theories for an understanding of geography, capital, and class in the operations of "the global" and of the state; and on feminism to uncover gender dynamics, and especially masculinities, in aspects of capitalist accumulation (and in militarism). I have applied standard social movement theory throughout the book but emphasized political economy more than is typically done in social movement theorizing. Chapter 1 summarized this book's main arguments, assumptions, and concepts in eight propositions, largely informed by the effects of globalization on social movements. Here I offer an additional five propositions to serve as food for (political) thought and suggestions for future research on social movements and the era of globalization.

1. *States and social movements:* Social movements or networks of contenders adopt a transnational form when (a) global opportunities for legitimation or growth present themselves or (b) collective action within domestic/national boundaries is foreclosed or repressed. We will continue to see social movements emerging throughout the world, and their tactics, scope, and prospects will depend on the combination of political opportunities, both domestic and global, as well as on the strength of their mobilizing and framing efforts. Movements are sometimes constrained from transnational activism and may choose strategically to remain domestically oriented. Movement opportunities and achievements will continue to be shaped by world-system location, the domestic structure of political opportunity, and the strategic choices of the actors involved. States will continue to surveil and co-opt challengers. But in the same way that states often work together to repress challengers (whether these are social movements, revolutions, or national states), movement capacity could withstand such tactics through cross-class coalitions and cross-movement alliances.

2. *Violence and social movements:* Women's movements are invariably nonviolent; labor movements and trade unions, too, have largely eschewed violence. Social movements or networks of contenders assume violent methods to achieve their goals when (a) state repression forecloses open forms of peaceful collective action or protest; (b) movements or networks interpret repression as weakness, betrayal, or an opportunity to gain adherents

to the cause; or (c) an extant cultural frame can be drawn upon to justify such actions. Violence as a tactic of contentious politics has been largely associated with revolutions or armed rebellions and less so with social movements, which typically make a strategic choice not to engage in violence even when states take repressive measures against them. The contrast between nonviolent movements and state repression could resonate with "fence-sitting" citizens.

3. *Feminism, masculinities, and social movements:* The more masculine the composition and the more violent the framings, the less likely it is that women will be involved as participants or leaders. Although some women will continue to identify with or support a masculinized movement, and the group may use some women in an instrumental fashion, such movements are unlikely to attract a critical mass of women or to incorporate them into leadership roles. With transnational networks in particular, which require a high degree of mobility, membership in movements and networks that deploy violence as the chief means of contention will continue to be overwhelmingly male. Place-based political movements that have embraced feminist goals, however, will attract large numbers of women adherents and even fighters.

4. *Social movements and political change:* The 2011 Arab Spring and the 2018–19 protests in Iran, Morocco, Algeria, Iraq, Lebanon, and Chile show that the semiperiphery of the world-system will continue to be the site of social movements for political change. At the same time, the Gilets Jaunes protests in France and the many teacher strikes in the United States suggest that core countries are not immune to social discontent. How to harness and connect the disparate movements in the direction of people-oriented systemic change remains the principal political challenge.

5. *Social movement analysis and globalization studies:* In recent years, political economy and class have returned to the study of social movements, and the field has overcome previous debates about costs and benefits, emotions and passions, constraints and strategic choices. To paraphrase Marx, women and men make history, but not always under conditions of their own choosing: structures may be a source of constraint, but agency operates even

within its limitations. Throughout history, women and men collectively have changed history, as the record of liberation movements, progressive revolutions, workers' movements, and feminist movements has shown. Today, as globalization appears to be under pressure and the corporate elites have lost legitimacy, the room for maneuver may be expanding. Future research in critical globalization studies could examine how local initiatives reflect and resist global processes, how nationally based movements and political parties coalesce to challenge corporate domination, how citizens' movements can democratize the institutions of global governance, and how feminist activism and values have inspired and informed movements, institutions, and norms.

Notes

CHAPTER 1: INTRODUCTION AND OVERVIEW

1. Karl Marx, "The Eighteenth Brumaire of Louis Bonaparte," in McLellan 1977, 300.

2. See della Porta 2007; Smith et al. 2008.

3. I have borrowed the term "New Global Left" from Christopher Chase-Dunn.

4. On "new social movements," see Melucci 1989; Eyerman and Jamison 1991; Rucht 1991. See McAdam, McCarthy, and Zald 1996 on theorization of political opportunities, mobilizing structures, and cultural frames.

5. Marx 1978, chapter 31. For studies on the world-system, see Chase-Dunn 1998; Wallerstein 1991; on the internationalization of capital, see Frobel, Heinrichs, and Kreye 1980.

6. See Chase-Dunn, Kawano, and Brewer 2000.

7. Political economist Susan Strange wrote trenchant critiques of the emerging reality of finance-driven markets and weak states; see Strange 1986, 1988, 1996. On transnational advocacy networks, see Keck and Sikkink 1998 and Smith et al. 1997.

8. On global restructuring, see Boswell and Chase-Dunn 2000; Cox 1992; Hopkins and Wallerstein 1996; Marchand and Runyan 2000; Moghadam 1995. See also Strange (as above).

9. On "globalism" and consumer capitalism as ideology, see Sklair 2001, 2002; Steger 2002, 2009; Steger and Roy 2010. See Fukuyama 1989 for a celebration of what he claimed was the triumph of liberal democracy and capitalism at the end of the Cold War.

10. On "world culture," see Meyer et al. 1997; Boli and Thomas 1997; Boli 2005; Moghadam and Elveren 2008; Paxton and Hughes 2014. On norm diffusion and advocacy/solidarity across borders, see Smith, Chatfield, and Pagnucco 1997; Keck and Sikkink 1998. See also Garrett 2006 on protest in an information age.

11. Benhabib 2006; Sassen 2001.

12. Arjomand 1986, 107; Wuthnow 1986; Klatch 1987; Blee and Creasap 2010, 273.

13. On the connection with global restructuring, see Moghadam 1995; on gender and fundamentalism, see Kandiyoti 1991 and Moghadam 1994b. On Islamist movements, see Zubaida 1993; Hafez 2003; Wiktorowicz 2004b; see also Beckford 1986 for comparative perspectives and Marty and Appleby's four volumes on comparative fundamentalisms (1991, 1992, 1993, 1994).

14. Keck and Sikkink 1998, 3. See also Smith, Chatfield, and Pagnucco 1997.

15. See Chase-Dunn, Morosin, and Álvarez 2015; Sanky 2016. On the financial crisis in Argentina and the rise of social movements, see Di Marco 2011a and Ozorow 2019.

16. On labor protests in Egypt and Tunisia, see Beinin 2009a, 2009b, 2012, 2015. The Arab Spring generated a prodigious scholarship.

17. Supportive of the NATO "humanitarian intervention" were Middle East specialists such as Gilbert Achcar, Rami Khoury, and, most vociferously, Juan R. I. Cole, along with left-wing sociologists such as Lauren Langman and Michael Schwartz. Supporters cited the Arab League's endorsement of the Security Council resolution to allow a no-fly zone over Libya, but only nine of the twenty-two members voted in favor; two voted against, and the others abstained or were absent. Along with Samir Amin, Edward Herman, Gary Younge, Medea Benjamin, Alexander Cockburn, and others, I was adamantly opposed to both the NATO intervention and the violence of the rebels, leading to many impassioned e-mail exchanges and conversations. Veteran left-wing Egyptian economist Samir Amin criticized the intervention and the killing of Ghaddafi as imperialistic.

18. See Medea Benjamin and Charles Davis, "Instead of Bombing Dictators, Stop Selling Them Bombs," Antiwar.com, March 24, 2001, https://original.antiwar.com/medea-benjamin-davis/2011/03/23/instead-of-bombing-dictators-stop-selling-them-bombs.

19. On Afghanistan, see Cordovez and Harrison 1995; Moghadam 1994a; Rubin 1997.

20. Mouffe 2018.

21. Chase-Dunn and Inoue 2017.

22. Tarrow 1994, 48, cited in Keck and Sikkink 1998, 37.

23. McAdam, McCarthy, and Zald 1996; on "frames," see especially Snow 2004.

24. Gerlach 1999, 95.

25. See Goodwin, Jasper, and Polleta 2001; Flam and King 2005.

26. Cited in Barkawi 2006, 130. The quote is from a videotaped statement released on October 7, 2001. The mention of "eighty years" is a reference to the downfall and breakup of the Ottoman Empire and its caliphate.

27. Bhavnani, Foran, and Talcott 2005, 330.

28. Guidry, Kennedy, and Zald 2000a. See also Appelbaum and Robinson 2005; Chase-Dunn and Babones 2006; della Porta 2007; Juris 2008; Moghadam 2005; O'Brien et al. 2000; Podobnik and Reifer 2004; Smith, Chatfield, and Pagnucco 1997; Smith and Johnston 2002; Tarrow 2005.

29. On transnational feminism, see Eschle and Maiguashca 2010; Marchand and Runyan 2000; Meyer and Prugl 1999; Moghadam 2005; Stienstra 2000. On Middle East/North African feminism, see Berkovitch and Moghadam 1999; Moghadam 2003; Moghadam and Sadiqi 2006; Moghadam and Gheytanchi 2010.

30. Heckscher 2002.

31. Karl Marx, "The Eighteenth Brumaire of Louis Bonaparte," in McLellan 1977, 300.

32. Polanyi [1944] 2001; Arrighi, Hopkins, and Wallerstein 1989; Boswell and Chase-Dunn 2000; Chase-Dunn and Babones 2006; Chase-Dunn et al. 2009. Karl Polanyi's highly influential text was originally published in 1944. The 2001 edition includes contributions by economist Joseph Stiglitz and political sociologist Fred Block.

33. Smith 2008; see chapter 2 for further discussion.

34. Keck and Sikkink 1998, 38.

35. Moaddel 2005, 1.

36. Jayawardena 1986; Berkovitch 1999; Meyer 1999; Rupp 1998; Stienstra 1994; Plastas 2011. As noted by Boxer and Quataert 1978, the socialist movement organized predominantly working-class women, such as textile workers, for revolutionary causes, while the feminist organizations were largely middle class and reformist.

37. Marx, *The Eighteenth Brumaire of Louis Napoleon*, in McLennan 1977. I am grateful to Lauren Langman for reminding me of its relevance to contemporary right-wing populism.

38. See "About MoveOn.org," MoveOn.org, http://www.moveon.org/about .html; "About Azaaz.org," Avaaz.org, http://www.avaaz.org/en/about.php.

39. On Iran's protests and the internet, see Kamalipour 2010. On the use of mobile phones in protests, see Castells, Fernàndez-Ardèvol, and Sey 2006; on women's use of social media in Middle East protests, see Gheytanchi and Moghadam forthcoming 2020.

40. Stephen Moss, "Impresario of a New Journalism," *Guardian Weekly*, July 30, 2010, 28–29; BBC World Service, October 24, 2011; see wikileaks.org (accessed October 27, 2011). A Facebook posting by Catherine Savage (November 2011) featured a photo of Julian Assange with the comment, "I give private information on corporations to you for free and I'm the villain," juxtaposed with the image of Mark Zuckerberg and the comment, "I give your private information to corporations for money, and I'm the Man of the Year."

41. Walgrave et al. 2011; the quotes appear on pages 326 and 329. See also Langman 2005.

42. For examples and illustrations of anticorporate networking, see Juris 2008.

43. https://www.peaceaction.org, https://www.answercoalition.org, https://www.codepink.org, https://www.wilpf.org.

44. The term refers to the ability of individuals to take part in protest activity due to the absence of potential obstacles, which may be family responsibilities, a high-pressure job, the fear of being sacked, or physical incapacity. Young people's availability for activism is generally deemed to be high. On "biographical availability," see McAdam 1986; Goldstone and McAdam 2001.

45. Morozov 2011.

46. Burawoy et al. 2000.

47. In her feminist analysis of globalization, Spike Peterson (2003) has identified three gendered economic spheres: that of the production of goods and the provision of services; that of social, biological, and labor reproduction (sometimes known as the care economy); and the sphere of nonmaterial, speculative, and financial transactions (the virtual economy).

48. The phrase is from Guidry, Kennedy, and Zald 2000a, 17; however, I am not suggesting that they would agree with my recommendation. See also Appelbaum and Robinson 2005.

CHAPTER 2: GLOBALIZATION, ITS DISCONTENTS, AND COLLECTIVE ACTION

1. An early study was Barnet and Muller 1974. See Roberts and Hite 2007 for an elaboration of the evolution from development to globalization.

2. Harvey 2009, 39; Klein 2007b.

3. Soviet support was important to the South African and Palestinian liberation movements. In various parts of the world, some leftists who were appalled by US support for dictators and involvement in coups d'état, or who sympathized with the Palestinian national liberation cause, formed "revolutionary cells" in Germany, Italy, Japan, and elsewhere. Extremist leftists such as the German Red Army Faction (including the Baader-Meinhof group), the Japanese Red Army, and the Italian Red Brigades wreaked havoc but did not last long. French filmmaker Olivier Assayas's three-part miniseries *Carlos*, released in 2010, provides a good visual introduction to this episode.

4. On "the golden age of capitalism" and its end, see Marglin and Schor 1990.

5. I obtained some Cavtat Roundtable documents when I attended two of the meetings in the late 1980s. See also http://www.jstor.org/pss/29765806. On the NIEO, see "Declaration on the Establishment of a New International Economic Order," reprinted in Broad 2002, 99–102.

6. Loans also were taken out by dictators, which helped entrench their rule and benefited the lending institutions to the detriment of citizens. Such loans later came to be called "odious" by advocates of debt cancellation. See chapter 6.

7. Payer 1975.

8. For details on structural adjustments, see Cornia, Jolly, and Stewart 1989; Bakker 1994; Elson 1991; Moghadam 1995, 1998a; Sparr 1994.

9. On the Drexel Lambert Burnham scandal, see Zey 1993.

10. On the "deindustrialization of America," see Bluestone and Harrison 1982. See also Rupert and Solomon 2006, 42.

11. The United States also briefly withdrew from the International Labour Organization (1977–80). On the withdrawal from UNESCO, see Moghadam and Elveren 2008. In brief, the Reagan administration left UNESCO on December 31, 1984; the Bush administration returned on October 1, 2003. In 1997, the government of Tony Blair decided that the United Kingdom would rejoin UNESCO after the latter abandoned the NWICO idea and undertook administrative reforms. The United States rejoined UNESCO in 2004—but then withdrew again in 2011 when the Executive Board voted to allow Palestine to join.

12. See Williamson 2004. See also Steger and Roy 2010, 19–20.

13. ILO 2004; Oxfam 2002; Rodrik 1997; Stiglitz 2002.

14. Khor 2000; Korten 1995; Mander 1996.

15. See Tobin 1978. For a movement perspective on the Tobin tax, see Broad 2002.

16. Bello 2000.

17. Yaghmaian 2001; Sklair 2001, 2002; Steger 2002. "Globalizers" included academic economists, as seen in the 2010 documentary *Inside Job* by Charles Ferguson. See http://www.sonyclassics.com/insidejob.

18. Chase-Dunn 1998; Harvey 2003, 2004; Robinson 2004; Wallerstein 1991.

19. On inequalities, see the summary of Maddison's research in UNDP 1999; see also Atkinson 2001; Taylor 2000; Milanovic 2005, 2011; Korzeniewicz and Moran 2009.

20. Keefe 2017.

21. Monbiot 2011, 19; Foroohar 2011; Newman 1999; Wilkinson and Pickett 2009; UNDP 2005.

22. Case and Deaton 2017.

23. On the Millennium Development Goals, see http://www.un.org/millen niumgoals. For economists' perspectives on globalization, see Joseph Stiglitz, "Globalism's Discontents" (2002), in Roberts and Hite 2007, 295–304; Dani Rodrik, "Has Globalization Gone Too Far?" (1997), in Roberts and Hite 2007, 305–19, 314–15; Jeffrey Sachs, "The Antiglobalization Movement" (2005), in Roberts and Hite 2007, 356–59. See also Standing 1999b; Bhagwati 2004; UNDP 1999; Oxfam 2002.

24. For details on the global financial and economic crisis, see Chossudovsky and Marshall 2010; ILO 2011; IMF 2009; Tooze 2018; Walby 2015.

25. Peterson 2003; on the economic crisis and austerity, see Rubery 2015; Walby 2015.

26. On globalization and the state, see Mathews 1997, 50; Strange 1996, 4; Beck 2004, 144.

27. Castells 1996, cited in Zivkovic and Hogan 2007, 186.

28. Sklair 2001, 1; Sklair 1991; Robinson and Harris 2000, 20; see also Chase-Dunn 1998.

29. Hirst and Thompson 1996; Berger and Dore 1996.

30. Tarrow 2001; Johnston 2011.

31. These arguments are associated with, respectively, Harvey 2003; Robinson 2004; and Pieterse 2004.

32. Wallerstein 2000, 2003; see also Chase-Dunn and Inoue 2017.

33. On militarism and gender (in)equality, see Elveren and Moghadam 2019.

34. On "expulsions," see Sassen 2014.

35. Barkawi 2006, 10.

36. Lindekilde 2010.

37. On the "justice cascade," see Sikkink 2011. This is an important and impressively documented book, and Sikkink does have a chapter on the United States; however, the assumption that all states and officials are equally vulnerable to the new global norms and institutions of justice is flawed.

38. Morozov 2011; Dominic Rushe, "U.S. Ruling on Twitter 'a Blow to Privacy,'" *Guardian Weekly*, November 18, 2011, 12.

39. Santos 2006. See also chapter 6 in this book.

40. Barber 2001, 232, i.

41. Hardt and Negri (2000) theorized away the militarized state and coercive international relations and disputed the hegemonic role of the United States—incorrectly, in my view. For a summary discussion, see Howe 2002.

42. On the importance of the Afghanistan episode, see Cooley 1999; Rashid 2000; and Moghadam 2003, chapter 7.

43. American imperial expansionism predates its replacement of the United Kingdom as the world-system's hegemon and includes old-style territory grabbing (Hawaii in 1893, Puerto Rico in 1898, a group of islands in Asia-Pacific), the American war in the Philippines (1899–1902), and as purchases of territory (Louisiana, Alaska). Its early territorial expansion coupled with the devastation of European countries during World War II enabled the US rise to the position of hegemon.

44. On this latter point, see Elizabeth Drew, "The War in Washington," *New York Review of Books*, May 10, 2007, 53–55; Schumpeter, "The Civil War in Washington, DC, Is Damaging American Business," *Economist*, August 13, 2011, 66.

45. Connell 1998.

46. Runyan 2002, 362; Langman and Morris 2004.

47. Barber 2001; Kaldor 2003; Chua 2003.

48. Moghadam 2011b; Marx 1978, chapter 31. See also Walby 2015.

49. Eckstein and Wickham-Crowley 2003. See also Johnston and Almeida 2006.

50. Hadden and Tarrow 2007, 214; Tarrow 2005, 11.

51. Guidry, Kennedy, and Zald 2000a, 3; Alger in Smith, Chatfield, and Pagnucco 1997, 262, table 15.1.

52. Pianta and Marchetti 2007, 30–31.

53. Kaldor 2003, 44–45, 46; Anheier, Glasius, and Kaldor 2001, 21.

54. Taylor 2004, 4; Bauer and Hélie 2006.

CHAPTER 3: GLOBALIZATION
AND SOCIAL MOVEMENTS

1. Markoff 1999, 301; Runciman 2018, 5.

2. Guidry, Kennedy, and Zald 2000a; Johnston 2011; Meyer and Tarrow 1998. Park and Einwohner (2019) find some variations in support for social protests in the United States.

3. O'Donnell and Schmitter 1986.

4. Rueschemeyer, Stephens, and Stephens 1992.

5. Roberts 2016, 43. See also Roberts 1998. On Eastern Europe, see Bunce 2003, especially pages 171–74.

6. On South Korea, see Cummings 2000; Im 2000; Chang 2008. On Argentina, see Di Marco 2011a; Ozorow 2019.

7. Moghadam 2013b.

8. Keane 1996; Kenneth Bollen, cited in Korzeniewicz and Awbrey 1992, 612. See also Moore 1966; Lipset 1959; Huntington 1991; Welzel and Inglehart 2009.

9. Wejnert 2005.

10. On the ties between the April 6 Youth Movement and Otpor, see Kirkpatrick and Sanger 2011.

11. Keck and Sikkink 1998; Htun and Weldon 2018; Givan, Roberts, and Soule 2010.

12. Givan, Roberts, and Soule 2010. For a critique of US democracy promotion in Latin America, see Gill 2018, and on MEPI, see Salime 2010.

13. O'Donnell and Schmitter 1986, 7; cited in Korzeniewicz and Awbrey 1992, 618.

14. On egalitarian family relations, see Okin 1989; Di Marco and Tabbush 2011; Collectif Maghreb Egalité 95 2005.

15. Barber 1984; Schmitter and Karl 1991, 77. For more on formal and substantive democracy, politics, and citizenship rights, see Marshall 1964; Crick 2000; Lister 2003.

16. See the following: "Adbusters Occupy Wall Street," http://www.adbusters.org/blogs/adbustersblog/occupywallstreet.html; "Occupy Wall Street: The Resistance Continues at Liberty Square and Worldwide," http://occupywallst.org; Voigt 2011; Sánchez 2011.

17. See http://occupywallst.org/about.

18. "About," Occupy Wall Street, last accessed July 2019, http://occupywallst .org/about.

19. Fukuyama 1989; Huntington 1991.

20. Greshman 2011; Moghadam 2013a.

21. See Knapp, Flach, and Ayboga 2016.

22. See Lackner 1985; Molyneux 1985; Moghadam 2003.

23. Fraser 1995, 2000.

24. Beckwith 2010; Eschle 2000; Barron 2002; Di Marco and Tabbush 2011; Moghadam 2005; Vargas 2009.

25. On the democratic underpinnings of social movements, see Guidry, Kennedy, and Zald 2000b, 14; Costain 2005; della Porta 2005; Di Marco 2011a, 2011b; Dryzek 1990; Polletta 2002; Weldon 2011. On neoliberalism and its discontents in Latin America, see Silva 2010. On the Turkish feminist movement, see Arat 1994.

26. Prata 2010 on Portugal; Roces 2010 on the Philippines.

27. On Latin America, see Alvarez 1990; Jaquette 2001, 2009; Waylen 1994, 2007. On the Philippines, see Roces 2010.

28. Jaquette 2001, 114.

29. Moghadam 2018.

30. See Rueschmeyer 1998.

31. Bennoune 1995; Cherifati-Merabtine 1995; Messaoudi and Schemla 1998; Moghadam 2001; Salhi 2011.

32. UNDP 2002, 1.

33. Roberts 2016, 33.

34. On democracy and the semiperiphery, see Korzeniewicz and Awbrey 1992; Markoff 1999. On contagion, consent, control, and conditionality, see Przeworski et al. 1995, 6.

35. Vieceli 1997, 90. On democracy and structural adjustments in Africa, see also Bratton and Van De Walle 1992; Ake 1993.

36. Costas Douzinas, "In Greece, Democracy Is Reborn," *Guardian Weekly*, June 24, 2011, 20. For commentaries and comparisons of Argentina's 2001 default and the Greek dilemma, see http://www.guardian.co.uk/business/2010/apr/16/ argentina-to-repay-2001-debt and http://www.nytimes.com/2011/06/24/business/ global/24peso.html.

37. See https://www.dw.com/en/greece-central-bank-reports-brain-drain-of -427000-young-educated-greeks-since-2008/a-19373527-0.

38. *Economist* 2019a, 29–30.

39. *Economist* 2018f, 61.

40. Flassbeck and Lapavitsas 2015. See also Varoufakis 2017.

41. Yerkes and Ben Yahmed 2018.

42. Brown 2013.

43. Markoff 1999.

44. Gill 2018.

45. Dunn 2005; Przeworski et al. 1995, 4; Barber 2001; Habermas 1992.

46. Phillips 2003; see also UNDP 2011, which shows the extent to which US inequality lowers the Human Development Index (HDI) for the United States and its ranking among countries.

47. Chua 2003; Lukacs 2005.

48. According to Evgeny Morozov (2015), the agreement would enable corporations to sue governments for business-unfriendly laws and limit internet users' privacy. He quotes a conservative Swedish politician that "[b]arriers against the free flow of data are, in effect, against trade." See also https://en.wikipedia.org/wiki/Trade_in_Services_Agreement.

49. Walby 2004, and personal communications, summer 2019. In *How Will Capitalism End?*, Streek (2017) writes that the Western system of (neo)liberal democracy is in danger of going through a kind of "dark ages." See also Streek 2019.

50. O'Brien et al. 2000; Smith 2008, 41–44, 46.

51. Smith 2008; the quotes appear on pages 5, 106, 107. See also Smith and Wiest 2012.

52. della Porta 2005, 2009. See also Smith 2008; the quotes appear on pages 34, 214, 208.

53. Smith 2008; Moghadam and Elveren 2008.

54. On Saudi Arabia's "extortion" at the UN in connection with its violations of the Convention on the Rights of the Child and actions in Yemen, see Emmons and Jilani 2016.

55. See contributions in Moghadam, Franzway, and Fonow 2011.

56. See *Financial Times* 2019b.

57. Such proposals have been advanced by Senator Bernie Sanders, Senator Elizabeth Warren, and Congresswoman Alexandria Ocasio-Cortez.

58. Bello 2000. On the solidarity economy, see Allard, Davidson, and Matthaei 2008. Also see McBride 2001, especially chapter 8, and UNDP 2002, 3, on the Brazilian budgeting experiment.

59. Barber 2014; Smith 2017. On the Preston model, see https://blogs.lse.ac.uk/politicsandpolicy/local-democracy-with-attitude-the-preston-model. On Barcelona, see Gessen 2018; on Rojava, see Knapp, Flach, and Ayboga 2016. Rojova was attacked by Turkish forces in October 2019.

CHAPTER 4: ISLAMIST MOVEMENTS

1. Selections from the "Wave of Materialism" and "Crisis of Authority," in *Prison Notebooks*, by Antonio Gramsci (New York: International Publishers, 1971), 275–76.

2. Al-Muhajiroun was disbanded in 2004 and its leader, Omar Bakri Muhammad, has not been allowed back into the United Kingdom since August 2005. The group's tenet was "the use of military coups to establish Islamic states wherever

there are Muslims, including Britain" (Wiktorowicz 2005, 7). Considered by many UK Muslims as a "lunatic fringe," it managed to elicit considerable media attention.

3. Moaddel 2005, 1; Roberts 2003; Voll 1991, cited in Marty and Appleby 1991; Esposito 2002, 45–46. Salafists are literalists who also believe that Muslims should be ruled by an Islamic state similar to that established by the Prophet Muhammad and his successors (the Salaf). They formed partly in opposition to folkloric versions of Islam (maraboutism) practiced by rural people and the urban poor.

4. Gerges 2005; Hafez 2003; Wiktorowicz 2000, 2001, 2004a, 2004b, 15.

5. Abrahms and Glaser 2017; Gerges 2017; Stern and Berger 2015; Stevenson 2019. See also Roberts (2015, 10), who writes that US Intelligence was aware as early as summer 2012 that "an undeclared Salafist principality in eastern Syria" was in the making and that "this is exactly what the opposition wants, in order to isolate the Syrian regime." Roberts explains that the leak was published by a conservative watchdog organization called Judicial Watch. Abrahms (2017) has written of the Western media's bias in favor of Syrian (and foreign) rebels, and how the media have played down the rebels' extremism.

6. Clark and Schwedler 2003; Schwedler 2006; White 2003; Wickham 2002; Zeghal 2008.

7. See, for example, Rahman 1982. Fazlur Rahman was a critic of political and theological dogmatism whose career included a senior civil service post in Pakistan and a professorship at the University of Chicago. See Charles Kurzman's Liberal Islam project at http://www.unc.edu/~kurzman/LiberalIslamLinks.htm.

8. While they attracted many supporters in Iran and the diaspora, the "new religious intellectuals" were harassed or forced into exile by the authorities. For more information on these proponents of a liberal Islam, see Kurzman's online sources; see also Mir-Hosseini and Tapper 2006.

9. Internationally, the Swiss-born intellectual Tariq Ramadan is known as a proponent of nonviolent and liberal Islam, although some feminist groups have viewed him with suspicion. See Fourest 2004. (In 2017, he was accused of sexual assault, a charge he denied.) On the Ahmadiyya—who often are persecuted as heretics—see http://www.muslimsforpeace.org. The US-based ASMA society may be found at http://asmasociety.org/home/index.html.

10. The reformed law defines marriage as an equal partnership between spouses, with equal responsibility for the family. It gave women the right to divorce and also protected them from *talaq*, an Islamic practice that gives husbands the right to dissolve a marriage at will. See Sadiqi and Ennaji 2006; Moghadam and Gheytanchi 2010. On Musawah, see Segran 2013; https://musawah.org and Musawah September 2017 newsletter: http://www.musawah.org/sites/default/files/Vision%20Newsletter%20issue%20n%C2%AF22_final.compressed_0.pdf.

11. Al-Azm 1993, 117. See also Marty and Appelby 1991, 1994; Kepel 2002; Juergensmeyer 2003. On Islamic activists see Wiktorowicz 2004b, 2; Hafez 2003, 5.

12. Sadik Jalal al-Azm, "What Is Islamism?" (unpublished paper given to the author by al-Azm, Damascus, Syria, December 17, 2007). Al-Azm, retired professor of modern European philosophy at the University of Damascus, is one of the most prominent critical intellectuals in the Arab world.

13. Amin 2007, 2. That Islamist movements are right-wing as well as patriarchal has long been argued by transnational feminists such as Marième Hélie-Lucas, a founder of Women Living under Muslim Laws. See chapter 5 for details.

14. Regarding Iran, I have referred to two revolutions: the populist revolution against the shah in 1978–79 and the Islamic takeover in 1979–81 (Moghadam 1989). On the demonstration effect of Iran's Islamic revolution, see Esposito 1989.

15. On Western and Saudi support for Islamism, see Curtis 2010; Hegghammer 2010; Rubin 1997; Cooley 1999 (the quote appears on page 1). On Indonesia, see Hefner 2000; Dhume 2009.

16. Nakhleh 2009, 21–22.

17. On the assassination of Salmaan Taseer, see "Staring into the Abyss: Pakistan's Increasing Radicalization," *Economist*, January 8, 2011; the quote appears on page 39. See also Walsh 2011.

18. See Saad Eddin Ibrahim's pioneering sociological study of Islamists (Ibrahim 1980). On women, the veil, and male anxiety, see Mernissi 1987; Sabbah 1984. Other feminist studies on fundamentalism and Islamism include Kandiyoti 1991; Moghadam 1994b.

19. Wiktorowicz 2004a, 16.

20. Olesen 2007, 42. See also Klausen 2009 and Lindekilde 2010 for more on the Danish cartoon controversy.

21. On "blowback," see Johnson 2001. The origin of the name "al-Qaeda" is unclear; it may refer to a "base" used by bin Laden and his associates in Afghanistan; see Halliday 2005, 196. See also Gerges 2005 on transnational Islam.

22. Cesari 2004; Meer 2010. See also *Guardian Weekly*, "Cameron Cuts off Cash to Islamic Groups Suspected of Extremism," February 11, 2011, 13. In July 2010, the French National Assembly voted 335–1 to ban the wearing of the niqab or burka (which covers the face as well as the hair and body). The law is formally called "Forbidding the Concealing of the Face in the Public Space." See also *Guardian Weekly*, "Catalonia's 'Illegal' Islamic Court," December 18, 2009, 11.

23. Entelis 2005; Wiktorowicz 2004a, 20; Hafez 2004; Hafez 2003; Hafez and Wiktorowicz 2004, 62.

24. Hafez and Wiktorowicz 2004, 62.

25. The indented GIA quote appears in Hafez 2004, 52; others are found on pages 48–49, 50. On feminist concerns and activities in Algeria, see Moghadam 2001, 2011a; Salhi 2010.

26. See Goodwin 2007. Abrahms, in personal communication with the author, October 2019.

27. Ghannouchi, cited in Fadel 2011, 4.

28. Gulalp 2001, 434.

29. Gulalp 2001. See also Tugal 2009.

30. Rousselin 2015, 202; Cimini 2017, 52, 62, 63. See also Kienle 2015 and Saif and Rumman 2012.

31. Abdo 2000. For a sympathetic view of the Muslim Brotherhood, see Tariq Ramadan, in *The Fundamentalisms Project*, vol. 3.

32. Brown, Hamzawy, and Ottaway 2006; Komsan 2010a.

33. Komsan 2010a, 2010b. See also http://www.ecrwonline.org.

34. Kurzman 2012. On the class composition of MB members, see Masoud 2014, 6.

35. Pargeter 2010; El-Ghobashy 2005, 391. David Wroe, "Divisions in the Muslim Brotherhood," *The Age*, November 16, 2007, accessed December 12, 2007, http://www.theage.com.au/news/world/divisions-in-muslim-brother hood/2007/11/16/1194766965617.html.

36. Ghanouchi, 1993, 271–78.

37. See *Economist*, "Coptic Christians: Blue Christmas," January 5, 2019, 34–35; *Economist*, "Extremism in Pakistan: Standing up to Bigotry," November 3, 2018, 39; and *Economist*, "The World This Week," May 11, 2019, 9.

38. Siddiqui 2009.

39. *Economist*, "Dreaming of a Caliphate," August 6, 2011, 22.

40. Moaddel forthcoming 2020.

41. Wiktorowicz 2005, 85; Wickham 2002.

42. Tugal 2009.

43. In Islamabad, Pakistan, in July 2007, thousands of militants associated with the Red Mosque and its affiliated schools barricaded themselves with arms until military units eventually attacked.

44. Clark 2004; Harik 2004; Roy 2011. Sara Roy maintains that Hamas is at heart a political organization, albeit one that has encouraged the Islamization of Gazan society. Its social work and attention to the practical needs of those in Gaza is also a political move—especially in light of competition from the Palestine Liberation Organization and from newly formed Salafist groups.

45. Wiktorowicz 2004a. See also Davis and Robertson 2009 on how certain faith-based organizations can succeed at strategies of "bypassing the state" and building grassroots organizations.

46. Black 2007.

47. See *Economist* 2010. See also Steger 2003, 5, 2; Blunt 2009. The dissemination of extremist messages via the media, as well as radical mosques, may help explain the string of attacks on churches in the Muslim world. For example, nine churches were attacked in Malaysia in January 2010; the perpetrators, Muslim extremists, were angered by a court ruling overturning a ban on non-Muslims using

the word "Allah" for God. See the *Economist*, January 16, 2010, 8. The extremist Nigerian group Boko Haram went on a rampage in early 2012, killing Christians worshipping in church and then attacking police.

48. On the ISIS web presence, see Irshaid 2014 and https://www.wired.com/2016/03/isis-winning-social-media-war-heres-beat.

49. Khosrokhavar 2005.

50. Al-Azm 2004, 19. See also the miniseries *Carlos*, released by French filmmaker Olivier Assayas in 2010, which depicts the brief episode of Europe's experience with the extreme Left in the 1970s.

51. Al-Azm 2004, 19–20.

52. Al-Azm 2004, 20–21.

53. See Arab Barometer 2019.

54. Fuller 2002, 52–53.

55. Huntington 1996.

CHAPTER 5: FEMINISM ON A WORLD SCALE

1. World March of Women, declaration at World Social Forum, Porto Alegre, 2002; Fraser, Bhattacharya, and Arruzza 2018.

2. See, for example, Chafetz and Dworkin 1986; Dahlerup 1987; Margolis 1993; Basu 1995; Beckwith 2007; Molyneux 2001; Ferree and Tripp 2006.

3. Stienstra 1994, 2000; Naples and Desai 2002; Moghadam 2005.

4. Sperling, Ferree, and Risman 2001, 1157; Hawkesworth 2006, 27; Moghadam 2005, 2015.

5. Fraser, Bhattacharya, and Arruzza (2018), who offer eleven theses (as Marx did). The second epigraph at the beginning of this chapter is Thesis 10.

6. Thanks to Joan Ecklein, of WILPF-Boston, for this information. She attended a WIDF meeting in East Berlin in 1975. Joan Ecklein, personal communication with author, August 19, 2019.

7. The Palestinian question also divided participants, especially at the Copenhagen NGO Forum. See Fraser 1987.

8. Standing 1989, 1999a. Women-in-development (WID) began in the early 1970s and sought to bring attention to the problems facing women in the development process, including their marginalization from productive activities. Women-and-development (WAD) emerged as a more critical turn, and researchers raised questions about the nature of the development process into which women were to be integrated (see Beneria and Sen 1981; Elson and Pearson 1981). The gender-and-development (GAD) approach grounded itself more explicitly in feminist theorizing (see Young 1992).

9. For references to the prodigious literature, see Moghadam 2016. Two noteworthy examples are Sen and Grown 1987 and Elson 1991.

10. On female poverty, see Beneria and Feldman 1992; Chant 1995; Mogha-dam 1998b. On restructuring in the former communist bloc, see Moghadam 1993a; Rueschemeyer 1998. On global restructuring, see Marchand and Runyan 2010.

11. For an elaboration of various types of fundamentalism across the globe, their gender dynamics, and their impacts on women's legal status and social positions, see contributions in Kandiyoti 1991 and Moghadam 1994b.

12. Alvarez et al. 2002.

13. Moghadam 2003, chapter 7.

14. See Moghadam 1998b.

15. Women in Development Europe 1998; Wichterich 1999.

16. For more details on the activities of DAWN, WIDE, and WEDO, see Moghadam 2005, chapter 5.

17. International Confederation of Free Trade Unions (ICFTU), "3,000 Trade Unionists March in Protest at Poverty and Violence against Women in Durban on April 5," accessed April 15, 2002, http://www.icftu.org. The ICFTU is now known as the International Trade Union Confederation (ITUC), a nod to post–Cold War realities.

18. Moghadam 2005, 75–76. See also World March of Women 1999.

19. Dufour and Giraud 2007, 310; 318–19.

20. Author's personal observations at WSF Tunis.

21. Patricia Munoz Cabrera, "Globalising Gender Equality and Social Justice; WIDE—Women in Development Europe," prepared for the international Women's Studies North and South conference, Bellagio, Italy, September 13–17, 2011 (conference organized by the author).

22. WIDE+ 2015.

23. Kazi 1997, 141.

24. Shaheed 1994, 7–8.

25. Marieme Hélie-Lucas, personal communication with author, July 3, 2003. Charlotte Bunch, founder and first director of the Center for Women's Global Leadership at Rutgers University, was instrumental not only in raising funds for women's groups and their meetings but also in conceptualizing women's rights in the private sphere as human rights. For details on Algerian women's organizations, see Moghadam 2003, chapters 3 and 8, and Moghadam 2011a; see also Messaoudi and Schemla 1998.

26. The cautionary message about an Islamist international was stated at a conference I organized on comparative fundamentalisms and women, which took place at UNU/WIDER in Helsinki, Finland, in October 1990. See Moghadam 1994b; see also Hélie-Lucas 1993, 225. Disclosure: I provided some of the background information for a 2004 legal suit brought at the request of WLUML against an Algerian Islamist's request for political asylum in the United States.

27. Boix 2001, 6, 7.

28. See http://wluml.org/english/links.shtml (accessed January 16, 2008).

29. See http://wluml.org/english/pubsfulltxt.shtml?cmd[87]=i-87–549649 (accessed January 16, 2008).

30. See http://www.learningpartnership.org. Much of the information in this section comes from my observations and interviews conducted in March 2010 at the WLP offices in Bethesda, Maryland; a transnational partners' meeting that took place in Jakarta in April 2010; and a site visit to BAOBAB in Nigeria in July 2010.

31. WLP sometimes piggybacks on international conferences to bring its members together; an example is the World Democracy Movement conference, held in Jakarta, Indonesia, in April 2010. I attended the WLP meeting there and conducted individual interviews with WLP partners from Afghanistan, Morocco, and Nigeria.

32. Enloe 2007, 14. See also Confortini 2012; Enloe 1990; Reardon 1993; Tickner 1992; Accad 2007; Flamhaft 2007; Moghadam 2007.

33. Lucille Mathurin Mair was secretary-general of the UN's second conference on women, which convened in Copenhagen in 1980. The passage is cited in Bunch and Carillo 1992, 71. See also Pietila and Vickers 1994.

34. See http://www.un.org/docs/scres.

35. Jang Roko Abhiyan, "Rally on the 25th [of September, 2001]," circulated via the internet by socglob@topica.com.

36. See Eleanor Smeal (president of the Feminist Majority), "Special Message from the Feminist Majority on the Taliban, Osama bin Laden, and Afghan Women," Feminist Majority, September 18, 2001, http://feministmajority.org. It's unfortunate that this excellent statement came so late in Afghan developments.

37. See http://www.IWTC.org.

38. Starhawk 2003, 17.

39. See Kutz-Flamenbaum 2007.

40. MADRE statement communicated to author via e-mail in 2003.

41. *Ms. Magazine* (Spring 2003): 62, 65, 66.

42. This occurred on October 24, 2007, and was widely reported. Rice had been on Capitol Hill to testify before the House Foreign Relations Committee.

43. Milazzo 2005, 103. See also Brim 2003, 10–12.

44. See https://www.codepink.org/about.

45. See http://www.nobelwomensinitative.org. I was an invited participant. The six founders are Shirin Ebadi of Iran, Jody Williams of the United States, Betty Williams and Mairead Corrigan of Northern Ireland, Wangari Matthai of Kenya, and Rigoberta Menchu of Guatemala. The first international conference took place in Galway, Ireland, in May 2007, and was attended by roughly seventy-five women from across the globe.

46. MADRE, "MADRE Programs in Iraq," accessed November 28, 2007, http://madre.org/programs/Iraq.html.

47. See http://madre.org/programs/index.html.

48. MADRE, "Honor Crimes," November 28, 2007, http://www.madre.org/articles/int/honorcrimes.html. See also MADRE, "Mission | Vision," http://www.madre.org/index/meet-madre-1/who-we-are-49/mission—vision-160.html.

49. Eisenstein 2004; Enloe 2007.

50. Vargas 2005, 109–10.

51. Conway 2007, 50, 57, 63. In the latter quote, Conway is citing from a 2006 article by Nandita Gandhi and Nandita Shah.

52. WIDE Newsletter Special, April 2011, 1, http://www.wide-network.org.

53. Author's personal observation and notes, Tunis, March 26–30, 2013.

54. Author's personal notes, Tunis, March 27, 2013.

55. See Women Living under Muslim Laws 2005. Tariq Ramadan is considered by many observers to be an important intellectual and a representative of a liberal or moderate Islam. But others view him with skepticism. For a critique of Tariq Ramadan's Arabic-language statements, see Fourest 2004. Caroline Fourest—who also authored a scathing critique of the French Far Right nationalist leader Jean-Marie Le Pen—notes that in one of Ramadan's cassettes, Ramadan deliberately conflates "so-called secular Muslims" with "Muslims lacking Islam" (149). He also calls veiling a Muslim obligation and encourages young women to defend their right to veil, in part to protect themselves against the male gaze (see Fourest 2004, 212, quoting another cassette). At the First International Congress of Islamic Feminism, held in Barcelona in late October 2005 and organized by the Junta Islamica Catalan and the UNESCO office in Barcelona, Zainah Anwar of the Malaysian group Sisters in Islam told me that Tariq Ramadan had defended hijab at a meeting in Kuala Lumpur, leading to a spirited debate with the Islamic feminists who were themselves not veiled.

56. Author's personal observation, IAFFE conference, Glasgow, June 2019.

57. Vargas 2005, 109.

CHAPTER 6: THE GLOBAL JUSTICE MOVEMENT

1. This quote is from Franklin 2011, 13. Camila Vallejo, twenty-three, a member of the Communist Party, was elected leader of the University of Chile student union and led protests against the two-tiered system of education and the underfunding of public schools and universities. In 2019, as a member of Parliament representing the Communist Party, she was a leading figure in the renewed protests against the right-wing government of billionaire Sebastian Pinera, calling for a shorter work week, free education, and tax policies to reduce income inequality.

2. See, for example, della Porta 2007.

3. Taylor 1993, 2000.

4. Bello 2000, 55. On Ghana, see Njehu 2004, 103.

5. Mamdani 2018, 32.

6. Walton and Seddon 1994.

7. Subcomandante Marcos 2004.

8. Njehu 2004.

9. George 2004, 194. Susan George, a veteran international activist, adds that Jubilee 2000 dissolved itself in 2000, while other groups within the GJM continued to campaign for the abolition of all Third World debt.

10. George 2004, 196.

11. See Langman, Morris, and Zalewski 2002.

12. Bello 2004, 55. Bello adds that "the war on terror" resulted in a return of the US military bases.

13. Bello 2004, 64. Bernard Cassen of *Le Monde Diplomatique* and ATTAC and Susan George of the Transnational Institute and ATTAC were instrumental in working with the PT to launch the First WSF.

14. Pianta and Marchetti 2007, 40–41.

15. Podobnik 2005.

16. Moghadam 2005, 31–32; Pianta and Marchetti 2007, 40–41.

17. Various news reports covered the protest events of the early 2000s—for example, Tom Hundley, "Anti-Globalization Groups Gear Up," *Chicago Tribune*, July 15, 2001; Ben White, "An Elite Cast Debates Poverty," *Washington Post*, February 3, 2002; and Leslie Crawford, "Huge Protest March Passes Off Peacefully," *Financial Times*, March 18, 2002.

18. Pianta and Marchetti 2007, 39.

19. Cited in Franklin 2011, 13.

20. See, for example, Esther Addley, "Local Action with Global Message," *Guardian Weekly*, October 21–27, 2011, 1.

21. Vargas 2005.

22. Reese, Gutierrez, and Chase-Dunn 2007, 4.

23. della Porta 2007, 44.

24. For example, in West Lafayette, Indiana, where I was based from January 2007 to December 2011, the GJM was present in the form of an anti-sweatshop student group at Purdue University called POLE (Purdue Organization for Labor Equality) and a community group called the Greater Lafayette Progressive Alliance. Members of both attended the United States Social Forum (USSF) that took place in Atlanta, Georgia, in July 2007. I also participated in the second USSF in Detroit, Michigan, in June 2010 and observed many student groups and community-based activist groups in attendance.

25. ATTAC, https://www.attac.org.

26. Ancelovici 2002.

27. https://www.attac.org/en.

28. Reese, Gutierrez, and Chase-Dunn 2007, 6.

29. See Brewer, Katz-Fishman, and Scott 2016.

30. Mertes 2004, 242.

31. Reese, Gutierrez, and Chase-Dunn 2007, 6. See also Smith et al. 2008.

32. Santos 2006, 95. Reese, Gutierrez, and Chase-Dunn (2007) surveyed 640 participants (out of 155,000 registered participants from 135 countries) at the 2005 WSF in Porto Alegre and found the following demographic breakdown: South Americans represented 68 percent of those surveyed (with Brazilians making up 58 percent of the total number); Western Europeans, 13 percent; North Americans, 9 percent; Asians, 8 percent; and Africans, 2 percent. Their sample included no participants from the Middle East or North Africa.

33. Smith and Smythe 2010. On Tunis 2015, see https://www.aljazeera.com/indepth/inpictures/2015/03/tunisia-hosts-world-social-forum-150328053159828.html and https://towardfreedom.org/archives/activism/making-a-better-world-the-2015-world-social-forum-in-tunis. The 2015 Forum opened just days after the March 18, 2015, ISIS attack on tourists at the Musée Bardo, which killed 22 people.

34. Santos 2006, 104, 188–95 (appendix 1). See also http://www.forumsocial mundial.org.br.

35. Borland 2006.

36. International Gender and Trade Network 2002.

37. Santos 2006, 53–54. Critiques by DAWN and WIDE are found in their online publications.

38. Santos 2006, 60.

39. See http://www.marchemondialedesfemmes.org/alliances_mondialisa tion/asamblea-movimientos-sociales/declarations/poa-2012/en. On women in Via Campesina, see Desmarais 2007.

40. From author's copy of the program.

41. Santos 2006, 35. See also World Social Forum 2001 for the Charter of Principles.

42. Santos 2006, 92–93.

43. Santos 2006, 111–26.

44. Reese, Gutierrez, and Chase-Dunn 2007. Many European activists feel that a strong EU is needed as a counterweight to US hegemony, but others in the GJM are opposed and prefer a return to local democracy.

45. Danaher cited in George 2004, 98. See also Pianta and Marchetti 2007, 48.

46. For some of these ideas, see contributions in Podobnik and Reifer 2004; George 2004; Smith et al. 2008; the WSF Charter of Principles and other documents; various publications by WIDE and Marche Mondiale des Femmes/World March of Women.

47. George 2004. Susan George was among the participants in a landmark conference, organized by left-wing sociology professors and held at the University of California–Santa Barbara, in May 2003, that sought to define and advance "critical globalization studies." Her presentation focused on the responsibility of scholar-activists. See Appelbaum and Robinson 2005.

48. Santos 2006, 205–7 (appendix 3). For the Bamako Appeal, see http://mrzine.monthlyreview.org/bamako.html. See also chapter 7.

49. See Broad 2002, 42–46. The statement was issued and signed, inter alia, by Maude Barlow (Council of Canadians), Walden Bello (Focus on the Global South), Lori Wallach (Public Citizen), Vandana Shiva, and John Cavanaugh.

50. Shiva 2000, 123–24; Bello 2000, 90.

51. Klein 2007a. See also US filmmaker Oliver Stone's documentary *South of the Border*, released in 2010, which provides a good visual depiction of the Latin American "pink tide."

52. On the 2011 Montreal conference, see http://www.fiess2011.org/en; on the SEN, see http://www.ussen.org; for case studies of solidarity economy, visit http://aloe.socioeco.org/page70-studies_en.html, and https://transformadora.org/en/2020.

53. Tufekci 2016.

54. For a detailed set of essays by participants of the WSF, see Sen 2017, 2018. For a review essay and critical appraisal, see Moghadam 2019.

55. Moghadam 2005.

CHAPTER 7: POPULISMS IN THE WORLD-SYSTEM

1. Marx, "The Eighteenth Brumaire of Louis Bonaparte," in McLennan 1977, 300.

2. Schafer 2017, 1.

3. On Israel, see Ishay 2019; on India, see Bose 2017 and Burke 2014; on Turkey, see Dincsahin 2012.

4. Abrahamian 1993; Dorraj 1990; Moghadam 1993b; Tavakoli-Targhi 1988.

5. Laclau 2005; Skocpol and Williamson 2012.

6. Gidron and Bonikowski 2013.

7. Canovan 1999, 3; Archibugi and Cellini 2018; Ionescu and Gellner 1969; Aytac and Öniş 2014; Dincsahin 2012, 625.

8. Norris and Inglehart 2019, 66.

9. Mudde 2007.

10. Muis and Immerzeel 2017, 910; Norris and Inglehart 2019, 78.

10. Norris and Inglehart 2019, 78.

11. See Charlemagne, "Meet Marion Maréchal," *Economist*, March 16, 2019, 36.

12. *Economist*, "The AKK Era Begins," December 15, 2018, 44.

13. Ukraine is "a hotbed of far-right activity since the Maidan uprising in 2014. Quasi-fascist militia, such as the Azov Battalion, have fought Russia in the east and taken a role in policing." See *Economist*, "No Safe Places: White Nationalist Terrorism," March 23, 2019, 56–58.

14. See Runciman 2018. Albright's 2018 book is *Fascism: A Warning*.

15. Goodhart 2017; Hochschild 2016; Doerschler and Jackson 2018.

16. Hochschild 2016; Galston 2017.

17. On Muslim societies, see Moaddel 2002; Wiktorowicz 2000, 2004b, 2005. On Germany, see Garton Ash 2017. On Poland and Hungary, see Golebiowska 2017.

18. Orange 2018.

19. Harding 2019, 6.

20. Mudde and Kaltwasser 2017, 35. See also *Economist* 2018b.

21. *Economist*, January 26, 2019, 25.

22. Meret and Siim 2013a.

23. *Financial Times*, January 10, 2019. See also Judis 2016.

24. *Economist*, "When You Wish upon Five Stars: Italy's Populist Government Is Dreaming of Economic Growth," February 9, 2019, 28; Henly 2018, 10; See also https://en.wikipedia.org/wiki/Italian_general_election_2018.

25. See the following reports: https://www.theguardian.com/world/2010/oct/17/angela-merkel-german-multiculturalism-failed; https://www.independent.co.uk/news/uk/politics/cameron-my-war-on-multiculturalism-2205074.html; https://www.dailymail.co.uk/news/article-1355961/Nicolas-Sarkozy-joins-David-Cameron-Angela-Merkel-view-multiculturalism-failed.html.

26. See http://www.munkgc.com/europe/the-rise-of-right-wing-populism-in-the-nordic-countries; and Meret and Siim 2013a, 2013b.

27. Orange 2018.

28. Drohan 2019, 48.

29. Jayawardena 1986; Moghadam 1994b; Thapar-Björkert 2013; Yuval-Davis, 1997.

30. On Egypt, see Badran 1995 and Baron 2005; on Iran, see Afary 1996; on Turkey, see Kandiyoti 1989; on Palestine, see Gerner 2007.

31. Kandiyoti 1991; Moghadam 1994b; Taraki 1995.

32. See contributions in Moghadam 1994b by Alya Baffoun, Cherifa Bouatta and Doria Cherifati-Merabtine, Marieme Hélie-Lucas, and Binnaz Toprak.

33. Their contributions are in Moghadam 1994b.

34. See Power 2002 on Chile; Pratt 2012 on Egypt.

35. Kaufman, "Paradoxical Politics: Gender Politics among Newly Orthodox Jewish Women in the United States"; Klatch, "Women of the New Right in the United States: Family, Feminism, and Politics," both in Moghadam 1994b. See also Klatch 1987; Manning 1999; Stacey 1983.

36. Celis and Childs 2012, 214.

37. On the US women's votes in 2016, see Junn 2017 and Darby 2017; on the Turkish votes for Erdoğan, see Bostan 2011; see also Setzler and Yanus 2018.

38. Meret, Siim, and Pingeaud 2016. On voting patterns, see Spierings and Zaslove 2017.

39. Clark and Schwedler 2003; Shitrit 2016.

40. Chira 2018.

41. See Darby 2017; Junn 2017; Malone 2016; Strolovich, Wong, and Proctor 2017, 359.

42. Author observations and participation.

43. Harding 2019, 3.
44. Krizsán and Siim 2018.
45. See Graham-Harrison and Rasmussen 2018; *Economist* 2018e.
46. Inglehart and Norris 2016; Doerschler and Jackson 2018.
47. Connelly 2017, 4.
48. https://www.theguardian.com/world/ng-interactive/2017/sep/24/german
-elections-2017-latest-results-live-merkel-bundestag-afd.
49. Tyson and Maniam 2016.
50. Goodwin and Heath 2016.
51. See Lewis, Clarke, and Barr 2019.
52. Saif and Rumman 2012, 1.
53. Öniş 2004, 114, 118–19; Öniş 1997, 747–48.
54. Carkoglu 2002, 31–37. See also Özel 2003, 81–84.
55. Ayata and Tütüncü 2008, 468–70.
56. Elveren 2017, 4.
57. CNN Turk 2009.
58. Dincsahin 2012, 621. The enrollment in Imam-Hatip schools jumped from 65,000 when AKP came to power in 2002 to around 1.3 million in the 2016–17 school year (Elveren 2017, 5). Nawa and Sebzeci (2018) describe the creeping transformation of secular public schools into religious ones; evolution, for example, is rarely taught, ostensibly because students find it difficult to understand.
59. Dincsahin 2012, 636.
60. *Economist* 2018a, 48.
61. Peterson 2018.
62. Ilkkaracan 2012, 2017; Elveren 2017; Ayata and Tütüncü 2008; see also Çitak and Tür 2008.
63. *Economist* 2019b, 31–32.
64. Henley 2017.
65. Oltermann 2018.
66. Szabo 2015, 301–3, 310, 313.
67. *Financial Times* 2019a; Wilkin 2018.
68. Jasiewicz 2008, 7–8.
69. *Economist* 2018b, 43.
70. Jasiewicz 2008, 9.
71. *Economist*, March 2, 2019, 29; see also *Economist* 2018b, 43–44, citing a World Bank study; and *Economist* 2018d, 33.
72. Peto and Grzebalska 2016.
73. Cocotas 2017; Moore 2017.
74. Data from *Human Development Indices and Indicators, 2018 Statistical Update*. See UNDP 2018.

75. The paragraph draws on Ishay 2019, 109–10.

76. See *Times* (London), "Jewish Fauda Actor Sparks Row by Marrying a Muslim," October 20, 2018.

77. Shelev 2019.

78. Both quotes from Tharoor 2016.

79. Rodrik 2017.

80. Müller 2016a.

81. Bageant 2007; Hedges 2010; Lasch 1994; Müller 2016a, 2016b.

82. Langman 2020, and personal communication, August 2019.

83. Johnstone 2018; Rockhill 2019.

84. Harding (2019, 8) is referencing Guillot's *Twilight of the Elites: Prosperity, the Periphery and the Future of France*, trans. Malcolm Debevoise (New Haven, CT: Yale University Press, 2019).

85. Harding 2019, 11.

86. Harding writes that he observed the hammer-and-sickle flag on display, and members of the pro-communist trade union CGT were among the marchers. The leftists were "steering their comrades away from dangerous distractions [xenophobia, etc.] and sharpening the focus on inequality" (Harding 2019, 11).

87. Harding 2019, 5–6.

88. Oumlil 2017.

89. Salime 2019.

90. Kadivar and Sotoudeh 2018; Kalb 2018; Niknejad 2019.

91. See Bajoghli 2018; Ehsani and Keshavarzian 2018.

92. Serres 2019.

93. See Oxfam blog post by Sofia del Valle, "The Protests in Chile's Streets Are about Inequality," *Politics of Poverty* (blog), November 6, 2019, https://politicsof poverty.oxfamamerica.org/2019/11/protests-chile-inequality-social-justice.

94. Schafer 2017.

95. Piñeiro, Rhodes-Purdy, and Rosenblatt 2016.

96. See https://www.laprogressive.com/andres-manuel-lopez-obrador.

97. The "Squad" refers to Alexandria Ocasio-Cortez, Ayanna Pressley, Rashida Tlaib, and Ilham Omar. See also https://www.politico.com/interactives/2018/women -rule-candidate-tracker.

98. Councillor Alasdair Rankin (Scottish National Party, Edinburgh), letter to the editor, *Economist*, August 2, 2014, 12.

99. See *Economist*, January 5, 2018, 21.

100. Wallerstein 2011.

101. Wallerstein 2011; Mouffe 2018.

102. Corbyn 2018.

CHAPTER 8: CONCLUSIONS AND PROGNOSTICATION

1. Marx, *Theses on Feuerbach*, probably 1845, as cited in McLennan 1977, 156.
2. Sanders 2010.
3. Barber 1998.
4. Granovetter 1983; Langman 2005; Castells 1996; Giddens 1999.
5. Morozov 2011; Tufekci 2016.
6. Scheffer 2011.
7. Right-wing extremists have attacked politicians (the murder of member of Parliament Jo Cox in the United Kingdom in June 2016) and demonstrators (the August 2017 death in Charlottesville, Virginia, of protester Heather Heyer, run over by a car driven by a neo-Nazi).
8. Karl Marx, *The Eighteenth Brumaire of Louis Bonaparte*, in McLennan 1977, 322.

REFERENCES

Abdo, Geneive. 2000. *No God but God: Egypt and the Triumph of Islam.* Oxford: Oxford University Press.

Abrahamian, Ervand. 1993. *Khomeinism: Essays on the Islamic Republic.* Berkeley: University of California Press.

Abrahms, Max. 2017. "Syria's Extremist Opposition: How Western Media Have Whitewashed the Rebels' Record." *Foreign Affairs*, October 30, 2017. https://www.foreignaffairs.com/articles/middle-east/2017-10-30/syrias-extremist-opposition.

Abrahms, Max, and John Glaser. 2017. "The Pundits Were Wrong about Assad and the Islamic State: As Usual, They're Not Willing to Admit It." Op-ed, *Los Angeles Times*, December 10, 2017.

Accad, Evelyne. 2007. "Gender and Violence in Lebanese War Novels." In *From Patriarchy to Empowerment: Women's Participation, Movements, and Rights in the Middle East, North Africa, and South Asia*, edited by V. M. Moghadam, 293–310. Syracuse, NY: Syracuse University Press.

Afary, Janet. 1996. *The Iranian Constitutional Revolution 1906–1911: Grassroots Democracy and the Origins of Feminism.* New York: Columbia University Press.

Ake, Claude. 1993. "Rethinking African Democracy." In *The Global Resurgence of Democracy*, edited by Larry Diamond and Marc Plattner. Baltimore, MD: Johns Hopkins University Press.

Al-Ali, Nadje, and Latif Tas. 2017. "'War Is like a Blanket . . .': Feminist Convergences in Kurdish and Turkish Women's Rights Activism for Peace." *Journal of Middle East Women's Studies* 13 (3): 354–75.

Al-Azm, Sadik. 1993. "Islamic Fundamentalism Reconsidered: A Critical Outline of Problems, Ideas and Approaches." *South Asia Bulletin: Comparative Studies of South Asia, Africa, and the Middle East* 13 (1–2): 93–121.

———. 2004. "Islam, Terrorism and the West Today." Essay written for the Prae-
mium Esarmianum Foundation on the occasion of the award of the Erasmus
Prize, Amsterdam, November 2004. Naarden: Foundation Horizon.

Allard, Jenna, Carl Davidson, and Julie Matthaei, eds. 2008. *Solidarity Economy:
Building Alternatives for People and Planet.* Papers and Reports from the US Social
Forum 2007. Chicago: ChangeMaker Publications.

Alvarez, Sonia. 1990. *Engendering Democracy in Brazil: The Women's Movements in
Transition Politics.* Princeton, NJ: Princeton University Press.

Alvarez, Sonia, Elisabeth Jay Friedman, Ericka Beckman, Maylei Blackwell, Norma
Chinchilla, Nathalie Lebon, Marysa Navarrro, and Marcela Rios Tobar. 2002.
"Encountering Latin American and Caribbean Feminisms." *Signs: Journal of
Women in Culture and Society* 28 (2): 537–73.

Amin, Samir. 2007. "Political Islam in the Service of Imperialism." *Monthly Review*
59, no. 7 (December): 1–18.

Ancelovici, Marcos. 2002. "Organizing against Globalization: The Case of ATTAC
in France." *Politics & Society* 30, no. 3 (September): 427–63.

Anheier, Helmut, Marlies Glasius, and Mary Kaldor, eds. 2001. *The Global Civil
Society Yearbook.* Oxford: Oxford University Press.

Appelbaum, Richard, and William I. Robinson, eds. 2005. *Critical Globalization
Studies.* New York: Routledge.

Arab Barometer. 2019. "Findings Revealed from the Big BBC News Arabic Survey."
June 24, 2019. https://www.arabbarometer.org/media-news/findings-revealed
-from-the-big-bbc-news-arabic-survey.

Arat, Yesim. 1994. "Toward a Democratic Society: The Women's Movement in Turkey in the 1980s." *Women's Studies International Forum* 17 (2): 241–48.

Archibugi, Daniele, and Marco Cellini. 2018. "How Dangerous Is Populism for
Democracy?": *Global-E* 11, no. 21 (April 10, 2018). http://www.21global.ucsb
.edu/global-e/april-2018/how-dangerous-populism-democracy.

Arjomand, Said Amir. 1986. "Social Change and Movements of Revitalization in
Contemporary Islam." In *New Religious Movements and Rapid Social Change*,
edited by James Beckford, 87–112. Beverly Hills and Paris: Sage Publications
and UNESCO.

Arrighi, Giovanni, Terence K. Hopkins, and Immanuel Wallerstein. 1989. *Antisystemic Movements.* London: Verso.

Atkinson, Anthony. 2001. "Is Rising Inequality Inevitable? A Critique of the Trans-
atlantic Consensus." *WIDER Annual Lectures* 3 (November).

Ayata, Ayşe Günes, and Fatma Tütüncü. 2008. "Critical Acts without a Critical
Mass: The Substantive Representation of Women in the Turkish Parliament."
Parliamentary Affairs 61 (3): 461–75.

Aytac, Selim Erdem, and Ziya Öniş. 2014. "Varieties of Populism in a Changing
Global Context: The Divergent Paths of Erdogan and *Kirchnerismo*." *Comparative Politics* 47 (1): 41–59.

Badran, Margot. 1995. *Feminists, Islam, and the Nation*. Princeton, NJ: Princeton University Press.

Bageant, Joe. 2007. *Deer Hunting with Jesus: Dispatches from America's Class War.* New York: Three Rivers Press.

Baiocchi G., Patrick Heller, and M. K. Silva. 2011. *Bootstrapping Democracy: Transforming Local Governance and Civil Society in Brazil*. Stanford, CA: Stanford University Press.

Bajoghli, Narges. 2018. "Behind the Iranian Protests." *Jacobin Magazine*, January 4, 2018. https://www.jacobinmag.com/2018/01/iran-protests-hasan-rouhani-green -movement.

Bakker, Isabella, ed. 1994. *The Strategic Silence: Gender and Economic Policy*. London: Zed Books, in association with the North-South Institute.

Bal, Selin. 2016. "Aile Bakanı Ensar Vakfı'na sahip çıktı." *Genç Gazete*, March 22, 2016. http://gencgazete.org/aile-bakani-ensar-vakfina-sahip-cikti.

Barber, Benjamin. 1984. *Strong Democracy: Participatory Politics for a New Age*. Berkeley, Los Angeles, and London: University of California Press.

———. 1998. "More Democracy! More Revolution!" *Nation*, October 26, 1998, 11–15.

———. 2001. *Jihad vs. McWorld: How Globalism and Tribalism Are Reshaping the World*. New York: Ballantine.

———. 2014. *If Mayors Ruled the World: Dysfunctional Nations, Rising Cities*. New Haven, CT: Yale University Press.

Barkawi, Tarak. 2006. *Globalization and War*. Lanham, MD: Rowman & Littlefield.

Barnet, Richard J., and Ronald Muller. 1974. *Global Reach: The Power of Multinational Corporations*. New York: Simon & Schuster.

Baron, Beth. 2005. *Egypt as a Woman: Nationalism, Gender, and Politics*. Berkeley: University of California Press.

Barron, Andrea. 2002. "The Palestinian Women's Movement: Agent of Democracy in a Future State?" *Middle East Critique* 11 (1): 71–90.

Basu, Amrita, ed. 1995. *The Challenge of Local Feminisms: Women's Movements in Global Perspective*. Boulder, CO: Westview.

Bauer, Jan, and Anissa Hélie. 2006. *Documenting Women's Human Rights Violations by Non-state Actors: Activist Strategies from Muslim Communities*. Québec: International Centre for Human Rights and Democratic Development and WLUML.

Bayat, Asef. 2007. *Making Islam Democratic: Social Movements and the Post-Islamist Turn*. Stanford, CA: Stanford University Press.

Beck, Ulrich. 2004. "The Cosmopolitan Turn." In *The Future of Social Theory*, edited by Nicholas Gane, 143–66. London: Continuum.

Beckford, James, ed. 1986. *New Religious Movements and Rapid Social Change*. Thousand Oaks, CA, and Paris: Sage and UNESCO.

Beckwith, Karen. 2007. "Mapping Strategic Engagements: Women's Movements and the State." *International Feminist Journal of Politics* 9 (3): 312–38.

————. 2010. "Introduction: Comparative Politics and the Logics of a Comparative Politics of Gender." *Perspectives on Politics* 8, no. 1 (March): 159–68.

Beinin, Joel. 2009a. "Egyptian Workers from Arab Socialism to the Neo-liberal Economic Order." In *Egypt: The Moment of Change*, edited by Rabab El-Mahdi and Philip Marfleet, 68–86. London: Zed Books.

————. 2009b. "Workers' Protest in Egypt: Neo-liberalism and Class Struggle in the 21st Century." *Social Movement Studies* 8, no. 4 (November): 449–54.

————. 2012. "The Rise of Egypt's Workers." Washington DC: Carnegie Endowment for International Peace.

————. 2015. *Workers and Thieves: Labor Movements and Popular Uprisings in Tunisia and Egypt*. Stanford, CA: Stanford University Press.

Bello, Walden. 2000. "Building an Iron Cage." In *Views from the South: The Effects of Globalization and the WTO on Third World Countries*, edited by Sarah Anderson, 54–90. Chicago: Food First and the International Forum on Globalization.

————. 2004. "The Global South." In *A Movement of Movements: Is Another World Really Possible?*, edited by Tom Mertes, 49–69. London: Verso.

Beneria, Lourdes, and Shelley Feldman, eds. 1992. *Unequal Burden: Economic Crises, Persistent Poverty, and Women's Work*. Boulder, CO: Westview.

Beneria, Lourdes, and Gita Sen. 1981. "Accumulation, Reproduction and Women's Role in Development: Boserup Revisited." *Signs* 8, no. 2 (Winter).

Benhabib, Seyla. 2006. *Another Cosmopolitanism*. Oxford: Oxford University Press.

Benjamin, Medea, and Charles Davis. "Instead of Bombing Dictators, Stop Selling Them Bombs." Antiwar.com, March 24, 2001. https://original.antiwar.com/medea-benjamin-davis/2011/03/23/instead-of-bombing-dictators-stop-selling-them-bombs.

Bennoune, Karima. 1995. "S.O.S. Algeria: Women's Human Rights under Siege." In *Faith and Freedom: Women's Human Rights*, edited by Mahnaz Afkhami. Syracuse, NY: Syracuse University Press.

————. 2010. "Remembering the Other's Others: Theorizing the Approach of International Law to Muslim Fundamentalism." *Columbia Human Rights Law Review* 41:635–98.

Ben Shitrit, Lihi. 2015. *Righteous Transgressions: Women's Activism on the Israeli and Palestinian Religious Right*. Princeton, NJ: Princeton University Press.

Berger, Suzanne, and Ronald Dore, eds. 1996. *National Diversity and Global Capitalism*. Ithaca, NY: Cornell University Press.

Berkovitch, Nitza. 1999. *From Motherhood to Citizenship: Women's Rights and International Organizations*. Baltimore, MD: Johns Hopkins University Press.

Berkovitch, Nitza, and Valentine M. Moghadam. 1999. "Middle East Politics: Feminist Challenges." Introduction to special issue, *Social Politics: International Studies in Gender, State, and Society* 6, no. 3 (Fall).

Bhagwati, Jagdish. 2004. *In Defense of Globalization*. New York: Oxford University Press.

Bhavnani, Kum-Kum, John Foran, and Molly Talcott. 2005. "The Red, the Green, the Black, and the Purple: Reclaiming Development, Resisting Globalization." In *Critical Globalization Studies*, edited by Richard Appelbaum and William I. Robinson, 323–32. New York: Routledge.

Black, Ian. 2007. "Al-Qaida Chief Launched 'Any Questions' Sessions on Web." *Guardian*, December 20, 2007, 22.

Blee, Kathleen M., and Kimberly A. Creasap. 2010. "Conservative and Right-Wing Movements." *Annual Review of Sociology* 36:269–86.

Bloom, Ester. 2017. "EU Parliament Member: Women Must Earn Less because They Are Weaker, Less Intelligent." CNBC, March 7, 2017. https://www.cnbc.com/2017/03/07/polish-mep-women-must-earn-less-since-they-are-less-intelligent.html.

Bluestone, Barry, and Bennett Harrison. 1982. *The Deindustrialization of America: Plant Closings, Community Abandonment, and the Dismantling of Basic Industry.* New York: Basic Books.

Blunt, Gary. 2009. *iMuslims: Rewiring the House of Islam.* Chapel Hill: University of North Carolina Press.

Boix, Monserrat. 2001. "Women's Networks: Islamists' Violence and Terror." *WLUML Newssheet* 13, no. 4 (November–December).

Boli, John. 2005. "Contemporary Developments in World Culture." *International Journal of Contemporary Sociology* 46 (5–6): 383–404.

Boli, John, and George M. Thomas. 1997. "World Culture in the World Polity." *American Sociological Review* 62, no. 2 (April): 171–90.

Borland, Elizabeth. 2006. "The Mature Resistance of Argentina's Madres de Plaza de Mayo." In *Latin American Social Movements: Globalization, Democratization, and Transnational Networks*, edited by Hank Johnston and Paul Almeida, 115–44. Lanham, MD: Rowman & Littlefield.

Bose, Mihir. 2017. "Seventy Years after Independence, the India I Know Is Losing Its Way." *Guardian Weekly*, August 11, 2017.

Bostan, Yahya. 2011. "İşte % 50'nin sırrı." *Sabah*, October 3, 2011. https://www.sabah.com.tr/gundem/2011/10/03/yuzde-50-oyun-nedeni-sekuler-secmenler.

Boswell, Terry, and Christopher Chase-Dunn. 2000. *The Spiral of Capitalism and Socialism: Toward Global Democracy.* Boulder, CO: Lynne Rienner.

Boxer, Marilyn J., and Jean H. Quataert. 1978. *Socialist Women: European Socialist Feminism in the Nineteenth and Early Twentieth Centuries.* New York: Elsevier.

Bozkurt, Umut. 2013. "Neoliberalism with a Human Face: Making Sense of the Justice and Development Party's Neoliberal Populism in Turkey." *Science & Society* 77 (3): 372–96.

Bratton, Michael, and Nicholas Van De Walle. 1992. "Towards Governance in Africa: Popular Demands and State Responses." In *Governance and Politics in Africa*, edited by Goran Hyden and Michael Bratton. Boulder, CO: Lynne Rienner.

Brewer, Rose, Wanda Katz-Fishman, and Jerome Scott. 2016. "USSF3 Evaluation and Documentation: United States Social Forum." April 10, 2016. https://usso cialforum.net/ussf3-eval-and-documentation.pdf

Brim, Sand. 2003. "Report from Baghdad." *Off Our Backs* (March–April): 10–12.

Broad, Robin, ed. 2002. *Global Backlash: Citizen Initiatives for a Just World Economy.* Lanham, MD: Rowman & Littlefield.

Brown, Nathan. 2013. "Egypt's Failed Transition." *Journal of Democracy* 24, no. 2 (October): 45–58.

Brown, Nathan, Amr Hamzawy, and Marina S. Ottaway. 2006. "Islamist Movements and the Democratic Process in the Arab World: Exploring Gray Zones." Paper no. 67 (March). Washington, DC: Carnegie Endowment for International Peace. http://www.carnegieendowment.org/files/cp_67_grayzones_final.pdf.

Bunce, Valerie. 2003. "Rethinking Recent Democratization: Lessons from the Post-communist Experience." *World Politics* 55, no. 2 (January): 167–92.

Bunch, Charlotte, and Roxanna Carillo. 1992. *Gender Violence: A Development and Human Rights Issue.* Dublin: Atlantic Press.

Burawoy, Michael, Joseph A. Blum, Sheba George, Zsuzsa Gille, and Millie Thayer. 2000. *Global Ethnography: Forces, Connections, and Imaginations in a Postmodern World.* Berkeley: University of California Press.

Burke, Jason. 2014. "Narendra Modi and BJP Sweep to Power in Indian Election." *Guardian,* May 16, 2014. https://www.theguardian.com/world/2014/may/16/narenda-modi-bjp-sweep-power-indian-elections.

Canovan, Margaret. 1999. "Trust the People! Populism and the Two Faces of Democracy." *Political Studies* 47 (1): 2–16.

Carkoglu, Ali. 2002. "Turkey's November 2002 Elections: A New Beginning?" *Middle East Review of International Affairs* 6 (4): 30–41.

Case, Ann, and Sir Angus Deaton. 2017. "Mortality and Morbidity in the 21st Century." Brookings Papers on Economic Activity (Spring). https://www.brookings .edu/bpea-articles/mortality-and-morbidity-in-the-21st-century.

Castells, Manuel. 1996. *The Rise of the Network Society.* Oxford: Oxford University Press.

Castells, Manuel, Mireia Fernàndez-Ardèvol, and Araba Sey. 2006. *Mobile Communication and Society: A Global Perspective.* Cambridge, MA: MIT Press.

Celis, Karen, and Sarah Childs. 2012. "The Substantive Representation of Women: What to Do with Conservative Claims?" *Political Studies* 60:213–25.

Cesari, Jocelyne. 2004. *When Islam and Democracy Meet: Muslims in Europe and in the United States.* New York: Palgrave Macmillan.

Chafetz, Janet S., and Gary Dworkin. 1986. *Female Revolt: Women's Movements in World and Historical Perspective.* Totowa, NJ: Rowman & Allanheld.

Chang, Paul Y. 2008. "Unintended Consequences of Repression: Alliance Formation in South Korea's Democracy Movement (1970–1979)." *Social Forces* 87 (2): 651–77.

Chant, Sylvia. 1995. "Women's Roles in Recession and Economic Restructuring in Mexico and the Philippines." In *Poverty and Global Adjustment: The Urban Experience*, edited by Alan Gilbert. Oxford: Blackwell.

Charrad, Mounira. 2001. *States and Women's Rights: The Making of Postcolonial Tunisia, Algeria, and Morocco*. Berkeley: University of California Press.

Chase-Dunn, Christopher. 1998. *Global Formation: Structures of the World Economy*. 2nd ed. Lanham, MD: Rowman & Littlefield.

Chase-Dunn, Christopher, and Salvatore Babones, eds. 2006. *Global Social Change: Historical and Comparative Perspectives*. Baltimore, MD: Johns Hopkins University Press.

Chase-Dunn, Christopher, and Hiroko Inoue. 2017. "Long Cycles and World-Systems: Theoretical Research Programs." IROWS Working Paper 115. Riverside: University of California–Riverside, Institute for Research on World-Systems. https://irows.ucr.edu/papers/irows115/irows115.htm.

Chase-Dunn, Christopher, Yukio Kawano, and Benjamin Brewer. 2000. "Trade Globalization since 1795: Waves of Integration in the World-System." *American Sociological Review* 65 (1): 77–95.

Chase-Dunn, Christopher, Alessandro Morosin, and Alexis Álvarez. 2015. "Social Movements and Progressive Regimes in Latin America: World Revolutions and Semiperipheral Development." In *Handbook of Social Movements across Latin America*, edited by Paul Almeida and Allen Cordero Ulate. Dordrecht: Springer Netherlands.

Chase-Dunn, Christopher, Richard Niemeyer, Preeta Saxena, Matheu Kaneshiro, James Love, and Amanda Spears. 2009. "The New Global Left: Movements and Regimes." IROWS Working Paper 50. Riverside: University of California–Riverside, Institute for Research on World-Systems. https://irows.ucr.edu/papers/irows50/irows50.htm.

Cherifati-Merabtine, Doria. 1995. "Algerian Women at a Crossroads: National Liberation, Islamization, and Women." In *Gender and National Identity: Women and Politics in Muslim Societies*, edited by Valentine M. Moghadam, 40–62. London: Zed Books.

Chira, Susan. 2018. "Women Don't Think Alike. Why Do We Think They Do?" *New York Times*, October 12, 2018. https://www.nytimes.com/2018/10/12/sunday-review/conservative-women-trump-kavanaugh.html.

Chossudovsky, Michel, and Andrew Gavin Marshall, eds. 2010. *The Global Economic Crisis: The Great Depression of the XXI Century*. Montreal: Global Research Publishers, Centre for Research on Globalization.

Chua, Amy. 2003. *World on Fire: How Exporting Free Market Democracy Breeds Ethnic Hatred and Global Instability*. New York: Doubleday.

Cimini, Giulia. 2017. "The Economic Agendas of Islamic Parties in Tunisia and Morocco: Between Discourses and Practices." *Asian Journal of Middle Eastern and Islamic Studies* 11 (3): 48–64.

Çitak, Zana, and Özlem Tür. 2008. "Women between Tradition and Change: The Justice and Development Party Experience in Turkey." *Middle Eastern Studies* 44 (3): 455–69.

Clark, Janine. 2004. *Islam, Charity, and Activism: Middle-Class Networks and Social Welfare in Egypt, Jordan, and Yemen.* Bloomington: Indiana University Press.

Clark, Janine, and Jillian Schwedler. 2003. "Who Opened the Window? Women's Activism in Islamist Parties." *Comparative Politics* 35 (3): 293–312.

CNN. 2013. "Kentucky Dems Demand McConnell Apologize for *Golden Girls* Quip." CNN Politics, March 15, 2013. http://politicalticker.blogs.cnn.com/2013/03/15/kentucky-dems-demand-mcconnell-apology-for-golden-girls-quip.

CNN Turk. 2009. "Kriz teğet geçti dedim, etkilemedi demedim." CNN Türk, April 3, 2009. https://www.cnnturk.com/2009/ekonomi/dunya/04/03/kriz.teget.gecti.dedim.etkilemedi.demedim/520810.0/index.html.

Cocotas, Alex. 2017. "How Poland's Far-Right Government Is Pushing Abortion Underground." *Guardian*, November 30, 2017. https://www.theguardian.com/news/2017/nov/30/how-polands-far-right-government-is-pushing-abortion-underground.

Collectif Maghreb Egalité 95. 2005. *Guide to Equality in the Family in the Maghreb.* Translated by Chari Voss. Bethesda, MD: Women's Learning Partnership for Rights, Development and Peace.

Confortini, Catia Cecilia. 2012. *Intelligent Compassion: Feminist Critical Methodology in the Women's International League for Peace and Freedom.* New York: Oxford University Press.

Connell, R. W. 1998. "Masculinities and Globalization." *Men and Masculinities* 1 (1): 1–20.

Connelly, Kate. 2017. "Weakened Merkel Begins the Tough Job of Forming Coalition." *Guardian Weekly*, September 29, 2017.

Conway, Jane. 2007. "Transnational Feminisms and the World Social Forum: Encounters and Transformations in Anti-globalization Spaces." *Journal of International Women's Studies* 8, no. 3 (April): 49–70.

Cooley, John. 1999. *Unholy Wars: Afghanistan, America and International Terrorism.* London: Pluto Press.

Corbyn, Jeremy. 2018 (Dec.). "The Other Path Ahead." Special issue, *Economist*.

Cordovez, Diego, and Selig S. Harrison. 1995. *Out of Afghanistan: The Inside Story of the Soviet Withdrawal.* New York: Oxford University Press.

Cornia, Giovanni Andrea, Richard Jolly, and Frances Stewart. 1989. *Adjustment with a Human Face: Protecting the Vulnerable and Promoting Growth.* Oxford: Clarendon Press and UNICEF.

Costain, Anne. 2005. "Social Movements as Mechanisms for Political Inclusion." In *The Politics of Democratic Inclusion*, edited by Christina Wolbrecht and Rodney Hero, 108–21. Philadelphia: Temple University Press.

Cox, Robert W. 1992. "Global Perestroika." In *Socialist Register 1992*, edited by Ralph Miliband and Leo Panitch, 26–43. London: Merlin Press.

Crick, Bernard. 2000. *Essays on Citizenship*. London: Continuum.

Cummings, Bruce. 2000. "Democracy and Civil Society in Korea." In *Pathways to Democracy: The Political Economy of Democratic Transitions*, edited by James F. Hollifield and Calvin Jillson, 133–46. New York: Routledge.

Curtis, Mark. 2010. *Secret Affairs: Britain's Collusion with Radical Islam*. London: Serpent's Tail.

Dahlerup, Drude, ed. 1987. *The New Women's Movement: Feminism and Political Power in Europe and the USA*. London: Sage.

Darby, Seyward. 2017. "The Rise of the Valkyries: In the Alt-Right, Women Are the Future, Not the Problem." *Harper's Magazine*, September 2017. https://harpers.org/archive/2017/09/the-rise-of-the-valkyries.

Darom, Naomi. 2017. "What Did the Women in the Women's March March About?" Paper written for Sociology 7225: Gender and Social Movements. Northeastern University, December 2017.

Davies, Christian. 2018. "Polish MPs Back Even Tougher Restrictions on Abortion." *Guardian*, January 11, 2018. https://www.theguardian.com/world/2018/jan/11/polish-mps-reject-liberalised-abortion-laws-but-back-new-restrictions.

Davis, Nancy J., and Robert V. Robertson. 2009. "Overcoming Movement Obstacles by the Religiously Orthodox: The Muslim Brotherhood in Egypt, Shas in Israel, Communione e Liberazione in Italy, and the Salvation Army in the United States." *American Journal of Sociology* 114 (5): 1305–49.

della Porta, Donatella. 2005. "Deliberation in Movement: Why and How to Study Deliberative Democracy and Social Movements." *Acta Politica* 40 (3): 336–50.

———, ed. 2007. *The Global Justice Movement: Cross-National and Transnational Perspectives*. Boulder, CO: Paradigm.

———. 2009. "Making the New Polis: The Practice of Deliberative Democracy in Social Forums." In *Culture, Social Movements and Protest*, edited by Hank Johnston, 181–208. Farnham, UK: Ashgate.

Desmarais, Annette Aurélie. 2007. *La Via Campesina: Globalization and the Power of Peasants*. Halifax, Canada, and London, UK: Fernwood Publishing and Pluto Press.

Dhume, Sadanand. 2009. *My Friend the Fanatic: Travels with a Radical Islamist*. New York: Skyhorse.

Diamond, Larry. 2010. "Why Are There No Arab Democracies?" *Journal of Democracy* 21 (1): 93–104.

Diamond, Larry, Juan Linz, and Seymour Martin Lipset, eds. 1989. *Democracy in Developing Countries: Asia*. Boulder, CO: Lynne Rienner.

Di Marco, Graciela. 2011a. "Gendered Economic Rights and Trade Unionism: The Case of Argentina." In *Making Globalization Work for Women: The Role of Social*

Rights and Trade Union Leadership, edited by Valentine M. Moghadam, Mary Margaret Fonow, and Suzanne Franzway, 93–122. Albany: State University of New York Press.

———. 2011b. "Claims for Legal Abortion in Argentina and the Construction of New Political Identities." In *Feminisms, Democratization, and Radical Democracy: Case Studies in South and Central America, Middle East, and North Africa*, edited by Graciela Di Marco and Constanza Tabbush, 167–89. Buenos Aires: UNSAM Edita.

Di Marco, Graciela, and Constanza Tabbush, eds. 2011. *Feminisms, Democratization and Radical Democracy*. San Martin, Argentina: UNSAMEDITA Press.

Dincsahin, Sakir. 2012. "A Symptomatic Analysis of the Justice and Development Party's Populism in Turkey, 2007–2010." *Government and Opposition: An International Journal of Comparative Politics* 47 (4): 618–40.

Diner, Cagla, and Sule Toktas. 2010. "Waves of Feminism in Turkey: Kemalist, Islamist and Kurdish Women's Movements in an Era of Globalization." *Journal of Balkan and Near Eastern Studies* 12 (1): 41–57.

Doerschler, Peter, and Pamela Jackson. 2018. "Radical Right-Wing Parties in Western Europe and Their Populist Appeal: An Empirical Explanation." *Societies without Borders* 12 (2). https://scholarlycommons.law.case.edu/cgi/viewcontent.cgi?article=1327&context=swb.

Dorraj, Manochehr. 1990. *From Zarathustra to Khomeini: Populism and Dissent in Iran*. Boulder, CO: Lynne Rienner.

Dorraj, Manochehr, and Michael Dodson. 2009. "Neopopulism in Comparative Perspective: Iran and Venezuela." *Comparative Studies of South Asia, Africa, and the Middle East* 29 (1): 117–31.

Drohan, Madeleine. 2019. "Populism Moves North." In "The World in 2019." Special issue, *Economist*.

Dryzek, John. 1990. *Discursive Democracy: Politics, Policy, and Political Science*. Cambridge: Cambridge University Press.

Dufour, Pascale, and Isabelle Giraud. 2007. "The Continuity of Transnational Solidarities in the World March of Women, 2000 and 2005: A Collective Identity-Building Approach." *Mobilization* 12, no. 3 (November): 307–22.

Dunn, John. 2005. *Setting the People Free: The Story of Democracy*. New York: Atlantic Books.

Eckstein, Susan E., and Timothy Wickham-Crowley. 2003. "Struggles for Social Rights in Latin America: Claims in the Arenas of Subsistence, Labor, Gender, and Ethnicity." In *Struggles for Social Rights in Latin America*, edited by Susan E. Eckstein and Timothy Wickham-Crowley, 1–56. London: Routledge.

Economist. 2010. "Satellites in the Arab World: Stop Their Orbit." October 30, 2010, 50.

———. 2017. "Movements in EM Major: How Populism Can Shape Emerging Markets." October 7, 2017, 19.

————. 2018a. "Checking Up on the Imams." January 20, 2018, 48.

————. 2018b. "Europe's Welfare States: Battle of the Benefits." January 27, 2018, 43–44.

————. 2018c. "Threat and Opportunity: European Populism." February 3, 2018, 12.

————. 2018d. "Zlotys for Tots: Social Policy in Poland." May 12, 2018, 33.

————. 2018e. "Situations Vacant: Employing Refugees in Germany and Sweden." June 16, 2018, 69.

————. 2018f. "Greece: Far from the Finish Line." August 12, 2018, 61.

————. 2019a. "The Twilight of Syriza," March 23, 2019, 29–30.

————. 2019b. "A Long Way from Home: Syrians in Turkey." April 27, 2019, 31–32.

Edson, Henry. 2017. "The Political Economy of a Populist Backlash." Final paper written for INTL 5200: Political Economy: Interdisciplinary Perspectives. Northeastern University, December 2017.

Ehsani, Kaveh, and Arang Keshavarzian. 2018. "The Moral Economy of the Iranian Protests." *Jacobin Magazine*, January 11, 2018. https://jacobinmag.com/2018/01/iranian-protests-revolution-rouhani-ahmadinejad.

Eisenstein, Zillah. 2004. *Against Empire: Feminisms, Racism, and the West*. London: Zed Books.

El-Ghobashy, Mona. 2005. "The Metamorphosis of the Egyptian Muslim Brothers." *International Journal of Middle East Studies* 37:373–95.

Elson, Diane, ed. 1991. *Male Bias in the Development Process*. Manchester, UK: Manchester University Press.

Elson, Diane, and Ruth Pearson. 1981. "Nimble Fingers Make Cheap Workers: An Analysis of Women's Employment in Third World Export Manufacturing." *Feminist Review* 7, no. 1 (March): 87–107.

Elveren, Adem Y. 2017. "The Pious Predator State: The New Regime in Turkey." *Challenge* 61 (1): 85–91.

Elveren, Adem, and Valentine M. Moghadam. 2019. "The Impact of Militarization on Gender Inequality and Female Labor-Force Participation." ERF Working Paper 1307. Cairo: Economic Research Forum for the Arab Countries, Iran and Turkey, June 2019.

Emmons, Alex, and Zaid Jilani. 2016. "UN Chief Admits He Removed Saudi Arabia from Child-Killer List Due to Extortion." *Intercept*, June 9, 2016. https://the intercept.com/2016/06/09/u-n-chief-admits-he-removed-saudi-arabia-from-child -killer-list-due-to-extortion.

Enloe, Cynthia. 1990. *Bananas, Beaches and Bases: Making Feminist Sense of International Politics*. Berkeley: University of California Press.

————. 2007. *Globalization and Militarism: Feminists Make the Link*. Lanham, MD: Rowman & Littlefield.

Entelis, John. 2005. "Islamist Politics and the Democratic Imperative: Comparative Lessons from the Algerian Experience." In *Islam, Democracy and the State in*

Algeria: Lessons for the Western Mediterranean and Beyond, edited by Michael D. Bonner, Megan Reif, and Mark Tessler. London: Routledge.

Eschle, Catherine. 2000. *Global Democracy, Social Movements, and Feminism.* Boulder, CO: Westview.

Eschle, Catherine, and Bice Maiguashca. 2010. *Making Feminist Sense of the Global Justice Movement.* Lanham, MD: Rowman & Littlefield.

Esposito, John, ed. 1989. *The Iranian Revolution: Its Global Impact.* Gainesville: University Press of Florida.

———. 2002. *Unholy War: Terror in the Name of Islam.* Oxford: Oxford University Press.

Euractiv. 2011. "EU Funds Used for Hungarian Anti-abortion Campaign." Euractiv, June 17, 2011. https://www.euractiv.com/section/justice-home-affairs/news/eu-funds-used-for-hungarian-anti-abortion-campaign.

Eyerman, Ron, and Andrew Jamison. 1991. *Social Movements: A Cognitive Approach.* University Park: Pennsylvania University Press.

Fadel, Leila. 2011. "Islamists' Win Tests Tunisia Democracy." *Guardian Weekly*, November 4, 2011, 4–5.

Farris, Sara. 2017. *In the Name of Women's Rights: The Rise of Femonationalism.* Durham, NC: Duke University Press.

Ferree, Myra Marx, and Aili Marie Tripp, eds. 2006. *Global Feminism: Transnational Women's Activism, Organizing, and Human Rights.* New York: New York University Press.

Financial Times. 2019a. "Baby Boosters: Orbán Unveils Family Reform." February 11, 2019, 1.

———. 2019b. "G20 Speeds up New Tax Regime for Big Tech." June 10, 2019, 1, 4.

Flam, Helena, and Debra King, eds. 2005. *Emotions and Social Movements.* New York: Routledge.

Flamhaft, Ziva. 2007. "Iron Breaks, Too: Israeli and Palestinian Women Talk about War, Bereavement, and Peace." In *From Patriarchy to Empowerment: Women's Participation, Movements, and Rights in the Middle East, North Africa, and South Asia*, edited by V. M. Moghadam, 311–26. Syracuse, NY: Syracuse University Press.

Flassbeck, Heiner, and Costas Lapavitsas. 2015. *Against the Troika: Crisis and Austerity in the Eurozone.* London: Verso.

Foroohar, Rana. 2011. "Whatever Happened to Upward Mobility?" *Time*, November 14, 2011, 25–34.

Fourest, Caroline. 2004. *Frère Tariq: Discours, stratégie et méthode de Tariq Ramadan.* Paris: Grasset et Fasquelle.

Fox, Jon E., and Peter Vermeersch. 2010. "Backdoor Nationalism." *European Journal of Sociology* 51 (2): 325–57.

Franklin, Jonathan. 2011. "Camila Takes on Chile's Elite." *Guardian Weekly*, September 2, 2011, 13.

Fraser, Arvonne. 1987. *The U.N. Decade for Women: Documents and Dialogue.* Boulder, CO: Westview.

Fraser, Nancy. 1995. "From Redistribution to Recognition? Dilemmas of Justice in a 'Postsocialist' Age." *New Left Review* 212:68–93.

———. 2000. "Rethinking Recognition: Overcoming Displacement and Reification in Cultural Politics." *New Left Review*, n.s., 3 (May–June): 107–20.

Fraser, Nancy, Tithi Bhattacharya, and Cinzia Arruzza. 2018. "Notes for a Feminist Manifesto." *New Left Review* 114 (November–December). https://newleftreview .org/issues/II114/articles/nancy-fraser-tithi-bhattacharya-cinzia-arruzza-notes -for-a-feminist-manifesto.

Frobel, Folker, Jurgen Heinrichs, and Otto Kreye. 1980. *The New International Division of Labor.* Cambridge: Cambridge University Press.

Fukuyama, Francis. 1989. "The End of History?" *The National Interest,* 16, 3–18.

Fuller, Graham. 2002. "The Future of Political Islam." *Foreign Affairs* (March–April): 48–60.

Galston, William A. 2017. "The 2016 US Election: The Populist Moment." *Journal of Democracy* 28 (2): 21–33.

Garrett, R. K. 2006. "Protest in an Information Society." *Information, Communication & Society* 9:202–24.

Garton Ash, Timothy. 2017. "Populist Ills Demand We Think of the 'Left Behind.'" *Guardian Weekly*, October 6, 2017.

George, Susan. 2004. *Another World Is Possible If . . .* London: Verso.

Gerges, Fawaz. 2005. *The Far Enemy: Why Jihad Went Global.* Cambridge: Cambridge University Press.

———. 2017. *ISIS: A History.* Princeton, NJ: Princeton University Press.

Gerlach, Luther. 1999. "The Structure of Social Movements: Environmental Activism and Its Opponents." In *Waves of Protest: Social Movements since the Sixties*, edited by Jo Freeman and Victoria Johnson, 85–98. Lanham, MD: Rowman & Littlefield.

Gerner, Deborah. 2007. "Mobilizing Women for Nationalist Agendas." In *From Patriarchy to Empowerment: Women's Participation, Movements, and Rights in the Middle East, North Africa, and South Asia*, edited by Valentine M. Moghadam. Syracuse, NY: Syracuse University Press.

Gessen, Masha. 2018. "Barcelona's Experiment in Radical Democracy." *New Yorker*, August 6, 2018. https://www.newyorker.com/news/our-columnists/barcelonas -experiment-in-radical-democracy.

Ghannouchi, Rachid. 1993. "The Participation of Islamists in a Non-Islamic Government." In *Power-Sharing Islam*, edited and translated by Azzam Tamimi, 270–78. London: Liberty for Muslim World Publications.

Gheytanchi, Elham, and Valentine M. Moghadam. Forthcoming, 2020. *Women and the New Media Activism.* In *Gender and Sexuality in the Middle East and North Africa*, edited by Helen Rizzo and Michael Ryan. Boulder, CO: Lynne Rienner.

Giddens, Anthony. 1999. *Runaway World: How Globalization Is Reshaping Our Lives*. London: Profile Books.

Gidron, Noam, and Bart Bonikowski. 2013. "Varieties of Populism: Literature Review and Research Agenda." Working Paper Series. Harvard University, Weatherhead Center for International Studies, Cambridge, MA, 2013. https://scholar.harvard.edu/files/gidron_bonikowski_populismlitreview_2013.pdf.

Gill, Timothy. 2018. "From Promoting Political Polyarchy to Defeating Participatory Democracy: U.S. Foreign Policy towards the Far Left in Latin America." *Journal of World-Systems Research* 24 (1): 72–95. http://jwsr.pitt.edu/ojs/index.php/jwsr/article/view/750.

Girgin, Fatma. 2016. "Bakan Ramazanoğlu'nun 'Kadına Şiddet Yoktur, Algıda Seçicilik Vardır' Söylemi Başlı Başına Bir Skandaldır." *Baro Türk–Türk Hukuk Merkezi*, 2016. Accessed February 15, 2018. http://www.baroturk.com/bakan-ramazanoglunun-kadina-siddet-yoktur-algida-secicilik-vardir-soylemi-basli-basin-18693h.htm.

Givan, Rebecca Kolins, Kenneth Roberts, and Sarah A. Soule, eds. 2010. *The Diffusion of Social Movements: Actors, Mechanisms, and Political Effects*. New York: Cambridge University Press.

Glasco, Madlyn. 2017. "A Political Paradox." Paper written for Sociology 7225: Gender and Social Movements, Northeastern University, December 2017.

Goldstone, Jack A., and Doug McAdam. 2001. "Contention in Demographic and Life-Course Context." In *Silence and Voice in the Study of Contentious Politics*, edited by Ronald Aminzade, Jack Goldstone, Doug McAdam, Elizabeth Perry, William Sewell, Sidney Tarrow, and Charles Tilly, 195–221. Cambridge: Cambridge University Press.

Golebiowska, Ewa. 2017. "The Links between Gender Role Belief, Conceptions of the Family, Attitudes toward Poland's Membership in the European Union, Religiosity, and Polish Support for Gay and Lesbian Rights." *Politics, Groups, and Identities* 5 (4): 599–617.

Goodhart, David. 2017. *The Road to Somewhere: The Populist Revolt and the Future of Politics*. London: Hurst.

Goodwin, Jeff. 2001. *No Other Way Out: States and Revolutionary Movements, 1945–1991*. Cambridge: Cambridge University Press.

———. 2007. "Explaining Revolutionary Terrorism." In *Revolution in the Making of the Modern World*, edited by John Foran, David Lane, and Andreja Zivkovic, 199–221. London: Routledge.

Goodwin, Jeff, James M. Jasper, and Francesca Polleta, eds. 2001. *Passionate Politics: Emotions and Social Movements*. Chicago: University of Chicago Press.

Goodwin, Matthew, and Oliver Heath. 2016. "Brexit Vote Explained: Poverty, Low Skills and Lack of Opportunities." London: Joseph Rowntree Foundation. https://www.jrf.org.uk/report/brexit-vote-explained-poverty-low-skills-and-lack-opportunities.

Goulard, Hortense. 2016. "Germany's Anti-Islam Pegida Movement Launches Political Party." *Politico*, July 19, 2016. https://www.politico.eu/article/germans -anti-islam-pegida-movement-launches-political-party.

Graham-Harrison, Emma, and Janus Engel Rasmussen. 2018. "Inside Denmark's Official Ghettos, a Life of Isolation." *Guardian Weekly*, August 17, 2018, 6.

Granovetter, Mark S. 1983. "The Strength of Weak Ties: A Network Theory Revisited." *Sociological Theory* 1:201–33.

Greshman, Carl. 2011. "The Fourth Wave: Where the Middle East Revolts Fit in the History of Democratization—and How We Can Support Them." *New Republic*, March 14, 2011. http://www.tnr.com.

Gross, Jan T. 2017. "Poles Cry for 'Pure Blood' Again." *New York Times*, November 16, 2017. https://www.nytimes.com/2017/11/16/opinion/poland-pure-blood -march.html.

Guardian. 2016. "Turkish President Says Childless Women Are 'Deficient, Incomplete.'" June 6, 2016.

Guidry, John A., Michael D. Kennedy, and Mayer N. Zald. 2000a. "Globalizations and Social Movements." In *Globalizations and Social Movements: Culture, Power and the Transnational Public Sphere*, edited by John A. Guidry, Michael D. Kennedy, and Mayer N. Zald, 1–32. Ann Arbor: University of Michigan Press.

———, eds. 2000b. *Globalizations and Social Movements: Culture, Power and the Transnational Public Sphere*. Ann Arbor: University of Michigan Press.

Gulalp, Haldun. 2001. "Globalization and Political Islam: The Social Bases of Turkey's Welfare Party." *International Journal of Middle East Studies* 33:433–48.

Habermas, Jurgen. 1992. "Further Reflections on the Public Sphere." In *Habermas and the Public Sphere*, edited by Craig Calhoun. Cambridge, MA: MIT Press.

Habibi, Nader. 2012. "The Economic Agendas and Expected Economic Policies of Islamists in Egypt and Tunisia." Middle East Brief no. 67. Brandeis University, Crown Center for Middle East Studies, Waltham, MA, October 2012.

Hadden, Jennifer, and Sidney Tarrow. 2007. "The Global Justice Movement in the United States since Seattle." In *The Global Justice Movement: Cross-National and Transnational Perspectives*, edited by Donatella della Porta, 210–31. Boulder, CO: Paradigm.

Hafez, Mohammed. 2003. *Why Muslims Rebel: Repression and Resistance in the Islamic World*. Boulder, CO: Lynne Rienner.

———. 2004. "From Marginalization to Massacres: A Political Process Explanation of GIA Violence in Algeria." In *Islamic Activism: A Social Movement Theory Approach*, edited by Quintan Wiktorowicz, 37–60. Bloomington: Indiana University Press.

Hafez, Mohammed, and Quintan Wiktorowicz. 2004. "Violence as Contention in the Egyptian Islamic Movement." In *Islamic Activism: A Social Movement Theory Approach*, edited by Quintan Wiktorowicz, 61–88. Bloomington: Indiana University Press.

Halliday, Fred. 2005. *100 Myths about the Middle East.* London: Saqi.

Harding, Jeremy. 2019. "Among the Gilets Jaunes." *London Review of Books* 41, no. 6 (March 21): 3–11.

Hardt, Michael, and Antonio Negri. 2000. *Empire.* Cambridge, MA: Harvard University Press.

Harik, Judith. 2004. *Hezbollah: The Changing Face of Terrorism.* London: I. B. Tauris.

Harris, Chris. 2017. "Women's Day Sparks Soaring Support for Action over Polish MEP's Sexism." *Euronews,* March 8, 2017. http://www.euronews.com/2017/03/08/support-soars-for-polish-mep-to-be-sacked-over-sexist-comments.

Harvey, David. 2003. *The New Imperialism.* Oxford: Oxford University Press.

———. 2004. "Neoliberalism and the Restoration of Class Power." *Via Portside,* August 6, 2004. http://www.scribd.com/doc/63941056/HARVEY-David-Neoliberalism-and-Class-Restore.

———. 2009. *A Brief History of Neoliberalism.* Oxford: Oxford University Press.

Hawkesworth, Mary. 2006. *Globalization and Feminist Activism.* Lanham, MD: Rowman & Littlefield.

Heckscher, Zahara. 2002. "Long before Seattle: Historical Resistance to Economic Globalization." In *Global Backlash: Citizen Initiatives for a Just World Economy,* edited by Robin Broad, 86–91. Lanham, MD: Rowman & Littlefield.

Hedges, Chris. 2010. *Death of the Liberal Class.* New York: Nation Books.

Hefner, Robert. 2000. *Civil Islam: Muslims and Democratization in Indonesia.* Princeton, NJ: Princeton University Press.

Hegghammer, Thomas. 2010. *Jihad in Saudi Arabia: Violence and Pan-Islamism since 1979.* Cambridge: Cambridge University Press.

Held, David, ed. 2000. *A Globalizing World? Culture, Economics, Politics.* London: Routledge.

Hélie-Lucas, Marieme. 1993. "Women Living under Muslim Laws." In *Ours by Right: Women's Rights as Human Rights,* edited by Joanna Kerr. London: Zed Books, in association with the North-South Institute.

Henley, Jon. 2017. "Europe Casts Anxious Eyes East as Liberal Values Flounder." *Guardian Weekly,* December 22, 2017, 22–23.

———. 2018. "Italy at Odds with EU over Immigration." *Guardian Weekly,* June 15, 2018.

Herszenhorn, David. 2010. "Congress Now Has a 'Tea Party Caucus.'" *New York Times,* July 20, 2010. https://thecaucus.blogs.nytimes.com/2010/07/20/congress-now-has-a-tea-party-caucus.

Hirst, Paul, and Grahame Thompson. 1996. *Globalization in Question: The International Economy and the Possibilities of Governance.* Cambridge, UK: Polity.

Hochschild, Arlie Russell. 2016. *Strangers in Their Own Land: Anger and Mourning on the American Right.* New York: New Press.

Hopkins, Terence K., and Immanuel Wallerstein. 1996. "The World System: Is There a Crisis?" In *The Age of Transition: Trajectory of the World-System 1945–2025*, coordinated by Terence K. Hopkins et al., 1–10. London: Zed Books.

Howe, Stephen. 2002. *Empire: A Very Short Introduction*. Oxford: Oxford University Press.

Htun, Mala, and S. Laurel Weldon. 2018. *The Logics of Gender Justice: State Action on Women's Rights around the World*. Cambridge and New York: Cambridge University Press.

Hungarian Spectrum. 2013. "Sexism in the Hungarian Parliament." September 12, 2013. https://hungarianspectrum.wordpress.com/2013/09/12/sexism-in-the-hungarian-parliament.

Hunt, Alex. 2014. "UKIP: The Story of the UK Independence Party's Rise." BBC News, November 21, 2014. http://www.bbc.com/news/uk-politics-21614073.

Huntington, Samuel. 1991. *The Third Wave: Democratization in the Late Twentieth Century*. Norman: University of Oklahoma Press.

———. 1996. *The Clash of Civilizations and the Remaking of World Order*. New York: Simon & Schuster.

Ibrahim, Saad Eddin. 1980. "Anatomy of Egypt's Militant Islamic Groups: Methodological Notes and Preliminary Findings." *International Journal of Middle East Studies* 12, no. 4 (December): 423–53.

Ilkkaracan, Ipek. 2012. "Why So Few Women in the Labor Market in Turkey?" *Feminist Economics* 18 (1): 1–37.

———. 2017. "The Economic Gender Gap and the Political Gender Gap: Implications for Path Dependency in Gender Inequalities and Sustainable Growth." Paper presented at the 26th annual meeting of the IAFFE, Seoul, Korea, June 29–July 1, 2017.

Im, Hyung Baeg. 2000. "South Korean Democratic Consolidation in Comparative Perspective." In *Consolidating Democracy in South Korea*, edited by Larry Diamond and Byung-Kook Kim, 21–54. Boulder, CO: Lynne Rienner.

International Gender and Trade Network (IGTN). 2002. "With Women, Another World Is Possible." IGTN statement, World Social Forum, Porto Alegre, Brazil, February. Accessed January 16, 2008. http://www.wide-network.org/index.jsp?id=198.

International Labour Organization (ILO). 2011. *The Global Economic Crisis: Causes, Responses, and Challenges*. Geneva: International Labour Office. http://www.ilo.org/wcmsp5/groups/public/---dgreports/---dcomm/---publ/documents/publication/wcms_155824.pdf.

———. 2004. *A Fair Globalization: Creating Opportunities for All*. Geneva: World Commission on the Social Dimensions of Globalization. https://www.ilo.org/public/english/wcsdg/docs/report.pdf.

292   REFERENCES

International Monetary Fund (IMF). 2009. *World Economic Outlook, April 2009: Crisis and Recovery.* Washington, DC: IMF. http://www.imf.org/external/pubs/ft/weo/2009/01/pdf/text.pdf.

Ionescu, Ghita, and Ernst Gellner. 1969. *Populism: Its Meanings and National Characteristics.* New York: Macmillan.

Irshaid, Faisal. 2014. "How ISIS Is Spreading Its Message Online." BBC News, June 19, 2014. https://www.bbc.com/news/world-middle-east-27912569.

Ishay, Micheline. 2019. *The Levant Express: The Arab Uprisings, Human Rights, and the Future of the Middle East.* New Haven, CT: Yale University Press.

Jaquette, Jane. 2001. "Regional Differences and Contrasting Views." *Journal of Democracy* 12, no. 3 (July): 11–125.

———. 2009. "Feminist Activism and the Challenges of Democracy." In *Feminist Agendas and Democracy in Latin America*, edited by Jane Jaquette, 208–18. Durham, NC: Duke University Press.

Jasiewicz, Krzysztof. 2008. "The New Populism in Poland: The Usual Suspects?" *Problems of Post-communism* 55 (3): 7–25.

Jayawardena, Kumari. 1986. *Feminism and Nationalism in the Third World.* London: Zed Books.

Johnson, Chalmers. 2001. "Blowback." *Nation*, October 15, 2001. http://www.thenation.com/doc/20011015/Johnson.

Johnston, Hank. 2011. *States and Social Movements.* London: Polity.

Johnston, Hank, and Paul Almeida, eds. 2006. *Latin American Social Movements.* Lanham, MD: Rowman & Littlefield.

Johnstone, Diana. 2018. "Yellow Vests Rise against Neo-Liberal 'King' Macron." *Consortium News*, December 5, 2018. https://consortiumnews.com/2018/12/05/yellow-vests-rise-against-neo-liberal-king-macron.

Judis, John. 2016. *The Populist Explosion: How the Great Recession Transformed American and European Politics.* New York: Columbia Global Reports.

Juergensmeyer, Mark. 2003. *Terror in the Mind of God: The Global Rise of Religious Violence.* Berkeley: University of California Press.

Junn, Jane. 2017. "The Trump Majority: White Womanhood and the Making of Female Voters in the U.S." *Politics, Groups, and Identities* 5 (2): 343–52.

Juris, Jeffrey. 2008. *Networking Futures: The Movements against Corporate Globalization.* Durham, NC: Duke University Press.

Jussim, Lee. 2015. "Conservative Feminism: Liberals Have No Monopoly on Advancing Women's Interests." *Psychology Today*, August 19, 2015. https://www.psychologytoday.com/blog/rabble-rouser/201508/conservative-feminism.

Kadivar, Mohammad Ali, and Abolfazl Sotoudeh. 2018. "Development, Politics, Democracy, and Diffusion: A Wave of Anti-regime Protests in Iran." Paper delivered at Harvard University, Transnational Studies Initiative, Cambridge, MA, October 15, 2018.

Kaftan, Gizem. 2017. "Turkish Women's Movement in Abeyance." Paper written for Sociology 7225: Gender and Social Movements. Northeastern University (December).

Kalb, Don. 2009. "Headlines of Nationalism, Subtexts of Class: Poland and Popular Paranoia, 1989–2009." *Anthropologica* 51 (2): 289–300.

Kalb, Zep. 2018. "Iran Braces for More General Strikes as Budget Negotiations in Sight." *Al Monitor*, October 23, 2018. http://www.al-monitor.com/pulse/ originals/2018/10/iran-teachers-union-strike-collective-action-truckers-budget .html#ixzz5Uq3NlyEx.

Kaldor, Mary. 2003. *Global Civil Society: An Answer to War*. Cambridge, UK: Polity.

Kamalipour, Yahya R., ed. 2010. *Media, Power and Politics in the Digital Age: The 2009 Presidential Election Uprising in Iran*. Lanham, MD: Rowman & Littlefield.

Kandiyoti, Deniz. 1989. "Women and the Turkish State: Political Actors or Symbolic Pawns?" In *Women-Nation-State*, edited by Nira Yuval-Davis and Floya Anthias. Basingstoke: Macmillan.

———, ed. 1991. *Women, Islam, and the State, and Islam*. Basingstoke: Macmillan.

Kazi, Seema. 1997. "Muslim Laws and Women Living under Muslim Laws." In *Muslim Women and the Politics of Participation*, edited by Mahnaz Afkhami and Erika Friedl, 141–46. Syracuse, NY: Syracuse University Press.

Keane, John. 1996. *Reflection on Violence*. London: Verso.

Keck, Margaret E., and Kathryn Sikkink. 1998. *Activists beyond Borders: Advocacy Networks in International Politics*. Ithaca, NY: Cornell University Press.

Keefe, Patrick Radden. 2017. "The Family That Built an Empire of Pain." *New Yorker*, October 30, 2017. https://www.newyorker.com/magazine/2017/10/30/ the-family-that-built-an-empire-of-pain.

Kepel, Gilles. 2002. *Jihad: The Trail of Political Islam*. Cambridge, MA: Harvard University Press.

Khor, Martin. 2000. "How the South Is Getting a Raw Deal at the WTO." In *Views from the South: The Effects of Globalization and the WTO on Third World Countries*, edited by Sarah Anderson, 7–53. Chicago: Food First Books.

Khosrokhavar, Farhad. 2005. *Suicide Bombers: Allah's New Martyrs*. Translated by David Macey. London: Pluto Press.

Kienle, Eberhard. 2015. "Changed Regimes, Changed Priorities? Economic and Social Policies after the 2011 Elections in Tunisia and Egypt." Working Paper 928. Cairo: Economic Research Forum.

Kim, Hee-Kang. 2009. "Should Feminism Transcend Nationalism? A Defense of Korean Feminist Nationalism." *Women's Studies International Forum* 32 (2): 108–19.

Kirk, Ashley, and Patrick Scott. 2017. "Dutch Election: How the Far Right Could Win but Not Rule in a Country Known for Its Liberal Values." *Telegraph*, March 17, 2017. http://www.telegraph.co.uk/news/0/dutch-election-far-right-could -win-not-rule-country-known-liberal.

Kirkpatrick, David D., and David E. Sanger. 2011. "A Tunisian-Egyptian Link That Shook Arab History." *New York Times*, February 13, 2011. http://www.nytimes.com/2011/02/14/world/middleeast/14egypt-tunisia-protests.html.

Klatch, Rebecca. 1987. *Women of the New Right*. Philadelphia: Temple University Press.

Klausen, Jyttle. 2009. *The Cartoons That Shook the World*. New Haven, CT: Yale University Press.

Klein, Naomi. 2007a. "Latin America's Shock Resistance." *Nation*, November 26, 2007. http://www.thenation.com/doc/20071126/klein.

———. 2007b. *Shock Doctrine: The Rise of Disaster Capitalism*. New York: Henry Holt.

Knapp, Michael, Anja Flach, and Ercan Ayboga. 2016. *Revolution in Rojava: Democratic Autonomy and Women's Liberation in Syrian Kurdistan*. Translated by Janet Biehl. London: Pluto Press.

Koerner, Brendan I. 2016. "Why ISIS Is Winning the Social Media War." *Wired*, March 2016. https://www.wired.com/2016/03/isis-winning-social-media-war-heres-beat.

Komsan, Nehad Aboul. 2010a. "The Muslim Brotherhood . . . Returning Egypt to an Age without Law." Press release issued by the Egyptian Center for Women's Rights, Cairo, December 15, 2010. https://ecwronline.org/index.php/2010/12/15/the-muslim-brotherhood-returning-egypt-to-an-age-without-law.

———. 2010b. "Who Judges the Judges? A Black Day in the History of Justice in Egypt." Press release issued by the Egyptian Center for Women's Rights, Cairo, November 16, 2010. http://www.ecwronline.org.

Korten, David. 1995. *When Corporations Rule the World*. San Francisco, CA: Kumarian.

Korzeniewicz, Roberto, and Kimberley Awbrey. 1992. "Democratic Transitions and the Semiperiphery of the World-Economy." *Sociological Forum* 7 (4): 609–40.

Korzeniewicz, Roberto, and Timothy Patrick Moran. 2009. *Unveiling Inequality: A World-Historical Perspective*. New York: Russell Sage Foundation.

Krizsán, Andrea, and Birte Siim. 2018. "Gender Equality and Family in European Populist Radical-Right Agendas: European Parliamentary Debates 2014." In *Gender and Generational Division in EU Citizenship*, edited by Trudie Knijn and Manuela Naldini. Cheltenham: Edgar Elgar.

Kumar, Anurag. 2017. "OPINION-2017 Ends with Modi Wave: What 2018 Has in Offering for Rahul Gandhi?" ABP Live, December 20, 2017. https://www.abplive.in/india-news/opinion-2017-ends-with-modi-wave-what-2018-has-in-offering-for-rahul-gandhi-621285.

Kurzman, Charlie. 2012. "Votes versus Rights: The Debate That's Shaping the Outcome of the Arab Spring." *Foreign Policy*, February 10, 2012. https://foreignpolicy.com/2012/02/10/votes-versus-rights.

Kutz-Flamenbaum, Rachel. 2007. "Code Pink, Raging Grannies, and the Missile Dick Chicks: Feminist Performance Activism in the Contemporary Anti-war Movement." *NWSA Journal* 19, no. 1 (Spring): 89–105.

Lackner, Helen. 1985. *PDR Yemen: Outpost of Socialist Development in Arabia.* London: Ithaca Press.

Laclau, Ernesto. 2005. *On Populist Reason.* London: Verso.

Laer, Jeroen Van, and Peter Van Aelst. 2010. "Internet and Social Movement Action Repertoires." *Information, Communication & Society* 13 (8): 1146–71.

Langman, Lauren. 2005. "From Virtual Public Spheres to Global Justice: A Critical Theory of Internetworked Social Movements." *Sociological Theory* 23, no. 1 (March): 42–74.

———. 2020. "The Dialectic of Populism and Cosmopolitanism." In *On Cosmopolitanism in a Global Age*, edited by Vincenzo Cicchelli, Sylvie Octobre, and Estevão Bosco. Leiden: Brill.

Langman, Lauren, and Douglas Morris. 2004. "Hegemony Lost: Understanding Contemporary Islam." In *Globalization, Hegemony and Power: Antisystemic Movements and the Global System*, edited by Thomas Reifer. Boulder, CO: Paradigm.

Langman, Lauren, Douglas Morris, and Jackie Zalewski. 2002. "Globalization, Domination and Cyberactivism." In *The 21st Century World-System: Systemic Crises and Antisystemic Resistance*, edited by Wilma A. Dunaway. Westport, CT: Greenwood.

Langohr, Vickie. 2001. "Of Islamists and Ballot Boxes: Rethinking the Relationship between Islamisms and Electoral Politics." *International Journal of Middle East Studies* 33:591–610.

Lasch, Christopher. 1994. *The Revolt of the Elites and the Betrayal of Democracy.* New York: Norton.

Lewis, Paul, Seán Clarke, and Caelainn Barr. 2019. "Revealed: Populist Leaders Linked to Reduced Inequality." *Guardian*, March 7, 2019. https://www.the guardian.com/world/2019/mar/07/revealed-populist-leaders-linked-to-reduced -inequality.

Lindekilde, Lasse. 2010. "Soft Repression and Mobilization: The Case of Transnational Activism of Danish Muslims during the Cartoons Controversy." *International Journal of Middle East Studies* 42:451–69.

Lipset, Seymour Martin. 1959. "Some Social Requisites of Democracy: Economic Development and Political Legitimacy." *American Political Science Review* 53, no. 1 (March): 69–105.

Lister, Ruth. 2003. *Citizenship: Feminist Perspectives.* 2nd ed. London: Macmillan.

Lizardo, Omar. 2006. "The Effect of Economic and Cultural Globalization on Anti-U.S. Transnational Terrorism 1971–2000." *Journal of World-Systems Research* 7 (1): 144–86.

Lukacs, John. 2005. *Democracy and Populism: Fear and Hatred.* New Haven, CT: Yale University Press.

Malone, Clare. 2016. "Clinton Couldn't Win over White Women, but They Split along Educational Lines." FiveThirtyEight, November 9, 2016. https://fivethirty eight.com/features/clinton-couldnt-win-over-white-women.

Mamdani, Mahmood. 2018. "The African University." *London Review of Books* 4, no. 14 (July 19): 29–32.

Mander, Jerry. 1996. "The Dark Side of Globalization: What the Media Are Missing." *Nation* 15 (22): 9–29.

Manning, Christel J. 1999. *God Gave Us the Right: Conservative Catholic, Evangelical Protestant, and Orthodox Jewish Women Grapple with Feminism.* New Brunswick, NJ: Rutgers University Press.

Marchand, Marianne, and Anne Sisson Runyan, eds. 2010. *Gender and Global Restructuring: Sightings, Sites and Resistances.* 2nd ed. London: Routledge.

Marglin, Stephen, and Juliet Schor, eds. 1990. *The Golden Age of Capitalism.* Oxford: Clarendon Press.

Margolis, Diane. 1993. "Women's Movements around the World: Cross-Cultural Comparisons." *Gender & Society* 7, no. 3 (September): 379–99.

Markoff, John. 1999. "Globalization and the Future of Democracy." *Journal of World-Systems Research* 5, no. 2 (Summer): 277–309.

Marshall, T. H. 1964. *Citizenship and Social Class.* Cambridge: Cambridge University Press.

Marty, Martin E., and R. Scott Appleby, eds. 1991. *The Fundamentalism Project.* Vol. 1, *Fundamentalisms Observed.* Chicago: University of Chicago Press.

———, eds. 1992. *The Fundamentalism Project.* Vol. 2, *Fundamentalisms and Society.* Chicago: University of Chicago Press.

———, eds. 1993. *The Fundamentalism Project.* Vol. 3, *Fundamentalisms and the State.* Chicago: University of Chicago Press.

———, eds. 1994. *The Fundamentalism Project.* Vol. 4, *Accounting for Fundamentalisms: The Dynamic Character of Movements.* Chicago: University of Chicago Press.

Marx, Karl. 1978. *Capital.* Vol. 1. Moscow: Progress Publishers.

Masoud, Tarek. 2014. *Counting Islam: Religion, Class, and Elections in Egypt.* New York: Cambridge University Press.

Matfess, Hilary, Robert U. Nagel, and Meredith Loken. 2019. "Gendered Violence and Political Agendas." Political Violence @ a Glance, February 11, 2019. http://politicalviolenceataglance.org/2019/02/11/gendered-violence-and-polit ical-agendas.

Mathews, Jessica. 1997. "Power Shift." *Foreign Affairs* 76, no. 1 (January–February): 50–66.

Mazumdar, Sucheta. 1994. "Moving Away from a Secular Vision? Women, Nation and the Cultural Construction of Hindu India." In *Identity Politics and Women*, edited by Valentine M. Moghadam. Boulder, CO: Westview.

McAdam, Doug. 1986. "Recruitment to High-Risk Activism: The Case of Freedom Summer." *American Journal of Sociology* 92:64–90.

McAdam, Doug, John McCarthy, and Meyer Zald, eds. 1996. *Comparative Perspectives on Social Movements: Political Opportunities, Mobilizing Structures, and Cultural Frames.* Cambridge: Cambridge University Press.

McBride, William. 2001. *From Yugoslav Praxis to Global Pathos: Anti-hegemonic Post-Post-Marxist Essays.* Lanham, MD: Rowman & Littlefield.

McLellan, David. 1977. *Karl Marx: Selected Writings.* New York: Oxford University Press.

Meer, Nasar. 2010. *Citizenship, Identity and the Politics of Multiculturalism: The Rise of Muslim Consciousness.* New York: Palgrave Macmillan.

Melucci, Alberto. 1989. *Nomads of the Present.* Philadelphia: Temple University Press.

———. 1996. *Challenging Codes: Collective Action in the Information Age.* Cambridge: Cambridge University Press.

Meret, Susi, and Birte Siim. 2013a. "Gender, Populism and Politics of Belonging." In *Negotiating Gender and Diversity in an Emergent European Public Sphere*, edited by Birte Siim and Monika Mokre. Basingstoke: Palgrave.

———. 2013b. "Multiculturalism, Right-Wing Populism and the Crisis of Social Democracy." In *The Crisis of European Social Democracy*, edited by M. Keating and D. McCrone. Edinburgh: Edinburgh University Press.

Meret, Susi, Birte Siim, and E. Pingeaud. 2016. "Men's Parties with Women Leaders: A Comparative Study of the Rightwing Populist Leaders Pia Kjærsgaard, Siv Jensen and Marine Le Pen." In *Understanding the Populist Shift*, edited by G. Campani and G. Lazarides. London: Routledge.

Mernissi, Fatima. 1987. *Beyond the Veil: Male-Female Dynamics in Modern Muslim Society.* 2nd rev. ed. Bloomington: Indiana University Press.

Mertes, Tom. 2004. "Grass-Roots Globalism: Reply to Michael Hardt." In *A Movement of Movements: Is Another World Really Possible?*, edited by Tom Mertes, 237–47. London: Verso.

Messaoudi, Khalida, and Elisabeth Schemla. 1998. *Unbowed: An Algerian Woman Confronts Islamic Fundamentalism.* Philadelphia: University of Pennsylvania Press.

Meyer, David S., and Sidney G. Tarrow, eds. 1998. *The Social Movement Society: Contentious Politics for a New Century.* Lanham, MD: Rowman & Littlefield.

Meyer, John, John Boli, George Thomas, and Francisco Ramirez. 1997. "World Society and the Nation-State." *American Journal of Sociology* 103 (1): 144–81.

Meyer, Mary K. 1999. "The Women's International League for Peace and Freedom: Organizing Women for Peace in the War System." In *Gender Politics in Global Governance*, edited by Mary K. Meyer and Elisabeth Prugl, 107–21. Lanham, MD: Rowman & Littlefield.

Meyer, Mary K., and Elisabeth Prugl, eds. 1999. *Gender Politics in Global Governance*. Lanham, MD: Rowman & Littlefield.

Milanovic, Branko. 2005. *Worlds Apart: Measuring International and Global Inequality*. Princeton, NJ: Princeton University Press.

———. 2011. *The Haves and the Have-Nots: A Brief and Idiosyncratic History of Global Inequality*. New York: Basic Books.

Milazzo, Linda. 2005. "Code Pink: The 21st Century Mothers of Invention." *Development* 48 (2): 100–104.

Milne, Richard. 2019. "Lofven Takes Sweden into Unchartered Waters." *Financial Times*, January 18, 2019.

Minkenberg, Michael. 2002. "The Radical Right in Postsocialist Central and Eastern Europe: Comparative Observations and Interpretations." *East European Politics and Societies* 16 (2): 335–62.

Mir-Hosseini, Ziba, and Richard Tapper. 2006. *Islam and Democracy in Iran: Eshkevari and the Quest for Reform*. London: I. B. Tauris.

Mitchell, William, and Thomas Fazi. 2017. *Reclaiming the State: A Progressive Vision of Sovereignty for a Post-neoliberal World*. London: Pluto Press.

Moaddel, Mansoor. 2002. "The Study of Islamic Culture and Politics: An Overview and Assessment. *Annual Review of Sociology* 28:359–86.

———. 2005. *Islamic Modernism, Nationalism, and Fundamentalism: Episode and Discourse*. Chicago: University of Chicago Press.

———. Forthcoming, 2020. *The Clash of Values in the Middle East and North Africa: Islamic Fundamentalism versus Liberalism—a Study of People and Their Issues*. New York: Columbia University Press.

Moghadam, Valentine M. 1989. "One Revolution or Two? The Iranian Revolution and the Islamic Republic." In *Revolution Today: Aspirations and Realities. Socialist Register 1989*, edited by Ralph Miliband, Leo Panitch, and John Saville. London: Merlin.

———, ed. 1993a. *Democratic Reform and the Position of Women in Transitional Economies*. Oxford: Clarendon Press.

———. 1993b. "Revolutions and Regimes: Populism and Social Transformation in Iran." *Research in Political Sociology* 6:217–55.

———. 1994a. "Building Human Resources and Women's Capabilities in Afghanistan: A Retrospect and Prospects." *World Development* 22, no. 6 (June): 859–76.

———, ed. 1994b. *Identity Politics and Women: Cultural Reassertions and Feminisms in International Perspective*. Boulder, CO: Westview.

———. 1995. "Gender Dynamics of Restructuring in the Semiperiphery." In *Engendering Wealth and Well-Being*, edited by Rae Lesser Blumberg et al., 17–38. Boulder, CO: Westview.

———. 1998a. "Gender and the Global Economy." In *Revisioning Gender*, edited by Myra Marx Ferree, Judith Lorber, and Beth Hess, 128–60. Thousand Oaks, CA: Sage.

————. 1998b. "The Women's Movement in the Middle East and North Africa: Responding to Restructuring and Fundamentalism." *Women's Studies Quarterly* 26, nos. 3–4 (Fall/Winter 1998): 57–67.

————. 2001. "Organizing Women: The New Women's Movement in Algeria." *Cultural Dynamics* 13 (2): 131–54.

————. 2003. *Modernizing Women: Gender and Social Change in the Middle East.* 2nd ed. Boulder, CO: Lynne Rienner.

————. 2005. *Globalizing Women: Gender, Globalization, and Transnational Feminist Networks.* Baltimore, MD: Johns Hopkins University Press.

————. 2007. "Peace-Building and Reconstruction with Women: Reflections on Afghanistan, Iraq, and Palestine." In *From Patriarchy to Empowerment: Women's Participation, Movements, and Rights in the Middle East, North Africa, and South Asia,* edited by V. M. Moghadam, 327–51. Syracuse, NY: Syracuse University Press.

————. 2008. "Feminism and Nationalism in the Middle East: Friends or Foes?" Paper delivered at Global Studies Association conference, Pace University, New York, June 2008.

————. 2011a. "Algerian Women in Movement: Three Waves of Feminist Activism." In *Confronting Global Gender Justice: Women's Lives, Human Rights,* edited by Debra Bergoffen, Paula Ruth Gilbert, Tamara Harvey, and Connie L. McNeely, 180–99. Oxford: Routledge.

————. 2011b. "Women, Gender, and Economic Crisis Revisited: Perspectives on Global Development and Technology." *Perspectives on Global Development and Technology* 10 (1): 30–40. https://doi.org/10.1163/156914911X555080.

————. 2012. "Toward Human Security and Gender Justice: Reflections on Afghanistan and Iraq." In *Globalization, Social Movements and Peacebuilding,* edited by Jackie Smith and Ernesto Verdejo. Syracuse, NY: Syracuse University Press.

————. 2013a. *Globalization and Social Movements: Islamism, Feminism, and the Global Justice Movement.* 2nd ed. Lanham, MD: Rowman & Littlefield.

————. 2013b. "What Is Democracy? Promises and Perils of the Arab Spring." *Current Sociology* 61, no. 4 (June): 393–408.

————. 2014. "Democratization and Women's Political Leadership in North Africa." *(Columbia) Journal of International Affairs* 68, no. 1 (Fall/Winter): 35–53.

————. 2015. "Transnational Feminism and Movement-Building." In *The Oxford Handbook of Transnational Feminist Movements,* edited by Rawwida Baksh and Wendy Harcourt, 53–81. Oxford: Oxford University Press.

————. 2016. "Engendering Development Sociology: The Evolution of a Field of Research." In *Handbook of the Sociology of Development,* edited by Gregory Hooks, 21–47. Berkeley: University of California Press.

————. 2018. "Explaining Divergent Outcomes of the Arab Spring: The Significance of Gender and Women's Mobilizations." *Politics, Groups, and Identities* 6 (4): 666–89.

———. 2019. "*The Movements of Movements*: A Critical Review Essay." *Socialism and Democracy* 33 (1): 19–27.

Moghadam, Valentine M., and Dilek Elveren. 2008. "The Making of an International Convention: Culture and Free Trade in a Global Era." *Review of International Studies* 34, no. 4 (October): 735–53.

Moghadam, Valentine M., Suzanne Franzway, and Mary Margaret Fonow, eds. 2011. *Making Globalization Work for Women: The Role of Social Rights and Trade Union Leadership.* Albany: State University of New York Press.

Moghadam, Valentine M., and Elham Gheytanchi. 2010. "Political Opportunities and Strategic Choices: Comparing Feminist Campaigns in Morocco and Iran." *Mobilization: An International Quarterly of Social Movement Research* 15, no. 3 (September): 267–88.

Moghadam, Valentine M., and Fatima Sadiqi. 2006. "Women and the Public Sphere in the Middle East and North Africa." Introduction to special issue, *Journal of Middle East Women's Studies* 2, no. 2 (Spring).

Molyneux, Maxine. 1985. "Legal Reform and Socialist Revolution in Democratic Yemen: Women and the Family." *International Journal of Sociology of Law* 13:147–72.

———. 2001. *Women's Movements in International Perspective: Latin America and Beyond.* London: Palgrave.

Monbiot, George. 2011. "The 1% Are the Best Destroyers of All Time." *Guardian Weekly*, November 18, 2011, 19.

Moore, Barrington. 1966. *Social Origins of Dictatorship and Democracy.* Boston, MA: Beacon Press.

Moore, Jina. 2017. "This Is What Happens to Women's Rights When the Far Right Takes Over." BuzzFeed News, March 11, 2017. https://www.buzzfeed.com/jina moore/polands-far-right-is-trying-to-take-away-womens-rights-and-t.

Morozov, Evgeny. 2011. *The Net Delusion: The Dark Side of Internet Freedom.* New York: Public Affairs.

———. 2015. "What Happens When Policy Is Made by Corporations? Your Privacy Is Seen as a Barrier to Economic Growth." *Guardian*, July 12, 2015. https://www.theguardian.com/commentisfree/2015/jul/12/ttip-your-data-privacy-is-a-barrier-to-economic-growth.

Mouffe, Chantal. 2018. *For a Left-Wing Populism.* London: Verso.

Mounk, Yascha. 2018. *The People vs. Democracy: Why Our Freedom Is in Danger and How to Save It.* Cambridge, MA: Harvard University Press.

Mudde, Cas. 2007. *Populist radical right parties in Europe.* Cambridge: Cambridge University Press.

Mudde, Cas, and C. R. Kaltwasser. 2017. *Populism: A Very Short Introduction.* New York: Oxford University Press.

Muis, Jasper, and Tim Immerzeel. 2017. "Causes and Consequences of the Rise of Populist Radical Right Parties and Movements in Europe." *Current Sociology Review* 65 (6): 909–30.

Müller, Jan-Werner. 2016a. "Capitalism in One Family." *London Review of Books* 38, no. 23 (December): 10–11.

———. 2016b. *What Is Populism?* Philadelphia: University of Pennsylvania Press.

Nakhleh, Emile. 2009. *A Necessary Engagement: Reinventing America's Relations with the Muslim World.* Princeton, NJ: Princeton University Press.

Naples, Nancy, and Manisha Desai, eds. 2002. *Women's Activism and Globalization.* London: Routledge.

Nawa, Fariba, and Ozge Sebzeci. 2018. "Plan for 'Pious Generation' Drives Islam into Education." *Economist,* May 30, 2018.

Nelson, Rebecca. 2015. "The Conservative Answer to Feminism." *Atlantic,* May 6, 2015. https://www.theatlantic.com/politics/archive/2015/05/the-conservative -answer-to-feminism/451065.

Newman, Katherine S. 1999. *Falling from Grace: Downward Mobility in the Age of Affluence.* Berkeley: University of California Press.

Niknejad, Mohammad Reza. 2019. "Why Iranian Teachers Are Protesting." *Al-Monitor,* January 6, 2019. https://www.al-monitor.com/pulse/originals/2019/01/ iran-teachers-protest-strike-siting-working-conditions.html.

Njehu, Njoki. 2004. "Cancel the Debt: Africa and the IMF." In *A Movement of Movements: Is Another World Really Possible?,* edited by Tom Mertes, 94–110. London: Verso.

Norris, Pippa, and Ronald Inglehart. 2019. *Cultural Backlash: Trump, Brexit, and Authoritarian Populism.* Cambridge: Cambridge University Press.

O'Brien, Robert, Anne Marie Goetz, Jan Aart Scholte, and Marc Williams. 2000. *Contesting Global Governance: Multilateral Economic Institutions and Global Social Movements.* Cambridge: Cambridge University Press.

O'Donnell, Guillermo, and Philippe Schmitter. 1986. *Transitions from Authoritarian Rule: Tentative Conclusions about Uncertain Democracies.* Baltimore, MD: Johns Hopkins University Press.

O'Donnell, Guillermo, Philippe C. Schmitter, and Laurence Whitehead. 1988. *Transitions from Authoritarian Rule: Comparative Perspectives.* Baltimore, MD: Johns Hopkins University Press.

Okin, Susan Moller. 1989. *Justice, Gender, and the Family.* New York: Basic Books.

Olesen, Thomas. 2007. "Contentious Cartoons: Elite and Media-Driven Mobilization." *Mobilization* 12 (1): 37–52.

Oltermann, Philip. 2018. "Can a Continent's New Xenophobes Reshape Europe?" *Guardian Weekly,* February 9, 2018, 6–7.

Öniş, Ziya. 1997. "The Political Economy of Islamic Resurgence in Turkey: The Rise of the Welfare Party in Perspective." *Third World Quarterly* 18 (4): 743–66.

———. 2004. "Turgut Özal and His Economic Legacy: Turkish Neo-liberalism in Critical Perspective." *Middle Eastern Studies* 40 (4): 113–34.

Orange, Richard. 2018. "Denmark's Swing Right Leaves Muslims Feeling under Siege." *Guardian Weekly,* June 15, 2018.

Oumlil, Kenza. 2017. "Making Sense of Recent Protests in Morocco." Al Jazeera, June 4, 2017. https://www.aljazeera.com/indepth/opinion/2017/06/making-sense -protests-morocco-170604092533766.html.

Oxfam. 2002. *Rigged Rules and Double Standards: Trade, Globalization, and the Fight against Poverty*. Oxford, UK: Oxfam.

Ozcetin, Hilal. 2009. "'Breaking the Silence': The Religious Muslim Women's Movement in Turkey." *Journal of International Women's Studies* 11 (1): 106–19.

Özel, Soli. 2003. "After the Tsunami." *Journal of Democracy* 14 (2): 80–94.

Ozorow, Daniel. 2019. *The Mobilization and Demobilization of Middle-Class Revolt: Comparative Insights from Argentina*. London: Routledge.

Pargeter, Alison. 2010. *The Muslim Brotherhood: The Burden of Tradition*. London: Saqi.

Park, Soon Seok, and Rachel L. Einwohner. 2019. "Becoming a Movement Society? Patterns in the Public Acceptance of Protest, 1985–2006." *Sociological Focus* 52 (3): 186–200.

Pasha, Mustafa Kamal, and Ahmed I. Samatar. 1997. "The Resurgence of Islam." In *Globalization: Critical Perspectives*, edited by James H. Mittelman, 187–201. Boulder, CO: Lynne Rienner.

Paxton, Pamela, and Melanie M. Hughes. 2014. *Women, Politics and Power: A Global Perspective*. 2nd ed. Thousand Oaks, CA: Pine Forge Press.

Payer, Cheryl. 1975. *The Debt Trap: The International Monetary Fund and the Third World*. New York: Monthly Review Press.

Peterson, Scott. 2018. "In Turkey, Cruel Tradition Trumps 'Picture Perfect' Gender Laws." *Christian Science Monitor*, January 24, 2018. https://www.csmonitor .com/World/Middle-East/2018/0124/In-Turkey-cruel-tradition-trumps-picture -perfect-gender-laws.

Peterson, V. Spike. 2003. *A Critical Rewriting of Global Political Economy: Integrating Productive, Reproductive, and Virtual Economies*. New York: Routledge.

Peto, Andrea, and Weronika Grzebalska. 2016. "How Hungary and Poland Have Silenced Women and Stifled Human Rights." *Huffington Post*, October 14, 2016. https://www.huffingtonpost.com/the-conversation-global/how-hungary-and-po land-ha_b_12486148.html.

Phillips, Kevin. 2003. *Wealth and Democracy: A Political History of the American Rich*. New York: Random House.

Pianta, Mario, and Raffaele Marchetti. 2007. "The Global Justice Movements: The Transnational Dimension." In *The Global Justice Movement: Cross-National and Transnational Perspectives*, edited by Donatella della Porta, 29–51. Boulder, CO: Paradigm.

Pieterse, Jan Nederveen. 1998. "Hybrid Modernities: Mélange Modernities in Asia." *Sociological Analysis* 1 (3): 75–86.

———. 2004. *Globalization or Empire?* London and New York: Routledge.

Pietila, Hilkka, and Jeanne Vickers. 1994. *Making Women Matter: The Role of the UN*. London: Zed Books.

Piñeiro, Rafael, Matthew Rhodes-Purdy, and Fernando Rosenblatt. 2016. "The Engagement Curve: Populism and Political Engagement in Latin America." *Latin American Research Review* 51 (4): 3–23.

Plastas, Melinda. 2011. *A Band of Noble Women: Racial Politics in the Women's Peace Movement*. Syracuse, NY: Syracuse University Press.

Podobnik, Bruce. 2005. "Resistance to Globalization." In *Transforming Globalization*, edited by Bruce Podobnik and Thomas Reifer, 51–68. Leiden: Brill.

Podobnik, Bruce, and Thomas Ehrlich Reifer, eds. 2004. "Global Social Movements before and after 9–11." Special issue, *Journal of World Systems Research* 10, no. 1 (Winter). http://jwsr.ucr.edu/archive/vol10/number1.

Polanyi, Karl. [1944] 2001. *The Great Transformation: The Political and Economic Origins of Our Time*. Boston, MA: Beacon Press.

Polletta, Francesca. 2002. *Freedom Is an Endless Meeting: Democracy in American Social Movements*. Chicago: University of Chicago Press.

Power, Margaret. 2002. *Right-Wing Women in Chile: Feminine Power and the Struggle against Allende, 1964–1973*. College Park: Pennsylvania State University Press.

Prata, Ana. 2010. "Finding a Voice: Abortion Claim-Making during Portuguese Democratization." *Women's Studies International Forum* 33:579–88.

Pratt, Nicola. 2012. "The Gender Logics of Resistance to the 'War on Terror': Constructing Sex-Gender Difference through the Erasure of Patriarchy in the Middle East." *Third World Quarterly* 33 (12): 1821–36.

Przeworski, Adam et al. 1995. *Sustainable Democracy*. Cambridge and New York: Cambridge University Press.

Rahman, Fazlur. 1982. *Islam and Modernity: Transformation of an Intellectual Tradition*. Chicago: Publications of the Center for Middle Eastern Studies, University of Chicago.

Rashid, Ahmed. 2000. *Taliban: Militant Islam, Oil and Fundamentalism in Central Asia*. New Haven, CT, and London: Yale University Press.

Reardon, Betty. 1993. *Women and Peace: Feminist Visions of Global Security*. Albany: State University of New York Press.

Reese, Ellen, Erika Gutierrez, and Christopher Chase-Dunn. 2007. "Labor and Other Anti-systemic Movements in the World Social Forum Process." IROWS Working Paper 17. Riverside: University of California–Riverside, Institute for Research on World-Systems. http://irows.ucr.edu.

Reid, Edna, and Hsinchen Chen. 2007. "Internet-Savvy U.S. and Middle Eastern Extremist Groups." *Mobilization* 12, no. 2 (June): 177–92.

Reuters. 2017. "Support for Hungary's Ruling Fidesz Highest in Six Years in October: Pollster." November 2, 2017. https://www.reuters.com/article/us-hungary-politics-fidesz/support-for-hungarys-ruling-fidesz-highest-in-six-years-in-octo ber-pollster-idUSKBN1D21DE.

Roberts, Hugh. 2003. *The Battlefield: Algeria 1988–2002, Studies in a Broken Polity.* London: Verso.

———. 2015. "The Hijackers." *London Review of Books* 37, no. 14 (July 16): 5–10.

Roberts, J. Timmons, and Amy Bellone Hite, eds. 2007. *The Globalization and Development Reader.* London: Blackwell.

Roberts, Kenneth. 1998. *Deepening Democracy? The Modern Left and Social Movements in Chile and Peru.* Stanford, CA: Stanford University Press.

———. 2016. "Democracy in the Developing World: Challenges of Survival and Significance." *Comparative Studies in International Development* 51:42–59.

Robinson, William I. 2004. *A Theory of Global Capitalism.* Baltimore, MD: Johns Hopkins University Press.

Robinson, William I., and Jerry Harris. 2000. "Towards a Global Class? Globalization and the Transnational Capitalist Class." *Science & Society* 64, no. 1 (Spring): 11–54.

Roces, Mina. 2010. "Rethinking the 'Filipino Woman': A Century of Women's Activism in the Philippines, 1905–2006." In *Women's Movements in Asia: Feminisms and Transnational Activism*, edited by Mina Roces and Louise Edwards. London and New York: Routledge.

Rockhill, Gabriel. 2019. "One Question: Gilets Jaunes." *State of Nature* (blog), June 6, 2019. http://stateofnatureblog.com/one-question-gilets-jaunes.

Rodrik, Dani. 1997. "Has Globalization Gone Too Far?" Washington, DC: Institute for International Economics. http://j.mp/2ow2hqX.

———. 2017. "Populism and the Economics of Globalization." Cambridge, MA: Harvard University, Weatherhead Center for International Affairs. https://drodrik .scholar.harvard.edu/publications/populism-and-economics-globalization.

Round, Robin. 2002. "Controlling Casino Capital." In *Global Backlash: Citizen Initiatives for a Just World Economy*, edited by Robin Broad, 282–86. Lanham, MD: Rowman & Littlefield.

Rousselin, Mathieu. 2015. "In the Name of Allah and of the Market: The Capitalist Leanings of Tunisian Islamists." *Science and Society* 80 (2): 196–220.

Roy, Olivier. 2004. *Globalized Islam: The Search for a New Ummah.* New York: Columbia University Press.

Roy, Sara. 2011. *Hamas and Civil Society in Gaza: Engaging the Islamist Social Sector.* Princeton, NJ: Princeton University Press.

Rubery, Jill. 2015. "Austerity and the Future for Gender Equality in Europe." *International Labour Review* 68, no. 4 (August): 715–41.

Rubin, Barnett. 1997. "Arab Islamists in Afghanistan." In *Political Islam: Revolution, Radicalism, or Reform?*, edited by John Esposito, 179–206. Boulder, CO: Lynne Rienner.

Rucht, Dieter, ed. 1991. *Research on Social Movements: The State of the Art in Western Europe and the United States of America.* Boulder, CO: Westview.

Rueschemeyer, Dietrich, Evelyne Huber Stephens, and John D. Stephens. 1992. *Capitalist Development and Democracy*. Chicago: University of Chicago Press.

Rueschemeyer, Marilyn, ed. 1998. *Women in the Politics of Postcommunist Eastern Europe*. Armonk, NY: Sharpe.

Runciman, David. 2018. *How Democracy Ends*. New York: Basic Books.

Runyan, Anne Sisson. 2002. "Still Not 'at Home' in IR: Feminist World Politics Ten Years Later." *International Politics* 39 (September): 361–68.

Rupert, Mark, and M. Scott Solomon. 2006. *Globalization and International Political Economy*. Lanham, MD: Rowman & Littlefield.

Rupp, Leila. 1998. *Worlds of Women: The Making of an International Women's Movement*. Princeton, NJ: Princeton University Press.

Sabbah, Fatna A. [Fatima Mernissi]. 1984. *Woman in the Muslim Unconscious*. Translated by Mary Jo Lakeland. New York: Pergamon Press.

Sadiqi, Fatima, and Moha Ennaji. 2006. "The Feminization of Public Space: Women's Activism, the Family Law, and Social Change in Morocco." *Journal of Middle East Women's Studies* 2, no. 2 (Spring): 86–114.

Saif, Ibrahim, and Muhammad Abu Rumman. 2012. "The Economic Agenda of Islamic Parties." Carnegie Middle East Center, May 29, 2012. https://carnegie-mec.org/2012/05/29/economic-agenda-of-islamist-parties-pub-48187.

Salhi, Zahia Smail. 2010. "Gender and Violence in Algeria: Women's Resistance against the Islamist Femicide." In *Gender and Diversity in the Middle East and North Africa*, edited by Zahia Smail Salhi, 161–84. Milton Park, UK: Routledge.

———. 2011. "Algerian Women as Agents of Change and Social Cohesion." In *Women in the Middle East and North Africa: Agents of Change*, edited by Fatima Sadiqi and Moha Ennaji, 194–272. London and New York: Routledge.

Salime, Zakia. 2010. "Securing the Market, Pacifying Civil Society, Empowering Women: The Middle East Partnership Initiative." *Sociological Forum* 25, no. 4 (November): 725–45.

———. 2019. "Precarious Teachers Strike for Public Education in Morocco." *Middle East Report Online*, May 2, 2019. https://merip.org/2019/05/precarious-teachers-strike-for-public-education-in-morocco.

Sánchez, Juan Luis. 2011. "Dreaming of a 'New Global Citizen Power.'" *Periodismo Humano*, October 15, 2011. http://takethesquare.net/2011/10/13/october-15th-dreaming-of-a-%e2%80%9cnew-global-citizen-power%e2%80%9d.

Sanders, Bernie. 2010. "A Real Jaw Dropper at the Federal Reserve." *Huffington Post*, December 2, 2010. https://www.huffpost.com/entry/a-real-jaw-dropper-at-the_b_791091.

Sanky, Kyla. 2016. "What Happened to the Pink Tide?" *Jacobin Magazine*, July 27, 2016. https://www.jacobinmag.com/2016/07/pink-tide-latin-america-chavez-morales-capitalism-socialism.

Santos, Boaventura de Sousa. 2006. *The Rise of the Global Left: The World Social Forum and Beyond*. London: Zed Books.

Sarı, Diren Deniz. 2015. "AKP zihniyetinin kadına bakışı: 12 yılda kim, ne dedi?" BirGün, June 18, 2015. https://www.birgun.net/haber-detay/akp-zihniyetinin -kadina-bakisi-12-yilda-kim-ne-dedi-83051.html.

Sassen, Saskia. 2001. *The Global City: New York, London, Tokyo.* 2nd ed. Princeton, NJ: Princeton University Press.

————. 2014. *Expulsions: Brutality and Complexity in the Global Economy.* Cambridge, MA: Harvard University Press.

Sater, James N. 2007. *Civil Society and Political Change in Morocco.* London: Routledge.

Schafer, Armin. 2017. "Return with a Vengeance: Working-Class Anger and the Rise of Populism." Items, August 8, 2017. www.items.ssrc.org/return-with-a -vengeance-working-class-anger-and-the-rise-of-populism.

Scheffer, Paul. 2011. *Immigrant Nations.* London: Polity.

Schmitter, Philippe C., and Terry Lynne Karl. 1991. "What Democracy Is . . . and Is Not." *Journal of Democracy* 2, no. 3 (Summer): 75–88.

Scholte, Jan Aart. 2000. *Globalization: A Critical Introduction.* London: Palgrave.

Schwedler, Jillian. 2006. *Faith in Moderation: Islamist Parties in Jordan and Yemen.* New York: Cambridge University Press.

Scott-Clark, Cathy, and Adrian Levy. 2010. "Lost Boys of Pakistan." *Guardian Weekly,* November 5, 2010, 25–27.

Seçim Haberler. 2015. "1 Kasim 2015 AK PARTİ Genel Seçim Sonuçları." Seçim Haberler, 2015. https://secim.haberler.com/2015/ak-parti-secim-sonucu.

Secular Hungary. 2013. "Top 10 Sexist Hungarian Politicians." Secular Hungary, September 22, 2013. https://secularhungary.wordpress.com/2013/09/22/top -10-sexist-hungarian-politicians.

Segran, Elizabeth. 2013. "The Rise of the Islamist Feminists." *Nation,* December 4, 2013. https://www.thenation.com/article/rise-islamic-feminists.

Selk, Avi. 2017. "Poland Defends Massive Far-Right Protest That Called for a White Europe." *Washington Post,* November 12, 2017. https://www.washington post.com/news/worldviews/wp/2017/11/12/pray-for-an-islamic-holocaust-tens -of-thousands-from-europes-far-right-march-in-poland.

Sen, Gita, and Caren Grown. 1987. *Development, Crises, and Alternative Visions: Third World Women's Perspectives.* New York: Monthly Review.

Sen, Jai, ed. 2017. *The Movements of Movements.* Part 1, *What Makes Us Move?* New Delhi and Oakland, CA: OpenWord and PM Press.

————, ed. 2018. *The Movements of Movements.* Part 2, *Rethinking Our Dance.* New Delhi and Oakland, CA: OpenWord and PM Press.

Serres, Thomas. 2019. "Understanding Algeria's 2019 Revolutionary Movement." Briefing no. 129. Brandeis University, Crown Center for Middle East Studies, Waltham, MA, July 2019.

Setzler, Mark, and Alixandra B. Yanus. 2018. "Why Did Women Vote for Donald Trump?" *Political Science* 51, no. 3 (July): 523–27.

Shaheed, Farida. 1994. "Controlled or Autonomous: Identity and the Experience of the Network Women Living under Muslim Laws." Women Living under Muslim Laws Occasional Paper 5. WLUML, July 1994.

Shelev, Chemi. 2019. "Netanyahu's Trump-Inspired Embrace of the Racist Right Is Repulsive, but Gantz-Lapid Threat Means You Ain't Seen Nothing Yet," *Haaretz*, February 21, 2019.

Shitrit, Lihi B. 2016. "Authenticating Representation: Women's Quotas and Islamist Parties." *Politics & Gender* 12:781–806.

Shiva, Vandana. 2000. "War against Nature and the People of the South." In *Views from the South: The Effects of Globalization and the WTO on Third World Countries*, edited by Sarah Anderson, 91–124. Chicago: Food First and the International Forum on Globalization.

Sidahmed, A. Salam, and Anoushirvan Ehteshami, eds. 1996. *Islamic Fundamentalism*. Boulder, CO: Westview.

Siddiqui, Mona. 2009. "Call for Change, but All Too Quiet." *Times Higher Education* (London), April 2, 2009, 54.

Sikkink, Kathryn. 2011. *The Justice Cascade*. New York: Norton.

Silva, Eduardo. 2010. *Challenging Neoliberalism in Latin America*. New York: Cambridge University Press.

Skalli, Loubna Hanna. 2007. "Women, Communications and Democratization in Morocco." In *Empowering Women: Participation, Rights, and Women's Movements in the Middle East, North Africa, and South Asia*, edited by Valentine M. Moghadam. Syracuse, NY: Syracuse University Press.

Sklair, Leslie. 1991. *A Sociology of the Global System*. Baltimore, MD: Johns Hopkins University Press.

———. 2001. *The Transnational Capitalist Class*. Oxford: Blackwell.

———. 2002. *Globalization: Capitalism and Its Alternatives*. 3rd ed. Oxford: Oxford University Press.

Skocpol, Theda, and Vanessa Williamson. 2012. *The Tea Party and the Remaking of Republican Conservatism*. Oxford: Oxford University Press.

Slawson, Nicola. 2017. "Austrian President Approves Far-Right Freedom Party Joining Coalition Government." *Guardian*, December 16, 2017. https://www.theguardian.com/world/2017/dec/16/austrian-president-approves-far-right-freedom-party-role-in-coalition-government.

Slyomovics, Susan. 2005. *The Performance of Human Rights in Morocco*. Philadelphia: University of Pennsylvania Press.

Smeal, Eleanor. "Special Message from the Feminist Majority on the Taliban, Osama bin Laden, and Afghan Women." Feminist Majority, September 18, 2001. http://feministmajority.org.

Smith, Alex Duval. 2016. "Polish Prime Minister Favours Total Ban on Abortion." *Guardian*, March 31, 2016. https://www.theguardian.com/world/2016/mar/31/polish-prime-minister-favours-ban-on-abortion.

Smith, Jackie. 2008. *Social Movements for Global Democracy*. Baltimore, MD: Johns Hopkins University Press.

———. 2017. "Local Responses to Right-Wing Populism: Building Human Rights Cities." *Studies in Social Justice* 11 (2): 347–68.

Smith, Jackie, Charles Chatfield, and Ron Pagnucco, eds. 1997. *Transnational Social Movements and Global Politics*. Syracuse, NY: Syracuse University Press.

Smith, Jackie, and Hank Johnston, eds. 2002. *Globalization and Resistance: Transnational Dimensions of Social Movements*. Lanham, MD: Rowman & Littlefield.

Smith, Jackie, Marina Karides, Marc Becker, Dorval Brunelle, Christopher Chase-Dunn, Rosalba Icaza, Jeffrey Juris, Lorenzo Mosca, Donatella della Porta, Ellen Reese, Peter Jay Smith, and Rolando Vásquez. 2008. *The World Social Forums and the Challenge of Global Democracy*. Boulder, CO: Paradigm.

Smith, Jackie, and Dawn Wiest. 2005. "The Uneven Geography of Global Civil Society: National and Global Influences on Transnational Association." *Social Forces* 84:621–51.

———. 2012. *Social Movements in the World-System: The Politics of Crisis*. Rose Series. Washington, DC: Russell Sage Foundation for the American Sociological Association.

Smith, Peter J., and Elizabeth Smythe. 2010. "(In)Fertile Ground? Social Forum Activism in Its Regional and Local Dimension." *Journal of World-Systems Research* 16 (1): 6–28.

Snow, David A. 2004. "Framing Processes, Ideology, and Discursive Fields." In *The Blackwell Companion to Social Movements*, edited by David A. Snow, Sarah Soule, and Hanspieter Kriesi, 380–412. Malden, MA: Blackwell.

Sparr, Pam, ed. 1994. *Mortgaging Women's Lives: Feminist Critiques of Structural Adjustment*. London: Zed Books.

Sperling, Valerie, Myra Marx Ferree, and Barbara Risman. 2001. "Constructing Global Feminism: Transnational Advocacy Networks and Russian Women's Activism." *Signs* 26 (4): 1155–86.

Spierings, Niels, and Andrej Zaslove. 2017. "Gender, Populist Attitudes, and Voting: Explaining the Gender Gap in Voting for Populist Radical Right and Populist Radical Left Parties." *West European Politics* 40 (4): 821–47.

Stacey, Judith. 1983. "The New Conservative Feminism." *Feminist Studies* 9 (3), 559–83.

Standing, Guy. 1989. "Global Feminization through Flexible Labor." *World Development* 17 (7): 1077–95.

———. 1999a. "Global Feminization through Flexible Labor: A Theme Revisited." *World Development* 27 (3): 583–602.

———. 1999b. *Global Labour Market Flexibility: Seeking Distributive Justice*. Basingstoke, UK: Macmillan.

Starhawk. 2003. "Why We Need Women's Actions and Feminist Voices for Peace." *Off Our Backs* (March–April): 16–17.

Steger, Manfred. 2002. *Globalism*. Lanham, MD: Rowman & Littlefield.

———. 2003. *Globalization: A Very Short Introduction*. Oxford: Oxford University Press.

———. 2009. *Globalization: A Very Short Introduction*. 2nd ed. New York: Oxford University Press.

Steger, Manfred, and Ravi K. Roy. 2010. *Neoliberalism: A Very Short Introduction*. New York: Oxford University Press.

Stern, Jessica, and John M. Berger. 2015. *ISIS: The State of Terror*. New York: HarperCollins.

Stevenson, Tom. 2019. "How to Run a Caliphate." *London Review of Books* 41, no. 12 (June 12): 9–10.

Stienstra, Deborah. 1994. *Women's Movements and International Organizations*. New York: St. Martin's.

———. 2000. "Dancing Resistance from Rio to Beijing: Transnational Women's Organizing and United Nations Conferences, 1992–1996." In *Gender and Global Restructuring: Sightings, Sites and Resistances*, edited by Anne Sisson Runyan and Marianne Marchand, 209–24. London: Routledge.

Stiglitz, Joseph. 2002. *Globalization and Its Discontents*. New York: Norton.

Strange, Susan. 1986. *Casino Capitalism*. Manchester, UK: Manchester University Press.

———. 1988. *States and Markets*. London: Bloomsbury.

———. 1996. *The Retreat of the State: The Diffusion of Power in the World Economy*. Cambridge: Cambridge University Press.

Streek, Wolfgang. 2017. *How Will Capitalism End?* London: Verso.

———. 2019. "The European Union Is a Liberal Empire and It's about to Fall." *London School of Economics Blog* (blog). https://blogs.lse.ac.uk/brexit/2019/03/06/long-read-the-european-union-is-a-liberal-empire-and-it-is-about-to-fall.

Streeten, Paul. 1997. "Globalization and Competitiveness: Implications for Development Thinking and Practice?" In *Economic and Social Development into the XXI Century*, edited by Louis Emmerij, 107–47. Washington, DC: Inter-American Development Bank.

Strolovich, Dara Z., Janelle S. Wong, and Andrew Proctor. 2017. "A Possessive Investment in White Heteropatriarchy? The 2016 Election and the Politics of Race, Gender, and Sexuality." *Politics, Groups, and Identities* 5 (2): 353–63.

Subcomandante Marcos. 2004. "The Hourglass of the Zapatistas." Interview with Gabriel García Márquez and Roberto Pombo. In *A Movement of Movements: Is Another World Really Possible?*, edited by Tom Mertes, 3–15. London: Verso.

Subramanian, Narendra. 2007. "Populism in India." *SAIS Review of International Affairs* 27, no. 1 (Winter–Spring): 81–91.

Sundberg, Jan. 2015. "Who Are the Nationalist Finns Party?" BBC News, May 11, 2015. http://www.bbc.com/news/world-europe-32627013.

Szabo, Maté. 2015. "From Anticommunist Dissident Movement to Governing Party: The Transformation of Fidesz in Hungary." In *Movements in Times of Democratic Transition*, edited by Bert Klandermans and Cornelis van Stralen, 301–16. Philadelphia: Temple University Press.

Taraki, Lisa. 1995. "Islam Is the Solution: Jordanian Islamists and the Dilemma of the 'Modern Woman.'" *British Journal of Sociology* 46 (4): 643–61.

Tarrow, Sidney. 2001. "Transnational Politics: Contention and Institutions in International Politics." *Annual Review of Political Science* 4:1–20.

———. 2005. *The New Transnational Activism*. Cambridge: Cambridge University Press.

Taskin, Yuksel. 2008. "Upsurge of the Extreme Right in Turkey: The Intra-Right Struggle to Redefine 'True Nationalism and Islam.'" *Middle Eastern Studies* 44 (1): 131–49.

Tavakoli-Targhi, Mohamad. 1988. *Emergence of Two Revolutionary Discourses*. Chicago: University of Chicago Press.

Taylor, Lance. 1993. *The Rocky Road to Reform: Adjustment, Income Distribution and Growth in the Developing World*. Cambridge, MA: MIT Press.

———. 2000. "External Liberalization, Economic Performance, and Distribution in Latin America and Elsewhere." WIDER Working Papers 215. Helsinki, Finland, December 2000.

Taylor, Rupert. 2004. "Interpreting Global Civil Society." In *Creating a Better World: Interpreting Global Civil Society*, edited by Rupert Taylor, 2–10. Bloomfield, CT: Kumarian Press.

Tekeli, Sirin, ed. 1994. *Women in Modern Turkish Society: A Reader*. London: Zed Books.

———. 2010. "The Turkish Women's Movement: A Brief History of Success." *Quaderns de la Mediterania* 14:119–23.

Tessler, Mark. 2007. "Do Islamic Orientations Influence Attitudes toward Democracy in the Arab World? Evidence from the World Values Survey in Egypt, Jordan, Morocco, and Algeria." In *Values and Perceptions of the Islamic and Middle Eastern Publics*, edited by Mansoor Moaddel, 105–25. New York: Palgrave Macmillan.

Thapar-Björkert, S. 2013. "Gender, Nations and Nationalisms." In *The Oxford Handbook of Gender and Politics*, edited by G. Waylen, K. Celis, J. Kantola, and S. L. Weldon. Oxford: Oxford University Press.

Tharoor, Ishaan. 2016. "Trump's Victory Places U.S. at the Front of a Global Right-Wing Surge." *Washington Post*, November 9, 2016. https://www.washingtonpost.com/news/worldviews/wp/2016/11/09/trumps-victory-places-u-s-at-the-front-of-a-global-right-wing-surge.

Tickner, Ann. 1992. *Gender in International Relations: Feminist Perspectives on Achieving Global Security*. New York: Columbia University Press.

Tobin, James. 1978. "A Proposal for International Monetary Reform." *Eastern Economic Journal* 4, nos. 3–4 (July/October): 153–59.

Tooze, Adam. 2018. *Crashed: How a Decade of Financial Crises Changed the World.* London: Allen Lane.

Traub, James. 2016. "The Party That Wants to Make Poland Great Again." *New York Times*, November 6, 2016. https://www.nytimes.com/2016/11/06/magazine/the-party-that-wants-to-make-poland-great-again.html.

Tufekci, Zeynep. 2016. *Twitter and Tear Gas: The Power and Fragility of Networked Protest.* New Haven, CT: Yale University Press.

Tugal, Cihan. 2009. "Transforming Everyday Life: Islamism and Social Movement Theory." *Theory and Society* 38, no. 5 (September): 423–58.

Tyson, Alec, and Shiva Maniam. 2016. "Behind Trump's Victory: Divisions by Race, Gender, Education." Pew Research Center, November 9, 2016. https://www.pewresearch.org/fact-tank/2016/11/09/behind-trumps-victory-divisions-by-race-gender-education.

UNDP. 1999. *Human Development Report 1999: Globalization with a Human Face.* New York: Oxford University Press.

———. 2002. *Human Development Report 2002: Deepening Democracy in a Fragmented World.* New York: Oxford University Press.

———. 2005. *Human Development Report 2005: International Cooperation at a Crossroads: Aid, Trade and Security in an Unequal World.* New York: United Nations Development Programme.

———. 2011. *Human Development Report 2011: Sustainability and Equity: A Better Future for All.* New York: United Nations Development Programme.

———. 2018. *Human Development Indices and Indicators, 2018 Statistical Update.* New York: United National Development Programme.

van Bruinessen, Martin. 1996. "Kurds, Turks and the Alevi Revival in Turkey." *Middle East Report* 200 (July–September): 7–10.

Vargas, Virginia. 2005. "Feminisms and the World Social Forum: Space for Dialogue and Confrontation." *Development* 48, no. 2: 107–10.

———. 2009. "International Feminisms: The World Social Forum." In *Feminist Agendas and Democracy in Latin America*, edited by Jane Jaquette, 145–64. Durham, NC: Duke University Press.

Varoufakis, Yanis. 2017. *Adults in the Room: My Struggle with the European and American Deep Establishment.* New York: Farrar, Straus and Giroux.

Vieceli, Jacqueline M. 1997. "Assessing the Impact of Structural Adjustment on Prospects for Democracy in the 'Third World.'" *Comparative Studies of South Asia, Africa, and the Middle East* 17 (2): 82–99.

Voigt, Kevin. 2011. "Beyond Wall Street: 'Occupy' Protests Go Global." CNN, October 7, 2011. http://edition.cnn.com/2011/10/07/business/wall-street-protest-global.

Waddington, David, and Mike King. 2007. "The Impact of the Local: Police Public-Order Strategies during the G8 Justice and Home Affairs Ministerial Meetings." *Mobilization* 12, no. 4 (December): 417–30.

Walby, Sylvia. 2004. "The European Union and Gender Equality: Emergent Varieties of Gender Regime." *Social Politics: International Studies in Gender, State & Society* 11, no. 1 (Spring): 4–29.

———. 2009. *Globalization and Modernities.* London: Sage.

———. 2015. *Crisis.* London: Polity.

Walgrave, Stefaan, W. Lance Bennett, Jeroen Van Laer, and Christian Breunig. 2011. "Multiple Engagements and Network Bridging in Contentious Politics: Digital Media Use of Protest Participants." *Mobilization: An International Journal* 16 (3): 325–49.

Wallerstein, Immanuel. 1991. *Geopolitics and Geoculture: Essays on the Changing World-System.* Cambridge: Cambridge University Press.

———. 2000. "Globalization or the Age of Transition? A Long-Term View of the Trajectory of the World-System." *International Sociology* 15 (2): 249–65.

———. 2003. *The Decline of American Power: The U.S. in a Chaotic World.* New York: New Press.

———. 2011. "Structural Crisis in the World-System: Where Do We Go from Here?" *Monthly Review*, March 1, 2011. https://monthlyreview.org/2011/03/01/structural-crisis-in-the-world-system.

Walsh, Declan. 2011. "Pakistan's Liberal Dream Has Died with the Assassination of Taseer." *Guardian Weekly*, January 14, 2011, 9.

Walton, John, and David Seddon. 1994. *Free Markets and Food Riots: The Politics of Global Adjustment.* Oxford: Blackwell.

Waylen, Georgina. 1994. "Women and Democratization: Conceptualizing Gender Relations in Transition Politics." *World Politics* 46, no. 3: 327–54.

———. 2007. *Engendering Transitions: Women's Mobilizations, Institutions, and Gender Outcomes.* London and New York: Oxford University Press.

Wejnert, Barbara. 2005. "Diffusion, Development, and Democracy, 1800–1999." *American Sociological Review* 70 (February): 53–81.

Weldon, S. Laurel. 2011. *When Protest Makes Policy: How Social Movements Represent Disadvantaged Groups.* Ann Arbor: University of Michigan Press.

Welzel, Christian, and Ronald Inglehart. 2009. "Development and Democracy: What We Know about Modernization Today." *Foreign Affairs* (March–April): 33–41. http://www.worldvaluessurvey.org/wvs/articles/folder_published/publication_593/files/inglehart-welzel-modernization-and-democracy.pdf.

West, Lois. 1997. *Feminist Nationalism.* London: Routledge.

White, Jenny B. 2003. *Islamist Mobilization in Turkey: A Study in Vernacular Politics.* Seattle: University of Washington Press.

Wichterich, Christa. 1999. *The Globalized Woman: Notes from a Future of Inequality.* London: Zed Books.

Wickham, Carrie Rosefsky. 2002. *Mobilizing Islam: Religion, Activism, and Political Change in Egypt.* New York: Columbia University Press.

WIDE+. 2015. "Changing Global Policy Paradigm for Women's Rights: Report of WIDE+ Meeting 18 June 2015, Barcelona, Spain." WIDE+, September 28,

2015. https://wideplus.org/2015/09/28/wide-2015-report-womens-rights-need-a-transformation-of-the-global-development-paradigm.

Wiest, Dawn. 2007. "A Story of Two Transnationalisms: Global Salafi Jihad and Transnational Human Rights Mobilization in the Middle East and North Africa." *Mobilization* 12, no. 2 (June): 137–60.

Wiktorowicz, Quintan. 2000. "The Salafi Movement in Jordan." *International Journal of Middle East Studies* 32: 219–40.

———. 2001. *The Management of Islamic Activism: Salafis, the Muslim Brotherhood, and State Power in Jordan*. Albany: State University of New York Press.

———. 2004a. "Introduction: Islamic Activism and Social Movement Theory." In *Islamic Activism: A Social Movement Theory Approach*, edited by Quintan Wiktorowicz, 1–36. Bloomington: Indiana University Press.

———, ed. 2004b. *Islamic Activism: A Social Movement Theory Approach*. Bloomington: Indiana University Press.

———. 2005. *Radical Islam Rising: Muslim Extremism in the West*. Lanham, MD: Rowman & Littlefield.

Wilkin, Peter. 2018. "The Rise of 'Illiberal' Democracy: The Orbánization of Hungarian Political Culture." *Journal of World-Systems Research* 24 (1).

Wilkinson, Richard, and Kate Pickett. 2009. *The Spirit Level: Why Greater Equality Makes Societies Stronger*. New York and London: Bloomsbury Press.

Williamson, John. 2004. "A Short History of the Washington Consensus." Institute for International Economics, September 4, 2004. http://www.iie.com/publications/papers/williamson0904-2.pdf.

Witt, Michael. 2019. "De-globalization: Theories, Predictions, and Opportunities for International Business Research." *Journal of International Business Studies* 50:1053–77. https://link.springer.com/content/pdf/10.1057%2Fs41267-019-00219-7.pdf.

Women in Development Europe (WIDE). 1998. *Trade Traps and Gender Gaps: Women Unveiling the Market. Report on WIDE's Annual Conference Held at Jarvenpaa, Finland, May 16–18, 1997*. Brussels: WIDE.

Women Living under Muslim Laws (WLUML). 2005. "WLUML Appeal against Fundamentalisms." WLUML, January 21, 2005. http://www.wluml.org/english/newsfulltxt.shtml?cmd%5B157%5D=x-157-103376.

World March of Women. 1999. "Advocacy Guide to Women's World Demands." https://www.rapereliefshelter.bc.ca/sites/default/files/imce/World%20March%20of%20Women%20-%20World%20Demands.pdf.

World Social Forum. 2001. "Charter of Principles." http://www.universidadepopular.org/site/media/documentos/WSF_-_charter_of_Principles.pdf.

Wuthnow, Robert. 1986. "Religious Movements and Counter-Movements in North America." In *New Religious Movements and Rapid Social Change*, edited by James Beckford, 1–28. Beverly Hills, CA, and Paris: Sage Publications and UNESCO.

Yaghmaian, Behzad. 2001. "The Political Economy of Global Accumulation and Its Emerging Mode of Regulation." In *Labor and Capital in the Age of Globalization:*

The Labor Process and the Changing Nature of Work in the Global Economy, edited by Berch Berberoglu. Lanham, MD: Rowman & Littlefield.

Yan, Holly. 2015. "Donald Trump's 'Blood' Comment about Megyn Kelly Draws Outrage." CNNPolitics, August 8, 2015. http://www.cnn.com/2015/08/08/politics/donald-trump-cnn-megyn-kelly-comment.

Yerkes, Sarah, and Zeineb Ben Yahmed. 2018. "Tunisians' Revolutionary Goals Remain Unfulfilled." Carnegie Endowment for International Peace, December 6, 2018. https://carnegieendowment.org/2018/12/06/tunisians-revolutionary-goals-remain-unfulfilled-pub-77894.

Young, Kate, ed. 1992. *Gender and Development Reader.* Ottawa: Canadian Council for International Cooperation.

Yurdakul, Hasan. 2015. "2008 Küresel Ekonomik Krizi Ve Türkiye'ye Etkisi." *Sahipkıran Stratejik Araştırmalar Merkezi*, January 12, 2015. http://sahipkiran.org/2015/01/12/kuresel-ekonomik-kriz.

Yuval-Davis, Nira. 1997. *Gender and the Nation*. London: Sage.

Zeghal, Malika. 2008. *Islamism in Morocco: Religion, Authoritarianism, and Electoral Politics*. Princeton, NJ: Markus Wiener.

Zey, Mary. 1993. *Banking on Fraud: Drexel, Junk Bonds, and Buy-Outs*. Piscataway, NJ: Transaction Books.

Zivkovic, Andrea, and John Hogan. 2007. "Virtual Revolution? ICTs and Networks." In *Revolution in the Making of the Modern World*, edited by John Foran, David Lane, and Andreja Zivkovic, 182–98. London: Routledge.

Zubaida, Sami. 1993. *Islam, the People and the State: Political Ideas and Movements in the Middle East*. London: I. B. Tauris.

INDEX

Note: Page numbers followed by "f" or "t" refer to figures and tables, respectively.

About the Author

Valentine M. Moghadam is professor of sociology and international affairs at Northeastern University, Boston, and former director of the International Affairs Program and the Middle East Studies minor and concentration (2012–17). The author of many books and journal articles, she has lectured widely and consulted many international organizations. Born in Tehran, Iran, she received her higher education in Canada and the United States. In addition to her academic career, Dr. Moghadam has been a senior researcher with the WIDER Institute of the United Nations University, Helsinki, Finland, and a section chief at UNESCO in Paris. She also has served as a board member of Massachusetts Peace Action.

GLOBALIZATION

Series Editors

Manfred B. Steger

University of Hawai'i–Mānoa and Western Sydney University

and

Terrell Carver

University of Bristol

"Globalization" has become *the* buzzword of our time. But what does it mean? Rather than forcing a complicated social phenomenon into a single analytical framework, this series seeks to present globalization as a multidimensional process constituted by complex, often contradictory interactions of global, regional, and local aspects of social life. Since conventional disciplinary borders and lines of demarcation are losing their old rationales in a globalizing world, authors in this series apply an interdisciplinary framework to the study of globalization. In short, the main purpose and objective of this series is to support subject-specific inquiries into the dynamics and effects of contemporary globalization and its varying impacts across, between, and within societies.

Globalization and Sovereignty, 2nd ed.
John Agnew

Globalization and War
Tarak Barkawi

Globalization and Human Security
Paul Battersby and Joseph M. Siracusa

Globalization and the Environment
Peter Christoff and Robyn Eckersley

Globalization and American Popular Culture, 4th ed.
Lane Crothers

Globalization and Migration
Eliot Dickinson

Globalization and Militarism, 2nd ed.
Cynthia Enloe

Globalization and Law
Adam Gearey

Globalization and Feminist Activism, 2nd ed.
Mary E. Hawkesworth

Globalization and Postcolonialism
Sankaran Krishna

Globalization and Media, 3rd ed.
Jack Lule

Globalization and Social Movements, 3rd ed.
Valentine M. Moghadam

Globalization and Terrorism, 2nd ed.
Jamal R. Nassar

Globalization and Culture, 4th ed.
Jan Nederveen Pieterse

Globalization and Democracy
Stephen J. Rosow and Jim George

Globalization and International Political Economy
Mark Rupert and M. Scott Solomon

Globalization and Citizenship
Hans Schattle

Globalization and Money
Supriya Singh

Globalization and Islamism
Nevzat Soguk

Globalization and Urbanization
James H. Spencer

Globalisms, 4th ed.
Manfred B. Steger

Rethinking Globalism
Edited by Manfred B. Steger

Globalization and Labor
Dimitris Stevis and Terry Boswell

Globalization and Surveillance
Timothy Erik Ström

Globaloney 2.0
Michael Veseth

Globalization and Health
Jeremy Youde